The Complete Book of
GREENHOUSE GARDENING

The Complete Book of
GREENHOUSE GARDENING

IAN G. WALLS

*With contributions from E. W. Curtis, A. G. Channon,
R. A. Martin, and J. W. Newbold*

Preface to the American Edition by Jerome A. Eaton

Quadrangle/The New York Times Book Co.

First published in Great Britain by Ward Lock Limited, 116 Baker Street, London, WIM 2BB

Library of Congress Catalog Card Number: 75-8291

International Standard Book Number: 0-8129-0577-6

Book design: Denis Wrigley MSIA

SB
415
.W29
1975

Contents

PART I

On the Design and Running of Greenhouses

PART II

On the Growing of Plants in Greenhouses

SOME USEFUL DEFINITIONS

I SPECIAL COMPOUNDS

Cheshunt compound	An anti-damping off fungicide to protect young seedlings made up of a mixture of 2 parts copper sulphate and 11 parts ammonium carbonate and dissolved: ½ oz. in one gallon of water.
Hoof and Horn Meal	A source of 12% to 14% nitrogen released to the plant over several months. Any equivalent commercial nitrogen fertilizer will provide an acceptable substitute.
John Innis Growing Composts	Enriched potting soils prepared as to usage.

JIP$_1$ (John Innis Potting Compost No. 1)★   This basic potting formula can be approximated by the following:

parts by volume
- 7 sterilized loam
- 3 peatmoss
- 2 builder's sand

plus

per bushel of compost
- 4 oz. of 5-7-10 complete commercial fertilizer
- ¾ oz. ground limestone

JIP$_2$ (John Innis Potting Compost No. 2)★

parts by volume
- 7 sterilized loam
- 3 peatmoss
- 2 builder's sand

plus

per bushel of compost
- 8 oz. of 5-7-10 complete commercial fertilizer
- 1½ oz. ground limestone

JIP₃ (John Innis Potting Compost No. 3)*

parts by volume
$\begin{cases} 7 \text{ sterilized loam} \\ 3 \text{ peatmoss} \\ 2 \text{ builder's sand} \end{cases}$
plus

per bushel of compost
$\begin{cases} 12 \text{ oz. of 5-7-10 complete} \\ \quad \text{commercial fertilizer} \\ 2\frac{1}{2} \text{ oz. ground limestone} \end{cases}$

JIS (John Innis Seedling Compost)*

parts by volume
$\begin{cases} 2 \text{ sterilized loam} \\ 1 \text{ peatmoss} \\ 1 \text{ builder's sand} \end{cases}$
plus

per bushel of compost
$\begin{cases} 1\frac{1}{2} \text{ oz. superphosphate} \\ \frac{3}{4} \text{ oz. ground limestone} \end{cases}$

JIS_A (John Innis Seedling Compost for Acid Loving Plants)*

To produce a PH of between 5.0 and 6.0

parts by volume
$\begin{cases} 2 \text{ sterilized loam} \\ 1 \text{ peatmoss} \\ 1 \text{ builder's sand} \end{cases}$
plus

per bushel of compost
$\begin{cases} 1\frac{1}{2} \text{ oz. superphosphate} \\ \frac{3}{4} \text{ oz. powdered sulphron} \end{cases}$

*These prepared potting soils are composed of specific ingredients. It is obviously ambiguous to prescribe 7 parts of loam without specifying, as does the British originator of these composts, that a medium garden loam should have 15 percent clay, 40 percent silt, and 45 percent sand. Such an exacting formulation is beyond the average amateur and it will be only after months of preparing small quantities of potting mixtures and watching their reactions to daily waterings that your *feel* will reinforce your judgment and such fine analyses will not be necessary.

Soil sterilization, another important ingredient in preparing composts, can also be a problem, since steam sterilizers are often uneconomical for treating small quantities, and the most effective gases and chemicals are a little tricky to use safely. It is often more convenient and economical to purchase five to ten bushels of sterilized loam from a local commercial greenhouse. This will provide you with sufficient base to prepare enough compost to last through many months of potting.

II ACCESSORIES AND MATERIALS

Air conditioning	Evaporative cooling — blowing air from outdoors through a moistened filter and into the greenhouse.
Parafin stove	Kerosene stove — recommended more for emergency standby use than for primary heat source.
Polythene	Polyethylene — sheet plastic used to cover temporary greenhouses or to retain moisture in a propagating bed.
Tallies and dibbers	Merely the English terms for flat wood labels and pointed sticks. The former carrying a plant's name or, painted, its color code says "resting" or "no water for this pot." Dibbers are painted sticks used to make planting holes for young plants or seedlings.
Tensiometer	Moisture meter — a device that automatically (and immediately) records on a dial the relative moisture in the soil of a potted plant.

III ·METHODS AND TERMS

Etiolated	Blanched — or lacking in vigor — usually a result of insufficient sunlight.
Genus	Equivalent to a plant's surname. Closely related plants are grouped into one genus. Plural is genera.

Species	Follows a plant's generic name and sets apart those plants with sufficient differences from others within the genus to make it a separate species. Spelled "species" in both singular and plural forms.

NOTE: Botanical nomenclature is recognized internationally and is far more dependable than common names. For example, in referring to Linden trees (as on page 19) the British use the name Lime. The American Lime tree is an entirely different genus. If the epithet Tilia is used in place of "Lime," it then becomes internationally uniform.

Stopping	Pinching—removing the growing tips of a plant to induce branching and thereby creating a bushier plant.

Preface
TO THE AMERICAN EDITION

Each country has within its borders certain products or services which the rest of the world looks upon and accepts as the highest expression of that form. So it is with greenhouse gardening and Great Britain, champagne and France, floating markets and Thailand, and fantastic wooden churches and Russia. In each case the environment furthered their intensive development.

Today, in spite of a short season of warm weather and bright sunlight, the British produce great quantities of fruits, vegetables, and flowers under glass structures. Many of these greenhouses are actually mounted on wheels which roll on tracks to cover the plantings in late summer after natural warmth has slackened. Such inventiveness in using greenhouses has made Great Britain the pacesetter in this specialized field of gardening.

British books on horticultural subjects were once shunned in the United States and thought not to speak to our special interests, problems, nor our available resources. However, anyone wanting the best in any specialized field would do well, first, to go to the most experienced resource and then adapt that expertise to his own needs. Mr. Walls' book is that outstanding font. In this volume he has taken special care to present thoroughly such mundane, though necessary, aspects of greenhouse construction as siting, step-by-step assembly, heating, and ventilation. All this material is both valid and extremely valuable to one's future greenhouse gardening success. We have added, wherever necessary, any explanations or translations that seemed appropriate to our climate, commercial availability, or language. Since the world has become smaller in recent years, a foreign word here or there no longer throws us, but merely adds a special charm to an already superior presentation.

In some instances editorial changes were made to clarify the usage of a familiar word. In others, such as the John Innis Composts, an entire concept required explanation. Having done so, we now feel certain that all the major elements for success in greenhouse gardening are yours.

The science of growing plants under glass by recreating any desired climate has among its variable factors those of temperature, humidity, light, and air to be considered and balanced. Nevertheless, this is accomplished through the same basic process everywhere in the world. Only local brand names or slight differences in the appearance of appliances and accessories will hint at their nationality.

Greenhouse books, regardless of their country of origin, are geared to one underlying objective — that of arming the reader with sufficient background in the many phases of greenhouse management to be able eventually to make his own decisions. Each of the forementioned variables effecting the plant's growth, also has an effect on one another. Mr. Walls' keen observations will lead you to recognize the symptoms of these effects, their cause, and the corrective measures that should be taken.

All of the information developed in the following chapters is based, first, upon the premise that we recognize or are willing to learn to recognize how each of the plant species we choose to grow should look when grown to its fullest potential. Secondly, that by providing optimum conditions — all in proper balance — you will not merely duplicate nature's product but you will actually improve upon it. The particular microcosm that you create in your greenhouse will not be subjected to drought, unexpected rain or wind storms, plagues of debilitating diseases, or infesta-

1

tions of uncontrolled insects. Lacking these catastrophic events and given an ideal prepared soil and balanced nutrition, many plants will far surpass your expectations.

We urge you to accept this premise as one of reality based upon a clear, concise exposition of the facts and not naive optimism — the horticultural successes so commonplace in Great Britain will soon be within your grasp.

While the United States has a proliferation of swimming pools in backyards throughout suburbia, Britain has green-houses abounding everywhere. It is only logical, then, that we have greenhouse manufacturers numbering in the dozens from which to make a purchase, while England has over a hundred.

—But take heart. Among our fewer sources are some of the finest, most inventive, and dependable companies; and so it is with our seed houses and plantsmen. The following list, while not including all in each category, should prove helpful in getting you started.

Sources for Greenhouses

Aluminum Greenhouses, Inc.
14615 Lorain Avenue
Cleveland, Ohio 44111

Dome East
325 Duffy Avenue
Hicksville, New York 11801

Glass Garden Greenhouses, Inc.
P.O. Box 2329
Grand Rapids, Michigan 49501

Humex Ltd.
5 High Road
Byfleet, Weybridge, Surrey
England

or

E. & W. International
290 Sandringham Road
Rochester, New York 14610

Lord and Burnham
Irvington, New York 10533

or

Des Plaines, Illinois 60018

National Greenhouse Company
Box 100
Pana, Illinois 62557

J. A. Nearing Co., Inc.
10788 Tucker Street
Beltsville, Maryland 20705

Redfern's Prefab Greenhouses
55 Mt. Hermon Road
Scotts Valley, California 95060

Peter Reumuller Greenhouseman
P.O. Box 2666
Santa Cruz, California 95060

Stearns Greenhouses
98 Taylor Street
Neponset, Massachusetts 02122

Sturdi-Built Manufacturing Company
11304 S. W. Boones Ferry Road
Portland, Oregon 97219

Texas Greenhouse Co., Inc.
2710 St. Louis Avenue
Ft. Worth, Texas 76110

Turner Greenhouses
P.O. Box 1260
Goldsboro, North Carolina 27530

The Vegetable Factory
Box 2235
Grand Central Station Post Office
New York, New York 10017

Vendors of Greenhouse Accessories

George J. Ball, Inc.
West Chicago, Illinois 60185

plants, rooted cuttings, and greenhouse supplies

Dillon Industries, Inc. P.O. Box 224 Melrose, Massachusetts 02176	soil sterilizers
Florist Products 1843 East Oakton Des Plaines, Illinois 60018	greenhouse supplies
H. P. Supplies Box 18101 Cleveland, Ohio 44118	lighting and watering equipment
Humex Ltd. 5 High Road Byfleet, Weybridge, Surrey England **or** E. & W. International 290 Sandringham Road Rochester, New York 14610	nonelectric watering and ventilating equipment, shading devices, and other greenhouse mechanisms
Walter F. Nicke P.O. Box 71 Hudson, New York 12534	general horticultural supplies
Al Saffer and Co., Inc. 130 West 28 Street New York, New York 10001	chemicals and greenhouse accessories
Shoplite Co., Inc. 566 Franklin Avenue Nutley, New Jersey 07110	fluorescent lighting fixtures and supplies
X. S. Smith Company Box 272 Red Bank, New Jersey 07701	shading fabrics
Sudbury Laboratory, Inc. Box 1028 Sudbury, Massachusetts 01776	soil testing equipment

Sources for Greenhouse Plants, Seeds, and Bulbs

Abbey Garden Box 167 Reseda, California 91335	succulents
Alberts and Merkel Bros. Boynton Beach, Florida 33435	wide variety of tropical plants
Antonelli Bros. 2545 Capitola Road Santa Cruz, California, 95010	tuberous begonias

Armacost and Royston 2005 Armacost Avenue West Los Angeles, California 90025	orchids
Buell's Box 218 Weeks Road Eastford, Connecticut 06242	gesneriads
John Brudy's Rare Plant House Box 1348 Cocoa Beach, Florida	rare seeds and plants
W. Atlee Burpee Co. Philadelphia, Pennsylvania 19132	seeds of annuals, biennials, and perennials
Butchart Gardens Ltd. P.O. Box 4010, Station "A" Victoria, British Columbia Canada	seeds
Fantastic Gardens 9550 S.W. 67 Avenue Miami, Florida 33156	tropical plants
Fischer Greenhouse Linwood, New Jersey 08221	African violets
J. Howard French Box 37 Lima, Pennsylvania 19060	bulbs
Joseph Harris Moreton Farm Buffalo Road Rochester, New York 14624	vegetable seeds
Alexander I. Heimlich 71 Burlington Street Woburn, Massachusetts 01801	miniature bulbs, corms, and tubers
Jack's Cactus Garden 1707 W. Robindale Street West Covina, California 91790	cactus in variety
Jones and Scully 2200 N.W. 33 Avenue Miami, Florida 33142	orchids
Michael Kartuz 92 Chestnut Street Wilmington, Massachusetts 01887	general assortment of plants
Logel's Greenhouses 55 North Street Danielson, Connecticut 06239	great assortment of exotics and standard greenhouse plants

4

Rod McLellan Co.
1450 El Camino Real
South San Francisco, California 94080

orchids

Merry Gardens
Camden, Maine 04843

wide variety of greenhouse plants

George W. Park Seed Co.
Greenwood, South Carolina 29646

wide selection of seeds

J. A. Peterson
3132 McHenry Avenue
Cincinnati, Ohio 45211

African violets

John Scheepers, Inc.
37 Wall Street
New York, New York 10005

bulbs and perennials

Seaborn Del Dios Nursery
Route 3, Box 455
Escondido, California

bromeliads

Sunnyslope Gardens
8638 Huntington Drive
San Gabriel, California 91775

rooted chrysanthemum cuttings

Thompson & Morgan Ltd.
London Road
Ipswich, Suffolk, England
or
P.O. Box 24
401 Kennedy Boulevard
Somerdale, New Jersey 08083

variety of seeds in all categories

Vetterle Bros.
P.O. Box 1246
Watsonville, California 95076

tuberous begonias

Wilson Bros.
Roachdale, Indiana 46172

geraniums

REGARDING THE USE OF CHEMICAL CONTROLS

Chemical materials used on plants for insect and disease control are constantly under re-examination by the United States Department of Agriculture. Between the editing of this book and the final proofreading, two previously acceptable chemicals have been withdrawn from commerce as too dangerous to use.

In view of the possibility of such reappraisal, we advise that you contact your County Extension Service (usually located in the county seat) for their current recommendations.

One has the option of purchasing a greenhouse and the necessary equipment for growing plants under glass from a convenient source almost anywhere in the United States. Additionally, British products are available at little extra trouble.

While a tremendous variety of plants can be ordered from any number of reliable American dealers, arrangements can also be made to import many of them (including some species that are otherwise hard to locate), as long as proper permission is obtained. Should you want to import plants or bulbs (seeds are usually admitted without a permit), write to:

U.S. Department of Agriculture
Animal and Plant Health Inspection
  Service
Plant Protection and Quarantine
Federal Center Building
Hyattsville, Maryland 20782

Tell them from what country you wish to import plants and list the genera and species if possible. Request an import permit and a few shipping labels. When placing your order abroad, send one of the labels. The plants will then be shipped to the nearest port of entry having a plant inspection station. They will be inspected, disinfected if necessary, repacked, and then delivered to your home via parcel post.

When traveling abroad do not try to sneak in any plants or cuttings, however healthy they may appear. Get a permit and you will find the Department of Agriculture inspectors extremely helpful and, more important, capable of protecting you —and all of us—from serious insect and disease problems.

JEROME A. EATON

Preface

Recent years have seen a tremendous increase in greenhouse gardening among non-professionals. It has been due partly to the now ready availability of factory-built greenhouse units, partly to the flood of automatic aids to environmental control which are so necessary for the part-timer, and also to the plant breeders who have produced heavy cropping and disease-resistant varieties of many popular crops.

The secret of success in this as in most aspects of gardening is attention to detail, and the detail necessary for satisfying and rewarding greenhouse cultivation in temperate latitudes is what this book sets out to provide. It takes into account the findings of recent horticultural research and the development of new cultural techniques, and attempts some reconciliation between amateur and commercial practice.

The author gratefully acknowledges the invaluable assistance he has received from numerous individuals, companies and research bodies in the preparation of the book. In particular he wishes to thank A. G. Channon B.Sc. Ph.D. and J. W. Newbold B.Sc. for the tables on the pests, diseases and physiological disorders of greenhouse plants; R. A. Martin, B.Sc. for the chapter on composts for greenhouse plants; J. R. Woodhams (Supervisor of the Fern Collection at the Royal Botanic Gardens Kew) for his assistance in preparing the chapter on the cultivation of ferns under glass; Susan Phillips for the chapter on the cultivation of cacti under glass, and Charles Simpson for his contribution on the cultivation of orchids in the greenhouse. He would also like to record his gratitude to R. Maclay Paton for his excellent line drawings and the late J. C. Raymond for his help in the planning and preparation of them and Roger Grounds for editing the manuscript, collecting the illustrations and seeing the book through press.

He would also like to thank the following for assistance with technical information and for allowing us to use their photographs: Hancock Aluminium Glasshouses Ltd, Wells Place, Merstham, Surrey; W. Godley, South of Scotland Electricity Board, Cathcart, Glasgow; Electricity Council, Trafalgar Building, London; the Ministry of Agriculture and Fisheries; Framptons Nurseries, Chichester, Sussex (chrysanthemums); Jacob L. Van Reison NV, Voorhout, Holland (bulbs); Vitax Ltd, Ormskirk, Lancs; Maxicrops Ltd, Northampton; Jiffy Pots (UK) Ltd, Trulls Hatch, Rotherfield, Crowborough, Sussex; SAI Horticulture Ltd, Leith, Edinburgh; Shell Chemicals Ltd; Murphy Chemicals; Humex Ltd; Wright Rain Ltd; D. McArthur, Scottish Field. The following seed houses and nursery firms have also kindly given information: D. T. Brown & Co Ltd, Station Road, Poulton-le-Fylde, Blackpool; Rivers of Sawbridgeworth, The Nurseries, Sawbridgeworth, Herts (indoor fruit); Scottish Chrysanthemum and Dahlia Society, Glasgow; Samen Mauser, PO Box 8022, Zurich, Switzerland; Hurst Gunson Cooper Taber Ltd, Witham, Essex; Vilmorin-Andrieux, 49750 La Menitre, France; W. W. Johnson & Son Ltd, Boston, Lincs; Finneys Toogoods Brydons, 94 Grainger Street, Newcastle-upon-Tyne; Suttons Seeds Ltd, Royal Seed Establishment, Reading, Berks; T. Sakata & Co, 2 Kiribatake, Kanagawa-ku, Yokohama, Japan; Asmer Seeds Ltd, Ash Street, Leicester; Webbs Garden Seeds Ltd, Sealand, Chester; Nutting & Thoday, Long Stanton, Cambridge.

Part 1

On the Design and Running of Greenhouses

Chapter I

The Historical Perspective

The growing of plants in covered houses, whether they be greenhouses, conservatories or orangeries, is essentially a northern hemisphere phenomenon. It is not, however, a new phenomenon, and the first attempts at growing plants under artificial conditions go back to at least early classical times. For countless generations much use has also been made of 'shade houses' or natural cover to allow the cultivation of many plants which are affected by excess sunlight.

The Greeks with their 'gardens of Adonis' appear to have had forcing houses in miniature. Plato in his *Phaedo* says that 'a grain, a seed or a branch of a tree placed in or introduced to these gardens acquired in eight days a development which could not be obtained in as many months in the open air'. Columella, a Roman writer on rural matters, speaks of Rome possessing 'within the precincts of her walls, fragrant trees, trees of precious perfumes such as grow in the open air in India or Arabia'. The implication of this is that they were not grown in the open air in Rome. It was Caesar Tiberius, however, who introduced a utilitarian note to these early attempts at covered gardening. Told by his doctor that he needed a cucumber a day to cure an illness, he instructed his gardener to produce a cucumber a day or else! The gardener succeeded in growing cucumbers *fere toto anno* by cultivating them in pits filled with fermenting dung and covered with frames or lights of talc or mica.

In later Roman times forcing was done by means of *specularia*, buildings covered with sheets of mica, thinly split, and it was mainly fruits, cucumbers and peaches among them, that were grown in this way; the epigrammatist Martial refers to peaches in *specularia*. Among the ruins of Pompeii a building of this kind has been discovered, with masonry staging for displaying plants and hot air flues in the walls; it was apparently originally glazed with talc or rough glass.

With the decline of the Roman empire the practice of forcing fruit in artificial conditions seems to have been abandoned in Europe, and not until the thirteenth century do we hear of any attempt to revive it. In 1295 Albert Magnus, a Paduan, is said to have entertained William of Holland, king of the Romans, in a garden maintained in flower and fruit by artificial heat. The wealthy merchants of Venice and Genoa, importers of many luxurious fruits, were probably the next to attempt glasshouse construction.

Farther north, the earliest development of the greenhouse appears to have taken place in France; the lead was subsequently taken by the Dutch when at the height of their maritime empire, and it passed ultimately to Britain. The first covered gardens were orangeries, normally without heat, built for sheltering citrus fruits during the winter months, but by the seventeenth century these had reached a fair degree of perfection. In 1685 Jules Mansard (or Mansart) built the noblest orangery in Europe for Louis XIV at Versailles. It had three arcaded galleries, the central portion of which was 508ft long, 42ft wide and 45ft high. In 1693 Fagon, Superintendent of the Jardin Royal, constructed the famous hothouse which he warmed with 'stoves and furnaces' for the preservation of tender plants, including the tea plant. The first successful attempt in Britain at greenhouse gardening was made at the Physic Garden at Oxford where the buildings were of wooden construction, very little better than cold frames.

In general, orangeries, which were unheated, came first; these were followed by conservatories, essentially houses for conserving tender plants; the stovehouse which was heated to a high degree came later. The credit for coining the word greenhouse (a house for conserving tender greens) goes to the diarist, Englishman John Evelyn.

In the early days the greatest problems related to heating, and all sorts of fantastic methods were used. The Dutch first used free-standing stoves which had to be fuelled from inside the greenhouse. It was fairly soon realised, however, that fumes from the stoves were destroying the plants, and quite a number of gardeners also appear to have been choked to death by these early furnaces. Even more primitive was the portable brazier, filled with burning coals and wheeled to and fro, used to heat the first greenhouses at the Oxford Physic Garden. Subsequent developments involved moving the stove outside and heating the back wall of the greenhouse by means of complicated flues.

At this time the only people who had greenhouses were the very wealthy. In Britain there was no real progress made in glasshouse development until the tax on glass was repealed in 1845. At that time when a gardener's day rate was 1s 6d (7½p) and a tradesman's 2s (10p), crown glass sections were 9d (4p) each and measured 9 × 20in approximately. Before 1845 a crate of crown glass cost £12, but by 1865 the price had dropped to £2 8s (£2.40). With such a reduction in the price of glass, development was rapid and greenhouses sprang up everywhere. Every gentleman with any self-respect had to have a greenhouse. The aristocracy really became enthusiastic and a number of structures similar to the Palm House at Kew were erected, perhaps the most famous being the huge conservatory built by Paxton for the Duke of Devonshire at Chatsworth.

Another major breakthrough occurred when hot water heating for greenhouses was invented. Incredible though it may

The great conservatory at Chatsworth House built by Paxton, one of the indefatigable pioneers of greenhouses. He was also one of the moving forces behind the Crystal Palace built for the Great Exhibition.

THE GREAT CHATSWORTH CONSERVATORY.

THE EXTERIOR, FROM THE ITALIAN TERRACE.

12

seem, until 1818 nobody realised that hot water circulated naturally. Once this principle had been understood all manner of boilers were invented, the manufacturers of each one claiming invariably that their boiler presented a larger area of water to the fire than anyone else's and was therefore a more efficient heat exchanger. One wonders what the proud possessors of the first boilers would have thought of a modern small bore, or mini-bore, heating system! The next problem, of course, was how to ventilate the heated greenhouse efficiently, while keeping it at an acceptable temperature to the plants being raised.

Once electricity became available, further advances followed in greenhouse development, and while it was cheap many greenhouses used it for heating to high levels. Today electricity is used mainly for heating to moderate levels, but is essential for the operating of almost everything in greenhouse mechanics. It is also used for artificial illumination, both so that one can see in the greenhouse after dark and to encourage the growth of plants with long-day requirements: for automatic ventilation and shading and for air circulation.

An interior view of Paxton's great conservatory at Chatsworth House. This was one of the great 'sights' of its day.

Thus, although greenhouses have developed rapidly and have come a long way from the earliest attempts by the Romans in classical antiquity, the basic problems faced by greenhouse designers and engineers today are still the same as they were in those days, and indeed throughout the whole history of the development of greenhouses, including the heyday of the Victorians. The giant conservatories such as that built by Paxton at Chatsworth House faced precisely the same problems as the eight foot by twelve foot greenhouse found so frequently in private gardens today. The difficulty has always been to find an effective balance between heating and ventilating, and between light and shade. Too much heat and the plants boil to death in their own condensation; too much ventilation and it becomes almost impossible to raise the temperature to the desired level; too much light and the greenhouse overheats in summer; too much shade and the plants become drawn and leggy. However, with modern electric and other automatic aids it is now possible to overcome all these problems and to have a greenhouse that is not only more efficiently heated, ventilated, lit and shaded than ever before, but also to have these elements in proper balance and so automatic in their running that the greenhouse can virtually be left to itself. All the modern greenhouse gardener need do is enjoy his plants.

Chapter 2

Some climatic factors in greenhouse siting

Careful consideration of terrain and climate is important in siting the commercial greenhouse if it is to be economically viable in face of competition from more favoured countries. The non-professional greenhouse gardener, though he may have no choice but to stay where he is, ought at least to be aware of basic climatic principles and their significance.

Latitude The nearer a country is to the equator the nearer it is to the sun; the farther one journeys away from the equator the colder it gets. Therefore in any country in the northern hemisphere it is theoretically warmer and lighter in the south than in the north (the converse is true of the southern hemisphere).

Effect of large areas of water Water like glass has reflective properties and large bulks of it add to the total amount of illumination available. This applies to both coastal and inland waters, and areas of land to the north of a large bulk of water derive more benefit from the reflected light than do areas to the south (the converse is true in the southern hemisphere). (Fig 1)

The thermal warmth of large areas of water is also of great significance, as heat is stored in the water and radiated back to the air. In the oceans this effect is heightened or modified by currents from tropical or polar regions. The influence of the

Fig 1

15

Gulf Stream or Mid-Atlantic Drift on the whole western coast of Britain is considerable in the raising of air temperatures and the reduction of winter frost.

Prevailing winds The prevailing wind for the whole of Britain is a south-westerly, coming from warm areas, and this, combined with the Gulf Stream, makes the whole western part of the country milder and wetter than the east.

Humidity Areas near large bulks of water and areas of high rainfall have high humidity; so do densely wooded areas due to transpiration of water through the leaves of the trees. A high moisture content in the air not only affects the growth of plants but also the incidence of disease. In dry districts, away from the sea or inland waters and where there are few trees, fungal diseases are a less frequent occurrence in the greenhouse.

Many gardeners erect a greenhouse and expect it to be (in terms of horticultural capabilities) the exact image of any other greenhouse. Such is not the case. An accurate assessment of weather patterns is an invaluable exercise which should under no circumstances be neglected, the paramount issues most certainly being light intensities and exposure.

Good light

While a dwelling house could conceivably be designed around a well-sited greenhouse or conservatory, it is more usual to design a dwelling house primarily for the living facilities it offers, and to relegate the greenhouse or conservatory to a position of less importance. There is, however, much to be said for incorporating the greenhouse or conservatory as a special feature in the home, both for aesthetic and practical reasons. It offers not only a pleasant and useful adjunct to the home but is also an economical way of greenhouse gardening since the heating can be linked to the domestic system.

These considerations, however, do not affect the fundamental importance of siting the structure where it will receive good light, though obviously if a conservatory is to be used mainly for leisure and pleasure one will wish to avoid having the temperature raised to an unacceptable level by the midday sun and will prefer a west orientation enjoying the evening sun. Even so, when a conservatory or greenhouse of conventional design adjoining a house has its longer axis facing west, the gable end will, unless obstructed in some way, be open to the south and therefore derive consider-

Fig 2

able sunlight. When a conservatory faces east the same applies, as one gable end is open to the south. A north-facing conservatory or greenhouse, if backed by a high building, will invariably receive very little sun at all, and its aesthetic and horticultural value could be questioned, for it will be of little use for any activity other than the growing of ferns or 'house' plants.

Good light is highly desirable for many horticultural activities, especially the propagation and growing of light-loving plants during the winter months. It is therefore elementary to choose a situation for the greenhouse which is as ideal as possible for light reception, especially during the winter months. There are many greenhouses so badly and hurriedly sited that results will never come up to expectations. Yet, given adequate information on sun angles, it is possible to calculate exactly what areas of shade will result from various buildings, trees or other obstructions at various times of the year. A site which lies in brilliant sunshine most of the day from March to October may be in real gloom for most of the winter when light is at a premium.

Make up a sighting angle (Fig 2) with two sections of wood, the angle between them being the same as the angle of incidence of the sun's rays in winter for that latitude. Place one leg of this sighting angle on the ground, using the other as a direction indicator. This will give fair guidance as to whether buildings or dense trees are likely to be a real problem.

Is shelter necessary?

Questions of light and shelter are obviously closely related. A greenhouse can be erected in a garden closely surrounded by tall hedges or fences and enjoy the very best of shelter yet the poorest of light as a result.

In many gardens shelter is in fact of no real consequence, as the whole general area does not have an exposure problem. There is no better natural guide to this than the 'shaping' of trees in the neighbourhood—better even than the advice of local gardeners, though this should not be discounted. Whether or not an exposure problem is bad enough to demand shelter for a greenhouse against excessive heat loss or structural damage is a matter for detailed assessment.

Wind can play many unpredictable tricks by bouncing off buildings and hills or creating areas of extreme turbulence on the lee side of walls and fences. A useful technique for checking on ploys of this kind is to select a number of very light battens of wood of equal thickness and height—perhaps $2\frac{1}{2}$ft long by 2–3in wide and $\frac{1}{2}$in thick. Measure off 2in or more at the base of these and mark this, then push them into the soil to exactly this mark in various situations in the garden. The stakes that always blow down first (allowing for different soil types) give a good guide to windy corners, and not only help in deciding whether or not shelter for the greenhouse is necessary but also in ensuring that the flue exit from oil or solid fuel boilers will not create a hazard to your own or your neighbour's home or greenhouse.

Providing shelter

Providing shelter is usually more concerned with the garden as a whole than specifically for a greenhouse. The same general rules apply for both (Fig 3a).

Solid wind barriers are now frowned upon. They do not 'stop' the wind at all. All they do is deflect it upwards, to descend later with some force, sometimes creating a considerable degree of turbulence immediately within the barrier. All

Fig 3a

17

Fig 3b

the evidence of recent research shows clearly that media about 50 per cent permeable are ideal for slowing the speed of the wind, thus avoiding both deflection and turbulence (Fig 3b).

Windbreaks are effective for a distance of approximately ten to twelve times the height of the barrier itself, which means that in practical terms a hedge 8ft tall will provide shelter for 80-100ft. The area of maximum shelter is in the region of five to six times the barrier height, or 40-50ft in the case of a hedge 8ft high, a distance which raises no shade problems. A tall hedge of densely planted poplars, on the other hand, would provide excellent protection for a large area but pose considerable shade problems in summer, especially if the hedge lay to the south of the intended greenhouse (north in the Southern Hemisphere).

The directional placement of the shelter in relation to the greenhouse will depend, as we have said, on the prevailing wind. The ideal arrangement in most areas of Britain is shown in Fig 4, a formula which can be fairly well adhered to in many gardens with a little planning.

A Dutch-style cedar greenhouse of glass-to-ground construction, permitting maximum light entrance from roof to soil level.

Natural shelter media
Hedges
    Beech
    Holly (common)
    Hornbeam
    Myrobalan *(Prunus cerasifera)*
    Privet
    Prunus cerasifera 'Nigra'
    Quickthorn (common hawthorn)
    Willow (trimmed as hedge)
    Yew, and many others

Will make thick impenetrable hedges 6–8ft in height. Should be cut regularly

Conifer hedges
    Chaemaecyparis lawsoniana
    Cupressocyparis leylandii
    Thuja lobbiiplicata

Grow fairly quickly to around 10–15ft

Trees
    Larch
    Limes
    Mountain ash
    Poplars *(Populus nigra* 'Italica'*; P. alba)*
    Scots pine *(Pinus sylvestris)*
    Silver birch
    Spruce *(Picea abies/excelsa; P. sitchensis)*
    and a great many others

Provide effective shelter belts but require sufficient room for development and are suitable only for the larger garden; seldom applicable to suburbia

Artificial shelter media
    Interwoven fencing
    Rustic fencing
    Plastic trellis
    Wood trellis
    Hollow blocks
    Alternate offset slats
    Horizontal cane
    Vertical cane
    Netlon
    Weldmesh
    Wire netting and straw
    Vertical lath
    Horizontal lath
    Single layer slats
    Polypropylene
    Rokoline

These are examples of materials in current use; all have their virtues and failings according to conditions

Fig 4

EXISTING SURFACE

HALVE THE DISTANCE

LEVEL

REMOVE 10″ TOP SOIL LAYER

EXCAVATE SUB SOIL AND REPLACE AT Ⓐ

Ⓐ

TOP SOIL REPLACED

Fig 5

Tree roots

Roots of trees or hedges situated adjacent to a greenhouse can be a problem particularly where the greenhouse border is used for crops, taking away moisture and nutrients and also disturbing foundations, poplars being notorious in this respect. The distance at which roots give rise to trouble depends on the species involved, but for privet, beech and other common hedges about 8–10ft should be allowed if at all possible, and considerably more for trees. Where such a distance is not possible constant deep digging is necessary to trim off any roots growing into the border or likely to impinge on foundations.

Drainage

Water shed from the roof of a greenhouse is best collected in a gutter and conveyed by a downpipe to a drain. With greenhouses of newer design and smaller size, rainwater is frequently allowed to run off into the soil, but only if natural drainage is sufficiently good, otherwise a rubble, tile or plastic drain must be run along the outside of the greenhouse to collect this rainwater and prevent seepage into the greenhouse. Drains should always have an effective outlet. The building of a greenhouse on a sloping site raises special drainage problems, particularly the disposal of moisture shed from higher land.

Site levelling and soil conditions

Since the physical and nutritional characteristics of soil and the whole question of soil analysis will be examined in detail in a later chapter, it is sufficient at this stage merely to draw attention to the importance of using a good soil, of even depth and good drainage, when growing plants in the greenhouse border. This matter is often airily dismissed as being of litte significance in the small amateur greenhouse, yet in fact even a moderately sized structure 18 × 12ft will require 24 sq yd of soil 1ft deep or, to put it another way, 8cu yd of soil—not the sort of soil bulk readily come across or physically easy to handle. For a benched greenhouse or for container or bed systems of culture, the importance of good soil diminishes.

When levelling a site there are several important points to be borne in mind, especially where it is intended to use the border soil for growing crops. Every attempt should be made to preserve the top layer of fertile soil and to replace it after levelling. Failure to do this will result in an intermingling of poor quality subsoil and top soil, with decidedly deleterious effects on the crops. Soil in its natural state has a porous structure due to the activity of micro-organisms, earthworms, and the action of plant roots. Subject this to pressure with heavy mechanical levelling equipment and much of the natural structure is destroyed by the breaking down of porous crumb formation and the compression of air and moisture channels. Many commercial greenhouse units are levelled irrespective of soil condition in an endeavour to keep to a tight erection schedule, with subsequent soil-structure problems.

Levelling methods currently used are as follows:

1 *Cut and fill* After stripping off the top soil, the difference in level is made up by splitting the difference between the lower and higher levels by movement of subsoil. What has been said about destruction of top-soil structure applies to subsoil, which can, if packed too hard, completely inhibit movement of water, either vertically or laterally, so that even if the top soil is replaced carefully drainage will never be effective. A banking is left and a retaining wall with a catchment drain may be necessary (Fig 5).

An aluminium greenhouse erected on a sloping site. Note the way a foundation has been created to level the actual standing for the greenhouse.

HIGH

REMOVE TOP SOIL

TAKE OUT SUB SOIL

SUB SOIL

LOW

TOP SOIL REPLACED LEVEL WITH LOW POINT

Fig 6

2 Levelling to lowest point (Fig 6). In this method the top soil is first removed and then the sub-soil is excavated to allow a level to be made at the lowest point. This will undoubtedly result in a much steeper banking than with the 'cut and fill' method, and this can give rise to proportionately greater drainage problems. Alternatively a retaining wall may be necessary. If it is, it should have a drain at its rear to catch the moisture shed from the higher land.

3 *Levelling to highest point* In this method, soil or ballast is used to bring up the level to the highest point. The advantages of this system are roughly counterbalanced by its disadvantages, though perhaps the gains are greater than the losses. While it avoids disturbing the existing soil structure it does, on the other hand, leave the greenhouse sitting proud of the natural levels and this can lead to over-effective drainage—a severe problem where crops such as tomatoes are to be border-grown (see Fig 7).

A point of some importance with regard to all levelling methods is that a suitable period of time must be allowed for sub-

sidence before the building of the greenhouse can commence. Alternatively, deeper foundations which allow contact with existing soil levels can be made, though this of course adds to the erection cost.

The disturbance of soil structure is of less importance where a slab floor is to be laid down and the greenhouse permanently benched, or where peat beds or similar growing systems are to be employed. There should, however, still be adequate provision for drainage, and sufficient time for subsidence should be allowed before building. If the top or subsoil is badly handled, drainage is bound to suffer, though this can be overcome if rubble is used instead of soil for the infill.

Weeds

Little account is usually taken of weeds when building a greenhouse, yet they can be a serious nuisance. There are several highly obnoxious weeds such as *Polygonum cuspidatum* (Japanese bamboo), *Equisetum* (horsetail), and *Agropyron repens* (couch grass)—to mention but a few—which are very difficult to control. If the site is infested with weeds of this character, mere physical levelling or the building of foundations will do nothing to control them. It can be argued that within the limited area of a greenhouse it is relatively easy to control any weed by mechanical means, but nevertheless the presence of bad weeds in the periphery of a greenhouse will always be a hazard and a nuisance.

The whole realm of weed control prior to greenhouse erection must be approached with caution, especially if the intention is to retain the existing soil as greenhouse borders. Many weed-controlling chemicals are extremely potent, but when used out of doors they are in time leached out by the rain; this will not be the case in a greenhouse so obviously it would be a much better practice to carry out a general weed-control programme some time before building the greenhouse, treating a sufficiently wide area to prevent the weeds from rapidly recolonising the greenhouse site.

The situation regarding weed-controlling chemicals is a constantly changing one; it is wise to consult official literature on the subject, strictly following instructions issued with the chemicals.

Services — water

Supplies of water and electricity are essential for the modern greenhouse. The volume and pressure of water required will depend on a number of circumstances. A critical factor is the size of the main pipe, as this dictates the amount of water available, providing there is a full and unrestricted flow. Whether a permanent supply pipe can be laid into the greenhouse and what diameter this may be will depend on the attitude of the local water board. Normally a 1in supply pipe will suffice for small greenhouses on an amateur scale, although if spraylines and mist irrigation are to be used then a larger pipe is desirable, it being remembered that the smaller the bore of the pipe, the greater the friction, which reduces pressure. This is perhaps difficult to appreciate, yet if one takes a half-inch supply from a 2in main, it is fairly obvious that the greater the length of the half-inch pipe, the greater the resistance to the flow. Gardeners frequently make temporary connections to a tap at the rear of the dwelling house or garage, using long lengths of small-bore hose, and wonder why they get only a trickle at the greenhouse. This is of course the result of friction.

When permanent pipes are laid into a greenhouse they must be at sufficient depth to avoid freezing. The take-off from a main *must* be approved by the water board (who will usually make a charge) and invariably must be connected by a qualified plumber. Whether the water used is individually

Fig 7

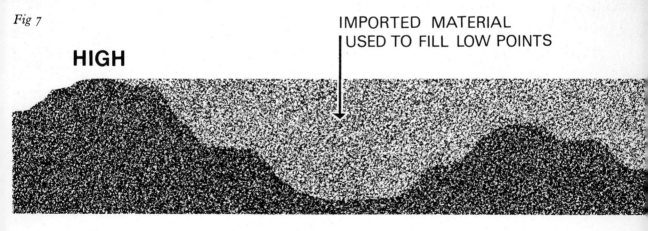

HIGH

IMPORTED MATERIAL USED TO FILL LOW POINTS

metered to the greenhouse or merely included in a flat water rate depends on local arrangements.

A compromise arrangement using a semi-permanent supply pipeline underground, but with a detachable connection to a tap, may be favoured and this may avoid the charges and complications of a permanent supply. Note that there should be facilities for draining this pipe in winter, especially if it is of steel. If it is not drained it may be split by frost. More usually these days pipes are of alkathene, and this tough material is not so badly affected by frost, but it can nevertheless be damaged.

The methods used to distribute the water within the greenhouse can vary considerably, problems of freezing being of importance once again. It may often be better to work with hosepipes from an outside tap which can either be drained off or lagged well during very cold weather, rather than from a fixed pipe. On the other hand, a deeply laid pipe and a standpipe in a correctly built and well-heated greenhouse will present few problems.

Electricity

The load necessary for a greenhouse will depend on its size and the range of equipment to be used. If an all-electric greenhouse is planned, the load can be quite heavy. The average small greenhouse of 10×8ft will normally require a $2\frac{1}{2}$kW heater, plus lighting, fan ventilation and possibly soil warming, adding up to a total of $3\frac{1}{2}$-4kW. Later in this book the formula

Fig 8

for working out the loading will be dealt with in detail, so it is enough at this stage to say that when all the calculations have been made, the gardener is then required by law to ensure that a qualified electrician carries out the necessary connection to the mains and that approved waterproof fittings are used throughout.

Access

There should always be ready, unobstructed access to any greenhouse, preferably a hard path of sufficient width to allow the use of a trolley or barrow. Inaccessible greenhouses tucked away in awkward corners are certainly not conducive to enthusiastic greenhouse gardening. Tool stores, potting sheds and supplies of soil should also be in reasonable proximity. There is a lot to be said for a greenhouse being attached to or as near the dwelling-house as possible, for the obvious reason that walking to and fro takes time and can be wet and unpleasant in bad weather.

Planning permission

It is usually wise to seek planning permission before embarking on any work connected with the erection of the greenhouse. For commercial greenhouses under

a certain size and over a permitted distance from a main road, planning permission may be completely unnecessary, but it is always advisable to check the situation with the authority or council involved. For amateur greenhouses under a certain size, planning permission may also not be needed, but here again it is better to make sure by approaching the planning body. Procedure differs under different authorities, but in most areas when making planning application it is obligatory to provide:

1 *A location plan* showing the exact siting of the greenhouse in relation to home, roads, and neighbouring buildings. It is often possible to obtain from the local planning authority, usually on payment of a small fee, a plan taken from the ordnance map of the area. The siting of the greenhouse in question can then be drawn in accurately and to scale in red ink, making sure that there is strict adherence to boundary lines (information on this should be requested beforehand from the planning body, and you should find out at the same time whether there are any local building regulations about the type of greenhouse allowed). (Fig 8).

2 *Full details of the greenhouse,* its foundations (if any), side and end elevations to

25

scale, details of materials and dimensions of the main structural members. Most greenhouse manufacturers have the necessary plans ready and in a form acceptable to the planning authority, but if you have designed your own greenhouse it will be necessary to draw up a set of plans or to enlist the services of a draughtsman.

3 *Notes on any drainage necessary*, especially if this involves linking up to an existing drainage system.

4 *A completed application form*, with the signatures of adjoining neighbours or their landlords or ground superiors certifying that they have no objection to the erection of the greenhouse. Permission may also be necessary from your own landlord or ground superior in the case of lets or feus, unless of course the ground is self-owned. A point of some interest is that where there is a building society involved with either land or house or both, they certainly must be told of your plans, especially if the greenhouse is to be attached to the house.

Chapter 3

Greenhouse Selection

Preliminary considerations

Before embarking on the erection of a greenhouse the following highly specific questions should be considered:

1 Is the district concerned well served with natural light, sheltered or exposed, and free from industrial pollution? In the same vein, is the area a very dry one, raising maintenance problems with wooden houses?

2 Does the proposed site receive the maximum amount of sunlight?

3 Is the greenhouse intended for use the whole year round or only for spring/summer?

4 What plants are to be grown and when—eg pot plants only, or general propagation followed by tomatoes and late chrysanthemums?

5 To what level is the greenhouse to be heated—fully, partly or not at all? A minimum of 55–60°F (13–16°C) all the year round, or merely to provide frost protection regardless of how cold it is out of doors?

6 What facilities are available for heat, with particular reference to the possibility of linking the greenhouse system with that of the dwelling house?

7 Is the greenhouse intended primarily as a room to relax in, or primarily for the growing of plants?

8 What size and shape of greenhouse is contemplated? Is money no object, or is there a strict budget involved? Might it in practice be better to consider a combined shed and greenhouse?

9 What constructional materials are considered suitable—wood, treated metal or alloy?

10 Must allowance be made for occasional absences from home, with vents, heating and perhaps watering and feeding being carried out in a semi-automatic manner?

11 Has any thought been given as to whether the greenhouse is to be fixed or mobile to allow a system of crop rotation?

Some of the more rudimentary principles relative to the questions asked will be discussed in the course of this and following chapters and summarised for reference in tabular form.

District

The level of natural illumination in any district varies not only according to latitudinal placement, but also with nearness to huge bulks of water, the presence of industrial pollution and in relation to several other factors. A garden may be situated at the top of a hill and so receive good light, yet be exposed to strong winds, making the maintenance of a high temperature all the year round both difficult and costly. Conversely, although good light, particularly in the winter months, is highly desirable for all greenhouse gardening activities, lack of it cannot be compensated for merely by increased temperatures, and artificial lighting involves a high initial capital outlay. Poor winter light makes the growing of light-demanding early tomatoes and winter lettuce, for example, extremely difficult in many northern districts, and in industrial areas atmospheric pollution detracts still further from the available light. Thus greenhouse gardeners in the more northerly latitudes are at a distinct disadvantage by comparison with those who garden in more southerly latitudes. While deficits in heat levels can be made good relatively easily, deficits in light intensity cannot so easily be remedied. These remarks apply not only to crop plants such as lettuce and tomatoes. Many pot plants such as pelargoniums and coleus also suffer when grown in conditions of poor winter light. The same is true of early-raised seedlings.

The all-glass types of greenhouse selected primarily for winter cropping are not going to be so generally acceptable to the northern gardener as they are to his southern counterpart. The northern gardener receiving poor winter light and often gardening under conditions of extreme exposure and winter cold may be better advised to have a permanently benched base-wall type of greenhouse which will not only reduce heat loss and keep fuel bills down, but serve better for spring propagation or year-round pot plant growing activities, followed by some later cropping. The same type of greenhouse would also be better for any gardener living in a very exposed situation. On the other hand in an area of good light with no exposure problem, an all-glass greenhouse could be used for a completely unrestricted production programme over the full year.

Desirable temperature levels

The amount of heating required in any greenhouse is usually determined with regard to the minimum winter temperature to be maintained. This in turn either determines, or is determined by, the type of plants to be grown in the greenhouse: the two factors are interdependent. The following are the four normally accepted levels for greenhouse heating.

Cool greenhouse
This provides frost protection only, keeping the temperatures between 45–50°F (7–10°C) in winter. This is a fairly frequent choice of temperature regime as it means that when the weather gets warmer, reasonably warm propagation is possible, to be followed by tomato growing at around the 60°F (16°C) level. Type of greenhouse is not critical, other than that a base wall reduces heat loss. On the other hand gardeners who want to grow lettuce or tomatoes will obviously do better with an all-glass structure for the better light

transmission it affords at ground-level, the final decision on this point depending largely on district.

The use of a separately heated propagating frame in the cool greenhouse is becoming very popular as it allows an intensive propagation programme at very low cost within the cooler atmosphere of the greenhouse.

Intermediate, or moderately warm, greenhouse
In this heat range a minimum temperature of between 55–60°F (13–16°C) is maintained continuously throughout the year. Such a temperature range is suitable for the great majority of greenhouse plants, and a wide variety of propagating activities can be carried on in the greenhouse itself (as opposed to within a separate propagating frame). In other words, a very full programme of activities can be embarked upon. It costs money to keep a greenhouse at these minimum temperatures, yet on the other hand there are great benefits in having a twelve-month gardening calendar. What has been said previously about natural light patterns is of special significance in this temperature range; the culture of light-sensitive crops such as early tomatoes or early lettuce should be avoided in poor light areas, irrespective of the heat level which can be achieved.

'Stovehouse'
This rather frightening title refers to a greenhouse for the culture of extremely heat-demanding plants such as some orchids, ferns and other epiphytes, in which the minimum temperature range is 65°F (18°C) or above. Few amateur gardeners think in these terms for very obvious economic reasons. A more localised concentration of heat such as that provided by the larger types of propagating case may be an acceptable compromise on grounds of cost.

Cold greenhouse
No artificial heat is involved at all, all heat being derived from the sun. The gardener in a very mild situation can derive great value from a completely cold greenhouse; in colder areas it is normally useless over

many of the winter months for anything other than hardy shrubs or plants.

A considerable amount of thought should be given to the temperature level at which one intends to run one's greenhouse, because once the decision has been taken it will, to a large extent, be irreversible. One will be limited to growing in that greenhouse only those plants which will grow in that particular temperature range. The real limitation is, in fact, one of cost: it is perfectly possible to heat what started as a cold greenhouse up to stove house level, but it would be very expensive to do so, because, ideally, the design and materials used in a greenhouse intended to be run at stove temperatures would be different from those used in a greenhouse intended to remain unheated. Because of the higher temperature required in a stove house, one would tend to go in for double-glazing and a house with brick half walls in order to minimise heat losses, whereas the greenhouse one might have purchased originally as a cold house might well have been of glass-to-ground design which would have a very high heat loss coefficient. Thus if one's desire is to move on from a cold house to a stove house, although it may seem sensible simply to heat the existing greenhouse to a higher level, it is in fact a highly uneconomic proposition. One would really do better to scrap the old greenhouse and start afresh with one better designed to do the job required. The initial outlay would obviously be greater than that of simply installing the necessary heating equipment, but in the long term there would be a considerable saving in cost.

A compromise may occasionally be reached, though this is really only practicable in fairly large greenhouses. This is a system that is sometimes adopted in the greenhouse of botanic gardens and other horticultural institutions, whereby the greenhouse is divided into two or more sections, each heated to a different temperature level. Some manufacturers of greenhouses will provide prefabricated partitions, while others provide for extensions to the greenhouse: either would enable one to divide the greenhouse satisfactorily. Alternatively heavy gauge translucent polythene can be used to create a curtain-type division, though this is not entirely satisfactory. However one sets about it, the actual calculating of the way in which the temperatures in the different sections are to be achieved is a job for a qualified greenhouse heating engineer and involves highly complex calculations. Unless these are done, and done correctly, one will fail to achieve the desired temperature differences.

Value for money

The cost of a proposed greenhouse is perhaps the most pertinent question of all. Prices of greenhouses are highly competitive, as perusal of catalogues, gardening papers or visits to flower shows or garden centres will prove. Value for money should always be sought after, and there can be an immense variation between different greenhouses, not so much in price but in respect of serviceability, lack of maintenance and other related matters. A wooden greenhouse constructed of white wood and glazed with putty and nails may be cheap, but how long will it last at the low level of maintenance which many gardeners are prepared to effect? If the policy is to spend as little as possible and strict attention is given to painting, then a cheap wooden house can last for a long while, and most certainly the putty glazed white wooden greenhouses are the cheapest. More sophisticated types of wooden houses constructed of Western Red Cedar or pressure-treated wood are excellent and economic buys (particularly if glazing systems avoid the use of putty and nails) for general greenhouse activities at low cost. Alloy and treated metal houses in their more sophisticated forms are generally more expensive than wooden houses.

Intensity of use

What has so far been said gives fairly clear guidance concerning the year-round use of a greenhouse. To think in terms of natural illumination only and disregard temperature would be wrong. In the more

29

southerly latitudes a completely unheated greenhouse can be reasonably effective in winter, allowing overwintering of pelargoniums, storage of dahlias, and the housing of quite a range of pot plants that are fully hardy, like fuchsias, primulas and many sub-tropical bedding plants. The situation can be very different in more northerly latitudes where, unless the winter is exceptionally mild, a completely cold greenhouse is virtually useless over the coldest winter months, with the possible exception of a few very mild coastal areas exposed to warm ocean currents, and even then winter dampness can be a real problem. Unheated base wall-type greenhouses certainly give much more frost protection than an all-glass greenhouse, and the same principle prevails even when the greenhouse is heated, no matter where it may be situated in the country. Gardeners in more southerly districts will not have to face such high fuel bills as those faced by gardeners farther to the north for any type of greenhouse.

Chapter 4

Design, Materials, Construction

Does shape matter?

A little research around the world, both into the past and the present, would no doubt bring to light greenhouses of every conceivable size and shape. Certainly with many of the earlier 'Botanic Garden' types of greenhouse, architects went to extremes; in modern idom the same may be said of some new plant houses.

Such diversity provokes the question: does shape or design really matter anyway? For most greenhouse gardening purposes what matters most is stability coupled with light transmission. Only where the absolute maximum light is sought for certain commercial crops, especially during the duller winter months, and when earliness of cropping or the quality of bloom is

A circular greenhouse. While these may be regarded as newfangled they do in fact provide a larger useful growing area than greenhouses of conventional design. This particular one is fully automatic, with capillary benches and self-regulating ventilation and blinds and thermostatically controlled heating.

crucial does glasshouse design become a critical matter.

Light is of two basic forms: the total illumination of the whole sky from all directions and the direct light transmitted by the sun as solar rays. The translucent material of a greenhouse will transmit about 90 per cent of the total illumination of the whole sky through the roof and sides of the greenhouse with almost equal efficiency. Direct readiation from the sun is only transmitted at maximum efficiency when the sun's angle is at 90° (normal) to the glass. Each degree away from normal results in a greater amount of deflection. A little thought along these lines shows the extreme difficulty of designing and erecting a greenhouse so that it will enjoy maximum light transmission at all times. The situation is, however, not quite so bad as it looks, since during the summer months the total radiation from the sun is usually far in excess of the requirements of many plants; it is only during the winter months that maximum light transmission is vital.

As the sun is never in the same position for long, any conventionally shaped greenhouse receives the maximum amount of light only for the very short period when the sun's rays penetrate the glass at 90°. Curved greenhouses were quite popular in earlier days, especially the all-important centre planthouse of the greenhouse range in the private estate garden; these offered a varied surface, part of which would always be at around 90° to the sun's rays (see Fig 12). Modern types of round greenhouses have been designed expressly to allow maximum light transmission over a period; the more sophisticated forms in fact turn to keep pace with the sun. Some years ago a tower greenhouse was devised in Germany in which plants were moved on a conveyor system round a tall tower to enable each plant to benefit from as much light as possible, but this system failed to develop to any great extent on economic grounds.

Much research has recently been concerned, however, with the conventionally shaped greenhouse. Assuming a roof pitch of approximately 30°, it can be seen that with a winter sun angle of approximately 15°, the angle of incidence at best is 180° −45°=135° (Fig 9). The vertical side of the greenhouse is better placed to transmit light with an angle of presentation of 75°. The higher the vertical side wall, the greater the amount of light transmitted, which in a single span house of normal width will reach the rear of the house easily. If the side wall is slightly angled off the vertical it is possible for the low-angled winter sun to have a 90° angle of incidence (see Fig 11). Recent experiments have aimed at making the roof pitch steeper on the side facing south, to transmit instead of deflecting the low-angled winter sun. A roof pitch of 60°, for example, gives an angle of incidence of 105° which is much more efficient in light transmission than the 135° of the normal roof pitch (see Fig 10).

Obviously there is more than winter to consider, and the normal roof pitch of 25–35° (Dutch light houses are often 20-25°) is much more efficient for light transmission in the spring and summer months than the 60° pitch, although as light transmission is so often in excess of the plants' needs, the steep roof pitch is not necessarily detrimental (Fig 12).

It becomes apparent that if a conven-

Fig 9

Fig 10

Fig 11

Fig 12

Fig 13

Fig 14

tionally shaped greenhouse is to derive maximum winter light it must be sited with the ridge running east-west; to have it running north-south would present only the south-facing gable end favourably for winter light, the sides and roof deriving very little owing to the very acute angle of incidence presented on two planes (Fig 14). The glazing bars or astragals also create a lattice blind effect (Fig 13).

A lean-to greenhouse of red cedarwood. Such greenhouses are particularly useful where space is confined.

Fig 15

Summary

1 The ideal greenhouse for light transmission would be completely rounded, but these have drawbacks in respect of size, cropping, etc.

2 The ideal greenhouse of otherwise conventional shape would have its roof pitched more steeply on the south-facing side, but I am unaware of any standard design in which this feature is incorporated.

3 For maximum light transmission in winter the conventional greenhouse should be orientated east-west to present its long axis to the south.

4 Where summer cropping only is concerned, north-south orientation is acceptable and indeed allows for a more equable distribution of light on both sides of the greenhouse.

Wooden greenhouses

The last ten years have seen rapid transition from wood to alloy as cladding material for greenhouses. Aluminium alloy has many advantages. It is strong (where extruded), light and extremely resistant to corrosion without any painting or other treatment. Superior or properly pressure-treated wood cannot, however, be discounted and is still viewed with much favour, since a tightly glazed wooden greenhouse is considerably 'warmer' than an alloy one, which means in effect that wooden houses cost less to heat. As cold is more rapidly transmitted from the outside through an alloy bar than through a wooden astragal (and conversely since heat is lost more rapidly), there are usually fewer condensation problems in a wooden greenhouse.

Main timbers available

The four timbers mainly used are Baltic redwood *(Pinus sylvestris)*, British Columbian pine *(Pseudotsuga menzieii/taxifolia)*, Western red cedar *(Thuja plicata)*, and Norway spruce *(Pices abies/excelsa)*. Hardwoods such as oak and teak are only used to a limited extent on account of their far higher cost.

Baltic redwood This is a desirable wood, even grained and, although fairly tough, easy to work with. Its strength to bulk ratio is good, being 31lb/cuft and it does not split badly when being nailed. It is readily impregnated with preservative.

British Columbian pine Similar in many ways to Baltic redwood, it can be obtained in long lengths, a point of more importance in the manufacture of large commercial greenhouses than in the making of smaller ones. It is reasonably free from knots, sap and other defects, but splits more readily than Baltic redwood when nailed, and is more difficult to impregnate with preservative. It has a bulk density of 33lb/cuft and is therefore broadly similar to Baltic redwood in its strength to bulk ratio.

Western red cedar This is an excellent wood for amateur greenhouse work when it is not used in long lengths, as it has a poor strength to bulk ratio (24lb/cuft); for this reason larger-sized members may

35

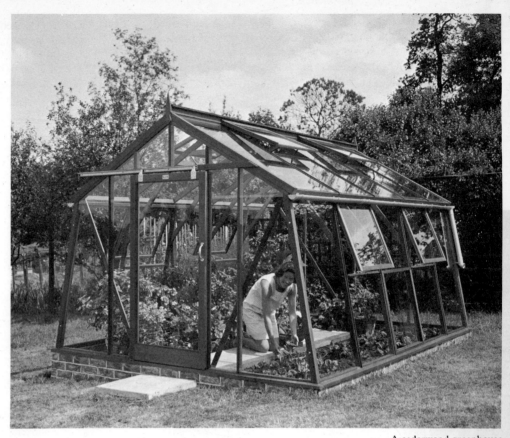

A cedarwood greenhouse with a sliding door. Note the sloping side-walls. These give greater penetration of winter light than vertical side-walls.

have to be used, particularly for astragals and ridge boards in exposed areas or where heavy snowfalls are frequent. Its chief virtues are inherent resistance to decay and excellent appearance, which makes it highly acceptable aesthetically for porches or conservatories adjoining the home. It has a tendency to split when being worked and, if possible, galvanised nails and screws, or copper nails and brass screws should be used. Western red cedar lends itself to treatment with oil. It is a little dearer than other woods mentioned.

Norway spruce Quite widely used for cheaper greenhouses on account of low cost, but for reasonably long life it must be treated or painted, preferably both. Being soft it is very easy to work and it does not split readily in the process. It has a strength/bulk ratio roughly similar to redwood.

Teak and oak Both of these are specialised woods of very high durability, having bulk to strength ratios of around 40–41lb/cuft. Easy to work, they are excellent where a greenhouse extremely resistant to varying climatic conditions is wanted, but when used in smaller sections they will make the greenhouse very expensive.

A greenhouse may be constructed of one type of timber, a variety of timbers, or a mixture of steel and timber.

36

Preservation of timber

This is a task best left to the timber or greenhouse supplier, but it is useful to know something about preservative treatment. Assessing the quality of timber is work for a specialist, but even the uninitiated can judge whether timber is free from small knots, large knots which may be loose, and 'splits', or whether it is too sappy (new). Many defects can be covered up with a coat of priming paint. Ideally timber should be both pressure treated and painted, unless of superior quality, although either will suffice in part. Paint protects the wood from the entry of moisture, which in turn protects it from decay, provided a perfect cover of paint is maintained. Preservatives impregnate the wood and immunise it against both the entry of moisture and decay, but obviously a painted greenhouse is more attractive than one which is merely preservative treated.

A small greenhouse with pre-cast concrete base-walls which are virtually indestructible and can be painted to blend in with the garden if required. The wall behind provides useful shelter for the greenhouse.

Timber preservatives are of three types —oil, water-soluble, and spirit-based. The oil types are largely creosote of one type or another and are not generally used for greenhouses because the fumes given off are toxic to many plants. Water-soluble preservatives are of various forms and based on copper sulphate (Woolmans salts), dinitrophenol, sodium dichlomate, sodium arsenate and sodium fluoride, which all form insoluble compounds when absorbed by the wood. Spirit-based preservatives are based on organic materials such as copper naphthenate or pentachlorphenol, dissolved in a spirit base which evaporates after application; because they are expensive they are usually painted on to the wood.

Water-based preservatives can be used when the wood is wet, whereas for spirit-based types the wood must be dry and free from any old paint, which must be removed if the preservative is to be effective. It is best to concentrate application in the region of joints or other areas where moisture can collect. Western red cedar is usually treated with linseed oil, which is simply brushed on when the wood is dry.

It should be realised that hand painting as a method of applying preservatives only results in penetration of the skin of the wood, which means that this will require fairly regular treatment.

Dip and pressure treatment
Timber can be completely immersed in preservative for a suitable period to allow reasonable penetration, which nevertheless can be negligible with certain types of

A half-boarded cedarwood greenhouse, permitting a very high degree of light penetration. Note again the arrangement of the staging on one side, leaving an area for a border on the side on which the glass reaches right down to ground level.

timber. Redwood will absorb preservative at the rate of about 1 in per week's immersion. Immersion in slowly heated preservative (180-200°F) (81-92°C), when thereafter the timber is allowed to cool in it, will result in fairly good absorption, following which the timber is allowed to dry. This is a method which will appeal to the amateur using an old bath with a fire below it. It is, however, far better to buy the wood already pressure treated, a practice carried out either by the glasshouse manufacturer or the firm supplying the timber.

Painting of timber

The painting of greenhouses is rather a boring task. Some manufacturers send their wooden greenhouses out either flat coated or fully painted, and the latter is to be preferred. The type of paint used for many years has been 'white lead' with the addition of zinc oxide against fungal growth and known as 'fungicidal paint'. White lead paints do, however, powder on the surface, and when sulphur is burned in the greenhouse to control fungal diseases, blackening can occur. If there is zinc oxide in the paint the burning of sulphur can cause zinc salts to form, which damage plants by contact.

Newer paints based on organic oils and synthetic resin with pigments other than lead, have considerably better light reflective qualities than those based on lead. They are also longer lasting and do not powder or dissolve. They must, however, be applied to *dry* timber, otherwise they will soon blister or flake off.

Paints containing cork can be used on metal gutters to prevent condensation. Aluminium paint was for a while much used on greenhouses, especially after the last war when lead was in short supply; though easy to apply, reasonably efficient, and giving good protection, it can flake off badly, especially if the timber is not sufficiently clean when it is applied. Rubber paints are excellent, and are better for metal, especially gutters, but are costly and difficult to apply.

When painting wood it is usual to apply a priming coat to timber which has not previously been painted. This should be wire brushed before applying the primer

A half-wall cedarwood greenhouse, with an inward opening door. Again the greenhouse has been placed close to a wall for shelter. The understaging can be used for storing greenhouse gardening implements.

if necessary. If you are erecting the greenhouse yourself, it is important to put on the priming coat before erection, otherwise joined surfaces are left unprotected. Next comes the undercoat, which may be put on after erection *but before glazing*. The final coat is put on after glazing, the usual practice when putty and nails are used being to lap the paint $\frac{1}{8}$–$\frac{1}{4}$in on to the glass over the putty to form a good waterproof seal.

Repainting will be necessary every three or four years on untreated or poor quality timber, perhaps more frequently in industrial areas. It is largely because they do not need painting that aluminium alloy, superior timber, and treated metal houses are now so popular.

Whatever type of paint is used, it is better not to bring plants into a newly painted greenhouse for a few days after painting since they could be damaged by fumes. Polyvinyl emulsion paints should not be used in a greenhouse as serious scorch damage to plants has been reported following their use.

Steel greenhouses

The high tensile strength of steel and its high strength/bulk ratio make it an ideal structural material for all buildings, and greenhouses are no exception. Most commercial greenhouses now use steel for the gutters and the supports, for purlin posts and rails, side and end supports, roof trusses and pitch frames whether they are cladded (the astragals holding the glass) with wood, steel or alloy. Steel is used as rolled sheets pressed into the appropriate shape for gutters, tubes, rectangular or box sections, and in RSJ, 'T' and angle for various construction members.

The main problem with many steel frame glazing bars lies in the fact that steel of sufficient thickness, unlike aluminium

A modern clip-glazed aluminium greenhouse with a sliding door. Note that staging has been used on one side, and space for a border left on the other.

40

alloy or expanded metal, cannot readily be pressed into a shape to allow a glazing method which secures the glass effectively without the use of a putty or bitumen type of glazing system. Nevertheless an excellent glazing system has been developed for steel glazing bars in recent years, using non-hardening glazing materials and plastic clips. Another system with dry glazing and a bar-cap and clip arrangement appears very effective in practice.

Steel must of course be properly treated against corrosion, otherwise it will quickly rust, and hot dip galvanising is essential *after* the steel has been cut to size, shaped and all holes bored. Alternatively cold galvanising can be carried out by painting with zinc powder taken up in a synthetic resin carrier, or simply old-fashioned red

lead. Aluminium paint is also very effective as a rust preventive for steel, provided the steel is reasonably clean before the aluminium paint is applied. Enamel is also used for painting over galvanised steel.

Personal experience over many years with the steel components of commercial and amateur greenhouses has shown the inadequacy in many cases of the metal galvanising treatment. A further problem with steel, especially if used in conjunction with aluminium alloy, is the bimetallic corrosion caused by electrolytic action. If a steel glazing bar is used in conjunction with alloy glazing clips, the galvanising will be broken down by this electrolytic action, allowing rust to form after a very short time. Even the water running from alloy glazing bars on to

The same greenhouse as shown in the previous illustration, but with an extension being added. The facility for extending greenhouses of this type is one reason for their popularity.

41

galvanised steel gutters can give problems, and certainly all manufacturers now ensure that plastic seal prevents the actual contact of the two metals, although nothing can be done about the shed water. Fortunately this is a problem which does not usually occur with amateur-sized greenhouses, as gutters on alloy greenhouses are also invariably of alloy.

Aluminium alloy

When first considered as a material for greenhouse construction, aluminium alloys were viewed with some suspicion. Earlier types of alloy were certainly subject to corrosion, especially in areas of salty air or industrial pollution. Even now considerable powder deposit may form on the alloy, but this need not give rise to concern. In recent years the quality of alloy used has improved so much that corrosion is only likely to be a problem in areas of unusually high industrial pollution. Aluminium alloy has an excellent strength/bulk ratio and, being a light metal, it can readily be extruded into sections of various shapes, the sections all being designed to give additional strength. It can also be shaped into complicated sections to form drip channels and to allow either clip or groove glazing, this latter being a system which has gained considerable favour in recent years since it gives a really tight seal and prevents air losses. In the UK aluminium alloys used must conform to British Standard specifications, which insist that they are resistant to corrosion.

As mentioned in the previous section, direct contact with steel must be avoided, and where this is impossible the steel should be protected with bitumen paint. Where aluminium alloy gutters are used, drip channels should be provided underneath to prevent the condensation droplets damaging crops owing to the high thermal conductivity of alloy. With commercial greenhouses it is advisable to use gutter support braces to ensure that the alloy gutter in a long section house does not sag, which can happen with snow load or under a man's weight when doing repairs.

Construction standards

Commercial greenhouses are manufactured to a code of practice based on the minimum acceptable standards. This takes into account (1) the structure as a whole, (2) individual structural elements such as truss, stanchions, purlins, joints, fixing, foundations, (3) cladding elements (glazing bars, etc). Amateur greenhouse manufacturers have not perhaps given such detailed study to their designs as these products are not subject to government approval for grants, but minimum construction standards should ensure that all greenhouses are stable enough to withstand very strong winds, snow load *and* crop weight, this last being of particular importance—greenhouses can, for example, easily be damaged by a very heavy crop of tomatoes.

To lay down section sizes for the component parts of a greenhouse poses problems, owing to the differing bulk/weight ratios involved; astragal bars of Western red cedar 2 × 2in will not be as strong as similar sections of Baltic redwood, for instance. Nor is it easy to give exact roof angles, height to ridge, height to eaves, size of doors, and all the other relevant measurements. A minimum *eaves height* of about 5ft gives adequate headroom but is not really sufficient; 5ft 6in to 6ft is better. The ridge height is commensurate with eaves height to give a roof pitch of from about 22° for Dutch light houses with no glass overlap, up to 35° for overlapped glass. There are, as with motor cars, many types of perfectly efficient models, but the price range varies widely and value for money is pretty consistent. Teething troubles can occur with a new model of motor car, and similarly with a new design of greenhouse, especially over mechanical items such as vents.

Do-it-yourself greenhouses

For the do-it-yourself enthusiast wishing to build a greenhouse there is a fairly wide margin of tolerance in design and most amateur joiners tend to err on the side of safety by using heavier timber than is really necessary.

For the average alloy greenhouse 8ft wide, alloy glazing bars which are stressed at 15lb per square foot are an acceptable norm. A steel greenhouse will have a much higher stress factor for similar glazing bar sizes, whereas for wood a comparable section size of Baltic redwood would require to have glazing bars approximately 3 × 2in thick, which would present shade problems.

Alloy houses can be self-built by buying the component parts, a procedure which I would hesitate to recommend in view of erection problems, it generally being better to buy the complete greenhouse in kit form. Steel houses are usually bought ready to erect, but they can be prefabricated by the gardener skilled with an electric drill or a welding plant, rust being the main problem following this procedure, even where galvanised steel component parts are originally used, although cold galvanising can do much to offset the rust problem on bored or cut sections (Fig 19)

All nails used in timber greenhouses should be galvanised, and screws and bolts in all alloy structures should be of alloy or brass.

Glazing systems

The type of glass used for greenhouses in Britain is drawn glass weighing 24oz per sqft (called 24oz horticultural glass) with a stress factor of up to 10lb per sqft. Continental types of glass are also used and these are slightly heavier, weighing 26oz

Acres of glass were flattened by the severe gales which hit Scotland in 1968. The phenomenon is a not infrequent one, and this picture stresses the importance of sound design, planning and construction in modern greenhouses.

43

per sq ft. A still heavier type of glass, 32oz per sq ft, is used for certain large-paned greenhouses, generally of commercial design. Commercially and in some amateur greenhouses the standard size of pane is 24 × 24in, while many amateur houses are 20 × 18in, or alternatively Dutch-size glass measuring 56 × 28¾in. There is certainly virtue in having larger pane sizes, as it increases the ratio of translucent to opaque material, which in turn ensures maximum transmission of light provided the greenhouse is orientated to the best possible advantage. The main drawback in having a large ratio of glass to structural material, and in particular no base wall is, as stated earlier, the increased heating costs.

Horticultural glass should be clear and unwarped, as 'bubbles' cause magnification and hot sun spots. It should allow a 90 per cent passage of solar radiation, but without the ultra-violet rays which in excess are damaging to plants. (Translucent glass is also used in warm countries to protect crops against excessive solar radiation.) Horticultural glass is only available in flat sheets, it not having the inherent strength necessary for use in curved form.

Alternatives to glass

Various forms of rigid plastics are available and can be used in lieu of glass in conventional greenhouses. They can readily be used in curved sections, which is a distinct advantage as far as light transmission is concerned. They perform the same function as glass, although it is claimed that they are more efficient in some respects in transmitting light. They are, however, more expensive than glass at present.

Several forms of clear polythene are available. The light gauge (38mu) is mainly used for 'double glazing' to reduce heat loss, and also for polythene tunnels; and the 125mu gauge for the construction of frames and greenhouses. The heavy grade, 150mm can also be used, though a double skin 125mu gauge is more in favour at present. PVC is also available and is clearer than polythene but tends to be more expensive.

Polythene is efficient in transmitting short-wave solar radiation, the light being all diffused and not directly admitted as in the case of glass. But normal grades of polythene, unlike glass, do not trap the long-wave radiation from heated objects within the greenhouse. Polythene destruction also occurs constantly due to ultra-violet rays (which tend to be stronger in areas of unpolluted air), but a degree of ultra-violet proofing is now incorporated into polythene, which makes it last longer. Another feature on the debit side is that dust adhesion resulting from the build-up of static electricity tends to cloud polythene and detract from its light transmission efficiency and general appearance.

The 'U' value or thermal coefficient of polythene is basically higher than that of glass, which results in a great deal of condensation unless the polythene has been treated to disperse moisture. Newer types of plastics, including polypropylene weave, have a similar or slightly lower 'U' value than glass and behave similarly as far as heat loss is concerned.

The problem of how to secure and tension without tearing has been successfully overcome in many of the latest designs: loose flapping polythene quickly deteriorates whereas tightly stretched polythene, even if of thinner grade, remains undamaged.

Glazing methods for glass

The simplest method of glazing is the use of putty and nails, as carried out on wooden glazing bars. Linseed oil putty is bedded in the channel of the glazing bar and the glass laid on this. The panes nearest the eaves in each section are laid first and the glazier then works upwards to the crest of the roof. Six brass sprigs are required per sheet (24 × 24in or 20 × 18in), two at the bottom of the lap, two 1-2in from the bottom of the pane, and two in the middle of each side. The next sheet of glass is laid on with a ¼-½in overlap (see Fig 15).

When necessary, glass is cut with a good straight edge and a sharp glass cutter, working on a flat wooden surface such as

44

Fig 16

the top of a table. Commercially the surplus putty pushed out by the glass is cut off with a putty knife, but on the amateur greenhouse it may be desirable to finish off the top of the glass with putty, running this the width of the astragal. This system of glazing has been in use for a great many years and is still favoured for the conventional wooden house construction. The putty should be painted over after a week or two when it has sufficiently hardened, but in time it will tend to crack and allow the entry of moisture.

The use of aluminium sealing strips has much to commend it on a new structure, to prevent rapid deterioration of the putty. They are often used after the glazing has already deteriorated, as a first-aid measure to avoid re-glazing, but this is really of very little use. A modification of conventional glazing which is quick and effective is to use strips of non-hardening mastic put down the grooves in the glazing bar, tacking the glass with *brass nails*—not sprigs.

Dry glazing is practised with all Dutch light greenhouses, the glass being held in a groove and consequently supported on all four sides. It might seem that this is a highly inefficient method of glazing since the glass rattles and the air space allows loss of heat, besides admitting water. In fact dry glazing is reasonably efficient, especially when the glass is held tightly. Vigorously blown rain *can* find its way into the structure but many gardeners have, after many years of experience, a high regard for the maintenance-free character of dry glazing and on balance the disadvantages are more than cancelled out by the advantages. Dutch greenhouses, if well

45

Fig 17

constructed, seldom suffer any damage
from gales or hurricanes, the severity of
that which occurred over central Scotland
in 1968 giving positive proof of the point.

Dry glazing systems are by no means
confined to wooden houses. In recent years
they have been adapted in alloy greenhouses in many different forms, the glass
being retained in an alloy glazing bar
extruded to form a groove which retains
the glass in a similar manner to the Dutch
light system (Fig 16).

Mastic and clips The more usual way of
glass retention with alloy glazing bars is to
bed the glass on a strip of mastic and retain
it with a stainless steel or alloy clip (see
Fig 18). 'Bar-caps' can also be fitted over
the clips to provide a tight seal and thereby

avoid a convenient lodgement area for
moss growth (a problem in dry districts
where sand or soil is blown around freely,
but less troublesome in wet areas where the
sand or soil is frequently dislodged by
heavy rain (see Fig 17). More sophisticated forms of glazing depend on a continuous bar-cap arrangement. Steel houses
are also usually glazed on the same system
of non-hardening mastic and clips, although one commercial system uses non-
hardening bitumen and plastic clips. It is
obviously more difficult to bar-cap a steel
bar than one of extruded alloy.

Modern glazing systems are remarkably
efficient apart from the problem of moss
lodgement, although on a small scale I
would doubt whether this is of great sig-

46

Fig 18

nificance, as the house can be brushed and washed down occasionally.

In very exposed districts something more sophisticated than the simple glazing clip system employed in many amateur structures would be advisable, owing to the degree of vibration of the glass which can be caused by persistent high winds. It needs merely one pane to loosen and slip for the wind to gain entry and rip out glass wholesale. Most glasshouse manufacturers will, I feel be prepared to provide bar-capping as a not-too-expensive extra where this is not standard.

Future trends in greenhouse design

While research in greenhouse design and the materials from which they are made is constant, the rising cost of all materials will undoubtedly accelerate matters greatly.

The great interest in the use of plastics primarily resulted because of their cheapness. Yet the massive rise in oil prices which has and will occur will tend to make oil derivative materials such as polythene highly suspect in the long term. It seems likely that for the foreseeable future conventional greenhouses will hold their place and any changes which occur will be simply refinements of existing design.

Greenhouses have in fact been with us more or less in their present form for a great many years.

Many gardeners have, in the last year or so, found that the use of corrugated plastic sheeting nailed to a wooden framework has made a reasonably satisfactory greenhouse, and it seems possible that rigid, reasonably priced, translucent sheeting of some form will be utilised in the next few years.

47

Summary of greenhouse materials

MATERIAL	TYPE	STRENGTH BULK RATIO	FURTHER COMMENTS
TIMBER On the whole 'warmer' greenhouses with less condensation provided glazing system is 'tight'	Baltic Redwood	Good	Good durable wood. Easy to work with. Readily impregnated with preservative
	British Columbian Pine	Good	Very similar in nature to Baltic Redwood. More difficult to impregnate with preservative
	Western Red Cedar	Poor but satisfactory in short lengths	Excellent appearance and resists decay. A most desirable wood for amateur structures unless in exposed situations
	Teak and Oak	Very high	Excellent woods with many qualities. Exposure is no deterent to their use
STEEL Makes very strong greenhouses. Excellent for internal structure	Must be well galvanised or enamelled	Very high	Excellent material but corrosion is a constant problem. Difficult to 'shape' for glazing purposes, (unlike alloy)
ALLOYS Light enough to work with & resists corrosion	Various types	Low	Good appearance (when new). Possibly the best material to use
CONCRETE Little used now. Not referred to in text	In reinforced form	Low	Makes very strong but clumsy greenhouses. Resists corrosion. Possibly best used for base of greenhouse only

Glazing systems

	Description	Comments
Putty and Nails On wood or metal houses	The conventional system still favoured by many gardeners	If well maintained gives a remarkably 'tight' greenhouse. Will in time deteriorate if not well maintained
Glazing Strips	The glass is laid on glazing strips instead of putty	A good system, the value of which is not yet fully appreciated. Very quick and simple
Dry Glazing	The glass is held supported in grooves in either wood or metal	Excellent maintenance free system even if it does allow a certain heat loss
Mastic and Clip	Clips are used to hold the glass on to strips of mastic or plastic	Most systems now satisfactory but additional 'Barcaps' necessary in exposed areas

Translucent materials

	Description	Comments
Glass Clear	24-26-32 oz. (thinner glass can be used but not advised	Glass is still the most effective transmitter of solar light and heat
Translucent	Cloudy glass which breaks up direct sunlight	Good for propagation activities and especially useful in very sunny climates
Plastic Rigid	In various forms in either curved or corrugated sheets	Apart from expense makes excellent greenhouses. Cheaper forms of corrugated sheeting can quickly make a useful structure
Polythene & P.V.C.	In various gauges. 38 mu, 125 mu, 150 mu	Deteriorate gradually but has a very useful role. Price will undoubtedly rise with increasing oil prices. Condensation still a major problem. Best used in double skin with a string or net separating the two sheets

Chapter 5

Types of Greenhouse

We turn now from the actual structural materials and their inherent strengths and design points to consider the basic forms of greenhouse. Before discussing them in detail there are a number of criteria for selection to be taken into account. These may be summarised as follows:

1 Maximum light transmission compatible with heat loss, bearing in mind the main purpose.

2 Freedom from maintenance, taking into account not only the structural materials, but also the glazing system.

3 Easy access to, and within, the greenhouse. Doors should be wide enough to permit entry of a barrow.

4 Reasonably easy and simple erection.

5 Cost. A relative matter. There is an excellent choice of structures to suit everyone's pocket.

6 Adequate ventilation, a really important issue which will be referred to in detail later.

7 Adaptability for automation, ie for ventilation, watering etc.

Fig 19

Span-roofed greenhouses

This is the conventional shape with straight sides and a sloping roof, fairly standard heights for amateur houses being about 7ft to 7ft 6in to the ridge and 5ft 6in to eaves. Most alloy greenhouses are glass-to-ground type. The length and breadth of the greenhouse varies from approximately 8ft long by 6ft wide, up to 12 × 8ft, which is an ideal width module as it allows two good sized widths of border or benches. There is a very wide range of sizes available and most are readily extendable in length.

Mobile greenhouses

A most interesting type of greenhouse for the amateur is the single-span Dutch light greenhouse constructed of interlocking Dutch light frames. The interlocking principle involving male and female lights fitting snugly into each other gives rigidity and avoids drip. The simplicity of the Dutch light structure is such that it can be erected very quickly. It also lends itself admirably to being mobilised by the fitting of pulley wheels to the bottom of the lights and running them on angle iron rails. If the ends of the greenhouse are hinged so that they can be raised clear of a crop the whole house can be moved en bloc and a system of crop rotation practised. For example one can crop with lettuce in site 1, then leave the lettuce to mature out of doors by pulling the house on to site 2 where a crop of tomatoes is planted. In the meantime a crop of mid-season chrysanthemums is planted out in April in site 3, the greenhouse being pulled over to cover this in September. A considerable number of cropping variations are practised commercially using mobile types of greenhouse. In Holland they are much used for the forced strawberry crop, the young plants being established in July by use of

Mobile greenhouses are still mainly used only in commercial circles, but smaller versions could be useful to the keen amateur.

irrigation out of doors, and after a suitable period of vernalisation (by cold weather) the mobile greenhouse is pulled over them in January and heat given to force the plants to crop from April onwards.

Mobile greenhouses need not, of course, be of Dutch light design, indeed many of those in Britain, Holland and Germany are not.

Commercial greenhouses

There is a vast range of sizes and types, and in this highly competitive business much experimentation. It is interesting to note that the massive ultra-wide-span houses erected in Britain in the sixties have given way recently under pressure of Continental competition to less costly narrower span structures and layouts designed to achieve maximum light transmission. In Europe however the popular Venlo-type (ie improved Dutch light) 3m houses are being superseded by a width module of 6m (21ft), again with economy of production in mind.

50

Variations in span-roofed greenhouses

Type	Design detail	Comments
1 Straight-sided span roof	Glass to ground level on very low base wall or base block	Good light transmission. Heating costs high in winter due to rapid heat loss
2 Sloping-sided span roof	As above but with sloping sides	Loss of headroom if side slope acute; orientate east-west for winter sun; stable
3 Span roof, sloping sides	Constructed of interlocking Dutch lights	Easy to erect; dry glazed; but can lose heat and be draughty
4 Conventional span roof, vertical or slightly sloping sides	Base wall 30–34in high	Best type for cold exposed area, especially for propagation; very stable
5 Span roof and vertical sides	Base of wood, asbestos or metal	No great advantage in respect of heat loss unless fibre-glass lined
6 Span roof and vertical sides	Roof half glass, half wood. Best done longitudinally	Dual purpose greenhouse/ shed at low cost; keep shed to north side or end

A Mansard or curvilinear greenhouse, in this case a mobile industrial one.

Mansard and curvilinear greenhouses

Mansard or curvilinear design simply sets out to provide a range of angles so that at any sun angle on the vertical plane there is a surface area of the glasshouse near the 'normal' angle (90°) for maximum solar radiation distribution if orientated east-west. This can give rise to problems in summer, necessitating shading, since variable-pitch roofs give more headroom for less air volume, and the increased solar radiation heats the air more than would be the case with a conventional greenhouse.

Mansard and curvilinear greenhouses have not found a great deal of favour in commercial circles, being more costly to build than span-roofed houses and not amenable to multi-span erection. For private gardens or parks' nurseries, however, the extra cost may be justified, especially when there is a lot of light-demanding winter work.

Greenhouses of this kind are available as glass-to-ground structures, or on a base block or wood or brick based wall. The mansard roof is also suitable for the lean-to greenhouse.

Lean-to greenhouses

The lean-to greenhouse was much favoured by earlier gardeners on account of the heat-reflecting and -storing qualities of the wall on which it was constructed. In recent years, lean-to greenhouses have fallen out of favour, largely because they pose tremendous ventilation problems in very hot weather, sited as they are invariably on a south-facing wall. But in the last year or so the high costs of fuel and the universal installation of central heating in the home have revived interest in the 'lean-to', since greenhouse heating can be linked to the domestic system and run very economically.

Lean to greenhouses can take three forms:

1 The three-quarter span, where it is preferable to extend the ridge of the greenhouse above the top of the wall and gain the full benefit of two-sided ridge ventilation.
2 The single pitch lean-to glass-to-ground, or on a base wall.
3 The curvilinear- and mansard-shaped lean-to, variable pitch.

There has been sufficient discussion on light transmission for the finer points of configuration to be appreciated. The variable pitch roofed structure is obviously best for good light transmission throughout the year, although excessively hot in summer. But both the three-quarter span and single-pitch types would suffer from excessive summer heating. Shading can be carried out, both outside and inside or a fan ventilation system installed to moderate temperatures.

An attractively designed lean-to greenhouse. This can be sited against a wall of any aspect depending upon the plants one wishes to grow in it. Ferns, for example, would thrive if it were sited on a north wall, the more popular exotics if it were sited on a south wall.

Circular greenhouses

Not a great deal can be said about circular greenhouses other than to extol their obvious advantages for light and solar heat transmission. They are more expensive to manufacture than conventional shaped houses offering comparable growing space. Nevertheless, the circular bench arrangement necessary with a circular greenhouse allows a high percentage of bench for pot plants or propagation under conditions of excellent light transmission and easy management. The more sophisticated forms of circular greenhouse have a turning mechanism by which the greenhouse revolves to keep pace with the sun. Effective ventilation can be a problem; fan ventilation or air conditioning is more or less essential if temperatures are to be kept to an acceptable level in very hot weather.

Plastic greenhouses

Plastic greenhouses made their enthusiastic debut in kit form in the early 1950s, and followed the basic design of a rigid tubular steel structure of conventional shape over which the plastic was stretched. At that time, however, plastic deteriorated very quickly due to the dual effects of ultra-violet rays and cold, being particularly vulnerable when in contact with structural members due to heat build-up. Modern experience has shown, however, that provided a good quality polythene is used and treated as being reasonably expendable (two years at the most) such greenhouses can be cheap and efficient for crop production. A basic fault is the condensation of moisture which occurs, necessitating very efficient ventilation if it is to be prevented. Double skin polythene helps in this respect

Simple forms of polythene walk-in tunnels in various forms have become very popular in Continental Europe and in Britain. The Lee Valley Horticultural Experimental Station has designed an excellent do-it-yourself structure where the polythene is lapped over hoops of galvanised barrel tubing.

Various types of polythene greenhouses can be bought ready to erect and the more

successful designs tension the polythene effectively, although the flapping of the polythene in some do-it-yourself tunnels is said to assist greatly with ventilation when the two end flap doors are left open. More recent recommendations, however, indicate the need to orientate plastic greenhouses so that prevailing wind can assist ventilation. Disease incidence should be no greater than in a glass greenhouse if correct ventilation is achieved. A recent criticism of plastic greenhouses is that carbon dioxide starvation occurs due to lack of air change when ventilation is poor. Water requirements in a properly ventilated plastic structure will be basically the same as those in an ordinary greenhouses.

While the majority of polythene greenhouses are of simple curved roof design, they can also be obtained in conventional multi-span form. In designs where wood is used for the structural members it is essential to use a wrap-round system of securing the polythene so that it does not tear at local stress points which occur when nails are used.

In commercial circles in Europe generally, there is a move towards polythene greenhouses, as the cost of traditional glasshouses rises constantly. The commercial grower must treat everything on a strict investment and return basis and the cost per square foot of a production unit capable of producing quantity and quality of crop is the vital issue. Much can be done by using polythene roofs and *hessian* sides for really cheap crop production! But naturally many growers much prefer a permanent glasshouse as a long-term investment without condensation, ventilation and renewal problems.

While a modicum of ventilation can be obtained in the polythene greenhouse by leaving doors or flaps open, orientating the house to catch the prevailing wind, or using vents, really effective ventilation can only be ensured by the installation of a suitably sized fan, and here of course is where the cost of the total structure starts to rise.

One of the most interesting types of polythene greenhouse is the 'bubble'.

Plastic greenhouses are still in their early days, but have a promising future ahead of them. Though at the moment mainly confined to commercial uses, they are bound to enter the domestic field fairly soon.

Here the polythene is kept inflated by a fan, ventilation being effected by an ancillary extractor fan, which brings a counterbalanced ventilator into use in an inlet. The true potential of 'bubbles' has, I feel, not been realised either in commercial or amateur gardening circles, no doubt because of the current interest in simple polythene greenhouses. Perhaps too the cost of running an electric motor constantly, as is necessary for inflation, tends to deter the gardener and grower alike. One type of plastic greenhouse has an inflated roof only.

54

Summary of greenhouse types

Greenhouse Type	Special Features	Range of Activities
SPAN-ROOFED (wood, alloy, steel)	Brick base wall	Pot plants, propagation chrysanthemums in pots
	Weatherboard base wall	Not so advantageous in respect of heat retention, but base wall can be lined with insulation materials such as fibre glass
	Glass to ground level	More costly to heat, but better light transmission makes them ideal for ground grown crops
LEAN-TO (single pitch, $\frac{3}{4}$ span or variable pitch)	With or without base wall	Will grow most crops. Ventilation and overheating problem unless extractor fans or air conditioning systems installed. Light distribution unequal. Excellent for peaches etc against wall
DUTCH LIGHT of simple design (including some of mansard design)	Static	Ideal for summer crops. Frequently used for lettuce and tomatoes. Heat loss occasioned by loose glazing system in some cases
	Mobile	Allows a system of crop rotation which can be highly advantageous
CURVILINEAR or MANSARD	On small base wall	Ideal for most activities, as in the case of glass-to-ground-level types. Heat loss high with the latter
CIRCULAR	Still in fairly early stages of development	Good for pot plants and propagation. Fan ventilation or air conditioning desirable
PLASTIC	Do-it-yourself type	Will grow most crops well if support adequate. Fan ventilation desirable
	Sophisticated type	Excellent for all activities with added advantages of mobility. Fan ventilation still desirable
	Bubble	Has great potential for professional and amateur. Continuous running electric motor for inflation

Summary of plastic greenhouses

Type	Design detail	Comments
Do-it-yourself types of various designs	Conventional span roofed shaped	As efficient a production unit as a conventional greenhouse, provided they are fan ventilated, although wear and tear of polythene is inevitable, necessitating fairly regular renewal. Cooler than a conventional greenhouse, especially at night.
	Tunnels	Reasonably stable in design and will suffer little damage by tearing until polythene weakens by ultra-violet deterioration. Ventilation problems still exist unless fans are used.
	Conventional shaped multi-span structures	More sophisticated forms are also stable and efficient. Crop supports require special consideration. Effective ventilation in all types may be a problem unless fans are used.
Bubble houses	Either total or part inflated	Likely to be developed to a great degree.

Chapter 6

Buying & Erecting Greenhouses

It is logical to think about the selection of a greenhouse before considering erection procedures, heating, ventilation, and other related matters, but it is imperative to understand the rudiments of these important matters before actually confirming the greenhouse order in precise detail. It far too often happens that people innocently buy greenhouses only to find out that they are insufficiently ventilated, not wide enough for two benches, or have other deficiencies.

Greenhouse buying can be approached in a variety of ways—you may send off for a catalogue you have seen advertised, or you may come across a greenhouse display at a flower show or garden centre. The information contained in greenhouse catalogues varies greatly: some are detailed in the extreme, some frustratingly unprecise. On the whole, however, they provide sufficient detail to enable one to make a selection even if technical issues such as stress and strain factors and general stability are seldom referred to.

Points to note when ordering

1 *Structural materials* Select for stability, lack of maintenance and aesthetic appearance. Glazing system is most important.

2 *Size and dimensions* Largely a question of suiting the greenhouse to the site, its size to intensity of use, and cost to money available. A frequent mistake is to purchase too small a greenhouse at the outset and find it bursting at the seams before long. Comparatively speaking, a larger greenhouse is a better investment than a smaller one on a square foot basis, this being readily ascertained by dividing the square foot area obtained into the total price. There is not a great difference in price between some alloys and conven-

tional wooden structures, especially if the latter are of superior treated wood.

3 *Ventilation* There is a distinct lack of reference in many catalogues to the actual ventilation area in relation to the actual area of the greenhouse, and this information is necessary in order to work out whether or not the design gives a satisfactory rate of air change. Methods of calculating ventilation requirements are given elsewhere and these should be studied before specifying the number of vents required. Very little reference is made in many amateur greenhouse catalogues to fan ventilation, although it is the most positive way of achieving air change.

4 *Number of doors* One door is standard in amateur greenhouses. Two doors would only be necessary where a greenhouse is large enough to merit them, being in the order of 15–20ft in length. Sliding doors are now available, and these have great advantages.

5 *Constructional base blocks* These are frequently offered, particularly with wooden greenhouses, and they are worth purchasing as they not only ensure a tight seal between the sill plate and the foundations, but make sure that the greenhouse is firmly secured to the ground. They also assist in simple, quick erection.

6 *Benching* This is usually available from manufacturers if required, there being merit in the fact that their benching will fit precisely into the greenhouse purchased.

7 *Other extras* Autovents, heaters, gutters and downpipes (if not standard), shades and other items can usually be ordered along with the greenhouse, and there is much to be said for buying them at the outset.

IMPORTANT NOTE Always double check the order, seeking the advice of a horticultural consultant or knowledgeable friend if in doubt on any important details. The cost of delivery should also be checked; some firms make a charge for delivery in certain areas, others include it in the basic price.

Delivery

Greenhouses are delivered in various forms, from the fully complete sections of prefabricated wooden greenhouses, glazed or unglazed, to the alloy structures neatly packed in a container. Where bulky and heavy sections are involved, some care should be taken to ensure that they are off-loaded from the delivery lorry relatively convenient to the erection site without impinging on it. These sections should be carefully stacked and adequately supported so that they are not likely to topple over in a gale; if in doubt lay them flat, but keep an eye on damage to the lawn!

Checking to see that everything is delivered undamaged and that no parts are missing is not always easy, but if at all possible it should be done, although this is not practical with alloy sections packed in boxes. The delivery note should be signed appropriately if there is any obvious damage, and the supplier informed immediately. Most reliable firms double check everything when it leaves the factory, as non-delivery of parts can cause a great deal of annoyance. Mistakes do occur however; new designs being particularly prone to missing parts, and in some instances sections do not fit properly together.

Plans and problems

Erection plans, in some cases very detailed indeed, should always be sent by the manufacturer, and they may in fact arrive before the greenhouse, which is a better arrangement as it allows the site and foundations to be prepared and the erection instructions and plans to be carefully studied. Note precisely whether centre to centre, outside to outside, or inside to inside measurements are quoted; outside to outside measurements are the most usual.

Consideration should be given to intended orientation for the greenhouse when making the actual purchase and most certainly when seeking planning permission. It can happen, however, that a different orientation seems preferable when the actual erection is in hand. It would then be better to delay work until the matter is corrected and I would imagine that most planning authorities would be fairly sympathetic to an alteration involving, in many cases, only a few feet one way or another with an amateur sized greenhouse. To ignore the tremendous implications of correct orientation would be folly.

Marking out the site

To peg out the position of the greenhouse on the ground, accurately cut pointed pegs 1 × 1in and at least 12in in length. Knock in the first peg lightly at the appropriate distance from some fixed line such as a fence, path or building, and by the use of a steel measuring tape tap in another peg to mark the length of the greenhouse, *using centre to centre* measurements for each peg. Check that the line of the pegs is in line with the fence or building, making sure at the same time that it follows the desired orientation. Note that it is the length of the greenhouse, the line of the ridge, which must conform to east-west or north-south orientation. A few degrees off the intended orientation one way or another is not vital, it being better, however, to err to the north for an east-west ridge orientation and to the east for a north-south orientation.

With a reasonably square greenhouse it is, on balance, marginally better to have the ridge running east-west for transmission of winter and spring light. Where, by necessity, the greenhouse has to be erected with an orientation between east-west and north-south to maintain a tidy line, there is not much one can do about it: the full implications of light transmission must, however, be appreciated.

The levels of the two pegs should now be set accurately, knocking them into the ground sufficiently to make them stable. With the average amateur sized greenhouse up to about 10–12ft in length, a long straight unwarped board and a spirit-level should suffice for level checking. For a longer greenhouse an intermediate peg or pegs is advisable, checking their line by the use of a light piece of cord or string which should always be set tautly between the two end pegs. If a Cowley level can be borrowed, set up and properly used, this helps to get the top of the pegs exactly level without the use of a spirit-level initially, although final checking with a spirit-level is always desirable.

Smaller greenhouses are usually erected dead level; a larger type with a gutter may have a slight fall in one direction, as advised by the manufacturer, to facilitate the run of water. With commercial greenhouses, especially in multi-bay form, a run is essential to ensure that the water moves quickly along the gutter and does not flow back through the glass. A fall of about 6–12in per 100ft length of greenhouse is usual.

Now tap a 2in nail *lightly* into the *centre* of each peg. Forming the right angle necessary to measure up the width of the greenhouse can be tricky and should never be guessed. A triangle carefully made up with pieces of straight unwarped wood 3ft, 4ft and 5ft in length may be used, checking that the right angle formed is exact by using a joiner's square. The triangle should be put exactly *to the nail* on one corner peg and one leg should be supported with bricks along the taut line between the two end pegs. After supporting the other right-angle leg, put a line along it and tie this to a peg set outside the width of the greenhouse. Then measure along the line and insert a peg at the exact width required. Repeat this procedure at the other corner and then check the two pegs longitudinally, also checking that the diagonals are equal. One usually finds it necessary to make slight adjustments so that everything tallies. (This task can also be undertaken with a site square, which is not perhaps the easiest instrument to use as it must itself be very carefully set up *dead level* over both of the first inserted

corner pegs in turn.) Now level up the corner pegs and tap nails into their centres. Finally set taut good-quality lines on each corner peg to make the outline of the house by using short pieces of wood, or more pegs, 2–3ft outside the house outline so that work can proceed on the foundations of the greenhouse without impediment by moving the corner pegs and lines out of the way as necessary (see Fig 20).

Foundations

With certain types of Dutch light greenhouses it is merely necessary to set down base blocks on levelled soil, though this is not a very satisfactory long-term arrangement either in the interests of stability or to prevent lateral movement of soil moisture. It is a practice adopted frequently by commercial growers taking short cuts in the interests of economy, or where a greenhouse site is being treated as temporary. A foundation of one kind or another is highly desirable to keep the greenhouse completely level and entirely stable in spite of the destructive forces of such things as gales and hurricanes. The precise nature of the foundation depends on a number of factors, and more specifically on the actual design of the greenhouse being erected. Study very closely the erection plans or booklet applicable to the greenhouse. Base blocks may be provided with the greenhouse if specially ordered; alternatively it may be necessary to build a brick base wall. For most amateur greenhouses a half-brick (4½in) wall will be adequate, and this is usually exactly the width of any special base blocks provided. In this case, after determining the exact centre line of the greenhouse base, take out a trench 8–9in wide and 5–6in deep, or deeper if the soil has recently been levelled in order to make contact with undisturbed soil. This may not always be practical. Using a mixture of 3 parts finely broken brick, 2 parts rough sand, and 1 part cement, run in a layer about 3–4in deep and 'dump' this as level as possible by the use of a fairly heavy straight board, using a spirit-level on top

59

of this to check levels regularly. Where a full brick foundation wall (9in) is necessary, as could be the case on a sloping site, or for a large greenhouse, the trench should be 12–14in wide and again 5–6in deep, although in many cases a half-brick wall would suffice if suitably reinforced with piles. Greenhouses can in certain circumstances be laid directly on the foundations without the base blocks, in which case any securing bolts will need to be inserted into the foundations at the appropriate points. Alternatively anchor cleats may be used. Special base blocks invariably have an in-built system of anchorage for the greenhouse. Always allow the foundations to harden sufficiently before starting building. In all cases it will be necessary to put the line back in position and keep this suitably taut when necessary to check that there is precise adherence to the stated outside measurement. Before building opposite walls, it is advisable to check the widths and length, as bricks tend to get out of alignment, especially if laid by someone who is not an experienced bricklayer.

Perusal of greenhouse catalogues frequently shows a complete perimeter wall with no allowance for doors, which involves an awkward step up unless there is a suitable ramp. Base blocks, when supplied, invariably leave the door flush with ground-level, a much more sensible arrangement, provided there is a concrete step.

It may seem that these items are trivial, yet they make a great deal of difference over the years to the easy management of a greenhouse, especially when wheeling barrows full of soil or debris. It is advisable to have a slight rise *up* to the door to avoid rain running into the greenhouse, which may happen if the ground slopes the other way.

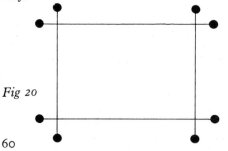

Fig 20

Skill in building even a low wall varies, but by using a 3:1 sand/cement mixture and checking the line and level of each brick or block carefully, it should be possible for even the rawest amateur builder to make a reasonably accurate job of it, failing which call in a builder or handyman. Note that if using faced bricks the faced side should be to the outside, otherwise they will quickly weather.

Building procedures

Where the type of greenhouse being built demands a low base wall of 30in or thereabouts, this must be carefully built, otherwise there can be erection problems. Very few prefabricated greenhouses intended for base walls now seem to be about, but they can be obtained if required and may be necessary on very exposed sites. Do-it-yourself enthusiasts frequently use the base-wall method of building a greenhouse, following conventional designs of sill plates on top of the wall to bear the astragals (see Fig 21). Second-hand ex-commercial structural material is often bought for the purpose of cutting down to build an amateur greenhouse, which is not usually a difficult job, provided care is taken to clean all the wood properly, giving it a good coat of paint before building commences, especially as the ends of the old astragal bars are generally removed. Galvanised nails should be used throughout, as steel nails can quickly rust.

There are seldom any problems in building a prefabricated greenhouse, particularly if time is taken to study erection plans. Some of the instruction booklets are detailed in the extreme, every part being marked and identified by a diagram, there being explicit erection diagrams bearing part numbers in addition. With alloy structures it is normal to build up the gable ends and one side on the ground; then, after putting up one gable end, proceed first with one side and then the other before putting up the other gable end. The roof and ventilators are generally left until last.

The completely glazed sections of a

prefabricated wooden greenhouse are erected in similar order, but it will be necessary to obtain help as the sections are often heavy. If building a greenhouse with wood on a do-it-yourself basis, it is merely a case of building the main framework first before putting in the astragals. When glazing, although procedures vary, it is often preferable to do the roof first, followed by the gable ends, leaving the sides until last so that if there should be a high wind it will blow through the structure. A very important point when building any type of greenhouse is to tie down loose vents at night, particularly if they are glazed, otherwise they can flap about and cause a lot of damage.

The need to anchor greenhouses securely cannot be emphasised too strongly, allowing cement to harden before fully erecting a valuable structure. There are frequent instances of

Fig 21

greenhouses being built on semi-hard brick base walls, and the whole thing being blown over in a strong wind, with devastating results.

Glazing should take place only during dry weather, as neither putty nor strips of mastic seal properly if the glazing bars are wet, in addition to which wet glass is very dangerous to work with. With alloy greenhouses all joins in gutters or main members should be properly sealed with mastic or other material.

Where there is a gutter the downpipe should be taken to an appropriate outlet or soakaway, and where the greenhouse is built on a slope it may be necessary to install a drain along the higher side to stop rain seeping into the greenhouse.

Installation of water
The installation of water has already been mentioned in connection with site preparation. If a supply pipe at low level is taken into the greenhouse, care should be taken not to damage the foundations. Ideally the water pipe should be laid before the greenhouse is built. The precise arrangements for water will depend on a number of circumstances, but a screw type tap is more or less a standard fitment. The most convenient place for the tap will again vary, but in the majority of cases the end opposite the door is most satisfactory (see Fig 22). For mist irrigation, capillary benches, spraylines, heating systems and other water-demanding equipment, special arrangements will be necessary, all readily accomplished with alkathene pipe and patent screw fittings.

Installation of electricity
Because greenhouses are damp places, *and with alloy greenhouses in particular,* plastic covered cable, preferably PVC conduit or PCP sheathed cable, must be used along with waterproof fittings for the installation of electricity. The complete installation should be supervised by a qualified electrician or someone with a sound knowledge of electrical installations, and properly earthed. An alloy greenhouse can fre-

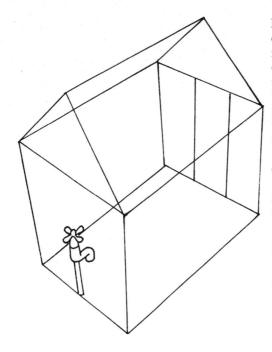

Fig 22

house will usually be dependent on the cropping arrangements. With a permanently benched greenhouse with a bench on each side, a slab path at least 2ft wide is the general rule. The area under each bench is usually left 'rough', although the fastidious gardener may well wish to slab the whole place. Slabs can be laid on a bed of sand, ashes or rubble, this last allowing the slabs to be held at the corners by cement (see Fig 23). Alternatively a concrete path can be run in using a 5:3:2 mixture and shuttering boards, making the concrete at least 2in thick.

When the borders are used for cropping purposes, a wooden 'cat walk' may be used instead of a slabbed centre path as it can be removed to allow complete soil sterilisation and cultivation. Where ring culture of tomatoes is practised, slabs are simply laid down the centre of the aggregate, unless some more permanent arrangement is preferred.

A point to note about slab paths set merely in sand or ash is that should excess moisture run about this can wash away the sand or ashes, allowing the slabs to become undermined or lose their level.

quently 'go live' because of the nearness of an open connection to the structure. With a wooden greenhouse, while the same care is not perhaps as necessary, the installation should be carried out to rigid standards of safety. Whether to bring power in overhead or by underground cable is a matter best decided by a qualified electrician who will also ensure that the supply cable is adequate for the load demanded by the equipment and taken right back to a suitably placed junction box and *not* a convenient plug.

Main path and greenhouse flooring

There should be a good slabbed path, or one of concrete or asphalt, to the greenhouse door or doors, there being nothing worse than a dirty wet path which, apart from being dangerous, constantly carries dirt and possible disease into the greenhouse.

The nature of the flooring in a green-

Maintenance of greenhouses

The painting procedure for greenhouses has already been referred to, as also have types of paint and frequency of painting. The current theme of erecting a green-

Fig 23

62

A firm, stable path is essential in any well-run greenhouse. It is rather a shame to clutter it up with large tubs, but it does provide a useful standing for plants like these that can be stood out of doors in summer and only need overwintering under glass.

house of materials and of a design which require little or no maintenance is founded on sound common sense, as there can be nothing more troublesome than constantly attending to the upkeep of buildings.

One of the main chores with any type of greenhouse is the cleaning of the glass, especially in industrial areas. Dust adheres to sticky deposits and in time a skin of dust develops on the glass, restricting light transmission very considerably. Moss and algae grow at any overlaps and on the glazing bars unless a carefully sealed bar-cap glazing system is used. Even then moss and algae can develop under the bar-cap if moisture gains access, which it usually does. The build-up of moss and algae, especially the former, can be extremely destructive and will literally push the glass out of position, causing leaks.

Glass cleaning can be carried out by using a proprietary glass cleaner or oxalic acid crystals dissolved in water, 1lb to 1 gallon, sprayed on and then washed off, the latter being especially necessary when a metal greenhouse is involved. The oxalic acid also burns off a fair proportion of the moss, the remainder being freely dislodged by a good strong jet from a hose pipe. Moss and algae also grow inside a greenhouse and the removal of these is better undertaken when the greenhouse is empty. The cleaning operation usually demands the wearing of protective clothing, including a waterproof hat. Cresylic acid used in a solution of 1 part to 39 parts of water is a useful material for cleaning down the inside as it burns off moss and algae very effectively. Moss and algae in glass overlaps may have to be removed physically with a piece of metal and a jet of water.

Base walls should be cleaned annually with a wire brush; if necessary paint them with whitewash or emulsion paint.

The maintenance of heating systems will be dealt with in another chapter.

63

Table of BTU requirements
For calculating approximate BTU requirements of larger greenhouses.

Floor area of glasshouse square ft.	HAG 'factor'	
	Narrow span up to 20 ft.	Wide span 20–60 ft.
1,000	1·87	2·09
5,000	1·45	1·52
10,000	1·35	1·42
15,000	1·30	1·37
20,000	1·27	1·34
25,000	1·25	1·31
30,000	1·24	1·30
35,000	1·22	1·29
40,000	1·21	1·28
45,000	1·20	1·26

Approximate BTU requirements to heat glasshouses are:—
(Floor area in sq. ft. × HAG 'factor' × lift in deg. F = BTU requirements.

Chapter 7

To study in depth the full implications of heat is well beyond the scope of this book. It will suffice to translate the three methods of heat distribution, ie conduction, convection and radiation, into practical terms in relation to greenhouse heating. Briefly, **conduction** is the transmission of heat through a substance from molecule to molecule, **convection** the transference of heat through a liquid or gas by circulation of the heated portion, and **radiation** the transference of heat energy by electromagnetic waves from heat source to absorbing object, and between objects.

Solar radiation

The short wave radiation from the sun passes through the glass of the greenhouse, warming everything it contacts, floor, soil, bench, plants, pots, and so on. These in turn re-radiate the heat back into the greenhouse on long waves which cannot pass through the glass. The heat trapped within the greenhouse sets up convection currents, establishing in effect a convection cycle of warmed air.

Artificial heating systems

Where an artificial heating system is introduced into the greenhouse it will operate independently of solar radiation, and more generally and preferably when solar radiation falls below an effective level. There are several forms of artificial heating available. Hot water pipes are a good method of heating greenhouses: the metal is a good conductor of heat and in turn transmits radiation heat; and both pipes and objects warmed by radiation set up convection currents. Hot pipes also transmit heat by conduction when they are in actual contact with the soil. Electric tubular heaters are another frequently used method of greenhouse heating and operate

in the same way as water heated pipes. Warm air heaters, free discharge or fan assisted, are becoming increasingly popular for greenhouse heating. The air on discharge sets up convection currents. Fans simply push the heated air out more quickly, though convection currents still subsequently develop.

Soil warming cables, used mainly for propagation benches, become warm by conduction, then transmit this heat by conduction and radiation to the soil or sand. Mineral insulated cables are used for warming the air.

Some variable factors in greenhouse heating

One important point which should be stressed is that these heating processes can readily be upset or disturbed. For example, one side of a greenhouse may be much colder than the other, despite a well-designed perimeter system of warm pipes, because a very cold wind blowing along that side is causing very rapid heat loss through the glass. Similarly, a fan heater may fail to direct warm air to all parts of the greenhouse, because a cold wind outside has produced an internal curtain of cold air.

Lack of uniformity in temperature throughout a greenhouse can be checked by the use of integrating jars (see Fig 24) or, less accurately, with a number of ordinary thermometers. These integrating jars, which are silver-foil-covered, water-filled bottles containing thermometers, are left in different areas of the greenhouse long enough for the water content in the jar to achieve uniform temperature (there may be difficulty in this respect during short summer nights). On inspection the temperatures recorded will be found to vary considerably.

Fig 24

The particular problems of greenhouse heating centre around the unavoidable rapid loss of heat through the glass by conduction, and inevitably also through leaks in the structure. There is therefore great need of a constant high output and uniform source of heat sufficient to overcome this rapid heat loss. A central source of heat, such as an oil heater or even an electric fan or convector heater, will not warm a greenhouse as uniformly as it would the room of a solid building. Ideally a greenhouse should have a complete ring of warm pipes to give off radiation heat and initiate convection currents, and in the centre there should be further radiation heat from pipes, which would also set up smaller convection currents (see Fig 25). Where there are benches there should be allowance for convection currents between the bench and the outside of the greenhouse (frequently this is prevented) in addition to radiation heat to plants on the bench by individual pipes. The diagrams referred to show the greenhouse longitudinally, but the ends of the greenhouse should develop similar convection currents, it being good practice to complete the circuit of pipes under the door by containing them in a grille.

Although a centrally sited unit heater is unable to achieve uniform heat distribution, this matters less as the season progresses and outside temperatures rise. Warm air fan heaters are slightly better than convector heaters (electrical, oil or gas), as they do move the air positively which assists with the mixing of warm and cold air, though there are inevitable cold spots. Warm air heaters, however, can be as efficient as warm pipe systems if the air is distributed in polythene ducts (see Fig 48).

Calculating heat losses

It is essential to make exact measurements of the greenhouse so that the heat loss through all external surface areas can be calculated accurately. The areas of glass (including glazing bars) and the areas of base walls of brick or wood or other mater-

Fig 25

ial should be measured separately since each will lose heat at different rates. Heat loss is calculated by the rate of thermal transmission (loss of heat by conduction) or ʮ value; different materials have different ʮ values. These are quoted in British thermal units, one unit being the amount of heat needed to raise the temperature of 1lb of water 1°F. The following are the accepted ʮ values for various materials and, in keeping with modern practice, they are quoted in slightly higher figures to allow for inadvertent heat loss. It should be noted that the same final figure can be worked out by taking the lower figures frequently quoted (eg in *Greenhouse Gardening*, I. G. Walls) and adding one-third to the final calculation. Note also that heat losses will be higher in exposed situations, lower in sheltered ones.

Average thermal transmission co-efficients of different materials

Glass (including glazing bars)		1.4Btu
Brickwork 4½in		.64 ,,
9in		.47 ,,
11in (ie dwelling house walls)		.30 ,,
Concrete 4in		.75 ,,
6in		.61 ,,
Wood 1in (tongued and grooved)		.5 ,,
Asbestos sheeting (corrugated)		1.4 ,,
Polythene 38mu		
125mu	For practical purposes taken as 1.4Btu	
150mu		
Polypropylene weave		

Technically there is also a heat loss through concrete or earth floors, but this is so small it can be ignored. In actual fact the floor can often serve as a considerable store of heat for re-radiation, but any heat loss is allowed for in the higher figures quoted above. It is now a relatively simple matter to calculate the total surface area of the greenhouse, eg the all-glass greenhouse shown in Fig 27.

Sides 2 × (8ft × 6ft)	=	96sqft
Ends 2 × (6ft × 6ft)	=	72sqft
Roof 2 × (8ft × 3ft 6in)	=	56sqft
Gable ends 2 × (3ft × 1ft 6in)	=	9sqft
		233sqft

Fig 26

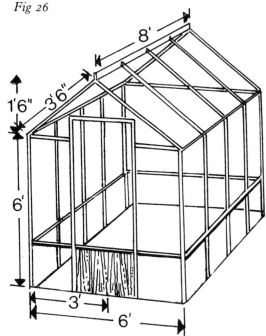

As this is an all-glass greenhouse the total heat loss is 233 × 1.4 = 326Btu. This figure is the difference per degree F between inside and outside temperatures and it is then necessary to calculate for the heat lift required; this is done by multiplying the 326 by the selected heat lift: a 20°F lift is adequate for frost protection and normal temperatures in spring; a 40°F lift will ensure a reasonable level of temperature throughout the year, even when it is 20°F out of doors; the 30°F lift is a compromise between the two. Thus the figures to be aimed at, eg 326 × 20 = 6,520Btu, 326 × 30 = 9,780Btu, and 306 × 40 = 13,040Btu, give the respective heat losses for the various lifts. These figures represent the actual heat requirements from the heating system, no matter what type or design this may be.

It is usual to have a slightly larger heat

Broad-bore heating pipes take a long time to cool down once the heat source has switched off.

production unit than necessary to allow quick response and to cope with periods of excessively low temperatures. Where a hot pipe system has the boiler sited away from the greenhouse (perhaps in a shed or garage), there will be some loss of heat en route to the greenhouse, a quarter to a third being the usual allowance for this loss. Allowance may also have to be made for an exposed situation. For a quick and *approximate assessment* of heat loss in small greenhouses only, multiply the number of square feet of floor area in the greenhouse by 125 for a 20°F lift, by 190 for a 30° lift and by 250 for a 40°F lift. In view of the many different sizes of greenhouse and types of structural material, there is no substitute for individual calculation.

Designing a heating system around the calculated heat requirement will depend on the type of crop to be raised and practical matters of the availability of electricity, oil or gas, and the possibility of linking the system to an existing one in the home.

Hot water systems
Large bore pipes
These were once normal installation for all greenhouses, but are not now considered economical for large units. Pipes are usually of 4in diameter and the water circulated by gravity, provided there is a gradual rise from the boiler to the highest point in the unit and a gradual fall-back to the boiler. There are design problems here, in avoiding obstruction to doors and in siting the boiler or heat source at a sufficiently low point—often below ground-level unless

Fig 27

the heating pipes in the greenhouse are fairly high (see Fig 27).

It is a slow and costly operation to heat up large volumes of water, but once hot it retains and radiates its heat for a considerable period. This, however, in combination with solar radiation often causes the temperature of the air in the greenhouse to rise excessively, which is not only wasteful but may be injurious to the plants, although it can help to encourage air currents through the crop. Once solar radiation ceases there may be a quick demand once again for heat, and the whole process of re-heating the now cool large volume of water has to be begun again.

Advantages of small bore pipes

Smaller bore pipe systems of 1–2in diameter are invariably installed now in greenhouses: there is much less water to heat, and thus the total bulk cools more rapidly. A further advantage of small bore pipes is that as they take up less room they can be readily taken to the crop and spread over the cropping area or under benches, between plants, and placed on the soil—especially important for plants such as early tomatoes which must be planted in a warm soil.

Accelerated hot water systems

The main disadvantage of small bore pipe systems is that as the diameter of the pipe decreases the friction increases, and it may be found that the hot water does not circulate rapidly enough or may not be capable of completing its circuit back to the heat source again. This can be overcome by the use of an accelerator pump—a matter for consultation with a heating engineer. Existing gravity systems can, in many cases, be greatly improved by the fitting of such a pump, although this will seldom be necessary on smaller installations.

High speed hot water systems

Accelerator pumps merely *assist* the circulation of the water but still allow natural circulation; high speed hot water systems, usually of small bore design, depend entirely on pumps for the circulation of the water, allowing no natural circulation. They include alkathene soil

warming pipes underground, and 'minibore' bench warming systems. Problems do exist with high speed water systems unless an entirely automatic system of firing is involved. The temperature of the greenhouse is usually controlled by a thermostat which operates the pumps and if a non-automatic solid fuel boiler is being used and the pump is shut off by the thermostat (due to a rise above the desirable temperature in the greenhouse) there can be serious overheating of he boiler. With automatically fired boilers, especially with oil or gas where there is no great residual heat involved, this situation does not arise. The problem can be overcome by using a non-return valve on a bypass which opens when the pump is nonoperative.

In high speed hot water systems, and to a limited degree with accelerated systems also, it is important to ensure that the pump is the correct size for the system. An inadequate size of pump would fail to overcome the frictional resistance of the pipes, but too powerful a pump would not only circulate the water, but could force it out of the system through the header tank. The design of pumps and accelerators and their selection for a specific task is a highly technical matter best taken up with a specialist supplier who will specify a particular size for the heating system involved after taking into account the length of pipe, its diameter, the calorific rating of the system, the acceptable temperature drop between flow and return pipes, and the design of the whole system.

Formulae exist which allow the ready calculation of pump sizes which are rated on what is called their 'circulating head' and it should be repeated that a pump with a larger circulation head than is necessary will give rise to problems. There are several ways of overcoming this such as fitting it on the flow pipe instead of, as is normal, on the return, or ensuring that the header tank is on the suction side of the pump, or alternatively raising the height of the header tank (see Fig 28). Pumps with variable circulating heads which allow some adjustment are available and may be the answer for smaller domestic greenhouse systems.

Types of piping

Cast iron piping is now seldom used for greenhouse heating, although there are still many older systems in existence. Steel pipes are invariably used and this has the distinct advantage of allowing screwed couplings or alternatively welding to be readily carried out—not possible with cast iron pipes. Before 1957 there were three classifications of pipes, A, B and C. Today it is enough to specify medium grade piping for all heating systems where screwed joints are to be used. Lighter continental European grades of piping are now being used in commercial installations. Pipes rust readily and while it was stated for a while that aluminium based paint should not be used as this reduced heat output, research has shown the reduction in heat transmission to be insignificant. Aluminium paint is therefore advised to reduce external rusting and general deterioration. Bitumastic paint should not be used as

this gives off fumes when the pipes are warm. Newer types of vegetable oil paint have also been developed.

Transmission of heat from different pipe sizes

The transmission of heat from pipes varies according to their diameter, the temperature of the water in them, and the external temperature of the air surrounding them. The following table shows the respective output of pipes of different diameters at an air temperature of 55°F (13°C), the varia-

Fig 28

tion of output for different air temperatures being shown in the accompanying table. To use this chart read upwards from the base to the line indicating pipe size, then move left to ascertain the output per foot of pipe. As the temperature of the water in a heating system varies, as indeed does the air temperature, it is necessary to accept a workable figure for design purposes. It can be seen, however, from the figure that the output from pipes can be considerably greater with a higher water temperature, especially when the water temperature rises above boiling point (see note under pressurised hot water systems). With smaller greenhouse systems one must be realistic and, considering the difference between the flow and return temperatures,

Fig 29

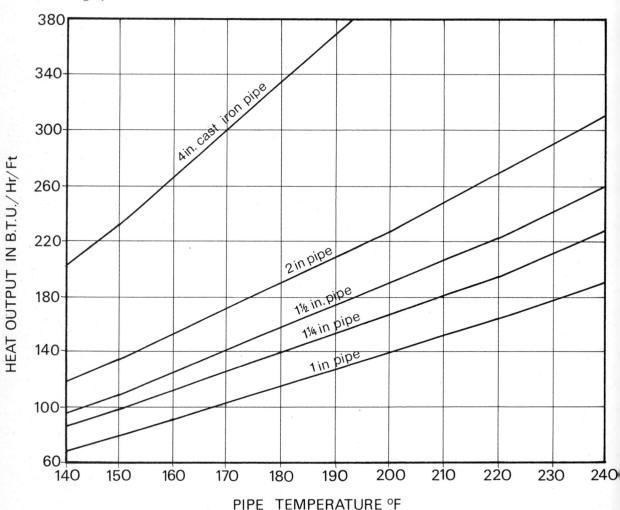

the following figures are reasonably work-able (see Fig 29).

Pipe emission at 100°F (37°C) temperature difference to nearest round figures

1in	80Btu
1¼in	100 ,,
1½in	110 ,,
2in	130 ,,
4in	230 ,,

Gilled pipes are available and these permit a much greater heat emission according to the design (up to four or five times as much as plain pipes).

Designing a hot water heating system

To design a pipe heating system the first stage is to determine the heat loss of the greenhouse and thereafter to calculate the length of pipe needed to supply the necessary heat in a form which will conveniently fit in with the type of cropping being prac-tised. To return to the 8 × 6ft greenhouse, and assuming a 40°F lift, we are concerned with the supply of some 13,000Btu. The respective lengths of piping of different diameters will be, to quote two examples,

$$\frac{13{,}000}{100} \qquad\qquad \frac{13{,}000}{230}$$

$$= 130\text{ft of }1\tfrac{1}{4}\text{in piping, or}$$

= slightly over 56ft of 4in (quite a few smaller systems are offered with a boiler and a length of 4in piping). If a 4in system was selected the normal arrangement of pipes will be a double run of pipe along each side and across the end, which comes

BREATHER

Fig 30

to 44ft, some 12ft short of the calculated figure. Assuming slightly hotter pipes in view of the nearness of the boiler, it is fair to assume that the required 13,000Btu could be supplied, bearing in mind that this allows for 60°F (16°C) in the greenhouse at 20°F (− 7°C) outside temperature. If, however, it is decided to use 1¼in pipes, the required 130ft will necessitate either spreading or banking on the sides (see Fig 30) requiring six lines of pipes along each side and across the end. There is virtue, therefore, for greenhouses of this small size, in using larger bore pipe, especially as to do this would also facilitate circulation without the fairly costly installation of a pump. As a compromise, 90 odd feet of 2in pipe would be required—four lines on the sides and at the end.

It will be noted that no provision has been made in this instance for heating in the region of the door and it would be difficult to allow for this where circulation depends entirely on gravity. Where a pump and small bore pipes are being used, these could conveniently be taken either below or above the door. Pipes can all be installed at high level and this has virtues for flower crops. Where larger greenhouses are concerned and spread heat is desirable for an early tomato crop, the pipes should be spaced out over the greenhouse. Commercially much use is made of flexible rubber couplings to allow the pipes to be raised or lowered as desired. When the soil is to be heated prior to planting tomatoes, the pipes are allowed to actually lie on the ground, and subsequently

Fig 31

when the soil is warm and more convection heat is necessary to warm the air, the pipes can be raised on bricks. On the Continent much use is made of underground alkathene pipes. A frequent practice in smaller houses is to install benches for the earlier part of the year for intensive propagation, removing these in the spring to make way for a ground-grown crop of tomatoes or chrysanthemums. In this case rubber coupled pipes capable of movement could be kept up a few inches below the bench to provide local heat for propagation, then dropped down to the ground to warm the soil for tomatoes or other crops (see Fig 31).

Low pressure steam heating systems
These have little place in small installations, a steam boiler being an expensive item, only economical between about 800–1,000lb of steam per hour, this being capable of supplying heat for a greenhouse of about one-quarter of an acre. As with medium pressure hot water systems less heating pipe is required.

Medium pressure hot water systems
In these systems hot water can be circulated through the heating pipes, if necessary above boiling point, the water being prevented from boiling because it is under pressure. The pressure is provided either by an ancillary unit or by a steam 'pad' in the boiler. Hot water boilers can be used where an ancillary unit is to be used, whereas with the pad system a steam boiler is necessary. As water temperatures in the pipes can be as high as 230–250°F (110–121°C), less radiation surface is needed in the greenhouse, so reducing the total length of pipe required, although the pipe layout will follow a similar pattern to a hot water system. A circulating pump is required to move the water round quickly. One advantage of the steam pad boiler system, where the heated water is taken off well below the steam level, is that steam for sterilisation is available simultaneously with the output of pressurised water for heating. Such systems have little place in smaller installations, although any gardener with an engineering turn of mind could well design a small system to operate very efficiently.

Low pressure steam systems (using steam boiler)
A problem with low pressure steam heating systems is how to achieve good control of pipe temperature, as the flow of steam into the pipe, while generally controlled by an electrically operated motorised valve, merely allows for the heat being either 'on' or 'off'. Temperature gradients are also liable to develop, as it is warmer nearer the boiler though this can be overcome if the length of heating pipe is kept short on each line and there is a large reserve of steam. It is also best to keep the diameter of the pipe as small as possible to keep the thermal inertia low. The steam condenses and is allowed to flow back to a condenser tank for piping back into the boiler. Steam is of course also available for sterilisation purposes.

Other systems centre round the injection of steam into water contained in 4in pipes, somewhat noisy but nevertheless quite effective.

Calorifiers or heat exchanger systems can also be used whereby steam is put through the calorifier, which in turn heats the water which is then pumped round the heating circuit. Low pressure steam injection systems have also been developed in recent years and have proved fairly efficient.

Systems linked to domestic heating
There are many instances where it is possible to combine home and greenhouse or conservatory heating, especially when the home system is of the small bore type. A normal pipe system may be designed in the greenhouse or conservatory served by the domestic system, although home-type radiators may be used. Provision must be made for night operation when domestic systems are frequently shut off and this is a matter best taken up with the heating contractor.

Warm air heating systems
There are a great many types of heaters

Ducted air heating is highly efficient in large commerical greenhouses, but has not yet been properly developed for use in smaller domestic greenhouses. Its great virtue is that it ensures an even distribution of warmth over the whole area of the greenhouse. In other applications the ducting can be laid on the ground, to warm both the soil and the plants.

suitable for greenhouse use. The advantages of warm air heating can be weighed against the disadvantages. Compared with pipe systems, installation costs are low; heaters are easily moved and so do not obstruct soil cultivation or sterilisation; they provide positive air movement, especially if fan-assisted; there can be a quicker response to changing temperatures than with a pipe system, especially where the latter has a high thermal inertia.

Some disadvantages of warm air heaters are as follows: temperature variations can

be much greater over the greenhouse area than with a well-designed pipe system, especially when heaters are of the free-discharge type; there is not the same ability to warm soil by radiation as with a well-designed pipe system (although recent experimental work has shown that a well-designed ducted system can give almost comparable results to a pipe system and also give positive air movement); where a number of warm air heating units are necessary, this adds considerably to the cost, but total cost may still be considerably less than a boiler and pipe system; running costs can be higher than with a well-designed pipe system, taking into account that warm air heaters are either on or off and there is no residual heat such as that contained in the water of a pipe system. Technically speaking, however, the lack of residual heat could be considered desirable in respect of achieving even temperatures.

Solid fuel units

Solid fuel warm air units take the form of a boiler with external flue and a heat exchange unit, the air being pulled in at the base of the unit and discharged through the top, either freely into the atmosphere or through ducts. Smaller types of these are hand-fired and are reasonably efficient but suffer from the disadvantage of inaccurate temperature control. While the combustion of the fuel can be controlled to a certain extent by the damper, it is obvious that this will leave much to be desired in the interests of accuracy.

Steam/air heat exchangers

Live steam passes through a heat exchanger, and warm air is discharged by a fan. These have little application in smaller units.

Oil-fired units

Many oil-fired warm air units are available, fired either by natural draught or pressure jet burners and of various sizes. The smallest economic size of pressure jet burner is in the 50,000–60,000 Btu range (but they go up to 100,000 or more), and this is capable of heating a fairly large greenhouse (800–900 sq ft). They lend themselves admirably to automatic control.

Small oil- or gas-fired warm air units

The smallest type of natural draught oil burner is a simple oil stove of which there are many types, which is in effect a warm air heater. It should be noted that the products of combustion are discharged into the atmosphere, and while the CO_2 (carbon dioxide) content of combustion could be useful as a means of CO_2 enrichment, the sulphur content of oil in excess could be damaging to crops. These small paraffin-burning stoves are suitable for small greenhouses and are in the range of 7,500–20,000 Btu output per hour and must of course have their burning rate manually adjusted to meet needs. Recent designs of oil heating units with very accurate heat control are available. They are generally placed centrally in the greenhouse, which has disadvantages for providing an even temperature throughout the greenhouse although some have 'arms' and other devices for more effective heat dispersal. In recent years gas-fired warm air units have become available, using either propane, town or natural gas. The sulphur content of all but natural gas can be a problem.

Electric warm air heaters

These are becoming increasingly popular for the heating of small greenhouses (see photograph). They are cheap to purchase, operate on a thermostat, and are reasonably efficient in use. They are available in different sizes, popular models being the 1,250 watt, 2,500 watt, and 3,000 watt (3kW). As 1kW is equal to 3,412 Btu, the respective Btu values are:

1,250 W model	4,262 Btu
2,500 W model	8,530 Btu
3,000 W model	10,236 Btu

A range of much larger models is also available.

It has been stated that the main disadvantage of unducted fan heater units is the fact that they must be sited at some central point, and this inevitably results in temperature gradients over the greenhouse. A further disadvantage is that the direct blowing of warm air on to plants immediately it is discharged by the heater should be avoided, as plants could be damaged. Nevertheless, the high efficiency of the small fan-assisted heaters and the advantages of built-in thermostats with which most of them are fitted can result in very efficient heating at low initial cost. Fan unit heaters are extremely useful for the cool greenhouse where frost protection is the aim. Large types of fan heater are available which have polythene ducts for distributing the warmed air, which largely overcomes the problem of even air distribution. With the increasing use of warm air heating units in the home, it could be possible to arrange for a duct to serve the lean-to greenhouse or conservatory built on to the house. This should be taken up with a qualified heating engineer, a basic problem being one of control (as with small bore heating systems) as the home heating system may be designed to shut off at night when there would be the biggest demand in the greenhouse or conservatory.

Electric convector heaters

These are generally fitted with thermostats and operate on the lines of taking air in at the base where it passes over a hot element and is discharged as warm air at the top of the heater. The warm air sets up convection currents and displaces the colder air, but it does this over a narrower zone than warm pipes distributed round the greenhouse. As with fan heaters, therefore, convectors have their limitations in respect of warming the greenhouse air uniformly and cold zones may frequently exist. Whether their shortcomings are acceptable depends largely on the range of crops being grown and whether these are particularly sensitive to temperature differences. The biggest drawback of convector heaters is the gentle movement of air compared to the positive distribution achieved by fan heaters, which encourages movement of both cold and warm air and minimises 'dead' pockets.

Storage heaters

Storage heaters operating on off-peak power are frequently fitted with fans which

Warm air heaters are probably the most efficient method of heating the greenhouse.

Modern aluminium
tubular heaters are
highly efficient. They are
non-corrosive and give
instant response to the
demands of a thermostat.

operate a thermostat and push out the warm air. So far there has been little use of storage heaters for greenhouse heating, as they offer temperature control problems; research work has been carried out on the feasibility of heating concrete paths, but it is likely that they would also offer temperature control problems.

Electric tubular heaters

Mains voltage waterproof tubular heaters are a very useful means of heating greenhouses, as they can readily be distributed round the perimeter. Of 2in diameter they can be installed standing 6in from soil-level, either singly or in banks of two or three. Special fixing brackets are generally supplied with them. For metal houses they are best put on the base wall, if any, or on a wooden support. Electricity loading is usually 60W per ft, which involves calculation of the exact Btu requirement, remembering that 3,412Btu—1kW (1,000W), which means just under 17ft for 1kW (3,412Btu). For calculating the length needed, the heat loss of the greenhouse is worked out and the footage of tubular heaters readily follows. Tubular heaters give off a fair amount of radiant heat which could scorch plants in the near vicinity, and this should be taken into account. Their operation should preferably be controlled through a thermostat. Mineral insulated (MI) cables have a useful application where thermal requirement is relatively low. They consist of a heating wire encased in an inert mineral material and protected by a copper sheath. Of only pencil thickness, the cables are secured to the sides of the greenhouse (as for tubular heaters) in porcelain holders, and are available in packaged units of 2, 3.3 and 5.2kW. MI cables cost less than tubular heaters of similar loading, but they cost more to install as this is invariably a task for an experienced electrician. Plastic-covered mains voltage heating cables are also available.

Heat production units for pipe systems

A very wide range of 'boilers' exists, extending from simple sectional boilers to sophisticated steel-packaged units complete with controls. The basic purpose of any boiler is to burn the selected fuel and then transfer the heat to the water contained in it. This is achieved with widely varying efficiency, resulting in a combustion loss in all cases, except where an electric boiler or immersion heater is used, as electricity operates at 100 per cent efficiency. To bring about combustion of oil, gas or solid fuel of various types, air is necessary, but this must be supplied in the correct amount to bring about efficient combustion. Where solid fuel is burned a great deal of the generated heat will be transferred to the water contained in the jacket of the boiler by radiation and conduction. In addition the hot gases given off by the burning fuel pass through the flueways en route to the chimney and in doing so further warm the water by the process of conduction. It is obvious that the more heat which can be 'extracted' from the hot gas before it reaches the chimney, the greater the efficiency, although too much extraction of heat and the discharge of too cool gases below around 400°F (204°C) can result in condensation in the chimney, especially if a metal unlagged chimney is involved. Combustion results in the production of the gas carbon dioxide (CO_2) and the efficiency of the circulation is directly related to the percentage of CO_2 contained in the flue gas. When this is measured with special instruments, in conjunction with flue temperature it is a means of determining the percentage efficiency of any boiler or appliance. With the high cost of fuel the various modern types of boilers take this fully into account and are designed accordingly. A simple and cheap boiler equipped merely with a grate for burning fuel allows the gases to pass directly into the flue at high temperature and can obviously never be as efficient as a boiler of such a design that the flue gas must travel as far as possible within the limit of design, often through tubes jacketed by water. This is applicable no matter what fuel is being burned, although there is little radiant heat where oil or gas are used. (See Fig 32 and Fig 33.)

Where there is an excessive 'pull' or draught in a chimney because it is of too large a diameter or too high, this can also be a frequent cause of excessive heat loss and low efficiency, as the gases are pulled out before their heat can be passed on.

There can be no overall formula for setting up a boiler for maximum heat transfer and combustion efficiency, as this depends on the precise requirements of each boiler. The same is true of chimney height; the outlet should of course be above the ridge height of the greenhouse. It is also advisable to site the boiler so that the prevailing wind takes flue gases away from the greenhouse (see Fig 34).

Draught diverters are essential particularly for oil-fired boilers as they break the solid column of air in the chimney and enable a stable draught or chimney 'pull' irrespective of wind speed out of doors.

Solid fuel boilers

These are available for hand-firing or automatic firing in a wide range of forms. The smaller inexpensive types used for smaller greenhouses are not noted for their high efficiency, being of very simple design. More expensive boilers are of course available which have a hopper feed and shaker grate and are remarkably efficient and reduce stoking and maintenance labour to the minimum. All solid fuel boilers are available in a very wide range of sizes and forms.

Natural draught oil burners installed in boilers

There are different ways of achieving 'automatic' heating in small heating units to avoid the constant necessity of hand-firing and cleaning. Natural draught burners are frequently installed in boilers intended for solid fuel burning with the fire grates removed, but the boiler can of course be bought complete with the burner. Natural draught burners are exceedingly simple in design and take several different forms, all of which rely on the natural intake of air for combustion. The burner must be installed completely level and the level of the oil control valve must be such that it cannot be over-filled. The simplest types must be manually lit and the level of heating controlled by a hand operated valve. For high efficiencies the flames should be baffled on to the sides of the boiler and a draught diverter must be fitted to reduce draught,

Fig 32

Fig 33

as any excessive chimney 'pull' will extract the hot gases before they have effected heat transfer to the boiler surface. Natural draught burners are available in a range of sizes to suit the smaller boiler unit for heating small greenhouses, ie 10,000–30,000Btu (see photograph).

Pressure jet and wall flame oil-fired burners A wide range of these exists and generally speaking the design of boiler is more sophisticated, as a pressure jet burner injects oil vapour and air under pressure which, on combustion, results in a surge of hot gases. Wall flame burners operate on a rotating system and are very efficient. Unless these hot gases can be directed through an efficient heat exchanging system they are expelled before they have given off a high proportion of their heat.

All oil-fired burners must be correctly installed with no air leaks and they must be set up so that the correct quantity of air is

Fig 34

used for efficient combustion. Simultaneously there should be correct adjustment of the flue draught—both matters for heating engineers or fuel consultants with the correct instruments. Pressure jet burners are of course fully automatic, which is a great boon to the busy gardener. Systems of control for boilers will be discussed in a later chapter.

Gas boilers

Basically gas boilers are similar in design to oil-fired boilers. Indeed the same design formula is frequently used for both, with the obvious difference that the gas requires a different burner. The availability of natural gas in many areas has led to an increased interest in gas firing for greenhouse heating, especially with the steep rise in oil prices over the years. Automatic control is more or less standard on all gas-fired boilers.

Low temperature corrosion of boilers

The problem of low temperature corrosion of boilers caused by the sulphur and possible chlorine content of fuels in conjunction with the temperature of the boiler heating surface is a major one. In essence what happens is that sulphuric acid is formed which corrodes the boiler surface, this occurring at operating temperatures below about 150°F (65°C), and there will, in greenhouse heating, be many occasions when pipes are required no hotter than this. A simple way of overcoming this, and at the same time enabling the pipe to be regulated to give a range of temperatures, is to install a mixing valve. This allows a close loop of heat to circulate through the boiler in a ratio dependent on the heat demand as called for by thermostat or by manual adjustment.

Note that a pump is required for circulation before close loop systems will operate. Mixing valves are frequently installed in domestic systems not only to keep the boiler at a high operating temperature, but to ensure a constantly warm domestic hot water supply.

Cost of heating greenhouses

Estimating the cost of heating a greenhouse is always open to some conjecture, although it is possible to arrive at a remarkably accurate figure. It is obvious that the prevailing outside temperature patterns for any country will greatly affect heating costs. Some reconciliation of the regional implications can be reached by checking on the degree day tables published by the Meteorological Office. These tables give estimates for average months, but variations are bound to occur seasonally and locally.

A 'degree hour' is the sum of the temperature difference between the inside and outside temperatures of the greenhouse (when it is cooler outside) multiplied by the time in hours which each temperature difference lasts. To keep the figures to a reasonable size they are divided by 24, and called 'degree days'. This tends to be a little complicated but should offer no difficulties to the competent mathematician. A more basic approach is to consult a table of costs which takes into account the varying operational efficiency of different equipment and different fuels.

For higher fuel costs add appropriate percentage: eg oil at 12p per gallon will cost 10p per therm; coal at 100p per cwt will cost 12p per therm. Note also that there will be the *extra* cost of electricity involved for pressure jet and wall flame oil burners, pumps etc (generally 5–10 per cent of fuel cost). It is thus relatively simple to calculate the running cost on a 24 hour basis assuming a 50–60 per cent demand overall, although it should be pointed out that this is assumption and nothing more and demand depends on exposure, region, tightness of greenhouse and other issues. If, for example, one has a greenhouse with a calculated heat loss of 8,000Btu, working on a 55°F (13°C) minimum, then using a $2\frac{1}{2}$kW (8,530Btu) fan heater, the cost of heating will be 50–60 per cent of the actual cost per hour, which is the cost of about $1\frac{1}{4}$–$1\frac{1}{2}$ units per hour, as electricity is 100 per cent efficient, there being no combustion heat loss. When calculating the cost of electrical heating it is usual to discount the primary unit rate, which tends

Table of Costs

Type of system	Average operational efficiency	Approx running cost per 100,000 Btu (therm) at fuel prices as stated
Simple solid fuel boiler (hard coal)	50%	Based on coal at 12,500 Btu/lb Cost of fuel/cwt 90p = 11p/therm 85p = $10\frac{1}{2}$p/ ,, 80p = 10p/ ,, 75p = $9\frac{1}{2}$p/ ,, 70p = 9p/ ,, 65p = $8\frac{1}{2}$p/ ,, 60p = $7\frac{1}{2}$p/ ,,
Refined solid fuel boiler (smokeless fuel or coke)	60%	Based on value of 12,000 Btu/lb Cost of fuel 90p = 11p/therm 85p = $10\frac{1}{2}$p/ ,, 80p = 10p/ ,, 75p = 9p/ ,, 70p = 9p/ ,, 65p = 8p/ ,,
	70%	75p = 8p/ ,, 70p = $7\frac{1}{2}$p/ ,, 65p = $6\frac{1}{2}$p/ ,,
Purpose-made oil-fired boiler and fan heaters	75%	Based on oil at 162,000 Btu/gal Cost of fuel per 10p = 8p/therm gal bulk purchase $7\frac{1}{2}$p = 6p/ ,, Small quantities 7p = 6p/ ,, (approx 25% extra) $6\frac{1}{2}$p = $5\frac{1}{2}$p/ ,, 6p = 5p/ ,, $5\frac{1}{2}$p = $4\frac{1}{2}$p/ ,,
Converted oil-fired with vaporiser type burner (costs fairly similar for free-standing oil heaters, perhaps slightly more advantageous)	70%	Based on oil at 158,000 Btu/gal Cost of fuel 10p = 9p/therm (remarks above 8p = 7p/ ,, apply) $7\frac{1}{2}$p = $6\frac{1}{2}$p/ ,, 7p = 6p/ ,, $6\frac{1}{2}$p = 6p/ ,, 6p = $5\frac{1}{2}$p/ ,,
Purpose-made gas fired boiler	75–80%	Based on cost of gas per therm, varies according to district, plus 20–25% loss of efficiency
All electrical heaters (storage heaters not considered here)	100%	Based on normal tariff Cost per unit $1\frac{1}{2}$p = 36p/therm 1p = 24p/ ,, $\frac{1}{2}$p = 12p/ ,,

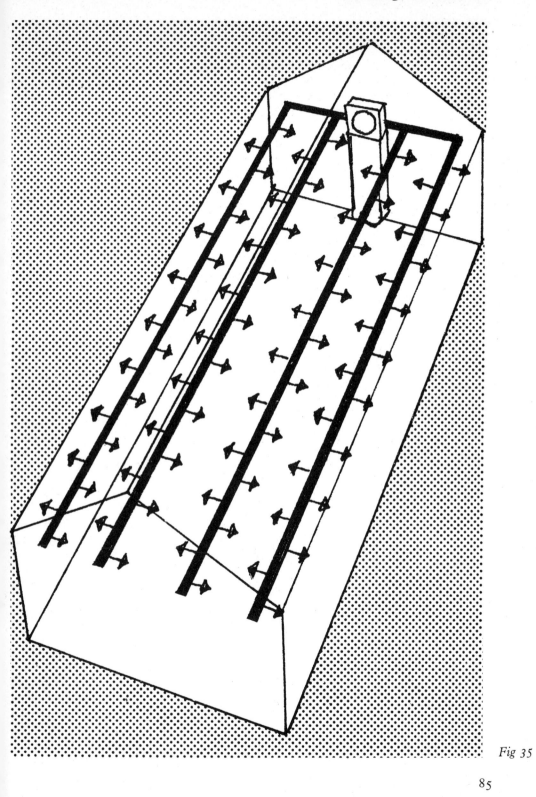

Fig 35

85

to be used up in the home, and simply calculate on the basis of a *flat rate* unless there is a separate meter. Where frost protection only is desired, ie 40–45°F (4–7°C) maximum, then there will obviously be a much lower demand than 50–60 per cent, as low as 10–12 per cent in some cases. For solid fuel, assuming 12,000Btu/lb of fuel and 60 per cent efficiency, one gets 60 per cent of 12,000 (7,200Btu) out of every pound of fuel, the cost of which can be calculated readily enough from the fuel price. It is of course again necessary to assume a figure for percentage loss of efficiency on combustion. In the absence of a properly carried out efficiency test, help is given in this direction by taking into account the calorific output of the boiler. With small boilers of around 15,000Btu capacity it is fair to assume an operational efficiency of about 60 per cent, when it will require 2lb of coal per hour on rapid burning, which would be 48lb per 24 hours. Rapid burning is seldom a constant necessity, however, and 20lb per day or 140lb per week is a fair average.

With an oil-fired boiler or oil stove the same sort of calculation can be made. Allowing 75 per cent of 160,000Btu (the approximate calorific value of 1 gallon of oil), which is 120,000 Btu, then an oil stove of 10,000 Btu will burn for 12 hours at full output. If the assumption of a 50–60 per cent usage is made, this figure becomes about 24–28 hours for 1 gallon. With a larger boiler rated at 120,000 Btu, then 1 gallon will burn for 1 hour at full capacity, experience showing that 1 gallon for $2\frac{1}{2}$ hours is a fair assumption.

It can perhaps now be appreciated that while it is possible to *estimate* running costs, so much depends on the temperature range desired in the greenhouse and, more important, on the outside temperature.

Linked systems

Where linked systems are involved there is no basic difference in calculation, it being a case of working out the heat loss for the greenhouse and, provided this is efficiently linked by small bore pipes or ducts, it should be possible to calculate the heating costs in the same way as for an independent system. A distinct advantage is likely to be the higher operational efficiency of the more expensive and sophisticated type of domestic heating units invariably used. In certain instances it may of course be possible to site the domestic boiler in the greenhouse or conservatory, the greenhouse then being kept heated by the radiant heat from the boiler, which could be completely lost if the boiler is sited out of doors. While there could be temperature control problems, these are not likely to be any greater than the problems which can arise with linked systems.

Boiler siting for greenhouses

In most instances where larger type solid fuel or oil-fired boilers are being used for a pipe heating system, space does not often permit the siting of the boiler in the actual greenhouse, although this is a highly practical course of action because of the radiation heat obtained from the boiler which will, as stated above, be lost if the boiler is sited separately. With smaller installations it is ideal if the boiler can be sited in the actual greenhouse. When sited elsewhere it should be protected from the elements and from wind which will interfere with the combustion rate. Care should always be taken to lag any exposed pipes running between the boiler and the greenhouse to avoid wasteful heat loss. Boilers and their housings should not shade the greenhouse; keep them to the north side if possible. As flue gases should be carried away by prevailing winds, north siting is doubly preferable.

All smaller self-contained heating units, including fan heaters of larger size, should be sited in the actual greenhouse, the flue pipes, if any, being taken through the roof by the fitting of a special waterproof gland. Free-discharge heaters are best sited centrally, but when polythene ducting is to be used it is better to keep the heater to the north end, if possible, and run the ducting out from this point (see Fig 35).

Modern plastic propagating cases like this one are easy to use and increase both the speed of germination and the number of seeds that germinate. The seed tray stands on a hot-plate warmed by coaxial cables.

Factor to be controlled	Manual	Type of Control Automatic without feedback	with feedback	Automated
Vents or fans	By handle, lever, or switch reference to thermometer	Thermostat opens vents fully and vice versa. Pulse control can be introduced. Fans operated until temperature drops. Time clock control for fans.	Thermostat or thermister in conjunction with monotronic control, but vents open only a certain amount as controller knows position of vents. same with fans	Solar radiation measured and applied, by light meter. Integrated control for all aspects.
Heat	By reference to thermometer Control valve or stoking	Thermostat + solanoid valve. Motorised or pump with no knowledge of conditions	Same as above with reference to actual temperature and conditions	As above
Irrigation Overhead and mist	Hoses, watering cans, trickle and spraylines in manual form or from taps. Light meter can be used at this level (e.g. 200 cal. per pint of water) (average)	Time clocks + sequence controller but no relation to actual crop state. Electronic leaf is also used at this level but can give rise to problems	Systems not yet designed which will give details on actual state of crop	Solar energy related to exact crop needs by means of light meter
CO_2	Not used a great deal in 'manual' form	Time clock control, possibly over-ridden by switch when vents open. No real knowledge of CO_2 level in greenhouse	Monitor which measures CO_2 content of atmosphere and controls imput	Solar light intensity related to level of enrichment

Chapter 8

Environmental Control

The ventilation of greenhouses is one of the most important facets of environmental control. It is necessary for the following reasons:

> to limit undue rise in temperature,
> to replace exhausted air with fresh,
> to maintain humidity at the required level.

Control of temperature

This is the most important consideration with many gardeners, as solar radiation between spring and autumn is very frequently in excess of needs on bright sunny days, necessitating frequent air changes to keep the greenhouse air temperature at an acceptable level for plants. When solar

Different thermostats are used for the heater and for the air-circulating fan.

short-wave radiation reaches the plants in a greenhouse about three-quarters of it is absorbed by the leaves and the remaining quarter reflected back to the greenhouse as long-wave radiation. As all other objects in the greenhouse reflect back the radiation, absorbing only a small proportion, the net effect is therefore to cause a rise in temperature of the plants' leaves and the surrounding area. The rise is reduced to a certain extent by the loss of heat by evaporation, caused by the process of transpiration. The total amount of foliage in any greenhouse varies considerably, and this in turn greatly affects the percentage of radiation absorbed and reflected, and in turn the amount of transpiration which takes place.

As air, when warm, becomes less dense and rises, an exit is allowed for it at the highest point in the greenhouse along the ridge. Cool air also gains entry into the greenhouse through the same 'exit' by a complicated interchange mechanism, provided there is enough air movement out of doors to give sufficient impetus for this interchange. If, however, cool air is allowed entry through lower vents this speeds up the whole process of interchange (see Fig 36).

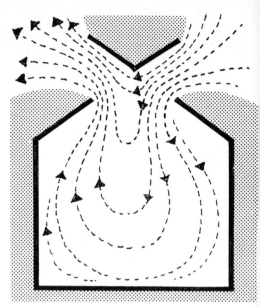

Fig 37

Ventilator size and position

The size of ventilator on the ridge is obviously critical and an actual ventilation area of at least one-fifth to one-sixth of the actual floor area (irrespective of lower vents) is the accepted commercial norm, although if a greater area can be provided this is better still. Lower vents or louvres should be proportionate in size with ridge vents. It helps greatly if ridge ventilators are capable of opening to an angle of 55°—in line with the slope of the opposite roof (see Fig 37) and well above the horizontal—as in this position they scoop in the wind while also allowing easier exit for warm air.

Correct provision of ridge vents is a critical point. For greenhouses of a width module of over 20 feet it is essential to have continuous ventilation on both sides of the ridge (see Fig 38) which allows effective air change under a wide range of conditions. On smaller greenhouses (which will include most amateur sized structures) continuous ridge ventilation is seldom fitted, it being usual to rely on alternate ridge ventilators, with fixed glazing opposite each vent. In this case, when a wind is blowing, air comes in on one side and is discharge out the other (see Fig 39). It is important to remember that the total area

Fig 36

Fig 38

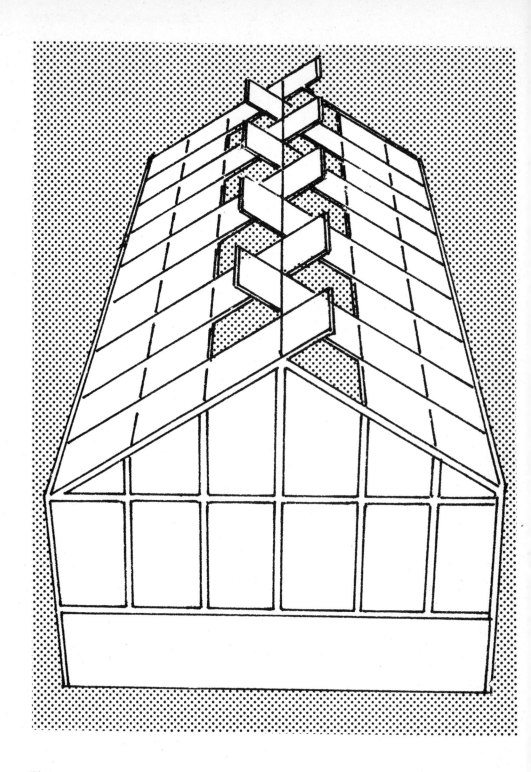

Fig 39

92

of these should still be at least one-fifth to one-sixth of the floor area. For a 10 × 8ft greenhouse with a ground area of 80sqft, one-fifth is 16sqft. This would allow for four 2 × 2ft ridge vents, provided they are capable of opening fully to that area. Most manufacturers are quite happy to provide additional ventilation up to the required ratio. Amateur greenhouses do, in fact, because of a higher glass/ground ratio, need a higher ventilation percentage than commercial greenhouses, possibly up to 30–40 per cent of the ground area.

With simple opening type vents on roofs or sides, draughts are unavoidable. Louvred types (see Fig 40), frequently used in sides and doors, are less liable to allow entry of draughts but it is doubtful whether any system of ventilation depending on the opening of a flap or louvres can be 100 per cent draught proof. Attempts at air-conditioning to allow 'perfect' ventilation without draughts will be referred to later.

Operation of ventilators

Ventilators can be operated by simple rack and pin or by pulley and cord. In recent years rack and pinion operation for commercial glasshouses has become almost standard (see Fig 41). To ensure as accurate a temperature regime as possible ventilators should operate automatically, either by electric motor or, on an amateur scale, by expansion type lifts which are cheap to purchase yet highly dependable in practice.

The mechanism for automatic ventilators is varied in design and depends much on the type of greenhouse and all the various design factors involved. Step control to give a quarter, one-third, three-quarter and full opening is available, the most sophisticated types of ventilator being linked to a proportional or modulating controller which sets the position of the vents according to the rate of change required in the greenhouse temperature. In addition there can be a wind gauge to open or shut vents in one direction to avoid draughts and a rain gauge to shut vents up when it rains.

Fig 40

Fig 41

93

Ventilators like the one
shown here will open
automatically as the
temperature rises.

Fan ventilation

Although this is still in its infancy in amateur greenhouses, fan ventilation is widely used in commercial spheres. When designing a fan ventilation system it must be remembered that most plants dislike rapid air movement which, like excessive wind out of doors, causes them to transpire too rapidly. It would be easy to fit a high output fan in a greenhouse to move the air at high speed, but this would inevitably cause turbulence and air movement to the detriment of the plants. Research work over many years has shown quite clearly that plants will tolerate an air flow rate of 7cuft per sqft maximum. This involves using relatively slow speed fans which are capable of moving a large volume of air slowly, rather than high speed fans which

suck air rapidly over a fairly localised area.

The basic design of an extractor fan ventilation system is to extract the air at one end or side of a greenhouse and provide for the entry of air at the opposite end or side. Where large units of greenhouses are involved, several fans are required, spaced to allow even, complete air extraction with no stagnant areas. With large commercial type greenhouses it is usual to have 4ft fans operating at 360–470rpm spaced evenly along the north or east side wall of the block, allowing for 60sqft per fan of inlet area on the opposite wall. This results in air movement as shown in Fig 42, which is achieved whenever the fans are in operation, irrespective of wind speed or weather conditions out of doors, generally maintaining an air flow of

94

An extractor fan. This
model is fully automatic,
switching on only when
the temperature rises to a
predetermined level. The
flaps open only under air
pressure from the fan,
and fall back into the
closed position once the
fan is switched off.

300ft per minute. The inlet can either be manually or automatically operated, it being important to ensure that the fans cannot operate until the vents are open. Fans are best operated from an aspirated thermostat or thermostats which can either operate all the fans simultaneously or in batches to come on at different temperatures. Time clocks are considered necessary on commercial holdings to give short periods of night ventilation, otherwise humidity can build up to a dangerous level, although fan operation can also be controlled by a humidistat. Variable speed fans are also available, worked by thermostatically operated variable speed controllers, but special types of fan motors are necessary, along with the sophisticated control gear for the inlet vents, which adds considerably to the cost of the installation.

While the installation height of a 4ft fan offers little difficulty as it invariably rests on the foundation wall choosing the height for small fans is not entirely straightforward. Experience has shown that with high set 24in fans on the side wall of smaller blocks of commercial greenhouses, the inlet being provided on the opposite wall, there is a tendency for the air to move over a dense crop such as tomatoes, rather than through it.

Amateur gardeners will almost certainly be using the smaller type fans, the specification for which must be carefully calculated by a firm specialising in fan ventilation of greenhouses, many domestic type fans being incapable of giving the requisite number of air changes. All fans should be louvred so that unwanted air cannot gain entry when the fans are not operating. It is convenient to install these fans fairly high in the greenhouse, a usual location being above the door.

Inlet for fans

The position of the inlet for fans has proved to be critical, experience showing that vents on the side wall rather than the roof are better for blocks of greenhouses. This allows the incoming air to make a quick loop before moving across the greenhouse. Single greenhouses lend themselves to the fitting of the fan in the gable end, either at both sides of the door if two are used, or above the door for one only. A further advantage in having side vent entry for fans is that heating pipes can partially warm the incoming air, a distinct advantage in cold weather as it tends to prevent any cold shock to the plants. Damp pads can also be used to wet incoming air, a technique practised in very warm countries, and gaining some favour in Britain for certain crops.

The temperature gradient which can exist between inlet and outlet in fan-ventilated greenhouses causes concern in certain quarters, the exact difference in temperature depending on length of travel of the air. In practice this seems to be of negligible proportions, certainly if compared to the temperature gradients which exist in greenhouses where conventional ventilators are fitted.

The positive air movement induced by fans ensures that humidity is kept at a low level and stagnant pockets avoided, there being ample experimental and practical cropping evidence to support this. The positive intake of air, especially in hot, still conditions when conventional vents cannot induce a sufficient number of air changes, results in a constant supply of carbon di-

Fig 42

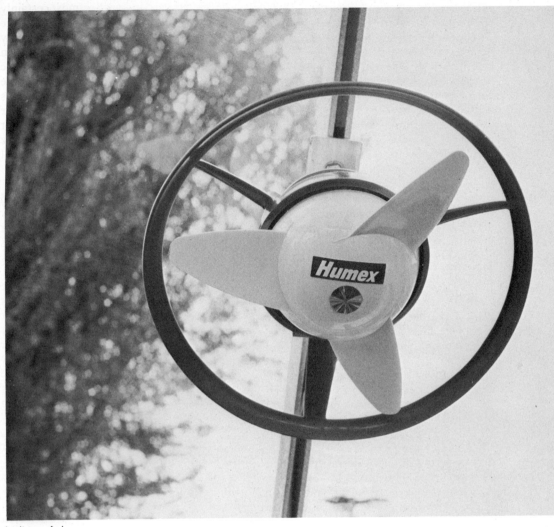

An internal air-
circulating fan. This only
circulates the air inside
the greenhouse.

oxide being brought to the plants. The form of air intake can vary from top-hinged ventilators to louvres, in both cases ensuring that there is sufficient inlet to cope with the fan capacity. Use has been made of mesh material, which allows entry of small amounts of air all the time and, with the suction developed when fans are in operation, acts as an efficient inlet. Flap arrangements are also possible, using sheets of plastic dropped down over the back of an inlet, which lifts up when the fans are in operation but prevents draughts when the fans are not in operation. A more recent development is polythene ducted fan in takes to try and minimise temperature gradient between intake and fans.

Air conditioning
In addition to conventional ventilation and

extractor fans, a more recent aspect of environmental control is air conditioning. This can take several forms, the most elementary of which is to pull air into the greenhouse thus pressuring it to a limited degree. The air is exhausted out of counterbalanced louvres. Such systems, although not complex, have proved effective, although temperature gradients in the greenhouse can be excessive if the design is not correct. Warm air can be introduced by the same basic system and humidity control can also be effected to a certain degree by using a humidistat to inject water into the moving air stream when necessary. These matters are, however, better taken up with specialist suppliers of equipment, as most systems need to be designed specially for each individual greenhouse.

Desirability of environment control

Plants have their own inbuilt requirements in respect of leaf temperature, air temperature, humidity, carbon dioxide and light required for photosynthesis. While a greenhouse creates an artificial environment, it is necessary to try to control this within reasonable limits in sympathy with the needs of the plants being grown in it. Under commercial growing conditions, where only one specialist cropping system may be involved, every attempt is made to conform to a blue-print in respect of environment, level of water and feeding requirement. The object of this is to ensure the maximum production of quality crops or plants on what can be a very tight schedule. Amateur or professional gardeners are not perhaps so deeply concerned with their greenhouse gardening, but there is still considerable virtue in calling on modern aids to control the environment automatically as far as this is possible, simply to ease the load of looking after plants and at the same time help to ensure quality despite enforced absence at business or elsewhere.

The full control of the greenhouse environment is a complex matter with a great many inter-related factors to be taken into account. Much research is still likely to take place over the next decade to try to discover what exactly constitutes the ideal environment for different plants and thereafter set out to achieve this effectively without too much complicated and expensive equipment.

Control of heating systems

With simple solid fuel hand-fired boilers and large diameter pipes where the water circulates entirely by gravity or thermosyphon, there is no real place for automatic control, and the usual control of temperature is to rely on the boiler damper and the level of firing in association with regulating air entry at the fire door. It may be possible to restrict the flow from the boiler by the use of a check valve situated on the flow pipe, although this could be dangerous and lead to overheating of the boiler. Solenoid valves electrically operated by thermostat can also be used, but suffer the same drawbacks. In practice and with experience a fair degree of control of actual temperature can be exercised, but only with constant vigilance, this showing the defects of such systems where strict environmental control is sought.

Where circulation of the water relies *largely* on a circulating pump, good temperature control can be achieved by linking the accelerator to an on/off thermostat set in the greenhouse, the amount of control which can be exercised varying according to the degree of dependence on pump circulation. Where the circulation of water depends *entirely* on the pump, there can be excellent temperature control, especially if the boiler is automatically fired by oil or gas.

Ideally there should be an independent on/off thermostat to control the boiler at a pre-set temperature (generally above 160°F/71°C) and an on/off or multi-step control (a combination of two or more on/off units arranged to operate in stages) sited in the greenhouse to call for heat. This operates the pump and sends water round the system. There are definite drawbacks to this system when large bore pipes are concerned, especially if these are of cast iron with cemented joints. Unless there can be arrangements to 'bleed' a small quantity of water into the pipes to keep them warm, especially adjacent to the boiler, the sudden rush of hot water when the pump is set in motion can split the pipes or loosen the cement joints. Arrangements to bleed in a small quantity of water usually consist of a pipe-fitted on/off thermostat, adjacent to the boiler on the greenhouse side of the pump and set to override the greenhouse thermostat when the temperature of the pipes falls below about 80°F (27°C).

Pump control is ideal for small bore systems of heating with their low thermal inertia and lack of complications from pipe damage. The methods of arranging a by-pass to ensure a continuously warm boiler

and simultaneously give a range of temperatures in the pipes, have been referred to earlier but an electrically operated modulating valve would ideally then require to be linked to a modulating controller. Modulating controllers can of course also be linked directly to pumps. They, like proportional controllers, operate on the principle that the amount of heat supplied is related to the variance of the greenhouse air temperature from the previous level, rather than by successive periods of full heat input followed by no heat, as dictated by an on/off thermostat. Night setback of temperature can also be manipulated according to average day temperatures.

A still further development is the use of integrating photometers or light sensors which control the input of heat according

Modern thermostats can usually be preset by the turn of a screw. Such thermostats can be used to control heating systems of almost any type.

to the prevailing light intensity and, still more sophisticated, relate this to the prevailing weather pattern in order to avoid sudden shocks to the plants' physiology. Night setbacks according to light intensity and temperature can also be incorporated.

Ventilators or fans can conveniently be operated on the same range of instruments as heating systems—independently but perfectly integrated.

What has been said about hot water heating systems applies equally well to other heating systems, whether these are steam or warm air supplied by direct firing or through heat exchange units. Reference has been made earlier to the complications of steam heating with regard to its on/off qualities, but in essence the same basic principles of automatic control apply.

Carbon dioxide enrichment and humidity control

The dispensing of carbon dioxide can be as simple as on/off and the shutting down of vents during the enrichment period to avoid wastage. Preferably, however, there must be integration between the two fac-

tors, so that ventilators are automatically closed and fans out of action when CO_2 is being dispensed. The amount of CO_2 supplied can also be related to light intensity.

Humidity control is not straightforward. When a rise in humidity is called for by a humidity sensor something of a dilemma may result, there being a choice of bringing into operation spraylines or mist jets and shutting the vents. Conversely, for lowering the humidity, are the vents to be opened, or the fans operated, or the heating called on to raise the temperature (warm air holding more moisture than cold air)?

It has previously been stated that allowance must be made in really sophisticated systems for damage to open vents caused by sudden winds, demanding a wind sensor, and a rain sensor to shut down the vents when it is raining heavily.

Automatic feeding and watering control

The supply of water and liquid feeding of plants and crops is also carried out automatically with sequence controllers operat-

A complex control panel, capable of masterminding all the automatic equipment in the greenhouse. The range of devices it controls can be increased simply by adding new banks to it.

Highly sophisticated
equipment is now being
used by commercial
growers for
environmental control in
greenhouses. More and
more of the equipment is
becoming available to
amateur growers.

ing solenoid valves, and this will be referred to in a later chapter.

Measuring and recording instruments

An accurate thermometer is an essential piece of equipment and these can take several forms, but undoubtedly the most useful is a maximum/minimum model, especially a push button re-set type. A humidity gauge or hygrometer is also a useful item. Ideally these instruments should be in an aspirated screen, failing which a metal foil shield is reasonably effective in shading them from direct sun.

No instrument, however, that is exposed freely to solar radiation, draughts, or radiation loss can be considered accurate. Solar radiation absorbed by the body of a thermometer or the case of a thermostat will result in a variance between the recorded and the actual conditions. For this reason the only way of ensuring accurate sensing is to use an aspirated screen for housing all instruments. This is an insulated box or section of large diameter PVC tubing fitted with a constantly operating small fan which pulls air gently through the box or tube over the thermostat or other instrument housed in the screen. This ensures that the actual air temperature or humidity is accurately recorded.

Aspirated screens are usually provided with the instrument installed, and the unit generally sited in the centre of the greenhouse; for greater accuracy it can be placed in the actual area of crop growth.

Control equipment and the amateur

The above items of control equipment in one form or another, and in various degrees of refinement and sophistication, are fully operational in many commercial and local authority units. Their application in amateur spheres is obviously more limited, and gardeners should confine their horizons to reasonable levels, seeking perhaps the automatic control of ventilation and heating on a simple on/off basis and little more. In recent years, however, mist and drip watering systems on automatic control have made a big impact in amateur circles.

Electric heating units of all types readily lend themselves to thermostatic control and it would be foolish not to take advantage of this. Manually operated appliances of any kind, and similarly hand-operated heaters, require constant regulation and, more important, the presence of the gardener if they are to be really successful in practice. But it would be wrong to imply that gardeners cannot get good results by relying entirely on manual management; many have achieved excellent results, especially those blessed with intuition and a good growing sense.

Chapter 9

Additional Equipment

Benching

The provision of benching or staging for a range of activities is invariably necessary, except when a greenhouse is being used exclusively for ground-grown crops. Even then propagation space is invariably demanded for a limited period of the year.

Benching must be strong as it has frequently to bear a considerable weight. Fixed benching is not so popular as it was owing to management problems, but it certainly allows better presentation and utilises space.

Conventional benching employs slatted

Benching can be contrived in a number of ways to suit individual requirements. The important thing is always that it should be stoutly constructed and completely secure.

wood of 4–5in and approximately $\frac{5}{8}$–$\frac{3}{4}$in section, set on bearers with approximately 1in between the slats. Ideally the wood for the slats should be of good quality such as Western red cedar, although preservative treated redwood would suffice. Benches from about 2ft 3in up to about 4ft permit ease of access, although centrally sited benches with both sides accessible can be much wider—up to about 5 or 6ft. A height of 30in (average table height) was previously thought to be ideal, but there is now commercial interest in knee-high benches of about 20in. These allow a much closer surveillance of the plants and their watering needs, a vital issue with the widespread use of plastic pots.

Wider spaced slats can be used where stock plants are being maintained so that there is no contact or run of moisture between the plants, so cutting down the risk of infection. Wood slats can also be inserted into angle iron or alternatively patent angle steel with a mesh top used. Benches can be made solid by using corrugated iron or asbestos, but they restrict air movement; they are considered to be more suitable for certain types of pot plants by some gardeners, though a difference of opinion exists. Solid benches are essential for mist propagation units or for the construction of capillary benches. Where solid benches are used there should always be a space between the bench and side of the greenhouse to allow the passage of air. The usual arrangement is to have benches on both sides of a central path. With a greenhouse 8ft wide, two benches each 2ft 6in wide would allow a 3ft path. In narrower houses one 3ft bench might be preferable, although two very narrow benches are possible but not always practical. Greenhouses 12ft in width could readily accommodate two side benches each 2ft 6in wide and a central bench of similar width, taking care that the central bench does not restrict access through the door or doors. The free opening of the door must also be taken into account when deciding on the width of the side benches. A sensible width of central path is always advisable to allow the entry

of a barrow or trolley.

Benches may be supplemented with shelving at higher levels, useful for ensuring maximum light for plants and utilising space. On vertical wooden-wall greenhouses they can be fitted with galvanised shelf brackets, while on alloy or metal houses manufacturers offer special shelf fittings.

Capillary benches

These involve the use of a completely level solid bench with 3–4in sides which is lined with inert washed sand of acceptable capillarity: a coarse gravelly sand to a depth of 1–1$\frac{1}{2}$in to give a free water zone is topped by 1in of finer sand. A perforated hose is laid down the centre of the bench before or during filling with sand, preferably under broken sections of drainage tiles so that water can pass through the perforations in the hose without restriction into the free water zone, or sections of curved asbestos can be used. Water can in fact be led in almost as satisfactorily at a single point in the free water zone, when it will spread effectively, although care should be taken to ensure that sand does not block the outlet. To control the level of water a plastic fish tank fitted with a ball and cock can be used so that the water level is held constantly 1–1$\frac{1}{2}$in below the top of the sand. Alternatively a float control unit can be used connected to a storage tank, adjusting the supply of water to the necessary level by adjustment of the control unit. More simply a slowly dripping hose or bleed-type irrigation units can be used to supply the water to the bench, or it can merely be kept topped up at regular intervals, although neither of the two latter methods is entirely satisfactory, owing to the varying degree of solar heat.

Plants in pots spaced out on a capillary bench extract water by capillary pull, plastic pots being rather better in this instance than clay pots. Plants can also be fed with liquid nutrients by this method, although there can be problems of local build-up of salts, causing chemical damage to plants. In recent years individual drip

The header-bottle for a capillary bench. Capillary benches have virtually eliminated the need for hand-watering the great majority of greenhouse pot plants—though one or two temperamental ones still need individual attention. These benches are most efficient when the plants are grown in plastic pots.

Benching can be
arranged in a number of
ways and for a number of
purposes. The benching
shown here is very deep
and contains coaxial
soil-warming cables in a
bed of sand. This makes
an ideal propagating
bench.

systems have tended to supersede capillary watering, one reason being that roots from the pots develop into the sand on capillary action, especially if the sand is too dry, resulting in severance and checks to growth when the plants are moved. A more recent development is the use of fibreglass mats to replace the sand—these proving highly successful.

Bench and soil warming

The escalating cost of all fuels has thrown new emphasis on the highly efficient localised application of heat directly to the propagating material. The use of alkathene pipe at 9–12in depth and 4–5ft apart linked to a pump-circulated hot water system has achieved certain favour in continental European countries for the production of early crops such as very early tomatoes or strawberries demanding soil warmth.

Electric soil warming using 12 gauge wire of known electrical resistance at 6–30 volts through a transformer at 9–10in depth and 3–9in apart, to give a loading of 5–10 watts per square foot, has also received little attention since the 1950s, possibly because of the high cost of electricity when used on the scale necessary to heat large bulks of growing media such as tomato borders. Such systems do, however, have an application for smaller border areas in many cases, using sheathed mains voltage cables.

The use of soil warming cables for bench application is, however, an entirely different matter, as the loading necessary at 8–12 watts per foot ensures that the level necessary (approximately 1kW per 100sq ft) is a highly efficient and economic operation. As the use of tools is unlikely, mains voltage cables are used, being laid on a 2in layer of sand over the cable. Control of the soil warming cable temperature can be achieved by several methods: (1) at off peak tariff by time clock operation (8 hours in 24), (2) according to the weather, by inspection with a soil thermometer, or (3) the best method, and essential for the higher temperatures necessary for mist propagation, by the use of 18in rod, or phial and capillary tube thermostats set across the run of the wires below the sand surface. It helps to induce warmth if spaces between pots or boxes on the bench are filled up with moist peat.

The local application of heat to either borders or benches (or plants or cuttings in pots) has little effect on the air temperature of the greenhouse, but such locally applied warmth to the media in which the plants are growing generally allows a lowering of the air temperature in the greenhouse, which has tremendous economic benefits. Indeed the success of mist propagation with the necessary attendant warmth in the actual rooting media has revolutionised propagation of many previously difficult-to-root plants.

Propagation cases and mist propagation units

Vegetative propagation is the production of young plants by inducing the formation of roots on sections of vegetative tissue removed from the parent plant. The more quickly this can be achieved the better, and it is therefore important to maintain the tissue in good condition. Soft tissue is particularly prone to rapid wilting when removed from the parent plant, simply because the leaves lose their moisture by rapid transpiration, which cannot be entirely replaced by the usual uptake of moisture because the water-absorbing tissue has been severed. While a certain amount of moisture can be obtained through the exposed xylem, the condition of all the

A propagating case like this one is one of the gardener's greatest assets. It needs a position in good light in the greenhouse and can be fitted with both soil and air-warming cables. An enormously varied range of plants can be raised in such cases.

tissue quickly deteriorates, which inevitably holds up the complicated process of forming new root tissue. If the air around the vegetative tissue (leaves, cuttings or other sections of plant) can be maintained in a very humid state, transpiration is considerably reduced and the tissue cells remain turgid. This can be achieved in several ways such as the use of a heated propagation case, by polythene drapes, or on a smaller scale in porch or conservatory by the use of polythene bags. Alternatively it can also be achieved by maintaining a fine film of moisture over the young plant sections, as achieved by mist propagation.

Propagating cases and polythene drapes both have the advantage of providing an environment which can be maintained independently of, and generally higher than, the greenhouse temperature, which offers considerable fuel savings. It is desirable also to have bottom heat which can either be provided by a pipe heating system beneath the bench on which the propagating case is placed or by the use of soil warming cables. Propagating cases can be of any convenient size and can be purchased complete, the larger sizes with soil warming cables and the smaller sizes with an electric bulb providing the warmth. Any handyman can make a propagating case with a sheet of glass and some wood, or even glass, for the sides, a convenient depth being about 10–12in. A distinct disadvantage of a propagating case is that condensation builds up on the underside of the glass, causing drips, but a good slope will encourage these to run to one end.

Plastic domes and germinating cabinets
Plastic dome cases for plastic seed trays have in many ways tended to replace propagating cases because of their cheapness and mobility, and if they are placed on a soil-warmed bench they achieve the same basic purpose as a propagating case.

Considerable heat build-up can, however, occur in propagating cases, polythene drapes and plastic domes, which can be detrimental to young plants; damage can usually be avoided because of the extremely high humidity but it is generally safer to shade with coloured polythene or other material.

Propagating cases and domes can of course be used for all other aspects of propagation, including seed germination. Germinating cabinets have, however, in recent years become popular for seed germination, and these are merely highly insulated shelved compartments fitted with a humidifier and heater, or on a less sophisticated scale merely a heater, the floor being maintained in wet condition to give the necessary humidity.

Mist propagation
This technique, originally developed in the USA, aims at overcoming many of the disadvantages of closed propagating cases by maintaining a constant fine film of water on the propagating material, so keeping the tissue cool by restricting the elementary process of loss of heat by evaporation and simultaneously preventing rapid transpiration. To be effective it must be used in conjunction with high level soil warming (15 watts per sq ft) to achieve 75°F (24°C), keeping the atmosphere moist by constant applications of water. A series of vertical mist nozzles 15–24in high are spaced 3–4ft apart (or according to water pressure available). Overhead mist lines can also be used.

It is highly important that the drainage in the bench is perfect to avoid saturation, which could have highly detrimental results. The film of moisture is maintained in relation to air temperature and solar radiation by using either a selenium cell light sensor, electrode-type 'leaf', or absorbent pad controller, all of which operate a solenoid valve to control water flow. Various types of 'leaf' are obtainable and it is necessary to obtain advice on which is the best for the particular type of water involved. A good pressure of water (40–60 lb psi) is necessary to operate the mist nozzles effectively, and if this is not available from the mains, a pressure tank will be necessary. In most areas, however, water pressure is adequate provided the

Mist propagation was invented in the United Kingdom but most of the development was done in the U.S.A. Many types of cuttings that proved impossible before the invention of mist propagation are now considered easy with its aid.

supply pipe is of sufficient diameter.

Weaning mist-rooted plants to become accustomed to growing naturally ideally involves a period of less frequent watering, and this can be achieved either by moving the 'leaf' nearer the nozzle, adjusting the particular type of leaf, or by a time control unit. Root temperatures should also be reduced gradually by altering the thermostat setting. In recent years however, much less attention has been paid to the whole process of weaning.

Shading equipment

The provision of shade restricts solar radiation very considerably and this in turn reduces air temperature. It may be necessary for propagating activities or for certain groups of plants, or crops such as tomatoes suffering from wilt diseases. The simplest method of shading is to apply proprietary shading material, usually green tinted, to the outside of the glass, or alternatively lime plus water which is less permanent. Much diluted emulsion paint is also useful but can be too persistent. All materials will invariably wash off by the end of the season, although some assistance with a long-handled brush may be necessary to ensure maximum light transmission in winter. Blinds can be fitted both outside and inside, and green polythene blinds, fitted at the ridge inside the greenhouse, are extremely useful. Slatted blinds can also be used for special plants such as orchids. It is important to ensure that the shading equipment purchased is suitable for the size of the greenhouse. As a temporary measure green polythene, plastic netting or other materials can be used, supported on wires, canes or any other suitable rigid stiffeners.

Shading has presented
problems to greenhouse
gardeners since the
earliest days. The roller
blinds shown here can be
operated automatically by
an electric eye.

Venetian blinds are one of the newer methods of shading a greenhouse. A simple patent invention keeps the blinds rigid in the same plane as the slope of the glass, and shading is created by changing the angle of the slats. This again can be done automatically by an electric eye.

Polythene lining

Double glazing, which has become very popular in domestic circles, involves the use of two sheets of glass hermetically sealed so that a layer of air is trapped, the net effect of which is to reduce heat loss considerably. This is not considered practical for greenhouses on account of cost, and such attempts as have been made by simply using two panes of glass on either side of wooden or metal glazing bars have not been successful, as it is difficult to ensure a tight enough seal to prevent the entry of dirt and moisture. Polythene lining of 38mu is frequently used for a simple form of double glazing, being tacked on to the inside of wooden glazing bars, using paper pads and drawing pins or staples. With metal houses a piece of wood inlaid into the groove in alloy glazing bars is usual, failing which a wooden framework can be used. Approximately a 25 per cent reduction in heat loss can be expected when all but the vent areas are covered. Problems of excess humidity can develop for certain crops, although this high humidity can of course be an advantage for propagating activities. Probably one of the greatest advantages of polythene lining is to prevent draughts and drips in older type greenhouses in poor repair. Light transmission is only marginally reduced by the polythene lining.

Carbon dioxide (CO_2) enrichment

The natural complement of the gas carbon dioxide in the atmosphere is 300 parts per million, and this is normally a sufficient concentration for the photosynthetic needs of plants. Research has shown, however, that under conditions of good light intensity and compatible temperatures, the growth rate of greenhouse plants may be restricted by lack of sufficient carbon dioxide. When the atmosphere is enriched up to approximately 600–900 parts per million (two- to threefold) the velocity of photosynthesis increases, or, more subtly, the quality of photosynthesis improves.

The breakdown of organic matter in the soil results in the production of CO_2, and this takes place in the soil continuously. Where cultural methods involve the use of large quantities of organic matter, such as 'hot' beds or straw bale culture of tomatoes or cucumbers, a considerable quantity of carbon dioxide is produced which enriches the air in the vicinity of the growing plants. Plants vary in their response to additional CO_2 and even certain varieties of the same species respond better than others.

The artificial enrichment of the atmosphere can be achieved in a variety of ways. The burning of paraffin stoves results in carbon dioxide in quantity, but unfortunately impurities such as sulphur are also produced and this can be harmful to plants if it reaches too high a concentration. The burning of propane gas in special burners is an efficient way of achieving carbon dioxide enrichment, propane gas being relatively pure. Natural gas greenhouse heaters would also produce CO_2 without any of the complications of sulphur production, as natural gas is pure. Liquid CO_2 piped into the greenhouse from bulk supply tanks is a popular commercial technique, as is the use of dry ice.

One of the problems of supplying extra carbon dioxide is checking the level of enrichment, this requiring specialised testing equipment. Ventilation should not proceed simultaneously with CO_2 enrichment for obvious reasons. Conflicting and confusing research reports in commercial circles still surround the whole issue of CO_2 enrichment, much depending upon the prevailing light levels and the particular and even variety of crop involved. Gardeners anxious to carry out carbon dioxide enrichment are advised to study all the reports, select their method of enrichment, and proceed on a cautious basis, seeking specialist advice if necessary from the fuel supplying bodies.

Watering and feeding equipment

The application of water and soluble nutrients is an essential part of greenhouse gardening. Watering methods may be as simple as a watering can filled directly from a tap or barrel or tank topped up by a hose, and liquid fertiliser used for each watering can application. Alternatively liquid fertiliser can be dissolved in barrels or tanks, but great care should be taken to measure both water and liquid fertiliser accurately.

Few modern commercial holdings are without some form of automatic or semi-automatic watering device, with the complementary use of bottle dilutors for liquid fertiliser application. Amateur gardeners are fast realising that there is great scope here, not only for reducing labour, but for ensuring greater accuracy in the realm of water and liquid fertiliser application.

Taps

A greenhouse should have a good tap supplying water at a fair volume and pressure. Screwed taps are preferable to plain types as they allow hose couplings.

Watering cans

These are available in tough plastic ranging from $\frac{1}{2}$gal capacity upwards, the most popular being the 1gal size, both for weight and for ease of measuring up liquid fertilisers. Enamelled metal cans are still very popular, although more expensive, and range from 3–8qt (2gal). Diminutive copper watering cans are useful for house plants and are generally 1–2pt capacity. A selection of roses is available to give fine or coarse droplets of water.

Containers for water

Old sinks or wooden barrels are frequently used as reservoirs for water, though modern plastic water baths holding from 25–40gal are available and are much more hygienic as they can readily be washed out. This is essential for all forms of water storage, as algae and scum can quickly grow on still water, a further problem being contamination with bacterial and fungal diseases. It helps if containers are left shaded.

Sprinkler lines

These provide large droplets of water from revolving nozzles spaced approximately 15ft apart. They are installed at a height of 6–8ft according to headroom available, and if sufficient volume and pressure of water is available, will dispense droplets over an area within a distance of approximately 20ft at a water pressure of between 20–40lb psi. Their main role is for the damping down of crops such as tomatoes, to shake the plants and assist with pollination, and they have therefore little general application. They are available generally in alloy with quick release couplings.

Spraylines

These can take several different forms and are available in both alloy and plastic, the latter tending to sag a little unless adequately supported. They can be used either at high or low level and are available with nozzle sprays spaced approximately 5ft to 7ft 6in apart with different sized jets for operating at different pressures. Typical output of $\frac{3}{32}$in jets ranges from 18gal per hour at 10lb psi up to 53 gal per hour at 40lb psi pressure. For larger jets of $\frac{7}{64}$ in the outputs are nearly doubled and range from 30gal per hour at 10lb psi to 80gal per hour at 40lb psi. The specification for spraylines varies according to manufacturer, as do the trajectories of the nozzles or jets. Fine atomisation is generally achieved at good working pressure, which saturates the whole growing area. The details given apply merely to commercial equipment, which of course can be utilised for large amateur greenhouses. For small amateur greenhouses spraylines of various types are available with much closer nozzle sprays, generally 3–4ft, for operating a 10ft sprayline from a $\frac{1}{2}$in hosepipe, and usually require a water pressure of 35lb psi. The output per hour of these units will obviously vary greatly according to the specification, and it is a matter which must be taken up with the supplier.

Control of spraylines can be effected either on a time basis with a solenoid valve through a sequence controller on a large scale or more simply with a hand-operated tap on a small scale. 'Automatic' waterers are also available which operate either on the saturation of a moisture sensitive pad or by a selenium light cell or other methods similar to those used to control mist irrigation units. The main drawback of spray-

Spraylines are an ideal
means of providing an
even supply of water in a
large greenhouse.
Smaller adaptations are
available for the amateur.

lines lies in their inability to spray water into containers or pots which are protected by foliage. Spraylines are therefore more useful for crops such as tomatoes, used at a high level until the plants reach 5ft then at low level generally at 12in on wire supports, and covering a smaller area. Lettuce crops and other border-grown plants are successfully watered with spraylines.

Damping down is effectively carried out with spraylines, increasing the humidity and reducing water needs, which is valuable for the gardener absent during the day, particularly when the spraylines are linked to an automatic device. A fair quantity of water can reach the pots in many instances. Liquid fertilisers can also be applied through spraylines in a form which makes them readily acceptable to the plants, either through their leaves or in the soil.

Trickle systems

These take several forms, all having in common the precise placement of droplets of water in a pot, container or growing border. The ability of water deposited in droplet form at a specific point to move through the growing medium varies within the type of medium. It has been found in certain free-draining light soils that trickle systems

Fig 43

do not adequately water a sufficiently wide zone, although this can be overcome by moving the position of the nozzle at regular intervals. There are two basic forms: those where plastic nozzles are used in a rubber hose, or 'spaghetti' systems where capillary tubes lead out to each plant and are held in position by a peg. Trickle systems can be used for either border-grown, container-grown or bench-grown plants (see Fig 43) and can be either manually operated or by a timing device operating a solenoid valve, or by a light cell.

Low-level watering systems

Perforated 'lay-flat' polythene tubing of 2in width throws out fine jets of water on expansion with a sufficient volume of water and is a useful system for tomatoes or other border-grown plants. It is not so suitable for container-grown plants. Round PVC tubing with small holes operates in a similar way, but is not usually so efficient as a trickle system.

Hosepipes

These are still indispensable for watering on a small scale, but care must be taken to avoid damage to soil structure by allowing an open-ended hose to splash on to the soil with force. Soil thus splashed on to tomato fruit is a frequent cause of fruit rotting. A rose or other attachment on the end of the hose can do much to avoid indiscriminate water dispersal, even a paraquat weed-killer dispenser being useful *(but used only for water application)* especially for tomatoes and other border-grown crops. Damping down is frequently practised with a hosepipe by pinching in the end, or preferably by using a fine rose.

Dilutors

While, as stated earlier, liquid fertilisers can be mixed as required in small quantities or prepared in bulk, a much more satisfactory arrangement is to use a dilutor into which the stock or concentrated solution of fertiliser is placed, the dilutor then being set at the correct dilution rate and placed in the supply line for spraylines or irrigation nozzles. Bottle dilutors are now used almost entirely on the displacement principle, although other systems work

Assessing water
requirements of pot
plants can be difficult.
Modern inventions like
this moisture meter are
ideal and fool proof—far
better than tapping pots
with one's knuckles.

on a capillary tube system. Problems arise where water pressures are erratic, as this can both damage the dilutor and alter the dilution rate. In addition, it is NOT permitted to connect dilutors direct to a mains supply. Proprietary liquid fertilisers are usually colour dyed so that a quick visual check on dilution is possible, although on a large scale the concentration check of the liquid fertiliser should be regularly carried out with a salt meter. Self-formulated feeds should also be colour dyed for visual checking. Note that a bottle of correctly diluted liquid feed should be available for colour comparison purposes. The quantities of water and soluble feed required by various plants is dealt with under cultural notes referring to each crop.

Assessing the water requirement of crops

In addition to controlling the application of water by solenoid valves, sequence controllers and other apparatus, various methods are used actually to determine the *needs* of the crop. The simplest of these is a tensiometer, a device which consists largely of a ceramic pot connected to a vacuum gauge, graduated in inches of mercury. This instrument indicates the suction necessary to extract water and can be related to the water requirement of the crop. The evaporimeter consists of sand in a thistle funnel connected to a graduated tube, so that the evaporation of water can be calculated and related to crop needs. More recently simple sensitive tipped water meters which state whether soil in pots or borders is 'wet', 'medium' or 'dry' have been available. Solarimeters are installed regionally at research stations and record the solar radiation, so that water requirements can be issued to the commercial horticulture industry.

Frames – cold and heated

With the advent of fan ventilation the greenhouse temperature can in fact be lowered to such an effective degree that acclimatisation can take place *in situ* without recourse to the frame. But although acclimatisation is the main role of a frame,

it can also be used very effectively as a production unit in its own right, like a small greenhouse—especially the elevated form with hessian sides used by specialist flower growers. Sophisticated types of frames, some of which are on rollers and capable of easy movement, can in fact achieve results commensurate in many ways with a greenhouse. In design, shape and orientation the same basic principles apply. Ventilation and watering are two problems, the former being achieved by lifting the sashes and the latter either by hand or by the use of low level spray lines. Heating can be by any of the methods already discussed, the heat loss being calculated in a similar manner to that for greenhouses, although with a brick base wall, for all practical purposes the square foot area of the frame sashes multiplied by 1.4 and ignoring the sides will give a fairly accurate figure. It is very easy to put the required amount of piping, mineral insulated cable or tubular heaters into the frame. Soil warming cables are also used at a loading of $7\frac{1}{2}$ watts per square foot, either by a mains voltage cable led in at 8–9in depth or by low voltage lines through a transformer.

Types and construction of frames

For many years the 6 × 4ft light sashes were standard items, but their weight plus their upkeep has made them a thing of the past. The Dutch light sash measuring approximately 2ft 6in × 5ft is ideal for frame construction. This has a single sheet of 24oz horticultural glass ($56 × 28\frac{3}{4}$in) and is simple and light to handle, being virtually maintenance-free if constructed in pressure treated wood. Bases for frames can be brick, concrete or breeze block, or wood (old railway sleepers serving on a large scale). The front of the frames should be approximately 9–10in high and the rear 12–14in to give a reasonable 'run'.

Frames can also be constructed against the base wall of a greenhouse, an ideal arrangement when the heating system is to be linked, a south orientation usually being preferable. Metal or alloy types come with directions, but there are no precise designs

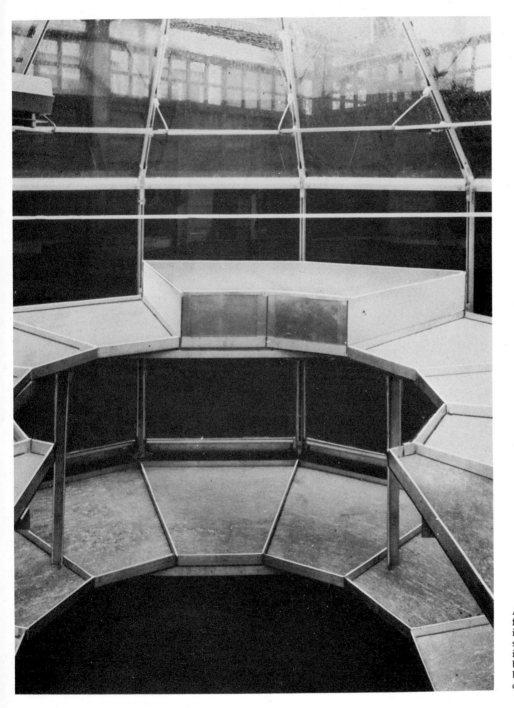

Additional equipment
for greenhouses can
include a wide range of
staging arrangements
including capillary
benches, some with
built-in soil-warming
cables.

otherwise; many gardeners simply adapt what materials they have to the best advantage. Polythene sashes (125mu) can readily be made up by using the wrap-round principle of construction in any convenient size. Wood should be preservative treated, this including both the sash spars and the groundwork. It is important to ensure that sashes are secure, otherwise they may be blown off in a high wind.

Potting sheds

Whether or not a special shed is desirable for compost mixing, potting and other activities will depend on the scale of operations, but a shed is certainly very useful for the storing of pots, tools, equipment and raw material for compost making. If work is to be carried out there, a good stout, level, well-placed bench, preferably with a window adjacent, is highly desirable.

The combined shed/greenhouse, either longitudinally or centrally, has its value, but the shade factor must invariably limit the scope of the greenhouse section, which may be undesirable.

Chapter 10

Lighting Greenhouses

Any discussion on illumination must be prefaced by the reminder of the precise role of light in plant growth. The intensity or level of light has a vital effect in the velocity of the photosynthesis process which is essential to all green plants; the duration of light, or day length, also has profound photoperiodic influences; and and sources of artificial light, as distinct from sunlight, have differing stimulative effects on plants.

Types of artificial lighting
Tungsten filament lamps
These lamps (the type frequently used for home lighting) produce light from a super-heated filament which contains a good deal of the far red in its spectrum and this will, in many plants, produce intense elongation. The intensity of light they produce is low but is sufficient to produce photoperiodic and photosynthetic reaction in extremely sensitive plants such as chrysanthemums, pelargoniums and many others. Tungsten filament lamps are also satisfactory for bringing many bulbs into flower.

Discharge lamps
These produce light by the discharge of electricity through a gas, and the colour varies according to the gas employed. Neon gives a largely red light, vaporised sodium a yellow light, and mercury a greeny blue. Neon is at present not thought to be a great deal of use for horticultural purposes, but sodium (SOX) is presently being experimented with. Mercury vapour lamps (MB) on the other hand are excellent for the production of high intensity lighting and are therefore used to supplement natural daylight where this is too low for optimum photosynthesis activity. The spectrum of light supplied by mercury vapour lamps appears to be adequately

balanced for most plants, although their use is not recommended for growing room cultivation entirely under artificial light as they produce a lot of heat. A 400W mercury vapour lamp is usually suspended at least 3ft above the bench or floor area being illuminated to give a high level of illumination compatible with maximum coverage of plants.

Fluorescent lamps
Types MBF or HLRG have a larger enclosed glass area than mercury vapour lamps and are coated entirely with fluorescent powder, so that some of the ultra-violet radiation is converted to visible light. This is an extremely useful light source for a wide variety of activities, including night-break or growing room techniques.

Tubular fluorescent lights (MCF) operate with mercury vapour at a much lower pressure than fluorescent lamps, and much of the ultra-violet radiation is successfully extracted and converted to useful light by the use of powders. By varying the powder coating, white, natural or warm white light is produced, the warm white being most suitable for horticultural purposes. A further advantage is that they do not produce much heat, having a low surface temperature.

Reflectors
Effective reflection ensures that the maximum amount of light is concentrated on the plants being treated, without at the same time directing too much heat upon them. Reflectors should not unduly restrict the entry of natural light, unless of course under growing room conditions.

Aluminium foil plates are used for tungsten filament lamps, whereas mercury vapour lamps need large reflectors. MBFR/U fluorescent lamps have a coating of reflective titanium oxide, and special

Supplementary lighting is essential in the growing of many greenhouse plants. Photoperiodicity is just as much a governing factor in growth as temperature, and both can be controlled to give flowers all the year round with many plants.

fluorescent tubes with a small reflector so that maximum illumination is concentrated through a 130° incidence.

Four main roles for lighting in greenhouses

1 To allow working on short winter days or in the evenings tungsten filament (the domestic type) lights or fluorescent strip lighting can be used, care being taken to position the lights so that standing at the potting or working bench on dull days or in the evening does not cast a shadow. Light fittings and control switches should be of waterproofed design.

2 To provide day-length manipulation or night-break techniques by the use of low intensity tungsten filament lights, 5–10W per sq ft, suspended above the plants.

3 To supplement the natural daylight when it falls below a level sufficient to maintain optimum photosynthetic activity, and to improve vegetative development and flower truss initiation a high intensity light source is used. This is mainly supplied by mercury vapour lamps—although fluorescent tubes are also employed—for a set number of hours per day over a limited period when the plants are at an early stage of development. Recently, however, more

The flowering of
chrysanthemums is
governed by the length of
daylight to which they
are exposed.

prolonged use of supplementary lighting has been made on more mature plants, with spectacular results in poor light areas. Reference to the precise use of supplementary lighting will be given in the respective crop notes.

4 To illuminate growing rooms.

Growing rooms

The term applies to a variety of techniques whereby artificial lighting supplants natural light. In most cases the waste heat generated by the lighting is used to provide a heat source. Low-intensity lights at 100 watts for every square yard of growing area are used in a building or cupboard of high thermal insulation. This is particularly suitable for bringing bulbs into flower: the tungsten filament lamps are kept suspended about 18in above the leaf tips of the bulbs, light being given for 12 out of 24 hours, preferably by time switch. In a well-insulated building, heat from the lamps may well be sufficient to keep the temperature sufficiently high, while during dark periods electric heaters are used.

Details of the construction of a growing room can be obtained by application to local electricity boards who have plans of standard growing rooms, although many different and varied designs of growing rooms are now in use, the basic objective being to increase the actual area available for the plants and at the same time reduce capital costs. The formula is a chamber within a building of high thermal insulation. The sides of the chamber are of pegboard to allow the passage of fan-circulated air, which avoids the local build-up of heat from the lights. A thermostatically operated ventilation vane allows entry of cooler air from outside when the temperature rises above the desirable level; when heat falls below the desirable level, a heating bank then comes into operation.

Some very rudimentary growing rooms involving banks of fluorescent lamps above benches have been installed, with suitable air outlets, in basements or rooms in older buildings and have been used successfully for many years. More recently growing rooms have been developed in black plastic greenhouses. The basis of the technique is the utilisation of light and heat in combination with low heat loss, thus avoiding the cost of heating a traditional greenhouse with its high heat loss.

The many technical issues which surround the construction of growing rooms and their use are beyond the scope of this book and are best taken up either directly with the Electricity Council or the agricultural/horticultural officers of the respective electricity boards, although reference will be made to their use in connection with crops such as tomatoes and bedding plants, which lend themselves admirably to growing room production.

Chapter 11

How Plants Live

It would be wrong to make a special issue of the physiological aspects surrounding plants being grown in a greenhouse, as the mechanics of growth and all the associated facets are common to all green leaved growing plants. The only special case which could be made for greenhouse plants is that they will, in most cases, be growing a lot quicker than they would out of doors, so that everything will generally happen faster. On the other hand it is possible to control the environment of a greenhouse to fairly fine limits, which is a distinct advantage, compared to the resigned acceptance of conditions as they occur out of doors. Perhaps then, taking all things into account, there does exist the need for a more complete understanding of basic physiological processes if greenhouse gardening is to be entirely successful.

Basic requirements

All green plants, given air and mosture in the absence of any inhibiting or restricting factor, will grow at a rate commensurate with the light level and temperatures to which that particular species or cultivar of plant is attuned. This rather complicated sentence perhaps requires some explanation. A tomato plant, a native of South America originally, has an inherent need for high light intensity and warmth. For it to grow, flower and produce fruit successfully, it is therefore incumbent on the gardener to provide for these conditions as far as possible. Plant a tomato plant outside in Britain during the month of March, instead of in the greenhouse, and if it does not die fairly quickly it will certainly not grow to any great degree, but will tend to debilitate. Conversely, plant a cabbage, a native of Europe, outside in March and, provided it has been suitably acclimatised, it will grow quite happily and in time pro-

duce a heart. Put the cabbage into the warm greenhouse environment suitable for the tomato and it will certainly grow at great speed, but it is unlikely that a heart will be produced, the plant developing vegatively and showing elongated growth.

These rather elementary examples by no means explain why the tomato and the cabbage must have an environmental regime compatible with their metabolism. One point, however, which does clearly emerge is that the velocity of growth of plants is invariably increased when they are put into an environment warmer than that to which they are attuned by inheritance. It is highly important to remember this elementary issue and to think of it categorically: the completely *hardy plant* which will survive out of doors all year in Europe in category 1; *half-hardy plants* such as the pelargonium in category 2; the tender tomato in category 3; and the very tender melon in category 4.

Basic plant processes

Any attempt to understand plant physiology must be prefaced by some discussion of the basic plant processes common to all green plants. While these will be grouped for convenience under separate headings, it should be appreciated that all processes are closely inter-related, each having a bearing on the other.

Respiration

Breathing is a function essential for all living organisms. In the case of green plants air is taken in through the pores on the leaves (and to a lesser extent through the stems and roots), its oxygen content extracted as energy for various chemical processes, and carbon dioxide gas expelled as a waste product—in a similar way to a fuel being burned by a fire or an internal combustion engine. The speed of respiration varies according to the age of the plant, the temperature of the atmosphere, and the rate of growth, this last activity not always being completely in keeping with temperature, as a combination of other factors may have a bearing on the growth rate irrespective of age or temperature.

Respiration is a continuous destructive process as compared with other functions such as photosynthesis which are carried out only during daylight hours. The destructive nature of respiration therefore draws on the reserves of the plant night and day, which means that food manufactured by the process of photosynthesis is utilised at night, a fact that has considerable significance in relation to day and night temperatures. If, for example, a warm bright day when a great deal of carbohydrate is manufactured in the plant leaves is followed by a cold night, there will usually be a surplus of carbohydrate, which in the case of the tomato plant will result in starch filled curled leaves. The converse is also true, and cool dull days with limited photosynthesis, followed by warm nights, will in fact dissipate the reserves of carbohydrate resulting in drawn spindly plants.

Process of respiration

Air taken in through pores in leaves, stem and roots	energy extracted for chemical processes	carbon dioxide expelled through pores

Photosynthesis

This is the process whereby the air taken in through the pores in the leaves has the carbon dioxide gas contained in it (at approximately 300 parts per million) extracted and the oxygen content of the air expelled, more or less the converse of respiration. Carbon dioxide is the vital source of carbon needed for the build-up of carbohydrates, which are synthesised with the aid of the catalyst chlorophyll, the green pigment present in all green plants. The supply of water and nutrients taken up by the plant roots (which will be discussed shortly) is also closely involved with photosynthesis.

Research has shown that there is a direct relationship between the velocity of photosynthesis and the prevailing light intensity, provided that temperature is sufficiently high and there is no restriction in water and nutrient supply. Adding to the natural complement of carbon dioxide, up to threefold enrichment, by various means under conditions of high light and temperature levels can, in certain cases, increase the rate of photosynthesis, which has various benefits largely centring round the increased supply of carbohydrates for the plant's vital processes.

No research has yet shown precisely what physiological processes are brought into play by carbon dioxide enrichment but it is quite clear that photosynthesis is an extremely complex function. The practical implication for greenhouse gardening is to ensure that there is no light restriction for light-demanding crops and that all other environmental factors must simultaneously be given strictest attention.

Process of photosynthesis

Air taken in by plant	carbon dioxide content extracted	oxygen expelled

Transpiration

Water absorbed by the plant roots and other parts of the plant passes up through the xylem tissue in the stem, and into the leaves where quantities in excess of requirements for various chemical processes are expelled as water vapour through the pores in leaves and stems, and to a limited degree through the epidermis or plant 'skin'. Apart from helping to keep the plant 'cool' by loss of heat through evaporation, a transpiration stream is created, this being essential for the movement of dissolved foodstuffs throughout the growing plant. Transpiration rate is controlled in an interesting way, as the pores or stomata are opened and closed by the activity of guard cells (see Fig 44) which close the stomata when flaccid and open it when turgid. Thus the rate of water loss is directly related to the temperature and humidity of the air. Once again it would be wrong to consider transpiration in strict isolation, as

epidermal cell

guard cell

stoma

Hot and dry-Open

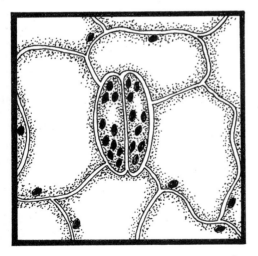

Cool and humid–Closed

Fig 44

there are in addition many other inter-related issues: (1) the healthy state of the roots and their ability to absorb sufficient water, (2) freedom from disease or restriction on the part of the xylem and other conducting tissue, (3) the age and size of the plant with particular emphasis on the leaf area, (4) the respective osmotic pressures of both soil and plant which will greatly affect the ability of the plant to take up moisture and nutrients in the first case (see below), (5) the species of plant involved and whether it is botanically adapted to moisture conservation, as indeed is the case with most cacti when the leaves are modified to 'needles'.

Process of transpiration   Water taken in through the process of osmosis passes up through the xylem and a proportion is given off as water vapour at a rate dependent on temperature, humidity, the osmotic pressures of plant and soil and other related issues.

Osmosis

This is undoubtedly not only one of the most important physiological processes, but an activity over which the gardener can exert considerable control. Any botany book will state that osmosis is the process whereby a higher concentration of salts in solution on one side of a semi-permeable membrane will absorb the water of a less concentrated solution by pulling it through the semi-permeable membrane. Relating this to plants, the stronger solution contained in the cell of the root (or other tissue) absorbs the water from the less concentrated solution of salts in the soil or growing medium, the net result of which is to set up suction pressures which are always endeavouring to equalise.

Botanists make much of the fact that only water is absorbed by osmosis and that soluble plant nutrients move in by diffusion and absorption, as few semi-permeable membranes are perfect; but for all practical purposes the two processes are so closely related that they can be considered simultaneously. Once the salt solution is contained in the cell of root or other tissue a chain reaction process goes on, as the cell receiving water has its concentration lowered, altering the osmotic pressure, which allows the more concentrated solution in the next cell to pull in the now less concentrated solution to even up the pressure, and so on.

The rate at which osmosis proceeds depends on many factors such as transpiration rate and the speed of other processes, but undoubtedly the salt concentration of the soil water is of paramount importance. When concentrated and soluble chemicals (some weedkillers and many fertilisers) are applied to the soil or growing medium, they alter the salt concentration. Where near equilibrium exists there can only be limited osmotic activity, if indeed there is any at all, whereas should the salt solution in the growing medium become more concentrated than that of the plant cell, osmosis in reverse can and will take place. The importance of salt concentration in the growing medium and successful osmosis on the part of the growing plant cannot be divorced from the availability of water supplies, as when water supplies diminish, salt solutions will become more concentrated and vice versa. This is a factor of considerable importance in greenhouse culture where the majority of plants will be growing in limited quantities of media. The sensitivity of plants to salt concentrations varies very considerably. Reference will be made to salt solution measurement in a later chapter when some scale of susceptibility for various plants will be stated. It must be further appreciated that some measure of growth control can be achieved by adjustment of the salt concentration of the growing medium, by applying either solid or liquid fertilisers, something which intuitive gardeners have been unconsciously carrying out for years.

Process of osmosis The stronger solution of salts in the plant cell pulls in the water from the weaker solution of the soil or growing medium and simultaneously there is absorption of liquid nutrients. A measure of growth control can be achieved by paying strict attention to the salt concentra-tion of the growing medium.

Translocation

This function relates to the transport of elaborated foodstuffs throughout the plant tissue, the main conducting tissue being the phloem. Many gardeners fail to realise that the food synthesised in the leaves is moved into the flower or swelling fruit as required, there often being the allusion that leaves and flowers or fruit have a separate unrelated existence. Further credence is given to this philosophy by the various feeding formulae prepared for the swelling of fruits or the size of flowers. Neither flower, fruit nor leaf of the plant exists in limbo, and it is the successful culmination of all processes in which translocation is merely one vital part which results in good flowers, fruits, or for that matter foliage.

Disruptions of any kind such as irregular watering, unsuitable or variable temperatures, or the wrong dilution of liquid feeding, can frequently affect the usual movement of elaborated foodstuffs around the plant, resulting in physiological trouble such as blotchy ripening or black bottoms of tomatoes, flower drop in many pot plants, lack of hearting in greenhouse lettuce, to mention only a few malfunctions which are closely linked to faulty circulation of elaborated foodstuffs or the direction of simple elements into their respective roles. Here again is a case, however, for emphasising that there is a very close relationship between all physiological factors and that compartmentalised thinking can be confusing.

Pollination and fertilisation

Sexual reproduction is a feature of most flowering plants and is a process which depends on the minute pollen grain or male sperm successfully and in good condition reaching the ovary of the same or other flower of similar species, and thereafter germinating, producing a pollen tube through which fusion between male gamete (sperm) and female gamete (egg or ovum) can take place, resulting in fertilisation and the production of new cells which form the fruit. Flowers which contain both male and female organs producing pollen capable of reaching and acceptable to the ovary are said to be self-fertile. When the pollen from another flower of the same species is necessary, a flower is said to be self-sterile, where male and female organs are produced on separate flowers, the flower is unisexual; both of these factors can give rise to problems when the fruit of the plant being grown is important. In some cases, however, fertilisation is not desirable and before it happens the flowers of male blooms are generally removed. There are many cases where fertilisation is unsuccessful, either because the pollen is not fertile or it dried out before germination, a frequent state of affairs in tomato growing due either to poor environmental conditions or the production of infertile pollen under conditions of poor light. Fertilisation of tomatoes can be aided by damping down frequently. In the case of peaches and nectarines pollination is assisted by collecting the pollen on a rabbit's tail or cotton wool and transferring this to open flowers, whereas with melons the male flower is removed and inserted into the female flower.

By contrast, it is inadvisable to allow fertilisation of cucumber flowers, as this results in the production of bitter fruit. Modern breeding programmes have now

Seeds need light, warmth and constant and even humidity to germinate rapidly and evenly. A little propagating case like this one provides an ideal environment for germination.

Fertilisation occurs in the flowers if pollen is fertile & compatible — the result being the fruit containing seeds

Photosynthesis, Respiration & Transpiration take place in the leaves of a plant

Hypogeal germination
(Bean)

Epigeal germination
(Sycamore)

Transport of water and nutrients takes place in the xylem and phloem contained in the stem

The root and root hairs absorbs water and soluble nutrients

Fig 45

130

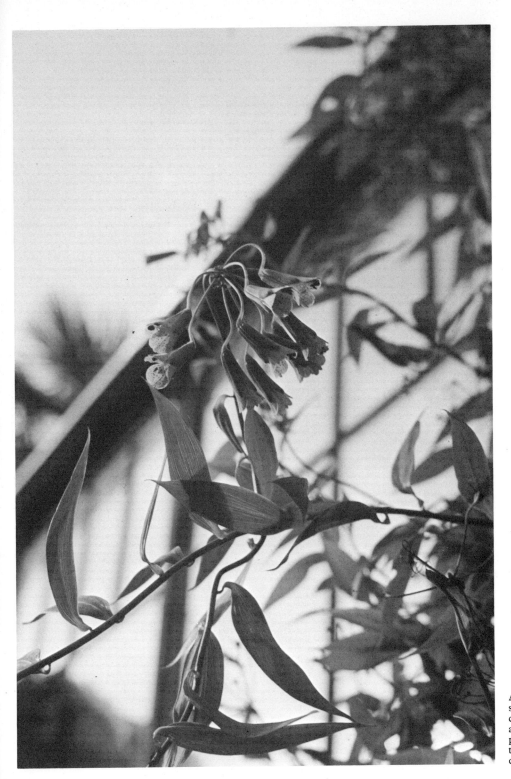

A bomarea hybrid. The
successful crossing and
cultivation of plants
always depends on a
proper understanding of
their basic growing
characteristics.

produced 'all female' cucumbers.

Germination of seeds

A seed contains a new plant in an embryo state, and given suitable conditions the young plant will develop into an adult plant. The initial awakening of the embryonic plant is called germination, which will occur when moisture has penetrated through the protective seed coat or testa to trigger it off. Air, moisture and suitable temperature are the prerequisites for successful germination, but these must be balanced to the particular inherent requirements of each species.

All seeds have a dormancy period during which they cannot be readily induced to germinate and this period varies according to species. Various ways and means are practised to break this dormancy period, for example by subjecting the seed to periods of low or high temperature. The time taken for a seed actually to germinate will vary with the species, and also the age of the seed. Seeds vary considerably in their viability or ability to germinate, and reference to both these facts will be made in the respective cultural notes where applicable, it being worth noting that the particular germinating procedure which has evolved for a particular type of seed has probably come partly by usage and partly by research over many years. Some seeds germinate below the compost surface (hypogeal), others above (epigeal), the botanical aspects being referred to in Fig 45.

Chapter 12

The subject of plant nutrition is very complex and it is not possible here to give more than an elementary background to it. In a great deal of what is written about plant nutrition, assumption rather than fact plays a very large part. As with the physiological aspects of plant growth, it is convenient to consider nutrition in a sectional manner. Here again there is such a complex relationship between all the nutritional elements and chemical processes that the ability of one chemical element to fulfil a role depends a great deal on the activity and presence of all the others. It could be said that each chemical element is a cog in a large wheel, and should a cog be missing some malfunction or complete breakdown of vital processes is likely. It is, however, true to say that the greenhouse gardener has matters under his control to a much greater extent than the gardener out of doors. He also has the ability to meter the quantity of each particular chemical element supplied to the plant.

All living organisms require a range of essential chemical elements if they are to generate the energy to carry out all the various processes concerned with their growth and development. Animals can take in food and drink in either solid or liquid form and digest the chemical elements in them, but living plants take their 'food' only in soluble or gaseous form, this being true even of insectivorous plants which 'digest' their prey. The majority of elements are assimilated by the roots, and carbon and oxygen are absorbed through the leaves. A plant nutrient is therefore a chemical which has a precise function in the plant's growth and a vital part to play in the plant's further development.

Soil types

Mineral soils are derived from the long-term chemical and mechanical breakdown of the earth's crust, a process which has been going on for millions of years. The size of particle to which the rock has been reduced varies greatly, from coarse gravel, through sand, down to silt and clay. Few mineral soils are, however, 'pure', having become interlaced with the organic remains of plants and animals, in addition to a vast population of micro- and macro-organisms such as bacteria, fungi, worms, and other forms of life. All these living organisms have differing functions and in the course of satisfying their own nutrient needs they decompose or chemically change a great many of the contents of the soil, rendering complex chemicals into a soluble form suitable for absorption by the living plant.

Mineral soils are classified largely according to their mineral particle size and are broadly divided into sandy soils or loams, which have a predominance of large particles; heavy clay loams, which consist of a large percentage of fine particles; and medium soils or loams, which have a reasonable proportion of all particle sizes. The size of particles in different soils is stated as follows:

	Particle size in mm
Coarse sand	2.000–0.200
Fine sand	0.200–0.020
Silt	0.020–0.002
Clay	less than 0.002

Particle size has a profound effect on the ability of air and moisture to penetrate freely through a soil, the sandy soil allowing free movement of air and moisture through the large pore spaces, the clay soil tending to lock up moisture and air because the particles adhere very closely together. Without movement of water, plants are unable to extract it for their needs and when there is a lack of air the chemical cycle is restricted, with profound effects on the availability of plant nutrients. This is why overwatered plants in pots frequently go yellow.

The organic matter content of the soil, coupled with chemical micro- and macro-organisms and worm activity can, however, greatly influence the behaviour of a soil, especially if of a clay type, by causing the particles to adhere together in a crumb formation instead of existing separately. This is due both to the adhesive effect of humic gums and to the electrolytic effect of positively and negatively charged chemical elements. When this can be encouraged to happen to a high degree, a soil is said to have a good structure. Conversely, when soil is badly lacking in organic matter or where micro-organism activity is reduced to a low level due to waterlogging or other factors, a soil may lose structure and become inhospitable to desirable plants. Organic as opposed to mineral soils are derived from plant and animal remains, fen or peat soils being classic examples, although few, if any, soils are 100 per cent organic.

It would be wrong to make too large an issue of the ideal soil or loam consisting of a good distribution of mineral particle size, organic matter in reasonable quantity, an excellent crumb structure, and a supply of both immediately available and long-term nutrients. While such soils do exist and are capable of growing excellent plants, research work and practical growing experience in recent years have shown that plants are grown highly successfully in a very wide range of soil types, from sandy soil with negligible organic matter content, to pure peat with barely any mineral content at all, provided there is a constant supply of readily available plant nutrients. It would be more correct to say that the nearer 'ideal' a soil is, the better the results from plants without so much attention and without recourse to additional nutrients. For greenhouse culture of border-grown plants, or culture in pots using soil-containing media, the same principles will apply.

The range of essential nutrients

The nutrient content of a mineral soil will vary according to the constituents of the native rock from which the soils were originally derived, the treatment which the soil has received over the years and the weather pattern. One could scarcely expect a cultivated light sandy soil in a very wet district to be rich in nutrients; these would tend to be washed or leached out. On the other hand, a light sandy soil which had supported a good cover of growth in a dry area could be surprisingly rich in plant nutrients. Clay soils tend to be richer in plant nutrients than light sandy soils, being invariably initially richer in plant nutrients which are not leached out so rapidly.

The range of mineral elements or plant nutrients varies from soil to soil in different regions, but they invariably contain the macro-elements phosphorus, potassium, calcium and magnesium, along with the micro-elements silicon, aluminium, sulphur, boron, manganese, copper, zinc, iron, molybdenum, chlorine, sodium, iodine, cobalt, selenium, and others less well known. In addition, the major element nitrogen is supplied by the breakdown of organic matter, and by fixation (synthesis from the atmosphere), and hydrogen and oxygen are supplied 90–95 per cent by water and carbon in gaseous form from the atmosphere.

While the natural complement of these elements may well suffice to sustain a plant growing naturally out of doors, this is not the case in realms of intensive greenhouse culture, which means resorting to the application or addition of these nutrients, particularly those of the macro category which are used in large quantities by most actively growing plants.

Macro-elements
Nitrogen (N)
The element nitrogen is a constituent of all forms of plant material, and is essential for the formation of proteins. It is taken up by the plant largely in the form of nitrate, but can also be absorbed as ammonia. The

effect of nitrogen on plants is to cause an increase in total bulk, which in practical terms generally means larger leaves and larger plants, although they may not necessarily be more productive of fruit and flowers; in fact, the reverse is often the case. Too much nitrogen in relation to other nutrients can also induce a lateness in flower or fruit formation. With tomatoes, a gross excess of nitrogen can, in the early part of the year when light intensity is low, induce such lush, soft vegetative growth that the plant fails to develop flower trusses, and, even if it does, these can 'miss' completely. The amount of nitrogen present naturally in soil can vary greatly, and soils rich in organic matter can contain up to 1 per cent or more, whereas an infertile soil will contain only .05 per cent. A usual figure would be in the order of .10 to .30 per cent.

The total nitrogen figure in the soil is no real guide to its availability to the plant, a lot depending on the rate of bacterial activity, which in turn depends on temperature, lack of competition from competing organisms such as protozoa, waterlogging, lack of air, excess consolidation and other factors. Partial soil sterilisation or pasteurisation by means of heat will result in a flood of available nitrogen because the pasteurisation heat kills off pests and diseases and destroys competing organisms, leaving the thick-walled spore-forming nitrogen bacteria free to carry on with their activities. The breakdown of organic matter in the soil results in the production of CO_2 (carbon dioxide) which will form a weak carbonic acid solution which is one of the main dissolving agents for nitrogen and other plant nutrients. As nitrate is highly soluble it can quickly be leached out of the soil by overwatering, which shows the folly of over-watering greenhouse plants. At the same time, flooding out of excess nitrogen can be a useful technique when there is known excess, as is the case following soil sterilisation methods which rely on heat. Ammonia is also washed out by flooding. While an excess of nitrogen generally results in lush

unproductive growth, prone to disease, shortage is quite clearly exhibited by pale sickly yellow leaves. Plants can also assimilate nitrogen as ammonium compounds, which can result in problems, a typical example being black bottom in tomato fruit.

Breakdown of nitrogen When a fertiliser such as hoof and horn meal is added to a *soil*, it is necessary for soil bacteria to attack the hoof and horn meal particles and break them down first into nitrite and then into soluble nitrate before the plant can utilise the hoof and horn's nitrogen content. Soilless media are initially sterile, containing few bacteria, and it takes time before the hoof and horn can be converted to nitrate. If, on the other hand, nitrogen is applied in the form of nitrate (eg potassium nitrate) the plant can absorb it immediately.

Nitrogen summary Required for all plants, especially those of a leafy nature. Taken up largely in the form of nitrate, but also as ammonia. Induces lush soft growth in many plants if applied in excess, especially tomatoes and other leafy crops early in the year when light intensity is low. Can also reduce flowering and fruiting potential of plants if over-applied. If in short supply, this results in small and often yellow leaves, along with a general lack of vigour.

Phosphorus (P and P_2O_5)

Phosphorus is associated with all life and is a constituent of every living cell in plants and animals. It might therefore be expected that large quantities are required by growing plants, but this is not the case; while it is constantly needed, the actual amount required is relatively small in proportion to the nitrogen and potash required.

Natural supplies of phosphorus are in most types of soil, a percentage of 0.15 being the amount present in an average loamy soil (a medium soil with a good proportion of organic matter). In chalky soil areas the amount present rises considerably to the order of 0.2–0.3 per cent, whereas in some types of infertile soil its presence may be minimal.

Phosphorus is frequently associated with successful root growth and early maturity, yet the need for it persists right through to flowering and subsequent fruit formation and ripening, where this is applicable. On the other hand many soils are heavily overloaded with phosphorus, indicating that its actual uptake by the plant can be relatively small. The surplus phosphorus remains in the soil because of its low solubility. Its availability to the plant is in the form of a weak phosphoric acid dissolved in a weak acid solution produced by micro-organism activity. In a very acid soil, phosphorus combines with iron and aluminium to form even less soluble components. The particular role of calcium in relation to phosphorus is by no means fully understood, as phosphorus would appear to be quite readily available to plants under the acid conditions of a soilless media (pH 5.5). The way in which phosphorus actually becomes available to plants is thought to be linked to the process through which previously insoluble phosphorus becomes available to the plant when more phosphorus is added, but, to confuse the issue still further, plants seem to exist quite happily in soils shown on analysis to have a high phosphorus content *without* the addition of any additional phosphorus.

The temperature of the soil or growing medium and the temperature of the air seem to be closely associated with the availability of phosphorus and the ability of the plant to assimilate it, this being illustrated quite clearly by the bluish coloration which results when many tender plants are subjected to cold. General lack of vigour and a distinct tendency towards poor rooting and late flowering are further symptoms of phosphorus shortage.

The effect of excess phosphorus on the plant is extremely difficult to define, no doubt because any excess phosphorus applied is rendered insoluble or is possibly lost by drainage in a free draining soil or growing medium.

Fertilisers are stated as having a percentage of soluble and insoluble phosphoric acid, a somewhat confusing state-ment; it is better if the percentage is stated as phosphorus (P) only.

Phosphorus summary Required by all plants in relatively small quantities. Has an effect on root development and early maturity. Shortage results in blue coloration; excess difficult to define.

Potassium (K and K_2O)

Potassium is required in very large amounts, particulary by flower and fruit producing plants. It is present initially in many soils in larger quantities than either nitrogen or phosphorus (1 per cent or more), although only a small proportion of the total quantity may be actually available to the growing plant. Excess results in hard stunted growth, whereas shortage gives rise to marginal leaf scorch and further encourages the soft lush growth typical of nitrogen surplus. There is therefore a very close relationship between the effects of nitrogen and those of potassium, and successful cultivation of most plants relies on the correct ratio of nitrogen to potash, phosphorus playing little part provided it is present in sufficient quantity.

Potassium is said to afford disease resistance qualities to plants, yet this is invariably associated merely with a hard or balanced growth which, apart from ensuring a good protection, has no surplus of carbohydrates for the disease organisms to plunder readily. Colour pigments develop well in the presence of adequate potash, which means clearer expression of colour in flowers, or better colour in fruit. An excess of soluble potash in the soil can also give rise to soluble salt problems, which can affect the osmotic process adversely, or burn the roots physically.

Potash summary Required in large amounts for most plants. Shortage is indicated by marginal leaf scorch. Excess results in stunted dark blue tinted growth, and in some cases burning of the leaf tips, no doubt because an excess in the growing medium results in a high soluble salt content.

Magnesium

The importance of magnesium varies according to the species of plant involved, but is essential for the photosynthesis process and the translocation of elaborated foodstuffs round the plant. Where this element is either in short supply or rendered insoluble, browny-orange areas appear *between* the veins, especially in older leaves. For those plants which make large demands on magnesium, this element is added regularly to the growing medium, often along with lime.

Excess of magnesium will create a salt problem in the growing media before its toxic effects, if any, are exhibited by the actual plant. The unavailability of magnesium to the plant is a complex subject, centred around the quantities of potassium and nitrogen in the growing media, and possibly other factors. Often when there is an excess of potash, or potash is used copiously, as with tomato soils, magnesium deficiency is at its worst. On soils of poor physical structure, potassium seems to be taken up in preference to magnesium, or alternatively the magnesium is rendered insoluble in some way. Magnesium deficiency is also worse in areas of strong light: in the case of tomatoes those along the outside areas nearest the glass seem to be the first to show deficiency symptoms.

Magnesium summary Required by all plants and in large amounts by some. Shortage results in interveinal chlorosis, with a yellowing or bronzing of the chlorotic area. Areas most exposed to strong light are usually first affected in a greenhouse. Plants in light soil heavily dressed with potassium are usually prone to magnesium deficiency. Excess is difficult to define, although excess salt concentration with all its side effects will usually result when it is over-supplied.

Calcium

Many authorities do not discuss calcium under plant nutrients, preferring to give this element a special consideration as a neutralising agent. Calcium is, however, an element needed by plants, especially for the cell walls, apart from its other functions—which are best pursued in a work on chemistry.

The exact causes of acidity in the soil or growing media have been studied for many years and are still not completely understood, but the gardener need merely think in terms of the amount of free lime available to the plants enabling the base exchange mechanism to operate whereby plants obtain their nutrients. A soil or growing medium may contain considerable amounts of calcium, but this may be 'held' by the organic content or humus content of the soil, a situation by no means unique in greenhouse culture, especially with soilless media.

A growing medium not supplied with lime will become considerably more acid, due to the acid-forming activities of microorganisms and chemical activity.

pH scale The measure of exchangeable calcium in the soil or other media (including of course liquids) is recorded on the well-known pH scale which, for the technically minded, is a logarithm of the calcium ion concentration. The pH scale runs from 1 to 14, most plants falling between about 4.5 and 7 for their particular preferences. However, matters have been further complicated by the lower pH range at which plants, in many cases, seem capable of growing satisfactorily in soilless media, no doubt because of the use of nutrients which are available to the plants without recourse to micro-organism activity. Unfortunately the amount of exchangeable calcium can greatly affect the availability of other nutrients and vice versa. Ammonium and potassium can, for example, immobilise the calcium if present in large quantities, whereas too much calcium can result in insolubility of manganese and iron, and too little can produce calcium toxicity of the same elements. It can be seen therefore that what might appear to be, on the surface, a simple question of acidity and alkalinity with calcium acting as the neutralising agent, is far from the case. At the same time there is much to be said for ignoring the complexities and pursuing the more simple course of relying on the pH figure, although deeper consideration will be given to the whole matter in a later chapter.

Calcium summary Required in varied amounts by most plants, especially for cell wall formation. Amounts needed vary and this translates itself into adjusting the soil or growing media to a suitable pH figure. Actual shortage of calcium in the plant will result in yellowing of leaves, rather typical of nitrogen shortage, or in extreme cases a whitening of the growing points. It is difficult to consider calcium shortage by itself, as there are so many associated issues involved, the same being true of an excess of calcium of which the yellow leaf coloration of iron deficiency is so typical.

Lesser or micro-elements
Sulphur
This element has a general role in plant nutrition, it being difficult to explain its exact function. Sulphur is present initially in most soils and in addition in many fertilisers used, so its shortage is seldom, if ever, a problem.
Iron
This is an important element in greenhouse culture and is greatly concerned with photosynthesis. It is very insoluble and is rendered still more so by *high* pH figures. Symptoms of shortage are yellowing of the whole leaf, although in extreme cases the leaf can turn white, the older leaves usually being more affected than the younger ones. Deficiency usually arises from an excess of exchangeable calcium in the soil or growing medium. Excess is difficult to detect, no doubt because excess iron combines with phosphorus to form insoluble compounds, but excessive iron application is not to be recommended.
Manganese
Like iron, this is much concerned with photosynthetic activity, which is why any shortage invariably produces a leaf-mottling effect. High pH figures usually spark off any deficiency of this element, although the mottling of the leaves of young plants caused by the invariably high pH figure of many growing composts usually disappears as the pH figure drops. Toxicity of manganese is a much more common problem, particularly in older tomato borders which are steam sterilised. Here a blue-black coloration develops on leaf tips, in addition to a general drooping.
Boron
Much more has been heard of boron in recent years, largely because its importance in tomato culture has been highlighted. It would appear to have a multifarious role to play in plant growth, as its shortage in many plants causes shrivelling of leaf tips and a blueing of stems and petioles. Tomato fruits develop a corky brown layer beneath the skin. In the majority of cases, and with properly formulated growing media, boron deficiency should not arise, although it is obviously an element which can cause considerable trouble. Care should be taken not to use boron to excess, as the efficiency of boron-based weedkillers is well known.
Other elements
The other elements referred to earlier do not usually give cause for great concern unless present in excess, or rendered so by general soil unbalance. There can also be a degree of substitution where the micro-element replaces the macro-element, resulting in deficiency symptoms of the latter in some cases, although they may serve admirably; eg silicon can replace phosphorus, and sodium can substitute for potash.

Main types of fertilisers for greenhouse culture

Fertiliser	N	P_2O_5	K_2O	Other elements	Comments & rates of use
Hoof and horn meal	12–14%				Organic form of nitrogen much used in tomato base fertiliser and composts; release of ammonia can be rapid, but complete release of nitrogen content is over a period. Use up to 4oz per sq yd
Dried blood	7–12%	1–2%	1%		A 'safe' top dressing for tomatoes, bulbs and other plants at 1–2oz per sq yd, as a quick-acting source of nitrogen. Also useful diluted at up to 2oz per gallon of water as a quick-acting stimulant
Nitro-Chalk	25%			carbonate of lime in varying amounts.	Inorganic quick-acting sources of nitrogen. Used for border-grown plants requiring an urgent boost
Nitra-Shell	34%				
Nitram	34.5%				
Nitro 26	26%				Useful where virus check occurs in tomatoes. Use at $\frac{1}{2}$–1oz per sq yd
Ammonium nitrate	35%				Inorganic. Used as a constituent of liquid fertilisers
Nitrate of potash or potassium nitrate	13%		44–46%		Inorganic, excellent source of readily available nitrogen. Used as liquid fertiliser—not dry
Urea	46%				Organic. Main use as a constituent of liquid feeds. Can be used dry at $\frac{1}{2}$oz per sq yd as an organic source of nitrogen. The more sophisticated form is

Fertiliser	N	P_2O_5	K_2O	Other elements	Comments & rates of use
					urea formaldehyde (Nitroform) which releases nitrogen over a period
Ammonium phosphate	11%	48%			Inorganic. Used mainly in slow-release type fertilisers and seldom as a separate fertiliser
Bonemeal	1–5%	15–32%			Organic. Not used greatly in greenhouse culture, but would be useful in a soil very low in phosphates, applied in addition to base feed. Use at 3–4oz per sq yd
Superphosphates of lime		18–21%			Inorganic. Best form of phosphates used generally as a constituent of base feeds and in composts. Can be used at up to 4oz per sq yd
Sulphate of potash			48%		Inorganic. Use dry at 1–2oz per sq yd as quick source of potash. Diluted in water at 1oz per gallon it is very quick acting
Epsom salts				*magnesium oxide* 16%	Inorganic. Use at up to 3–6oz per sq yd for tomatoes. Also used as foliar feed at 2lb per 10gal with a spreader.
Lime (hydrated) (ground)				*calcium oxide* 68% 47%	The main form of lime used for tomato culture is *ground limestone, a* relatively slow-acting form of calcium. *Magnesian limestone* is frequently used for tomato growing as it contains magnesium. Both forms are used according to soil

Compound fertilisers

There are many different types of proprietary compound fertilisers available. Typical analysis figures are as follows:

N	P$_2$O$_5$		K$_2$O	Comments (see cultural notes in Part II for rates of application)
	soluble	insoluble		
12%	5.5%	.5%	6%	High nitrogen base dressing for crops demanding a boost, eg lettuce or end-of-season tomatoes
6%	10%	.5%	17.5%	High potash for tomatoes in heat sterilised soil
9.5%	9%	.5%	13.2%	Balanced crop dressing for established crops
10.5%	7.5%	.5%	10·5%	For plants such as chrysanthemums demanding a balanced level of nutrients

N	P$_2$O$_5$		K$_2$O	Magnesium	
	soluble	insoluble			
John Innes Base Fertiliser					For John Innes composts see chapter on composts. Also as a base dressing for many crops
5.2%	7%	.5%	10%		
Enmag (SAI)—a mixture of magnesium, ammonium phosphate, sulphate of potash					
5%	.5%	23·5%	10%	10%	Slow-release general base dressing
Q4 (Vitax)					Manganese 30.36 ppm*
5.3%	6.8%	.7%	10%	1.73%	Iron 58.81 ppm*
					Zinc 42.50 ppm*
					Copper 30.36 ppm*
					Boron 15.13 ppm
					Molybdenum .41 ppm
					(*in chelated form—a widely used slow-release dressing especially suitable as it contains trace elements. Much used for composts)

Liquid feeds

These are either in liquid form or for dissolving. A very varied range is available but generally in the following regions:

	Nitrogen N_2	Sol. Phos. Acid P_2O_5	Potash K_2O	
Vitafeed-101 (Vitax)	26.00	—	26.00	⎫ Contain
Vitafeed-102 ,,	18.00	—	36.00	⎬ trace
Vitafeed-103 ,,	13.00	—	43.00	⎪ elements
Vitafeed-301 ,,	36.00	—	12.00	⎭

N	P_2O_5		K_2O
	soluble	insoluble	
Solufeed Standard			
23.3%	19.5%		16.0%
Solufeed Summer			
29.8%	9.9%		14.7%
Solufeed High Potash			
17.3%	8.5%		33.6%
Solufeed NK			
31.2%			20.8%
Solufeed AN 2/1			
28.5%			14.3%

Note: There are many proprietary liquid feeds; these from Vitax and ICI are merely examples. Use as directed. Different forms contain trace elements

Self-mix
Composition of feeds (oz/gal)

Nutrient
(% weight/vol)

K₂O to N ratio	Potassium nitrate	Urea or Ammonium nitrate		K₂O	N
3 : 1 (high potash)	24	—	—	6.3	2.0
2 : 1 (standard)	24	5	6	6.3	3.3
1 : 1 (high nitrogen)	24	16	20	6.3	6.3

Note: this is the stock solution prepared by careful mixing in warm water; it is diluted to 1:200, generally with a calibrated dilutor. When using a watering can the solution is 1 fluid ounce of the stock solution in $1\frac{1}{4}$ gallons of water. Use disulphine dye for easy colour identification of dilution strength.

Bulky organics used in crop culture

Precise recommendations regarding use are given in cultural notes, in Part II. Most of these organics contain trace elements in addition to those stated.

Average	Moisture %	Dry matter %	% in fresh manures			Comments
			Nitrogen (N)	Phosphorus (P)	Potash (K)	
Farmyard manure (FYM)	81	15	.43	.19	.44	Farmyard manure varies. Should be well decomposed. Contains reasonably balanced quantities of the main nutrients
Poultry manure	53	30	2.1	1.21	0.60	High nitrogen content, which can give rise to problems when used too liberally
Sewage sludge	40–75	65	2.32	1.29	0.25	More useful for crops grown out of doors. Nitrogen content not in such an available form as in FYM
Seaweed	70–80	10–20	.4–.8	0.1–.2	1–2	A useful form of organic matter fairly rich in potash. Use fresh or composted

143

Average	Moisture %	Dry matter %	% in fresh manures			Comments
			Nitrogen (N)	Phosphorus (P)	Potash (K)	
Peat	40–60	97	0·7–3	0·1–0·2	0·1–0·3	Used mainly to 'condition' soils intended for crop cultivation, also as top dressing or mulch, and as the main or sole ingredient of soilless composts. The pH of peat is in the 3.5–4.5 range

Liquid organics — seaweed

The use of liquefied seaweed offers an excellent organic source of macro- and micro-elements in readily available form. One such is marketed by Maxicrop, a typical example of which is as follows:

Total solids   8.5%
Organic matter   51.2%
Inorganic matter   43.6%
  containing

Nitrogen (N)	0.72%	Lime (CaO)	0.44%
Phosphate (P_2O_5)	2.0%	Iron (Fe_2O_3)	0.34%
Potash (K_2O)	3.0%	Alumina (Al_2O_3)	0.23%
Sulphate (SO_3)	6.1%	Copper	40 ppm
Chloride (Cl)	6.7%	Cobalt	4 ppm
Silica (SiO_2)	0.2%	Nickel	24 ppm
Iodine (I)	0.9%	Zinc	100 ppm
Bromine (Br)	0.8%	Molybdenum	10 ppm
Soda (Na_2O)	18.9%	Manganese	40 ppm
Magnesia (MgO)	0.58%	Boron	1 ppm

Also traces of vanadium, titanium, gold, silver, chromium, caesium, rubidium, ruthenium, rhenium, selenium, beryllium, lithium, tungsten, etc.

It has a wide range of uses, including straw bale treatment for tomatoes and cucumbers. A special feature of seaweed-based liquid feeds is that they contain the complete spectrum of nutrient content. An increase in pest and disease resistance is thought to be an important feature of seaweed-based fertilisers.

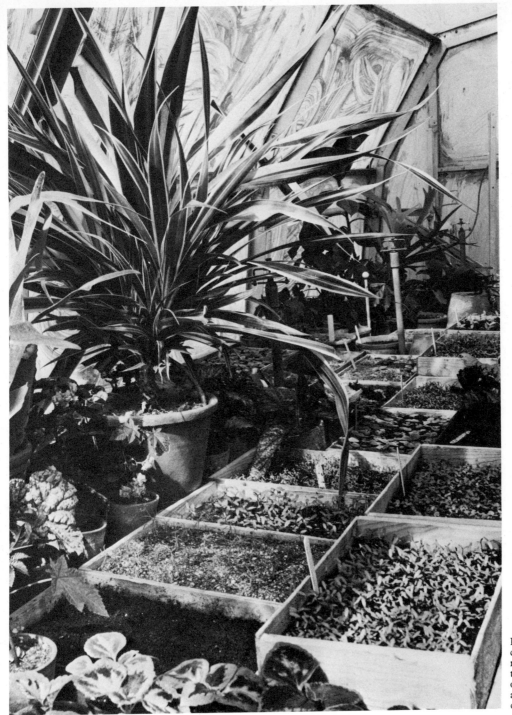

Different plants have different nutritional requirements. A thorough understanding of these requirements is an essential prerequisite of their cultivation.

145

Compressed peat blocks are now much in vogue but require the use of a special blockmaking machine.

Chapter 13

Soil & Compost Analysis

Most soil analysis procedures are based on the extraction of nutrients with a diluting agent which attempts to estimate the quantity of nutrient that the plant itself can extract from the soil. Whether the results of the analysis truly reflect the quantities of nutrients *actually available* to the plants is a matter of some conjecture.

This does not mean that soil analysis procedures can be set aside lightly, as they do have considerable value if interpreted correctly and linked to practical growing experience.

Testing kits

Several different types of kits are available: (a) litmus papers which indicate alkalinity or acidity when dipped into wet soil; (b) a series of litmus papers which indicate the approximate pH of the soil; (c) indicator fluids which, when used either separately with a solution of soil and water or with barium sulphate as a precipitant, give a remarkably accurate pH figure by comparison with a colour chart; (d) complete testing outfits which, by use of indicator fluids and colour comparison give, in addition to the pH figure, the relative availability or percentage deficiency of the three main elements—nitrogen, phosphorus and potash.

The value of these kits is that they give a fairly accurate indication of the fertility of a soil or growing medium without the inevitable wait associated with laboratory analysis. It should be pointed out, however, that these kits do not work entirely on the extraction principle and therefore do not indicate the *available* levels of nutrients in the soil but rather the total amounts of *soluble* nutrients.

Laboratory analysis

The availability of free laboratory analysis services varies greatly, but it is unlikely that there are any areas in Britain where laboratory analysis is not available on payment of a fee. The range of services carried out also differs according to the body concerned, but the following are the most important issues:

Organic matter Where a soil-based media for growing is involved, the percentage of organic matter is a useful figure, especially for border cultivation. Figures of 8–10 per cent (including moisture) are average, although some soils may have figures as high as 15–16 per cent, or indeed much higher. The significance of the organic matter content of soilless growing media will be discussed later.

Any gardener with a small crucible and accurate scientific-type scales can himself note the weight difference in a soil sample before and after combustion over a gas jet, and, by calculation, find out the percentage of organic matter content, which will include the moisture content unless the soil is oven-dried beforehand.

Lime requirement Exchangeable calcium is determined by several means, but usually by a pH meter, when lime requirement is then calculated by reference to a chart prepared by a series of buffering experiments. Most bodies report not only the pH figure, but the amount of calcium carbonate (ground limestone) necessary to achieve the required pH which, as stated earlier, will vary according to the plant species concerned.

Available nitrogen This is not a test carried out by every laboratory unless specially requested, as it varies so considerably according to temperature, season, whether soil has been heat sterilised, and other related issues. The analyst usually states whether his test indicates high, medium or low availability.

Available phosphorus (P$_2$O$_5$ or P)   This is reported as milligrammes (mg) per 100 grammes (g) P$_2$O$_5$, parts per million (ppm) P, or index factor; also stated as low, medium or high. The relativity of the figures is as follows:

1 ppm P = 2.3mg P$_2$O$_5$ per 100g × 10

or 1mg P$_2$O$_5$ per 100g = 0.437 ppm P ÷ 10

P$_2$O$_5$ = P × 2.3 or P = P$_2$O$_5$ × 0.437

Index factor P: 4–5 is standard for most greenhouse crops; below this, phosphorus is needed; above 4–5 little phosphorus required.

Available potassium (K$_2$O or K)   This is reported in a similar fashion to phosphorus in either mg per 100g K$_2$O or ppm K, or index factor; also stated as low, medium or high. The relativity of the figures in relation to one another is as follows:

1 ppm K = 1.2mg K$_2$O per 100g × 10

1mg K$_2$O per 100g = 0.83 ppm K ÷ 10

K$_2$O = K × 1.2 or K = K$_2$O × 0.83

Index factor K: 4–5 is standard for greenhouse crops.

NOTE: *Exact* conversions from P$_2$O$_5$ to P and K$_2$O to K and vice versa are complicated by differing extraction methods.

Magnesium   Some bodies now report magnesium, usually as an index factor, levels of around 3–5 being normal.

Soluble salt   This is a very important issue in greenhouse culture and is usually stated as low, normal or high. Some laboratories quote the figure as pC while others quote CF, the respective values of which are as follows, the index factor also being stated to give their true significance. Index 3 is the safe level for most greenhouse plants, up to 4 for tomatoes and chrysanthemums, but above this level there is danger of damage. These figures are equal to approximately pC 2.8–3.00, or CF 15–10. It cannot be over-emphasised how important these figures are; spot checks should be carried out on a regular basis before and after planting on a large scale. Salt concentration meters are considered a good investment by commercial growers, especially for checking the salt concentration of liquid feeds, and also of growing media to ensure even distribution of the fertilisers.

Spectrochemical analysis

This is used for determining the levels of trace elements in both soil and plant tissue. The elements mainly concerned are *zinc, manganese, copper and iron.* Spectrochemical analysis is generally used as a further check following normal soil analysis, more so with plant tissue than with soils.

Tissue analysis

In addition to spectrochemical analysis for the trace elements, tissue analysis ensures that the plant is assimilating the correct amount of nutrient. It is generally necessary to carry out a comparison between normal and abnormal tissue. Tissue analysis is becoming very much a part of commercial growing in countries such as the USA.

Observation of cultures

Fungal and other cultures are developed under laboratory conditions in specimens of soil. It is claimed that these methods give a much more accurate account of the nutrient levels actually available to the plant, as compared with those determined chemically. Visual assessment of plant response still remains a vital part of plant nutrition, and can be learned only by practical experience.

Eelworm determination

Soil or growing media infested with the cysts of the potato eelworm (*Heberodera rostochiensis*) are unsuitable for the culture of tomatoes, potatoes and other solanaceous plants, which crops it attacks with equal severity. A determination of the number of cysts per gramme (or 100g) of soil or growing media can be made by most advisory bodies, along with a similar statement of the number containing live larvae.

Taking samples of growing media

It is essential that any samples sent for analysis are representative of the main bulk of the growing media. For a greenhouse border, several small samples should be taken with a trowel, auger or other instrument, from a uniform depth of around 5–6in. Bulked together the sample should weigh about 2lb. Where batches of compost are being made up, the same basic

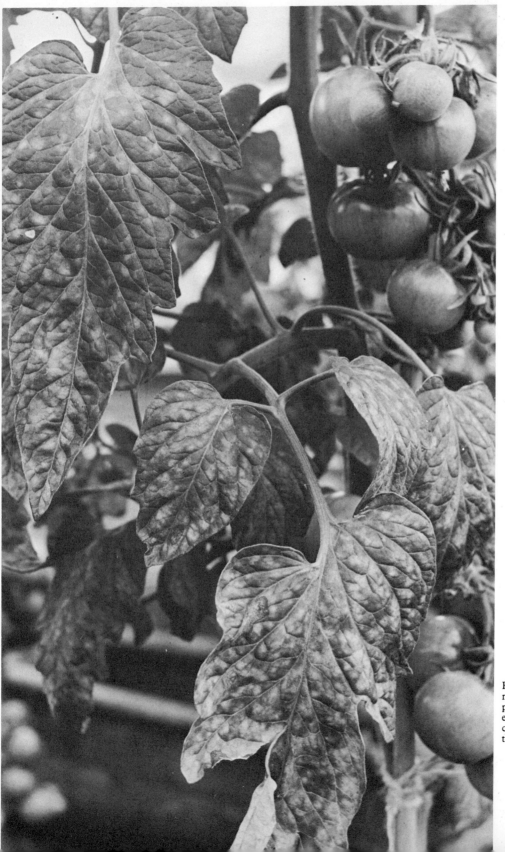

Regular analysis of growing media can prevent many phytopathogenic problems, especially where mono-culture of plants like tomatoes are concerned.

procedure should be followed, selecting small quantities of the media from various parts of the heap and bulking them together. It is sometimes advisable to have the basic ingredients analysed before mixing, especially if there is any doubt about extreme acidity, toxicity or other factors. Samples should be placed in a strong paper or polythene bag and clearly labelled for dispatch to the laboratory. One sample (2lb) will generally suffice for some 1,000 sqft of border. Always label samples clearly with the exact location and source, and give previous cropping history, if any, and proposed cropping programme, as this will assist the advisory body to give any corrective treatment that may prove to be necessary.

Analysis of solid or liquid fertilisers

Quality control is very strict at the manufacturing stage for all solid or liquid fertilisers, and analysis is seldom necessary, except in the case of doubtful identity. The checking of diluted liquid feeds for salt concentration (pC or CF) is useful, particularly if a doubtful dilutor/dilution method is involved.

Examination of soil for weeds, pests and diseases

It would obviously be folly to use a soil known to contain pests, diseases or weeds, yet it is not always possible to tell whether a soil is 'clean' or not, or for that matter to carry out sterilisation. The larger pests like wireworms, leatherjackets and other pests can of course be observed when working with the soil in any way, and particularly if putting it through a riddle or screen prior to mixing up a compost. Vegetative underground portions of many perennial weeds such as couch grass, horsetail, coltsfoot and others can also be fairly readily detected by visual examination, even if not specifically. Smaller pests and diseases, however can seldom be detected visually, most of the disease organisms or spores being microscopic in size. It is not feasible to examine soil for the presence of disease using the usual pathological techniques of plating and incubation, although an indicator plant could be grown and later sectioned and examined if a pathological service is able and willing to carry out this work, an unlikely situation unless a large commercial cropping enterprise was involved. Usually the previous history of a soil or growing media gives a good indication of what to look for in the way of both pest and diseases, and if in any doubt it is folly to use a doubtful growing medium unless it can be sterilised.

Where a 'new' soil is involved and there is some idea of the cropping pattern carried out in that soil previously, then this also gives guidance. If in any doubt about soil, or to make doubly sure that no trouble does overtake the plants which will be grown in it, the obvious answer, where possible, is to sterilise it either by heat or chemical means. Alternatively, prepared compost can be bought in.

The increasing popularity of soilless mixes owes much to the cleanliness of the basic ingredients (peat and sand) and to the fact that sterilisation is seldom, if ever, necessary. Peats, however, can carry rhizoctonia root rots which affect a wide range of plants.

Chapter 14

Sterilisation of Soil

The advantage of using a growing medium free of damaging pests, diseases and weeds cannot be over-emphasised in all spheres of greenhouse culture.

Soil sickness is a term which is difficult if not impossible to define accurately. Organic gardening adherents claim that soil sickness can be avoided by practising organic husbandry principles, so maintaining a soil 'in balance'. While this is an admirable solution, it gives rise to practical problems. Copious and regular supplies of properly made compost must be available, and even then there can often be a 'wait' period before the considerable forces of nature exert their influence, this taking longer than many gardeners have patience for.

Crop rotation principles would obviously do much to prevent the soil becoming sick in the first case, yet without a mobile or easily portable greenhouse, this cannot readily be accomplished. The use of a new soil or growing medium does of course achieve the same object, and provide the plants with an ideal start. This is why, under many circumstances, a strong case can be made out for container-growing of crops such as tomatoes.

The other answer is to pasteurise the soil, endeavouring to rectify the ills, while leaving behind beneficial elements to function to full advantage. The term sterilisation is most frequently used in this connection, whereas partial sterilisation or pasteurisation would be more accurate. Sterilisation implies rendering the growing media completely sterile, which would give rise to many problems with a soil-containing medium. Nevertheless it is a term which will be used for convenience.

Sterilisation of soil or soilless media can take several different forms, all of which have their limitations and drawbacks. The sterilised medium is not rendered immune from future trouble; it may in fact be more prone to invasion because competing organisms will have been killed off in the sterilising process. But heat sterilisation in most of its forms does help to render plant toxins soluble, so that they can be washed out, the same being true of toxic fertiliser residues; organic matter is usually broken down by heat sterilisation, rendering it more palatable to micro-organisms as a ready source of food. Perhaps the most significant advantage is in the survival of the thick-walled nitrosomonas and nitrobactor bacteria which, in the absence of competition, re-establish themselves completely uninhibited, resulting in a great flood of both ammonium and nitrate.

One vital aspect of sterilisation is that there are limits to the degree of penetration achieved over the growing medium. In the case of a greenhouse border, it is only practical to sterilise the top 10–12in of soil; if the lower depths contain pests and diseases they can act as a potent source of trouble for deep rooted crops. Virus disease of tomatoes, for example, can remain in the lower depths of a greenhouse border, ready to infect a subsequent tomato crop, even when the top 10–12in is sterilised, as the roots soon penetrate into the subsoil. Sterilisation can only be considered as 100 per cent efficient in connection with culture in troughs and containers, preferably when the ingredients of compost are being prepared for formulation—and even then contamination from airborne spores or pests cannot be ignored.

Sterilisation by heat

Most pests, diseases and weeds in both vegetative and seed form have a temperature at which they are organically destroyed, the same being true of micro-

Fig 46

organisms. The temperature aimed at during partial sterilisation, while taking into account the destruction temperatures of various organisms, also bears some relation to the sheer practicality of applying a certain temperature range. The boiling point of water is 212°F (100°C) and it is neither practical nor desirable greatly to exceed this. It is in this temperature range that most sterilisation processes operate and recourse to a detailed reference book on fungal and virus diseases will show that such a temperature range is highly effective. Indeed many of the weaker parasitic diseases are destroyed at temperatures as low as 160–170°F (70–76°C); but many virus diseases require fully 200°F (92°C) to be completely destroyed, the same being true of the eelworm cysts *Hederodera rostochiensis.*

One of the greatest problems when applying a heat process to a soil or growing media is achieving a uniform temperature throughout the bulk. It merely requires the centre of a lump of soil to remain at low temperature for it to act as a potent source of re-infection for the sterilised area of the growing medium. Over-sterilisation also raises problems of sterility and formation of toxic substances. Obviously too it is undesirable to incorporate doubtful bulky organics until they also have been sterilised.

The moisture content of a growing medium will greatly affect the passage of heat and the degree of penetration achieved in a given time.

Methods of applying steam
Hoddesdon grid method (Fig 46)
Named after the town of Hoddesdon, Herts, where the system was originally developed at the then existing Cheshunt Research Station, this process is used for borders in commercial greenhouses and involves the leading of steam under pressure into perforated steel pipes laid below the soil surface, which has previously been rendered moist and friable by deep cultivation. The many technicalities connected with the grid process can be studied in detail in *Ministry of Agriculture Bulletin No. 22.* The sheer cost of providing steam and the labour for digging in the grids have caused concern in recent years.

Sheet steaming (Fig 47)

This process was developed originally in the Netherlands and involves leading pressurised steam into either a coffin-type box with outlet holes or perforated hose-pipe under a heavy grade PVC sheet secured at the edges by long sandbags or other means. With a boiler output of 1,000lb steam per hour it is possible to sheet steam an area of approximately 800-1,000sq ft in one operation (Fig 47).

One of the obvious advantages of sheet steaming over the grid method is the tremendous saving in labour, whereas its main disadvantage lies in the difficulty of achieving adequate penetration of the steam, which may take several hours to reach sufficient depth.

Low pressure steam sterilisation

This has much more application for smaller growers, professional and amateur gardeners, although it is doubtful whether the setting up of the apparatus can now be merited in view of ready and reasonably

Fig 48

Fig 47

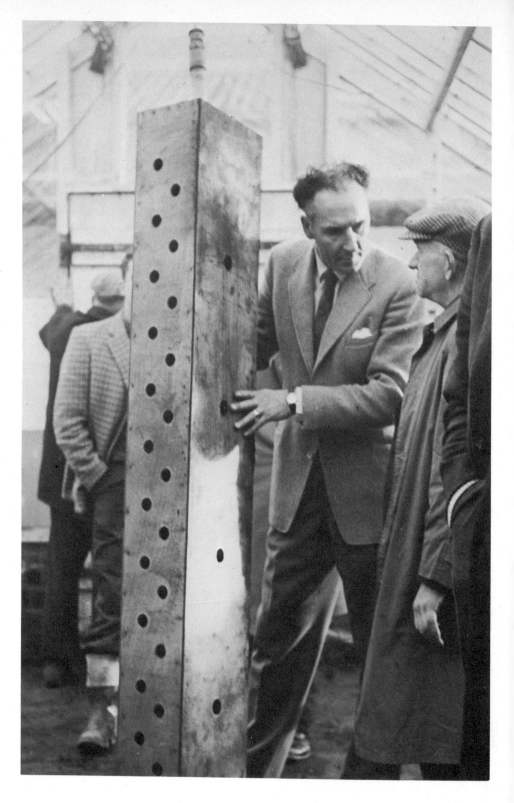

Part of the equipment
used in sheet steaming,
one of the most efficient
of all methods of
sterilising soil.

154

cheap availability of prepared composts. When the John Innes composts were originally formulated and the specifications laid down, the John Innes low pressure sterilisers were built in their thousands all over Britain (see Fig 48). Here shredded loam was evenly spread in a 10–12in layer on perforated sheeting over a shallow tray of water kept boiling by a coal fire, the steam passing slowly through the soil, being trapped by a tarpaulin or sack covering (now PVC). It took several hours for the soil at the top of the layer to reach the necessary 180–190°F (82–88°C) and careful checking was necessary to ensure that the whole batch of soil was evenly sterilised. Various models were available, most of which are no longer manufactured; low pressure sterilisers are now usually improvised.

Another form of steam sterilisation is to drench shallow layers of soil on a clean surface with boiling water, covering with clean sacks or PVC sheets to retain the heat. On a still smaller scale suspending small sacks of soil in the steam given off by a water boiler can be remarkably successful. The efficiency of all these methods depends much upon the care which is exercised in ensuring even distribution of temperature.

Dry heat sterilisation
By the application of dry heat to the soil at a sufficiently high temperature, its moisture content is converted to steam. The crudest form of this method is the use of a fire under a sheet of metal on which is placed a shallow layer of soil. The soil should be wet and care must be taken not to over-sterilise it. It is usual to stir the soil constantly to keep it from burning. The careful use of a flame gun can achieve the same result if the wet soil is spread in a shallow layer on a clean surface.

Rotary drum sterilisers rely on sterilisation at 'flash point', the soil being rotated round a metal drum and falling through a fierce flame. The angle of the drum determines the number of times the soil is subjected to 'flash point' heat before being ejected out of the other end of the drum. The efficiency of rotary drum sterilisers depends not only on the correct adjustment of the burner and the angle of the rotating drum, but very much on the moisture content of the soil, which if too wet will 'ball' badly. Conversely if the soil is too dry it tends to burn, which destroys its structure. The ejected soil must be carefully checked to ensure that it has reached a temperature of at least 160–170°F (71–76°C) and that this is maintained in the heap for a reasonable period. Where potato eelworm or virus is a problem, higher sterilisation temperatures are advisable.

Electric soil sterilisers are available in different sizes, the soil being heated by panel type elements to a uniform 180°F (82°C); although the soil in the vicinity of the panels may be overheated and rendered sterile, it is soon reconstituted by the bulk of soil.

Chemical soil sterilisation

Various chemicals are used for this purpose, and in commercial spheres these have become extremely popular for economic reasons. They are also useful for the amateur gardener, but great care must be taken to follow the directions implicitly. The fumes, however, can be toxic to young plants, which raises problems in greenhouses where there is mixed cropping.

The chemicals, to be effective, must give off gas which is sufficiently toxic to ensure the destruction of pests, diseases and weeds, yet without harming the beneficial organisms in the soil. The efficiency of chemical sterilisation varies greatly, not because of the precise chemicals involved, but because of the condition of the soil, its moisture content and, most important, the prevailing temperature. It is also important to ensure even distribution throughout the soil being sterilised.

Formaldehyde This is reasonably effective on some fungal diseases, but relatively ineffective against many pests. It is used at a strength of 1 part formalin 38–40 per cent to 49 parts water (approximately 1 pint to 6 gallons) and the soil is thoroughly drenched (approximately 5 gallons being required per square yard to 9in depth).

There is a wait period of 20–40 days according to temperature (which must be sufficiently high otherwise the formaldehyde will become polymerised) before the soil can be used.

Phenols Several forms are available, including cresylic acid, and here again they must be used according to directions (generally 1 in 39). They are used in a similar manner to formaldehyde, the wait period in this case being 18–20 days. They are mainly effective against pests, but there is also some fungicidal action. Usually about 5–6 gallons of the prepared solution is required per square yard.

Other chemicals used commercially are D-D (mainly for nematodes) and carbon bisulphide, both of which are injected into the soil, dithane, chloropicrin, methyl bromide and metham-sodium, the latter

Sterilisation chart

Material	Root eel-worm	Root rots	Fusarium & verti-cillium wilts	(TMV) Mosaic virus	Damp-ing-off disease	Weeds	Treatment to planting days
Carbon bi-sulphide (by injection)	C	X	X	X	X	X	7
Chloropicrin**	X	C	C	X	C	X	20
Cresylic acid	P	X	P	X	P	X	18–20
D-D (by injection)	C	X	X	X	X	X	40
Dithane	X	P	X	X	P	X	3–14
Formaldehyde	X	P	P (good at 60°F/ 15°C)	X	P	X	20–40
Metham sodium* (variable results)	C	C	P	X	C	C	40
Methyl bromide**	C	C	P	X	C	C	4
Steam, including correctly applied dry heat and hot water (180°F/82°C)	C	C	C	C (good at 194° F/ 90°C)	C	C	7–14

* amateurs may only be able to obtain certain forms
** only available to bona fide horticulturalists
C control
P partial control
X no control

Sterilisation of soil can
present problems, yet
sterilised soil is essential
for most aspects of
greenhouse cultivation.

being widely used commercially. All these chemicals must be used strictly according to directions, which generally state that the soil should be cultivated, the sterilants applied and, with the powdered or prilled form, rotovated in before 'sealing' with water.

To ensure that these chemicals are effective, the temperature of the soil must be above 49–50°F (9.5°C). The soil should be rotary cultivated or forked to release the fumes after a few weeks. Heaps of potting soil can be treated with chemicals in the same way as border soil. Methyl bromide has found favour in recent years because of its effectiveness on pests and diseases and also its rapid dissipation. *It must be applied by a contractor.*

Chapter 15

Greenhouse Growing Composts

The need for good compost

The soil in the garden is usually satisfactory for growing plants there but it is not so suitable for use as a growing medium in pots or boxes, particularly under intensive culture under glass. The reason is that the soil will settle into a compacted state in the pot, especially when watered continually. In the garden the soil is constantly being turned and agitated by the action of worms and insect life within the soil (not to mention larger beings using a spade or hoe!) but these creatures are not generally present in the plant pot, the result being that the soil settles, becomes inadequately aerated and therefore increasingly difficult for water to penetrate; growth will be poor and eventually the plant may die. It is therefore necessary to improve the soil as a growing medium if it is to be used successfully in a pot. This is normally done by the addition of suitable materials to the basic soil and by correct treatment, but recently composts made without soil have become important.

The John Innes Composts

In 1939 W. J. C. Lawrence and J. Newell of the John Innes Horticultural Institution published the results of their intensive research into the characteristics of compost, and the John Innes Composts, which were to revolutionise the growing of plants in pots and boxes, were born. The gardener for the first time had standard formulae that could be reasonably well reproduced and when properly used would give excellent results. Prior to this, he had had no means of deciding what particular factor a failure might be due to, whether it was a bad loam or diseased leaf-mould and so on.

The ingredients of these composts were neither expensive nor difficult to obtain, and the mixing of them was a comparatively simple job which did not require the use of such variable material as stable manure or leaf-mould.

There are two basic JI composts, one for seed sowing and one for potting, differing in their physical and nutrient make up. Two were considered necessary because of the differing conditions required. In the seed sowing composts, the structure had to be free-draining so that the compost was warm and free of excess moisture which can cause rotting. The potting compost was more moisture retentive but still well aerated to ensure good root action.

The basic formulae are given here for the mixes but the specifications of the individual raw materials given later must be studied. These are well and strictly defined so that the composts will be as uniform as possible.

Seed compost

This consists of two parts sterilised loam, one part peat and one part sand, by volume (ie using a bucket, pots, etc of known size). To this is added superphosphate of lime at $1\frac{1}{2}$oz per bushel and chalk or ground limestone at $\frac{3}{4}$oz per bushel.

During their early life, most of the nutrients required by seedlings are present within the seed itself but phosphates are required for the growth of new cells and good root action. The chalk is added to neutralise the acidity of the peat.

Potting composts

The John Innes potting compost No 1 strength was made to the following formula:

Parts by volume			J.I. base	4oz	per bushel of compost
	7 sterilised loam		chalk	$\frac{3}{4}$oz	
	3 peat	+	or		
	2 sand		J.I. base	5lb	per cu yd of compost
			chalk	1lb	

The No 2 strength was made by adding double the amount of John Innes base and chalk (ie 8oz and $1\frac{1}{2}$oz per bushel respectively), and the potting compost No 3 by adding three times the amounts (ie 12oz of John Innes base and $2\frac{1}{4}$oz of chalk per bushel of compost).

It should be noted that a mix of say 7 bushels of loam, 3 bushels of peat and 2 bushels of sand will not in all probability yield 12 bushels of compost. The reason is that particles of loam and sand will enter the pore spaces in the peat, thus reducing the volume of compost produced. Therefore, the compost volume, after mixing, will have to be measured, and the John Innes base and chalk added at the rates given above per actual bushel or cu yd of compost produced (see measurement of volume below).

For certain acid-loving plants such as the heathers (*Erica* varieties), etc, a special acid compost may be used. It is known as the John Innes seedling compost (A), the A standing for acid. As the name indicates, it is prepared by making the normal John Innes seed compost—2 parts sterilised loam, one part peat and one part sand, but the lime is omitted and replaced by $\frac{3}{4}$oz of flowers of sulphur per bushel of compost. The pH should then be between 5.0 and 6.0.

Measurement of volume

The most common unit of measurement of composts and their raw materials is the bushel. This is a volume, and one bushel is defined as 2,200cu in. For convenience, a standard bushel box may be made or purchased having a standard size 22 × 10 × 10in. One bushel is roughly equivalent to 8 gallons and, therefore, for convenience a bucket containing a 2 gallon mark may be used for measuring smaller quantities of compost ingredients as this represents one quarter of a bushel.

The other standard measurement of compost volume is the cubic yard. This is a volume of 36 × 36 × 36in and there are 21.7 bushels in a cu yd. This unit is rather large for the amateur and working with bushels is probably adequate for most purposes.

Specifications and preparation of the raw materials—loam

The main ingredient of a John Innes compost is the loam. It gives the compost body, and its chief function is to supply the clay and actively decomposing humus which are so essential for good plant growth.

A loam is defined as a soil in which the porportions of sand, silt and clay are well balanced, typically 7–27 per cent clay, 28–50 per cent silt with less than 52 per cent sand. A medium loam contains just enough clay to be slightly greasy when smeared between the fingers without being sticky. A light loam contains a greater amount of sand, and heavy loam a greater amount of clay. A medium loam should be used for a John Innes Compost; light, heavy and chalky loams should not be used; medium loam will have a good crumb structure and is usually a little acid (pH 5.5–6.3). The loam may be obtained either from arable or pasture land and is therefore known as arable loam and turf or garden loam.

The best loam is turf loam, which is the product obtained when turves cut from a *good* pasture on a loam soil are stacked in a heap until the grass and some of the roots have rotted. The turves should be cut from the top 4–5in of turf and soil, and measure roughly 12 × 9in for stacking.

Useful measurements of volume

1 bushel = 8 gallons = 2200 cubic inches = 1.28 cubic feet
21.7 bushels = 1 cubic yard = 27 cubic feet
$6\frac{1}{4}$ gallons = 1 cubic foot
1 gallon = $277\frac{1}{4}$ cubic inches

Approximate conversion

oz per bushel to lb per cu yd	lb per cu yd to oz per bushel
$\frac{1}{2}$oz/bushel = $10\frac{1}{2}$oz/cu yd	$\frac{1}{2}$lb/cu yd = $\frac{3}{8}$oz/bushel
1oz/bushel = 1lb 5oz/cu yd	1lb/cu yd = $\frac{3}{4}$oz/bushel
2oz/bushel = 2lb 10oz/cu yd	2lb/cu yd = $1\frac{1}{2}$oz/bushel
3oz/bushel = 3lb 15oz/cu yd	3lb/cu yd = $2\frac{1}{4}$oz/bushel
4oz/bushel = 5lb 4oz/cu yd	4lb/cu yd = 3oz/bushel
5oz/bushel = 6lb $8\frac{3}{4}$oz/cu yd	5lb/cu yd = $3\frac{3}{4}$oz/bushel
6oz/bushel = 7lb $13\frac{3}{4}$oz/cu yd	6lb/cu yd = $4\frac{1}{2}$oz/bushel
7oz/bushel = 9lb $2\frac{1}{2}$oz/cu yd	7lb/cu yd = $5\frac{1}{4}$oz/bushel
8oz/bushel = 10lb $7\frac{3}{4}$oz/cu yd	8lb/cu yd = 6 oz/bushel

---

Standardisation of the loam

The clay content is reasonably well standardised by choosing a medium or medium-heavy loam, and the humus content by choosing a turf loam as described above.

The pH value of the loam must be standardised to 6.3 (including moisture). If the soil is more acid than 6.3, ie if its pH is below this figure, calcium carbonate must be added in the form of ground limestone or chalk. For medium-heavy loams, the approximate amount of calcium carbonate in oz per sq yd for every 9in depth of turves is (6.3 − pH of loam) × 23. For example, if the pH of the loam is 5.8, the calculation is:

$$(6.3 - 5.8) \times 23 = 0.5 \times 23$$
$$= 11.5\text{oz per sq yd}$$

Therefore, as the loam is stacked (as detailed below), for every 9in depth of turves, $11\frac{1}{2}$oz of calcium carbonate should be evenly applied per sq yd.

For medium loams, the formula should be altered to (6.3 − pH) × 18. Taking the above example again, if the soil pH is 5.8, the amount of ground limestone to apply is:

$$(6.3 - 5.8) \times 18 = 0.5 \times 18$$
$$= 9\text{oz per sq yd}$$

The standardisation of the pH of the loam is very important, as excess acidity is a common cause of poor growth in pot plants.

The stacking

It is preferable to cut the turves in late spring or early summer as at these times the grass is thick and lush. The stack, which should not be more than 6ft in height or width, is built up in $4\frac{1}{2}$in layers (the approximate thickness of the cut turves). On top of the first layer is added a 2in layer of strawy animal manure or half-composted straw, on the next layer the lime is spread evenly—and so on alternately, until the stack is completed. The straw layer assists in the aeration of the stack and serves as an activator by providing a ready supply of bacteria. As moisture is essential to encourage rapid rotting the turves should be thoroughly wetted with a hose-pipe as stacking proceeds. Finally, the stack is covered against rain and is left undisturbed for about six months. At the end of this time the grass should have decomposed, the pH should have standardised to 6.3, and the whole thing dried out.

When the stack is being broken down, it should be cut with a spade downwards from the top to bottom so that mixing of the layers occurs to ensure a uniform material. The soil is sieved through a $\frac{3}{8}$in sieve and it is then ready for sterilisation. Care should be taken that the soil is not unnecessarily contaminated.

Sterilisation

This is necessary to ensure that the compost is free from harmful pests and diseases. Only the loam requires sterilisation, and it has been found that heating to 180°F (82°C) for ten minutes reduces the likelihood of high ammonia levels in the compost. The soil should be brought up to this temperature and cooled as quickly as possible.

Nature's way of dealing with soil nutrient deficiencies: the evolution of insectivorous plants which grow in anaerobic conditions of excessively high acidity and have to gain their nitrogen requirements from insects they catch and digest since these are not present in the growing medium.

Peat

The type of peat recommended for use in JI composts is known as granulated sphagnum moss peat. It should be graded so that most of the particles are of approximately ⅛in in size. Normally, this type of peat has a pH of between 3.5 and 4.0. Other peats, including sedge peat, are not recommended, although possibly cheaper. After purchase keep it dry and clean under cover so that it cannot be contaminated by weed seeds floating about in the air. Because it is comparatively sterile, it is not necessary to sterilise the peat before use in the compost.

Sand

As with the other raw materials, the sand should be chosen with care as its structure contributes much to the drainage of the

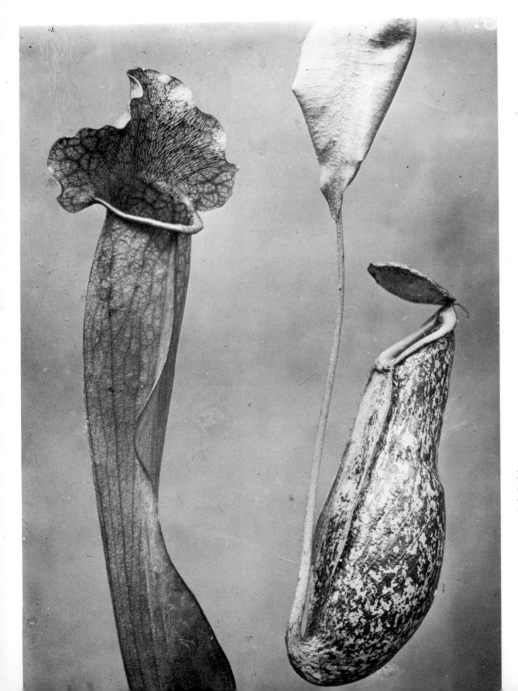

More carnivorous plants, which evolved their strange mode of life to overcome soil nutrient deficiencies. On the left *Sarracenia purpurea*, on the right a nepethes species. Both make unusual greenhouse plants.

compost and to its aeration. It should be grit/sand, clean, chemically inert, and sharp with little or no clay, silt, lime (such as sea shells) or organic matter. Between 60 and 70 per cent of the particles should be $\frac{1}{8}-\frac{1}{16}$ in, a typical grit/sand being sold as $\frac{1}{8}$ in down. Builder's sand and sea sand should not be used because they are usually too fine. To ease mixing, the sand should be dry. It does not require sterilisation.

The food supply—John Innes base
To grow plants well the compost must contain an adequate and well-balanced food supply.

John Innes base is made up of three fertilisers in the following proportions:

2 parts by weight hoof and horn, $\frac{1}{8}$ in grist (13 per cent nitrogen)

2 parts by weight superphosphate (18 per cent phosphoric acid)

1 part by weight sulphate of potash (48 per cent to 50 per cent potash)

It may be made up by the amateur from the raw materials or it may be purchased ready mixed. The analysis of the complete fertiliser is 5.1 per cent nitrogen, 7.2 per cent phosphate and 9.7 per cent potash. Note that no magnesium or trace elements were added as these were presumed to be adequately supplied by the loam.

Mixing and storing compost
The loam, with its pH standardised, has been sieved and sterilised. The peat from a compressed bale should be broken up by rubbing through a $\frac{3}{8}$ in sieve. Because it is usually very dry, the peat should be wetted, using a watering can or hosepipe, otherwise it may cause a temporary check to growth.

After the careful selection and preparation of the compost ingredients it would be senseless to spoil the compost by poor mixing. The correct method for hand-mixing is to spread the sterilised loam a few inches deep evenly over the mixing floor (which should be clean) with the moistened peat on top of the loam and the dry sand last. Part of the sand is kept back and the fertilisers and chalk added to this

and thoroughly mixed. This pre-mixes the fertiliser and chalk in some of the sand and makes their distribution through the compost easier and more even. The mixed sand and fertiliser is then spread as evenly as possible over the top of the rest of the sand. The pile of ingredients is cut down and turned over three or four times with a spade. When turning the soil over, it is important to scatter it as widely as possible, not just throw a shovelful from place to place. It cannot be stressed too much that the compost should be mixed as evenly as possible. Alternatively, a mechanical mixer, such as a concrete mixer, may be used.

Enough compost may be mixed for several weeks' use but it is not desirable to store compost for more than one month. In no case should it be stored for longer than six weeks or harmful ammonia fumes will build up from the breakdown of the hoof and horn meal and cause damage to the plants.

The disadvantages of soil-based composts
The John Innes composts had a profound effect on the quality of greenhouse and pot plants and on the success rate of growing them.

However, there are disadvantages with these composts today that were not so apparent in the early years of their use. They are as follows:

1 There is an increasing difficulty in obtaining turf loam. When it is obtainable it is often of indifferent quality and rather variable, producing results that may be disappointing.

2 The cost of loam is increasing because of the labour involved, and therefore not only is the compost becoming more expensive, but undesirable short cuts in production are practised.

3 As it is based on soil, the compost is heavy to move and its transport is costly.

4 The composts will not store as they become toxic due to the release of ammonia.

5 There is no source of readily available nitrogen (nitrate), magnesium or trace

elements. It is presumed that the loam will provide these but this is not always a valid assumption, especially nowadays.

If a good reliable source of loam can be found, the John Innes composts are satisfactory. They have stood the test of time and do have advantages, among them the gradual release of water and nutrients to the plants. However, for many commercial growers the disadvantages outweigh the advantages.

The development of soilless composts

The first pioneering work on soilless composts to make a big impact on the horticultural world was that done at the University of California and published in 1957. In fact, soilless composts are frequently referred to as UC composts or mixes (the UC standing for the University of California), even if they are not in fact following any UC formulae. Work was begun in the Department of Plant Pathology at the University of California, Los Angeles, in 1941 to find a better compost for growing plants in containers. Because of the difficulty of finding turf for composting and problems of toxicity after steaming, the John Innes method was not satisfactory and a substitute had to be found.

The UC composts

Eventually five basic compost mixes were evolved, ranging from all peat to all sand, with varying proportions of each in between. To these basic composts could be added one of six fertiliser formulae, three containing readily available nitrogen in the form of potassium nitrate and the others reserve, or longer-availability nitrogen.

When the UC system was first tried in Britain it was not very successful. It must be remembered that these composts were developed for conditions in California where the climate is distinctly Mediterranean. In Britain the lower temperature and light intensity resulted in nitrogen starvation in plants in UC composts as the breakdown rate of organic nitrogen was too slow. The fine structure of the compost, designed to retain moisture in the high transpiration conditions of California,

caused waterlogging in the cooler, more humid climate of Great Britain. The result was to make many people deeply suspicious of the whole idea of soilless composts; others however realised that it was just a matter of adjusting the formulations to the British climate, altering the water-holding capacity and the proportions of nitrogen to potash in the fertilisers.

Nitrogen supply in soil-based and soilless composts

The key to success in the nutrition of soilless compost is the supply of nitrogen, which must be provided in both readily available and slow release forms. When slow release nitrogen is added to soil or compost, it undergoes a number of changes into other compounds before it is available to the plants. Some of these compounds become toxic to plants in comparatively moderate concentrations and all of them are toxic in excess.

When an organic material such as hoof and horn is applied to the soil, the nitrogen it contains is made up of complicated protein-like compounds which are converted by the soil micro-organisms into inorganic ammonium form which is in turn converted into nitrate form—the form in which it can be taken up by the plants. The first stage is performed by what may be called the ammonifying bacteria and the second stage is performed by what may be called the nitrifying bacteria.

Obviously any condition which affects the population or the activity of these organisms will affect the rate of breakdown of the organic nitrogen into ammonium and nitrate compounds. The soil contains a very large number of micro-organisms including bacteria, fungi, actinomycetes, algae, nematodes and protozoa. All these forms of microscopic life exist in the soil in a state of dynamic equilibrium or ever-changing balance among themselves. Many of these organisms are harmful to plant life, therefore soil to be used in compost is sterilised to try to remove the harmful micro-organisms while leaving the beneficial micro-organisms as unaffected as possible.

In a soilless compost, the situation is rather different. The peat and sand are naturally almost sterile without sterilisation and hence the compost when made up will contain few, if any, of the micro-organisms that can convert organic nitrogen into the readily available nitrogen. Because of this it can be seen that readily available nitrogen must be provided in the compost in the form of nitrate until such time as the population of micro-organisms has been built up so that they in turn can provide the nitrates that the plants require. This is an important difference between soil-based and soilless composts and it led to the development of the starter solution for the UC composts. The use of calcium nitrate provided the readily available nitrogen until the hoof and horn began breaking down. The grade of hoof and horn would influence the speed with which nitrogen was released. Finer particles present a larger surface area for the bacteria to work on and hence the nitrogen release would be more rapid than from a coarser grade of hoof and horn.

Two other factors concerning the release of nitrogen must be pointed out. Firstly, the bacteria that convert the organic nitrogen to ammonium nitrogen are able to carry out the conversion even in the absence of oxygen. By contrast, the bacteria that convert the ammonium nitrogen into nitrate nitrogen must have an adequate supply of oxygen so that the ammonia may be converted to nitrate.

Secondly, the rate of nitrification is dependent on the pH of the compost and it occurs in two distinct stages:

$$\text{Ammonium} \xrightarrow{(1)} \text{Nitrite} \xrightarrow{(2)} \text{Nitrate}$$

The conversion of ammonium to nitrate goes through an intermediate stage known as nitrite. The first stage to nitrite will proceed up to a pH of 7.5 but the second stage from nitrite to nitrate will only proceed satisfactorily up to a pH of 7.0. It is obvious that between a pH of 7.0 and 7.5

the ammonium nitrogen will be converted as far as the nitrite but conversion of the nitrite to nitrate will be much slower, leading to a build-up of nitrite in the compost. Excess nitrite is damaging to all plants, but the most sensitive is antirrhinum. The first sign of damage is the yellowing of the younger leaves, turning to white in the presence of nitrite. On examination, the roots of the plants will be found to be brown and scorched.

Below a pH of about 5.5, the ammonium to nitrate conversion is slowed down but the breaking down of organic nitrogen to ammonium nitrogen continues. This time, at too acid a pH, ammonia will accumulate which is also particularly damaging to plants.

From the above, it can be seen that the rate and type of nitrogen applied to a compost must be carefully controlled. Composts containing organic sources such as the John Innes composts and the UC mixes with hoof and horn must not be stored for periods longer than one or two weeks before use, as ammonia will build up from the breakdown but nitrification of it cannot proceed as oxygen will not be able to penetrate the compost. The pH should be kept in the range of 5.5 to 7.0 because, above this pH, nitrite will accumulate while below this pH range ammonia will build up.

Further differences in the physical properties of soil-based and soilless composts

An important difference between soil-based and soilless composts is in the supply of nutrients. Soil-based composts contain relatively large quantities of nutrients supplied at rather infrequent intervals but soilless composts contain smaller quantities of nutrients which need to be supplemented more frequently. Incorrectly this is put down to the poor absorption of nutrients by the peat in the soilless compost. It is in fact because of the lower fixing capacity (storage) in peat. This may be best explained by a brief description of clay particles in the soil. These are very fine particles that contain nutrients within themselves which are not exchangeable in the normal soil solution. The exchangeable nutrients are held on to the surface of the clay particles by electrical charges and are removed into the soil solution to be taken up by the plant roots. This leaves a gap on the outside of the clay particle which is replaced from the nutrients within the clay particle. Thus the clay particle acts as a reserve or storage of nutrients. It is this reserve that peat itself lacks. Peat may be compared to a sponge that absorbs water and nutrients and releases them on demand, but once all the nutrients previously given have been removed, there is no reserve supply. The peat itself will gradually decompose but this breakdown is too slow to meet the needs of rapidly growing plants.

This is both an important weakness and strength in a soilless compost. Because of the lack of a reserve a wider range of nutrients must be added and added more frequently. But the grower has a tighter control over the growth of the plants because the plants will respond more readily to changes in nutrition since there is not that reserve of plant foods in the background.

A final difference between the two composts may aptly be mentioned now. Nearly all forms of peat suitable for use in compost have a higher water-holding capacity than loam. Again peat may be likened to a sponge as it contains very large quantities of space for holding water. In a soilless compost, which usually contains peat as the largest proportion of all the ingredients, this may result in over-watering. This is dangerous because the compost will become poorly aerated and this in turn will quickly lead to death of the roots. To overcome this, several precautions are usually taken when using a soilless compost in place of a soil-based compost. The pot should be loosely filled with soilless compost whereas a pot of soil-based compost should be pressed well in. *Pressing down a soilless compost will result in immediate trouble due to the lack of air*. It should be emphasised just how important the air is in a soilless compost. To prevent over-watering, the pot is filled to the top with compost, whereas with a soil-based compost approximately $\frac{1}{4}-\frac{1}{2}$in is left at the top of the pot to allow for watering.

The compost may be made free draining by adding a very coarse sand or grit to 'open up' the compost structure but it is not

Strictly for the largest greenhouses, the most magnificent of all the aroids, *Amorphophallus titanum*, whose flower is over eight feet high.

advisable to add too much otherwise the compost will require frequent watering and nutrients will be leached away, making high demands on the supplementary feeding. When watering a soil-based compost, the normal procedure is to allow the compost to become dry before watering well. Following this procedure with soilless compost will cause many problems, especially as the peat will be very difficult to re-wet. For soilless compost, the procedure is to water little and often, always keeping the compost more moist than a comparative soil-based compost.

Lastly, to keep the aeration good, the peat used should not be too fine or too decayed. Either would make the compost structure too close and result in a lower proportion of air to water.

The basic raw materials of soilless compost

Peat

By far the most important raw material is peat, and sphagnum moss peat is the most suitably structured for soilless compost, with good water retention and aeration characteristics. As it is naturally highly sterile and relatively free from pests, diseases and weed seeds, sterilisation is not necessary. Composts consisting of moss-sedge peat mixes or even sedge peat alone (*Carex* spp, not the dark, well-decomposed peat popularly referred to as sedge) have, however, been used successfully.

Sand or grit

Soilless composts may be made with peat alone but these are not as popular as the composts which have other materials added. Sand or grit is the most widely used additive, making mixing the nutrients easier and the structure of the peat less critical, although still important. Naturally, the compost is heavier with the inclusion of sand but the weight is still only half that of a John Innes compost. The increase in weight is helpful in that it improves the stability of pots.

Rate of addition With different formulations of compost (see later) there are different proportions of peat to sand. The most common ratios are three parts peat to one part sand, 2 parts peat to 1 part sand, 1 part peat to 1 part sand; all these are based on volume not weight, ie 1 bushel of peat to 1 bushel of sand, or 1 cu yd of peat to 1 cu yd of sand, or even 1 bucket of peat to 1 bucket of sand. Generally speaking, as the amount of sand is increased, the retention of water and nutrients will decrease. It is also reasonably safe to say that the aeration of the compost will be increased as the proportion of sand is increased. This is known as 'opening up' the compost.

Size The particle size of the sand has a great influence on aeration and water retention, permitting variations to suit the type of plant being grown. Three points should be considered in selecting particle size. Firstly, the fine sands as recommended in the original UC compost should be avoided. They were very successful in California but are not generally suitable for the moister and cooler climate in Britain. Secondly, if a coarser sand is being used, the peat should always be moistened before mixing to prevent separation of the peat and sand, which might give variabilities in the compost. Lastly, if the peat is fine, balance this by using a coarser sand; if the peat is coarse a finer sand may be included. However, such variability is not to be recommended as a general practice. It is preferable to standardise soilless compost by using a medium grade sphagnum moss peat (ie neither too fine nor too coarse) and a medium grade grit (say particles as in the John Innes recommendations of $\frac{1}{8}$ in down). This combination will give a free drainage compost that will retain adequate water but will not be easily waterlogged. In general practice, three parts peat to 1 part sand by volume is the preferred proportion of peat to sand.

Lime content The sand should be preferably lime-free for most subjects, and this is essential for growing the lime-hating plants such as heathers and azaleas. The compost formulations given in this book all contain lime as calcium carbonate and/or dolomite.

This assumes that sand is lime-free, usually with a pH between 6.0 and 6.5. As the pH of the sand rises, so the amount of lime added to the compost should be reduced, until with an alkaline sand having a pH of 8.3–8.5 (not normally recommended), no lime should be added to the mix.

It may be difficult for the amateur to assess the pH of the sand, unless the supplier is able to state it. The sand may be simply tested by using hydrochloric acid, which may be obtained in small quantities from a local chemist, but because it is a strong acid it should be handled with care. Hydrochloric acid reacts chemically with calcium carbonate (lime, chalk etc) to release carbon dioxide gas and this chemical reaction is used to test the sand for the presence of calcium carbonate. About one dessertspoonful of sand is placed in a non-corrosive (eg plastic) container and about a teaspoonful of hydrochloric acid is added to it. If no fizzing occurs (ie no carbon-dioxide gas is released), the sand will contain little (less than 0.25 per cent) or no calcium carbonate and it will thus be suitable for use in the compost. If fizzing occurs, the sand contains over 0.25 per cent lime and an alternative supply should preferably be found.

Occasionally, sands from the seashore are sold for horticultural use. These may contain common salt from the sea water, which is harmful to plants. However, these sands are usually washed and dried before sale, and provided they are structurally satisfactory they may be used in composts.

Alternative compost materials

Alternatives to sand or grit are usually more expensive and more difficult to obtain. Various advantages for them may be claimed and interest in them varies. These materials may be naturally occurring or they may be synthetic (man-made). Usually they are light, non-toxic, sterile, and slow to break down.

Vermiculite

This is produced from a naturally occurring material called mica which is a glassy type of mineral consisting of flat layers or wafers. It is mined, mainly in South Africa. When it is heated to a temperature of about 1,400°C it expands considerably, thus providing a very large surface area for water retention and rooting. It also has a good capacity for retaining the plant foods added to the compost and itself contains high levels of magnesium, calcium and potassium. Thus it is a useful additive at approximately 10 per cent by volume to composts, but it is expensive, so its advantages have to be weighed against the extra cost. Because of its light weight it has been used as a base for the production of lightweight fertilisers.

Perlite

Although very different from vermiculite this mineral is processed in a similar manner by heat. The basic raw material is a dense, glass-like rock formed by volcanic action in much the same way as pumice stone. The rock is crushed and heated so that it expands like popcorn to twenty or more times its original volume. This gives it water and air-retaining properties and, as in the case of vermiculite, lightens it. Unlike vermiculite, it naturally contains few nutrients and its capacity to absorb water is less. Perlite has been used as a base for lightweight fertilisers but its use in composts is limited because of its high cost and because the advantages gained by its incorporation have not been proven.

Polystyrene

Factories producing polystyrene products such as ceiling tiles and insulation boards have a waste problem that is an embarrassment to them because of difficulties of disposal of rejects and off-cuts. A small but increasing use for this waste has been in the addition of the broken-down pieces to composts. Various claims have been made as to the benefits obtained, such as improved aeration and drainage, even to increasing the temperature of the compost by 1–2°C but these are still early days and there is little experimental evidence to substantiate these claims. The material is very light and this causes problems as it tends to float to the surface of the compost during the mixing. There are little or no

Fertiliser lb/cuyd (or oz/bushel) compost	GLASSHOUSE CROPS RESEARCH INSTITUTE (GCRI) COMPOSTS			KINSEALY COMPOSTS				PEAT-LITE COMPOSTS		
	Seed sowing	Potting on or pricking out (High N reserve)	Potting on or pricking out (Low N reserve)	Seed sowing	Tomato composts (Potting)	Tomato composts (Growing on)	Potting or general compost	Mix A (Seed)	Mix A (Growing on)	Mix B
Peat / Sand etc	50 / 50	75 / 25	75 / 25	100 / —	100 / —	100 / —	100 / —	50 / 50 vermiculite	50 / 50 vermiculite	50 / 50 perlite
Ammonium nitrate	—	—	5oz (¼oz)	—	—	—	—	1lb (¾oz)	—	—
Calcium ammonium nitrate†	—	—	—	5oz (¼oz)	1lb 4oz (1oz)	1lb 4oz (1oz)	2lb 8oz (2oz)	—	—	•
Urea formaldehyde	—	1lb winter (½oz) 1¼lb spring (1oz) 2lb summer (1½oz)	—	5oz (¼oz)	1lb 4oz (1oz)	1lb 4oz (1oz)	—	—	—	—
Superphosphate	1lb 4oz (1oz)	2lb 8oz (2oz)	2lb 8oz (2oz)	9oz (½oz)	2lb 4oz (1¼oz)	2lb 4oz (1¼oz)	1lb 2oz (1oz)	2lb (1¼oz)	2lb (1¼oz)	2lb (1¼oz)
Potassium nitrate	1oz (¼oz)	1lb 5oz (1oz)	1lb 5oz (1oz)	—	—	—	—	—	1lb (¾oz)	1lb (¾oz)
Potassium sulphate	—	—	—	5oz (¼oz)	1lb 4oz (1oz)	2lb 4oz (1½oz)	1lb 4oz (1oz)	—	—	—
Kieserite	—	—	—	12oz (¼oz)	3lb (2¼oz)	—	3lb (2¼oz)	—	—	—
Dolomite lime	—	4lb (3oz)	4lb (3oz)	—	—	15lb 4oz (11½oz)	—	—	—	—
Ground limestone	5lb (4oz)	4lb (3oz)	4lb (3oz)	8lb 8oz (6½oz)	8lb 8oz (6½oz)	—	8lb 8oz (6½oz)	5lb (4oz)	5lb (4oz)	5lb (4oz)
Frit 253A	—	1oz (¼oz)	1oz (¼oz)	—	1oz* (¼oz)	1oz* (¼oz)	1oz* (¼oz)	‡	‡	‡

†Sold as Nitro-Chalk or Nitra-Shell but may be replaced by ammonium nitrate as follows: 5oz — 3½oz Ammonium nitrate, 1lb 4oz — 15oz ,, 2lb 8oz — 30oz ,,

*Frit added for convenience. Trace element mixture actually:
Sodium molybdate 0.07oz   Iron chelate 1.10oz
Copper sulphate 0.7oz   Iron sulphate 1.10oz
Borax 0.4oz   Zinc sulphate 0.45oz
Manganese sulphate 0.45oz

‡Trace elements added/cuyd of compost:
Borax   0.3oz (1 level tablespoon)
Iron chelate 1oz (3 level tablespoons)

1 bushel = 8 gallons (ie 4 two gallon bucketfuls)

plant foods present and the capacity to retain added plant foods is very low.

Polystyrene may be added to compost at up to 20 per cent by volume but the compost must not be heat sterilised, for example by steam, after incorporation, as the polystyrene will melt.

Pulverised fuel ash (PFA)

Large amounts of clinker-type materials must be disposed of by the large furnaces of power stations and one of the uses of this material is as a compost additive. The clinker is broken up (pulverised) and used as a replacement in whole or in part for the sand fraction of the compost. It is lighter than sand although heavier than the alternative materials mentioned above, and the PFA itself has some pore space within the particles. It is used with success by some growers but there have been reservations from certain authorities on its use because of possible excess levels of some trace elements.

Other materials

Synthetic foams have been used in the manufacture of composts as well as on land that is being reclaimed and for conserving water in dry areas. The most useful for horticultural purposes are the urea-formaldehyde foams as these have a cotton-wool-like texture. Shredded polyurethane foam can be obtained as a waste product of the cushion and bedding industry quite cheaply. Ideally, it should be shredded as finely as possible for addition to compost. Its addition is claimed to improve aeration and heat retention in the compost; roots appear to be attracted to the foam. Polyurethane blocks are also now produced for rooting cuttings. The blocks are available in sheet form, each block being a cube 3–4cm. They are wetted before use and the cuttings inserted into the blocks. Advantages claimed are that the rooting medium is light, sterile and uniform, maintaining the correct balance of air and water, giving even root development. It is likely that this type of medium will find increasing usage in the future. Indeed, the more these synthetic foams are used the more advantages are found for them.

Comparison of soilless compost mixes (see table)

Kinsealy composts

These were developed by the Glasshouse Crops Department at the Horticultural Research Centre of the Agricultural Institute, Kinsealy, Dublin, Eire, after the UC composts had been found unsatisfactory. The present formulae for the Kinsealy composts are based on peat alone. In the table of compost formulations will be found the current recommendations. Three basic composts are given, two specific tomato composts and a general potting compost. In addition, there is a tomato seedling compost, with a quarter of the plant food of the tomato potting compost. This division between the tomato and general composts would not appear to be too important because the nutrient content of both follow similar lines to composts from other organisations, the main difference lying in the proportion of readily available to slow-release nitrogen. It is interesting to note that the Kinsealy formulae are the only ones to specify the use of kieserite as the source of magnesium. The other formulae use dolomite lime as the magnesium source, which also neutralises the compost. Hence if kieserite is used, the rate of addition of ground limestone is higher than in a dolomite lime-ground limestone mixture, although the total amount of lime used will be similar.

Tomato seeds are sown in the seedling compost. The seedlings are then pricked out into the propagating compost where they remain until planting out. The tomato growing-on compost has a higher rate of potassium and magnesium addition and the magnesium source has been altered from kieserite to dolomite limestone which is available over a larger period of time. Owing to the high rate of addition of dolomite limestone, no ground limestone or chalk is required.

General potting compost was formulated after a wide range (over 70 species) of plants had been grown in it, including cucumbers. The basic formula is the tomato propagating compost, with half the

Streptocarpus, one of the most popular and colourful of greenhouse pot plants, available in a wide range of colours and ideal for growing in soilless compost.

rate of superphosphate, twice the amount of calcium ammonium nitrate and no source of slow-release nitrogen, so that the compost can be stored after mixing. Although higher rates of superphosphates have been tried, there has been no benefit reported by Kinsealy. It is interesting to note that this compost is similar in nutrient level to the GCRI compost described below. For ready mixed composts made to the Kinsealy formulae, see later under the section on ready-made compost.

Difficulty may be experienced with weighing out and evenly mixing the low trace elements in these formulae. The problems may be reduced by the replacement of these individual trace elements by 10oz of trace element frit 253A per cubic yard of compost.

GCRI mixes

These were first formulated by A. C. Bunt at the Glasshouse Crops Research Institute at Littlehampton in Sussex, England. There are three composts recommended at present, all adaptations of UC formulae: a seed-sowing or propagating compost based on equal volumes of peat and fine sand, and two 75 peat/25 fine sand composts for pricking out or potting on.

In the seed-sowing compost the only source of nitrogen is that readily available from potassium nitrate as seedlings are not in the compost long enough to require slower-release nitrogen. No source of magnesium has been found necessary by GCRI for seedlings.

The two potting composts vary in the nitrogen reserve. The compost known as High N Reserve Compost uses urea formaldehyde as the source of slow-release nitrogen and must be used fairly soon after mixing as it will not store. The organic nitrogen level is varied according to the season (see table); the readily available nitrogen level is higher than in the comparable UC compost and, to give a balanced growth, the phosphate and potash levels are also higher.

GCRI Low N Reserve Compost was developed as a compost that can be mixed and stored before use. It has a low level of readily available nitrogen and no slow-release nitrogen. Because of this, liquid feeding should commence earlier after potting up in this compost than in the High N Reserve Compost.

Both the GCRI potting composts use mixtures of dolomite lime and ground limestone for neutralising the compost to a pH of 5.5, the dolomite lime also supplying the necessary magnesium. They also contain fritted trace elements to rectify deficiencies of boron, zinc and manganese in the peat, as well as supplying copper and molybdenum.

Cornell lightweight composts (Peat-lite)

These were developed for the container growing of bedding plants at Cornell University, although subsequently they have been used for potting plants. Standardisation was the main theme and this was achieved by including 50 per cent vermiculite or perlite with the moss peat. This gave rise to the name of peat-lite for these composts, mix A containing vermiculite and mix B perlite.

The seed mix supplies nitrogen and phosphate as the major elements and boron and iron as trace elements, plus lime of course to neutralise the peat. Mixes A and B for growing on are fertilised with potassium nitrate and superphosphate but the potassium nitrate may be substituted by 2–12lb per cuyd of a compound fertiliser such as 5–10–5, 6–12–6 and 5–10–10. It must be remembered that the natural levels of potash and magnesium in vermiculite are high to supplement the added fertilisers but calcium content is variable. Because of this, ground limestone is used in preference to dolomite for the neutralising of the compost to provide calcium. These mixes may be safely stored. Peat-lite mixtures do not contain slow-release nitrogen, although MagAmp and urea formaldehyde were later used in the bedding plant mixes plus potash frit for slow release of potassium; however such composts should not be stored for long periods before use.

Problems may arise from the good drainage characteristics of the peat-lite

173

Primula obconica,
probably the most
popular of all primulas
for greenhouse
cultivation. Another ideal
candidate for a soilless
compost.

composts, the water tending to run through the compost before it is completely wetted. Watering should therefore be done only lightly initially. Generally the formulae suggested for this compost seem rather vague.

Other formulations

Above are given the better known of the compost formulations but there are many more, particularly from the various Experimental Horticultural Stations scattered throughout this and other countries. However, these are all rather similar to the GCRI type compost and it would serve no purpose to list them here.

Mixing composts—ready-made bases

The formulae given above can be rather bewildering for the commercial grower, let alone the amateur. Production of these composts requires the accurate weighing out of comparatively small quantities of fertilisers which have to be evenly mixed with large quantities of compost. This is not easily done and many of the composts used by the commercial growers are made from ready mixed compost fertilisers containing the major plant foods nitrogen, phosphates and potash with in some cases trace elements also. Most also include a balance between readily available and slow-release nitrogen. Obviously this is a great simplification and reduces the chance of error, with usually a single weighing out of the fertiliser plus a further weighing out of the lime (but see below on reduction of compost volume).

Lime in soilless composts

Lime is essential in a soilless compost and it performs two functions: it neutralises the acidity of the peat and supplies the nutrient calcium to the compost.

Sphagnum moss peat recommended for soilless compost has a pH of between 3.3 and 4.3 approximately, but commonly in the narrower range of 3.8 to 4.1. For a 3:1 peat-sand compost, the pH recommended is 5.5, ie approximately one pH unit lower than is recommended for a soil-based compost. If only the peat and sand are mixed together, the resultant pH will be about

4.3, assuming the use of an acid sand. To increase the pH to 5.5, 6oz of ground limestone will have to be added per bushel of compost or approximately 8lb per cu yd.

Ground limestone is chemically calcium carbonate. Chalk is also calcium carbonate but it is white and softer than limestone. Ground limestone is to be preferred for compost work as it will dissolve more slowly and maintain a reasonably consistent pH over the life of the compost. The grading (or size range) of the ground limestone is important: small particles will raise the pH initially but coarser particles (up to $\frac{1}{16}$ in) are needed to maintain the pH with time. Generally about ten days is required for the pH of the compost to reach 5.5. If the lime contains many fine particles, as in dolomite lime, the pH may reach 5.5 in only three days but the coarser particles must still be provided to maintain this level.

In some of the compost formulae, mixtures of ground limestone and dolomite are used. The reason for this is that dolomite provides magnesium, which may not be present in the other plant foods added to the compost. Dolomite is usually sold as a fine dust rather than as a graded material like ground limestone and it will therefore raise the pH of the compost initially quite quickly. All the formulae give mixtures of dolomite and ground limestone since ground limestone is necessary for the calcium. Both materials have similar neutralising powers, so that in a formula containing 9lb ground limestone per cu yd of compost, 5lb ground limestone and 4lb dolomite may be used instead if no other source of magnesium is included in the compost—$7\frac{1}{2}$oz per bushel.

Finally, the adjustment of the pH in an all-peat compost is a simple matter if the pH of the peat is known. It is known that 1lb of limestone will raise the pH of 1cu yd of peat by 0.3 of a pH unit. For example, if the peat has a pH of 3.5 and the compost pH required is 5.0 (the most suitable pH for an all-peat compost), the pH is to be raised by $5.0 - 3.5 = 1.5$. Therefore the amount of ground limestone required per

cuyd of peat is $\frac{1.5}{0.3}$ or 5lb per cuyd of peat.
If a smaller quantity of peat is being mixed, 5lb per cuyd is equivalent to 4oz per bushel.

Reduction in compost volume of peat/sand mixtures

When peat and sand are mixed, there is a reduction in the volume of compost produced. For example, if a normal 3 peat/1 sand mix is being made and say 9 bushels of peat and 3 bushels of sand are mixed together, 12 bushels of compost will not be produced since the particles of sand will tend to be absorbed into the spaces in the peat, resulting in an average reduction of one-sixth in volume. In the example quoted above, probably around 10 bushels of compost will be produced and it is this volume that is used to calculate the addition of lime and fertiliser. If 6oz ground limestone and 4oz compound fertiliser were being added to each bushel of compost, then the mix above would require 10 × 6oz lime (60oz) and 10 × 4oz (40oz) of fertiliser. Unless the reduction in volume is allowed for, too much lime and fertiliser will be added, causing damage to the plants.

Therefore for the first mix of compost, the peat and sand should be measured out and then mixed. The volume of the compost thus produced should be measured and the amounts of lime and fertiliser to be added calculated. These same amounts may then be added to further mixes without measurement of the final compost volume as this will be similar for the same volumes of peat and sand initially.

High salt levels in compost

Causes

The higher the fertiliser level in a compost, the higher the salt concentration and the more risk of plant injury. However, different fertilisers have a different effect on the salt level. Obviously slow-release fertilisers will have little effect on it initially, but as they are acted upon by the soil bacteria, the breakdown products which are soluble will contribute to the salt level. However, in the pot, part of this level will be removed as food by the plants and part will be washed away during watering. So that provided the release is not excessive, there is little risk of a dangerously high level accumulating. If such compost is stored in a bag the situation is rather different, because the system is closed and the salt and ammonia levels can build up as the slow release nitrogen becomes available.

The more readily available plant foods have the greatest effect on the salt level: ammonium nitrate comes first, closely followed by potassium nitrate and potassium sulphate. Superphosphate has the least effect on the salt level. Soilless composts can be more heavily fertilised than comparable soil-based composts without dangerous build-up, possibly because the peat acts as a sponge, absorbing the dissolved fertiliser which does not then harm the plant roots, possibly because soilless compost is better aerated.

The compost components may contribute to the salt level. Peat and sand have little effect but if soil is used it may contain a high level of salts. This is one reason why, when the John Innes composts were formulated, the soil was obtained from meadowland that had only low plant foods and hence a low salt level; an old greenhouse soil is not suitable because it is likely to contain fertiliser residues which may be harmful.

The last source of salt levels in compost is the water. Sometimes this may contain dissolved salts, particularly in bore-hole water. Tap water is usually safe but rain water is the safest of all.

Effect of high salt levels

The effect of a high salt level in a compost may vary from no apparent damage to rapid plant death. If the salt level is just on the limit of danger, there will probably be only a reduction in the rate of growth. As the salt level increases, the plant will absorb considerable quantities of fertiliser which will tend to accumulate in the leaf margins or tips, causing burning as the water evaporates and leaves the fertiliser behind.

Root damage also occurs. If the salt level becomes very high, water will actually be removed from the root into the growing medium, causing the root to brown and dry up. This will aggravate the problem since the plant will be able to take up less water, with the possibility of the leaves wilting and further damage to the leaf margins and tips. A frequent symptom is yellowing of the leaves which may be diagnosed by the inexperienced as a shortage of nitrogen and the plant may be promptly fed with liquid fertiliser, increasing the salt level of the compost still further and making the situation worse. Very often the first sign of root trouble is a yellowing of the foliage and if the plant is knocked out of its pot, the effect of the high salt level is evident by the browning of the roots. This must not be confused with damage due to over-watering.

Cure

If the damage is not too severe the compost can be leached out of its excess salt level by generously watering the compost. A free-draining well-aerated compost will help this. Alternatively, the plant should have as much of the damaging compost as possible removed from its roots and be re-potted into a fresh, safe compost. Damaged plants should be given plenty of shade and high humidity, thus reducing the rate of transpiration of water through the plant. The damaged roots are under less stress and new roots will be able to form. However, with most things prevention is better than cure and the compost should be made correctly in the first place.

Ready mixed composts

For the gardener who does not want the bother of mixing his own soilless compost either by the standard formulae or using one of the compost fertilisers given earlier, there are available on the market several ready-made composts. All the gardener has to do is to purchase a bag of compost from the local gardening shop, open it and start using it straight away. The disadvantage is that it is not known exactly what is in the compost, how much fertiliser it contains,

etc. However, it is sold to do a specific job and therefore it is presumed that it will do it well.

There are also many smaller firms who produce soilless compost and sell it through a few local garden shops and garden centres. Often, these producers supply the local commercial growers as well, or it may even be a local nurseryman who packs his own compost. It is obviously not possible to comment specifically on these locally available mixes. Some are excellent, based either on a GCRI type formula or a proprietary compost fertiliser but some may be rather variable in quality.

A general purpose mix is available in ready mixed compost, suitable for seed sowing, rooting cuttings and potting. This type of universal compost must contain only small amounts of plant food so that it will not be damaging to the tender seedlings. When it is used for potting, as it only contains these limited plant foods, the plants must have regular supplementary liquid feeding quite soon after potting if they are not to starve. The advantage in these products is simplicity, having only the one compost for all jobs, but the aftercare required is higher.

Other ready-mixed composts are available in two forms, one for seed sowing and rooting cuttings and the other for potting. The seed-sowing compost is similar to the general purpose compost already mentioned above, having low plant foods. The potting compost has higher plant foods that will sustain the plants longer but nevertheless, supplementary feeding is usually necessary in approximately six to eight weeks after potting. Occasionally, two potting strengths will be offered, as with the John Innes potting composts.

Plant propagation

A very important use for compost is in the propagation of plants. This may involve either seed sowing or taking cuttings and rooting them. The basic requirements of these composts are that they are free from pests and diseases, well aerated and well drained. The need for freedom from pest or diseases is obvious since at this stage both seedlings and cuttings are very susceptible to attack. The main danger is from the damping-off fungi or the so-called water moulds such as *Phytophthora* and *Pythium* either before or after the seedlings emerge from the soil. The damage caused by these fungi is usually most severe under conditions when germination of the seed, or rooting of the cutting is slow, for example, early in the season or in cold, wet soils. Keeping the compost well-aerated and free draining will keep it warmer and combined with less saturation with water, this will discourage the diseases. There are other means of giving protection such as the use of seed dressings containing fungicides such as captan or thiram and insecticides such as gamma-BHC (lindane). A fungicide may be added to the hormone rooting powders used for cuttings. Even these precautions will be less effective or even ineffective if the compost structure is not suitable.

For seed sowing, the soil-based John Innes seed compost is suitable. The soil is sterilised and, provided that has been done effectively, the soil will be free from harmful organisms, the grit is sterile anyway and the peat will be almost or completely sterile—so the compost should be satisfactory. Improved germination and growth have been obtained by using soilless seed sowing composts in place of the soil-based seed compost. There are several formulas that may be made up such as the G.C.R.I. and Kinsealy formulae or equal volumes of sphagnum moss peat and sharp sand may be mixed (50:50 peat:sand) together with a small amount (approximately 1 oz per bushel) of a compost fertiliser and ground limestone at 5 oz per bushel of compost for a lime-free (acid) sand.

For rooting cuttings, there is a whole variety of recommendations, ranging from all peat through various combinations of peat and sand to all sand, even using different composts for rooting different cuttings. However, this complication seems rather unnecessary as most subjects can be rooted very successfully in the 50:50 peat-

sand compost recommended above for seed sowing using one of the standard formulae or a compost fertiliser. Ready-made soilless composts can be obtained that are suitable for seed sowing and cuttings.

Cropping plants

Recently there has been an increasing interest in growing cropping plants such as tomatoes in compost in place of the more normal greenhouse soil. The main advantage is that the risk of pest or disease attack from the soil is prevented, as the compost is removed each year and replaced. The growing medium is known to be nutritionally good whereas there may be some doubt as to the suitability of the greenhouse soil, such as pH and fertilizer level, as well as the actual soil structure. The three different approaches to this method of growing-containers, modified ring culture and troughs, are dealt with in the chapters on tomato cultivation. In the container system, the compost is placed in pots (plastic), bags or tubes which are then spaced out in the greenhouse. Plants are put individually in pots but bags or tubes may have more than one plant. It is possible to buy the bags or tubes filled with compost such as Alexpeat. The main dangers of the bag method, the modified ring culture and the trough method are the drainage of water and the problems of the build up of the salt concentration in the compost. Watering must be done with care so that the compost does not become water-logged and feeding, whilst very necessary, must not be overdone in case the compost becomes toxic through excess fertilizer. One method of removing the problem is to slit the side of the growing bag or trough to allow excess water to drain away, but the disadvantage is that if the roots grow through the slits into diseased greenhouse soil, the plants will become infected. An alternative method with the bed for trough system is to place drainage tiles at the bottom of the trough, a system developed at the Kinsealy Institute in Ireland. A tile drain is laid in a central groove running along the bottom of the trough with a 1 in layer of gravel over the drain to prevent the compost entering it. The trough is topped up with not less than 6in of soilless compost. At Kinsealy, these troughs have been used successfully for three years without replacement, but the compost is sterilised by steam through the drainage tile at the end of each season to prevent the build-up of pests and diseases.

Compost strengths

Plants vary in their tolerance of the fertiliser level in the compost. In a ready-made compost the level of fertiliser is kept reasonably low so that the least tolerant plants may be grown. But problems arise when the gardener wishes to make up his own compost and has to decide on the strength of fertiliser to be used. In the lists below, the most commonly grown pot plants have been divided into two groups. The first group contains those plants that are not tolerant of high fertiliser levels and the second group plants that may be potted into a stronger compost.

Seed is sown or cuttings rooted in the standard composts detailed earlier. The plants in the first group are pricked out or potted into a compost with a strength of approximately John Innes Potting ½ or the equivalent in soilless. The final potting of these plants is done at John Innes Potting No 1 strength. In the second group the plants are pricked out into John Innes Potting No 1, and potted on into John Innes Potting No 2. All plants may be liquid fed after the roots have filled the pots (gently tap out the root ball to examine). Certain of these plants will tolerate higher levels of plant foods, but for the sake of simplicity the groupings have been kept to two.

Plants that are grown in the early stages in a greenhouse and later planted out in an outside soil, eg bedding plants, chrysanthemums, cucumbers, should be pricked out or potted on into John Innes Potting No 1 or its soilless equivalent. If the plants are to stay in the compost longer than approximately four weeks, some supplementary feeding should be given.

Group 1

Pricking out: John Innes Potting ½ or equivalent in soilless compost
Potting on: John Innes Potting 1 or equivalent in soilless compost
Adiantum (maidenhair fern)
Anthurium scherzerianum (painter's palette)
Aphelandra squarrosa
Asparagus (florist's fern) for smaller plants
Astilbe arendsii (spiraeas)
Begonia (winter-flowering)
Cacti (except epiphytes which require 6oz)
Camellia japonica (less lime)
Ceropegia woodii
Chlorophytum comosum 'Variegatum' (spider plant)
Cissus antarctica (kangaroo vine) 3½in pots
Codiaeum (croton)
Coleus blumei
Crassula coccinea (Rochea coccinea)
Crossandra
Dieffenbachia 3½in pots
Dracaena terminalis (Cordyline terminalis)
Ericas
Ficus pumila and *radicans* (small-leaved)
Fittonia
Geranium, ivy-leaved *(Pelargonium peltatum)*
Hedera (ivy)
Impatiens wallerana (busy Lizzie)
Kalanchoe
Maranta leuconeura kerchouiana (3½in pots)
Marguerites *(Chrysanthemum frutescens* and *coronarium)*
Monstera deliciosa
Nephrolepis (ladder fern)
Opuntia (prickly pear)
Orchids
Palms (3½in pots)
Pandanus veitchii
Pelargonium domesticum (regal pelargonium)
Peperomia
Philodendron (3½in pots)
Pilea cadieri
Platycerium bifurcatum (stag's horn fern)
Polyanthus *(Primula polyanthus)*
Polypodium (fern)
Primula malacoides, obconica and *sinensis* (winter)

Pteris (fern)
Rhoicissus rhomboidea (grape ivy) 3½in pots
Roses (fairy)
Saintpaulia ionantha (African violet)
Saxifraga stolonifera (mother of thousands)
Sedum sieboldii
Selaginella (selago, fern)
Setcreasia purpurea (purple heart)
Tradescantia albiflora and *fluminensis*
    (Wandering Jew)
Vriesea splendens (bromeliad)
Zebrina pendula (Wandering Jew)
Zygocactus truncatus (*Schlumbergera
    truncata*, Christmas cactus)
Group 2
Pricking out: John Innes Potting 1 or
equivalent in soilless compost
Potting on: John Innes Potting 2 or
equivalent in soilless compost
Achimenes (hot water plant)
Aechmea (bromeliad)
Asparagus (florist's fern) for large plants
Aspidistra
Asplenium (fern) 5in pots
Begonia rex, semperflorens and tuberous
Beloperone guttata (shrimp plant)
Calceolaria multiflora nana
Campanula isophylla
Capsicum (peppers)
Celosia
Cineraria

Cissus antarctica (kangaroo vine) 5in pots
Cyclamen persicum
Dieffenbachia (dumb cane) 5in pots
Euphorbia pulcherrima (poinsettia)
x *Fatshedera lizei*
Fatsia japonica
Ficus elastica (Rubber Plant)
Fuchsia
Genista (*Cytisus canariensis*)
Geranium, flowering (*Pelargonium zonale*)
Gloxinia (*Sinningia speciosa*)
Grevillea robusta (silk oak)
Hibiscus
Hippeastrum (amaryllis)
Hoya bella (wax flower)
Maranta (prayer plant) 5in pots
Palms 5in pots (mainly Collinia & Howe
    known as Kentia)
Philodendron 5in pots
Primula malacoides, obconica and *sinensis*
    (summer)
Rhoicissus rhomboidea (grape ivy) 5in pots
Ricinus communis (castor-oil plant, palma
    Christii)
Sansevieria hahnii and *trifasciata*
    (bowstring hemp, mother-in-law's
    tongue)
Scindapsus
Solanum capsicatum and *pseudocapsicum*
    (winter cherry)
Spathiphyllum wallisii

Chapter 16

Hydroponics in the Greenhouse

The name 'hydroponics' is derived from the work of Dr W. F. Gerische in California who in 1929 demonstrated the practicability of growing plants in balanced and aerated nutrient solutions in tanks. From this original work developed the more sophisticated techniques of hydroponics using either nutrient solution alone or in conjunction with aggregates such as sand, gravel, pebbles, vermiculite, or any one of a number of materials.

Hydroponics over the years has enjoyed mixed fortunes. It was initially received with enthusiasm and made steady progress as a cultural technique in sunny climates where soil is at a premium, but it did not receive universal attention in cooler northern regions. However, it is now making rapid headway in temperate climates, not only under glass but also out of doors for roof gardens and patios where it is often thought to be a cleaner and more convenient method of growing plants than the traditional soil beds.

While it is possible to obtain very high and uniform yields with a wide range of crops using hydroponic systems under strictly controlled conditions, there is very little margin of error: in other words, excess or deficiency of nutrients manifest themselves very strongly. Perhaps in this enlightened age, and particularly with experience of soilless cultivation and the liquid feeding necessary with it, gardeners are better able to accept hydroponics and understand its eccentricities.

As with soilless growing media or composts, the nutrients used in hydroponics must be soluble, aerated, palatable and capable of immediate absorption by the plants. Assuming this basic philosophy, therefore, all that is necessary is to arrange to grow plants in such a manner that they can be constantly supplied with such aerated solutions on a constant replacement basis. There are four basic methods which can be practised either in the greenhouse or out of doors.

Suspension in pure solution

Tanks approximately 8–9in deep are used. They can be any convenient size. Over the top is spread a fine mesh of wire netting, wood or glass wool to support plants so that their roots are suspended in the nutrient solution. This solution, despite regular pH tests, must be completely changed every 10–14 days.

Carnations, one of the most popular of all greenhouse plants. They are one of the most suitable plants for growing by hydroponics, which is the method by which they are being grown here.

This method is now little practised because of the obvious difficulty of plant support which it poses, coupled with the problem of ensuring accurate concentration and aeration (by compressor) of the nutrient solution. Plants also vary in their ability to grow in pure nutrient solution, especially where aeration is not adequate.

Flooded aggregate

Concrete tanks, boxes of galvanised metal protected with bituminous paint, or modern plastic-lined troughs, about 8–9in deep and any convenient width are used as containers for inert aggregates, eg sand (with neutral pH) preferably of coarse texture, crushed gravel (again inert), vermiculite (exflor grade), perlite, polystyrene or polyurethane chips, urea formaldehyde foam, clean ash or lignite in aggregate form a carboniferous material available in the UK, Germany, the USA and some other countries). The aggregate layer is 6–8in deep, depending on the root development of the crop grown. The nutrient solution is either fed from the top or pumped up from the bottom to flood the aggregate (with sub-irrigation systems coarser aggregates are desirable). In either case the nutrient solution is collected for redistribution. It is advisable to check the concentration and pH content regularly, making the necessary adjustments, or better still to replace the solution completely every 10–14 days, a rather costly and time-consuming operation. All the aeration necessary is achieved by the use of aggregates.

Drainage tanks

A compromise technique now in vogue for a wide range of plants is the use of polythene lined trenches or containers with drainage holes some 3in from the base, so that surplus moisture can drain out but leave a reservoir of moisture and nutrients in the bottom 3in of the trench. There is no collection of the surplus nutrients, which are lost through drainage and are applied on a regular basis. Containers or pots can also be used on a smaller scale with side drainage.

The aggregate chosen must be capable of moisture absorption, or in other words have an acceptable capillarity. This means quite simply that it must be capable of sucking up the water from below which tends to rule out coarse sand, gravel, polystyrene and polyurethane and, to a lesser degree, ashes. Vermiculite, perlite and lignite, particularly the last named, have excellent capillarity.

It is also desirable that the aggregate selected should remain open and porous over a period of time to admit air, and this to a certain extent rules out vermiculite in too fine a form (this applies also to the second system). While lignite remains porous for a long period if coarse enough at the outset, being organic it does suffer gradual breakdown over a period of time and requires riddling. Gravels and sands do of course remain porous but tend to lack capillarity.

Avoidance of soil sickness

One of the virtues of aggregate hydroponic culture is to allow re-use of the selected material simply by flushing it out with water or mild sterilant without recourse to sterilisation, the aggregate not developing soil sickness in a similar manner to soil. Should sterilisation be required to deal specifically with some pest or disease attack, aggregates lend themselves readily to *complete* sterilisation by heat or other means.

Controlled nutrient re-circulating systems

Several systems embodying controlled re-circulation of aerated nutrient solutions are now being developed at experimental level at various centres, including the Glasshouse Crops Research Institute, Littlehampton, England. Here lay-flat polythene tubing 10–12in wide is used, with nutrient solution constantly re-circulated through it from a storage tank. Plants (in this case tomatoes) are grown 14–16in apart in slits in the polythene. Plastic holders of a vertical design with elbows at 10–12in intervals are also being used for prostrate types of tomato, the nutrient solution, again, constantly being re-circulated.

It seems likely that other systems will quickly be developed, but it should be pointed out that they all suffer the disadvantage of constant checks or renewal of nutrient solutions and require apparatus such as tanks and submersible pumps.

Applying the nutrients

Complete spectrum nutrients containing major and trace elements are desirable and are available in proprietary form or can be self-formulated. The following are the more general formulae concerned. The salts are given in grammes per litre and are in hydrated form. They must be made up accurately in tanks.

Hoaglands solution

Potassium nitrate	0.51g/litre
Calcium nitrate	0.82 ,,
Magnesium sulphate	0.49 ,,
Potassium dihydrogen phosphate	0.136 ,,
plus Trace elements A–Z	

They are made up in 18 litres of water and 1ml of mixture is added per litre of above culture solution:

Aluminium sulphate	1.0g/litre
Potassium iodide	0.5 ,,
Potassium bromide	0.5 ,,
Titanium oxide	1.0 ,,
Stannic chloride	0.5 ,,
Lithium chloride	0.5 ,,
Manganous chloride	7.0g/litre
Boric acid	11.0 ,,
Zinc sulphate	1.0 ,,
Copper sulphate	1.0 ,,
Nickelic sulphate	1.0 ,,
Cobalt nitrate	1.0 ,,

1ml per litre of 0.5%
Solution of Ferric tartarate*
*Can be substituted by 1ml of 2.35%
Solution of Sequestrine 138 Fe.

Shive and Robbins—an alternative solution

Calcium nitrate	0.938g/litre
Ammonium sulphate	0.0924 ,,
Potassium dihydrogen phosphate	0.313 ,,
Magnesium sulphate	0.567 ,,

Schizanthus giant hybrids, one of the plants which people have tried to grow under hydroponics systems. The whole field of hydroponics is a very new one about which relatively little is known yet.

Ferrous sulphate	5.5mg/litre
Boric acid	0.57 ,,
Manganous sulphate	0.57 ,,
Zinc sulphate	0.57 ,,

Other feeding systems

There are a number of convenient packs available on the market involving the use of sachets, which are simply added to a stated amount of water, although some may be different in colour. In certain areas it may not be necessary to add trace elements as they are available from the water supply. Aggregate systems have the nutrient solution applied to flood stage when it is allowed to drain out slowly before being pumped back into the aggregate either from below or above. Much more simply, nutrients can be used in solid fertiliser form on top of the aggregate and simply watered in, a rather rough and ready method which seems to work best with the capillary systems (vermiculite, perlite, lignite).

A combination of base feeding with, for example, Vitax Q4 as a base, and ground limestone (according to pH of aggregate and type of plants) supplemented by NPK constant liquid feeding can be used with a reasonable degree of success, provided the gardener is of an observing nature and is capable of diagnosing deficiency or excess visually and taking the necessary evasive action. Where excess salt symptoms develop, it is generally advisable to flood out and start again from the beginning.

Solid dry feeding systems are perhaps much more applicable to the growth of longer term plants, including trees and shrubs, out of doors. It should be appreciated, however, that all hydroponic systems require constant vigilance, the least attention perhaps being required by capillary systems, and even they are *not* for the haphazard gardener unprepared to put some precision into his gardening.

Chapter 17

The word propagation literally means to increase by natural means, and this opens the flood gates for a discussion on what is 'natural' and what is 'artificial'. Setting aside this provocative argument there is, in the whole sphere of greenhouse culture, great scope for examining every facet of propagation under conditions where success is more likely than in the widely varying out-of-door conditions which prevail in most countries.

The living plant

Before propagation can be fully understood it is necessary to consider the basic morphology or botanical make-up of the living plant. Plants are divided broadly into two main groups: *dicotyledons* to which most broad-leaved plants belong, and *monocotyledons* which consist of narrow-leaved plants including lilies and most bulbous plants. The basic difference as far as propagation is concerned lies in the existence of a cambium layer in dicotyledons which is lacking in monocotyledons. The cambium cell layer exists between the vital xylem and phloem (see Fig 49) necessary for conducting water and nutrients in the plant, and its task is to replace worn-out cells and act as a source for regenerating the whole plant. Cambium cells are in fact the vital key to some aspects of successful propagation from miscellaneous sections of plant; it is mainly only the cambium cells which are able to bring about physical union between plants in grafting and give rise to the formation of new roots when rooting cuttings. It is fairly obvious therefore that one cannot propagate monocotyledons in the same way as they do not possess a cambium layer (see Fig 50), which imposes definite limitations in propagating methods (with the exception of *Dracaena*).

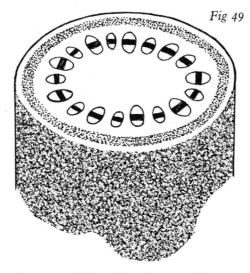

Fig 49

A young Dicotyledonous stem

Fig 50

A Monocotyledonous stem

In addition to monocotyledons and dicotyledons, a further grouping of plants relates to their longevity, there being three well-known groups:

1 *Annuals* These arise only from seed and die after forming seed, though not necessarily in the one calendar year, eg calendula, annual asters, clarkia, and thousands more (many annuals are of course half-hardy, living only a part of their lives out of doors).

2 *Biennials* These live for two seasons or, to be more specific, part of two seasons; in the first they prepare for flowering and in the second they flower, when thereafter they produce seed and die, eg turnips and foxgloves.

3 *Perennials* Plants in this group carry on flowering and producing seed for a great number of years, storing up their food in roots or stems, which enables them to survive the dormant period, although they may die down out of doors. Woody perennials have a permanent shoot system which usually does not die back to the ground (eg shrubs).

Annuals and biennials are rarely propagated by methods other than from seed, whereas perennials can be propagated either from seed, cuttings, or other parts of them such as roots, stems and leaves.

It must not be imagined that the gardener can choose the method of propagation he prefers, as plants exhibit considerable temperament in respect of how they increase themselves. A cutting from a large soft bush such as an elder may be extremely difficult to propagate, and likewise holly which has a very hard stem. Snips of coleus or tradescantia (wandering Jew or sailor) root in a few days, whereas many tender ericas (eg *Erica hymealis)* can be very tricky to root. The leaves of many plants can seldom be induced to root, whereas others such as those of *Begonia rex* produce roots with ease.

The eccentricities of seed are well known, where due to cross pollination and other causes the germinated offspring is different in colour or form from the parent plant. But though it may be assumed in the majority of cases that any portion of a plant's anatomy which can be successfully rooted will produce a plant of identical character and pattern of growth to the plant from which it was taken (setting aside 'sporting'), this is not always the case. Cuttings taken from mature plants produce plants which flower earlier than those produced from young plant cuttings. Where cuttings are taken from juvenile types of seed-raised conifers, the juvenile form persists. Straggly cuttings taken from older conifers will produce straggly plants, unlike those produced from young short-jointed cuttings from the terminal shoots. There would also appear to be a need to select particular types of chrysanthemum or carnation cuttings for stem propagation.

Propagation from seed

While propagation by seed appears to be an extremely cheap and simple method of producing new plants, it is not without drawbacks. Parentage and whether or not a seed is a true offspring of its parent is a critical matter. The grower of early commercial tomatoes purchases a certain variety of seed because of its special qualities in early fruiting, along with fruit size and quality, and the economic consequences of any performance variation are enormous, and this is true of many other plants at all centres of production. The exhibitor of a flower or vegetable, while not involved in economic results, stands to lose much if the seed he sows does not produce plants true to form. Indeed, the ordinary gardener seeking a special colour of flower or shape of turnip would be bitterly disappointed by considerable variation from inherent form. Conversely of course there is always the possibility of finding a form better than the parent. Fortunately there are many plants which produce seed that can, in most cases, be accepted as true to type because of many years of careful re-selection and controlled seed production. The whole secret of a seed house acquiring a good reputation lies in ensuring careful and rigorous selection.

Hybridisation

Matters are much more complicated today than in past years, due to the considerable degree of hybridisation which has taken place in an effort to produce better form, colour, size, shape, and indeed improve on every characteristic imaginable. The seeds of true species of plants such as common broom *Cytisus scoparius* and many others do however breed true to type from seed with little noticeable variation. In recent years much use has been made of F_1 (and F_2) hybrid seed. In the case of F_1 seed this is the result of controlled fertilisation between the two parents *annually* selected from those plants which are either annuals or treated as such. Mendel's Law refers to the true exhibition of the parent characteristics of both male and female parents in the first generation of seed produced, when thereafter segregation occurs in fixed proportions into respective male or female parent characteristics. The important issue with F_1 seed is the true and vigorous exhibition of the parents' qualities in 'blended' form, called hybrid vigour. This has very special significance also as far as the inbred resistance to disease is concerned, such resistances which are bestowed manifesting themselves strongly. The success which has been achieved with flowers and vegetables in F_1 seed form allows the seedsman to predict with certainty that certain qualities will be present in the offspring, whereas with ordinary seed there can be variations, loss of disease resistance, loss of vigour and many other deficiencies, particularly over a period of time unless vigorous re-selection is practised. It follows also that the same re-selection is required to maintain the qualities of the selected male or female parent of an F_1 hybrid. This perhaps serves to explain why seeds can give variable

Modern plastic propagating cases like this one are easy to use and increase both the speed of germination and the number of seeds that germinate. The seed tray stands on a hot-plate warmed by coaxial cables.

187

results, and the popularity of F_1 hybrids, but it must be emphasised once more that the careful selection and re-selection of 'ordinary' seed over a great many years will still, in many cases, give results of a high order.

It was said earlier that seed was cheap, and while this is true to a certain extent, the obviously high cost of producing F_1 seed, involving a re-cross annually, has raised the price of many seeds considerably. An example of this is the Carefree F_1 geranium, whose seeds are sufficiently expensive to cause gardeners some thought as to whether vegetative or seed propagation is cheaper, an issue still further complicated by the rather slower speed at which the F_1 geranium seed produces a flowering plant.

Speed of propagation

Where a plant can be propagated either from seed or vegetatively by cuttings or from other parts of the plant's anatomy, vegetative production is the quicker way of producing a *mature* plant. But the F_1 seedling may in turn overtake the vegetatively propagated plant and become bigger and more floriferous.

The advantage of seed is that it is an easily stored embryonic plant, and that a large number of plants can be produced from it in a small area with the minimum of trouble.

Transmission of disease

In the more technical aspects of disease transmission, it is obvious that seed offers a method of plant production much less prone to disease transmission than vegetative propagation. Virus and fungal diseases usually exist in the vegetative tissue of the plant, and it is not thought that the seminal reproductive section of the plant is affected, which means that the seed produced even by virus infected parents should be free from virus. One cannot, however, be too emphatic on this matter, as research is still probing into the facts surrounding the introduction of disease, but for all practical purposes non-transmission of disease by seminal means is a fact, although the importance of inherit-

In this greenhouse ideal conditions have been provided for the germination of seed. There is plenty of light, a well-ventilated atmosphere, warmth and a regular supply of moisture. Ventilation, heating and watering can all be operated automatically.

188

ance and disease susceptibility cannot be overlooked. It is also possible that the embryo itself may well be free of disease but the tissue surrounding it is not, which in practical terms gives rise to immense problems.

Containers for seed sowing, propagation and growing on

Pots are available in a wide range of sizes and shapes in plastic, clay, bituminised or treated paper, polystyrene or peat, in addition to which there are soil or peat blocks to consider.

Plastic pots

The swing to these in recent years has been dramatic, occasioned by hygiene, their very low manufacturing costs, transport, and their impermeability. When plastic pots made their debut they were viewed with considerable scepticism by older gardeners who failed to see how plants could grow in a non-sympathetic material incapable of admitting a sufficient supply of air to the roots. Clay with its porous nature seemed to offer all the advantages, yet practical experience has in the main shown otherwise. In a clay pot drying out occurs not only from the top but from the sides, whereas with a plastic pot the only area for evaporation is through the top surface. Plant physiologists have been at a loss to say whether or not this in itself is a good thing, but less water is certainly lost by plastic pots and this must surely be considered an advantage, though admittedly over-watering can occur by failure to take into account the respective differences in 'transpiration' loss. On the question of hygiene there can be no argument; plastic can be cleaned in warm water without scrubbing, and there is no risk of it absorbing disease as there is with clay. Plastic pots are, in addition, highly effective on capillary benches. They come in a wide range of sizes, round or square, light to handle and easy to store. Strips of small plastic pots are used commercially for a variety of purposes and are particularly useful for growing room activities where space is at a premium. The pot readily detaches by tearing, though some disturbance can occur when young plants require removal.

Paper pots

The role of paper pots is not so clear. While excellent as short-term containers for seeds or growing plants their cellulose content invariably results in a temporary nitrogen shortage until the cellulose decomposing fungi satisfy their own needs for nitrogen. There have been problems also with the saprophytic fungal agencies delaying the germination of seeds and the growth of plants. A major advantage of paper pots is that for seed sowing there is no disturbance on planting out or potting on, as the pot is planted intact, although the implications of temporary nitrogen shortage should not be overlooked. Paper pots are available in round or hexagonal shape, also in concertina-like strips from which pots can be taken as needed. Tubes of paper are very useful for sweet peas.

Red bituminised paper pots are available in large sizes and can be used for growing shrubs, tomatoes, chrysanthemums, and other long-term plants, lasting for about six months with normal handling.

Polythene

Being inert, polythene offers no nutritional problems. While young plants can be lined out with their polythene pots intact, removal on planting is advisable in most cases, and must be effected with care to avoid damage to roots.

Peat pots

Their main advantage is to allow plants to be grown and planted out without check. They are made from a mixture of approximately 75 per cent sterilised peat and 25 per cent wood fibre, the proportions varying with different manufacturers. Small quantities of nitrogen, phosphorus and potash are usually contained in the peat/wood fibre, which is compressed to form a thin wall. Experience is needed to get the best out of peat pots, which retain moisture with tenacity, thus necessitating less frequent watering particularly if the peat pots are housed in boxes or trays on top of a layer of peat. Space should be allowed between the individual pots, otherwise they can deteriorate quickly. They must not be handled any more than is strictly necessary, otherwise after a certain stage they disintegrate easily. Nutritionally peat pots do not present great difficulties, although extra nitrogen may be required at a certain stage of decomposition, as indicated by paler green leaves on the plant.

Peat pots are more suitable for pricking off and growing on than for seed sowing, although for single large seeds or pelleted seed they are excellent, as the roots penetrate the walls and are poised ready for action when the peat pot is potted on or planted out. They are also available in strip form to save space.

Jiffy 7s are compressed peat pots contained in a thin mesh net made from a mixture of polyethylene and polypropylene; they have made a tremendous impact in all spheres of propagation throughout Europe and further afield in recent years. The pots are expanded by saturating with water on a clean surface, or by standing in a tray of water or placing in a tub; the overhead method of expansion is said to be better for seed sowing. Capillary or tub expansion allows more air in the Jiffy 7 and provides better conditions for the rooting of cuttings. Plants as they develop can be fed with a complete liquid fertiliser high in nitrogen and potash. Seeds can be sown or cuttings rooted individually in each Jiffy 7, which is then potted on or planted out, avoiding all check to growth.

Plastic blocks

Developed in the early 1970s, these consist of foam plastic cut into blocks which serve for seed sowing, rooting cuttings, or pricking off. They simply provide a compatible and moist medium for the production of growth, but experience in their use is limited.

Soil and peat blocks

Soil blocks have been used for a great many years with changing popularity. Either soil-containing compost or peat can be blocked with suitable machinery, manually or automatically operated, the latter being essential for blocks required by the large scale commercial grower. In the early days of soil blocks they were used as a substitute

Jiffy 7s are compressed peat pots contained in a thin mesh net made of polythene. They come dry and compressed, and expand to their full size once soaked. They have proved extremely successful in rooting a wide range of greenhouse plants.

for pots, largely for pricking off seedlings, but in more recent years they have also been used for the rooting of cuttings and seed sowing. The automatic blockmaker not only makes the block but sows pelleted or split pill seeds automatically and is used mainly by large scale vegetable growers. Soil blocks must be sufficiently compacted otherwise they can disintegrate, and it is essential to hold the blocks in trays or boxes.

Bedding plant pots, trays, seed boxes and propagators

While wooden seed boxes suitably treated against rapid deterioration are still available in standard sizes ($14 \times 9 \times 2$in), these are tending to be ousted by plastic trays. Fish boxes have long been the main plant container for commercial bedding plant production, but the trend is now towards polystyrene trays complete with plastic dome lids. Drainage occurs in wooden boxes through the spaces left between the bottom spars, although some gardeners

make further holes. Ex-fish boxes tend to be both smelly and contaminated with salt, and they are best kept outside for a weathering period.

Plastic seed trays are usually available in the following sizes with slight variations according to suppliers: $8\frac{3}{4} \times 6\frac{1}{2} \times 2$in; $14 \times 9 \times 2$in (standard); $14 \times 9 \times 3$in; $10 \times 10 \times 2\frac{3}{4}$in; $24 \times 12\frac{1}{2} \times 3$in; $24 \times 12\frac{1}{2} \times 3$in (heavyweight). Polystyrene trays are generally of standard size ($14 \times 9 \times 2$in) although they are also available as break-up units (four units each constructed for 10–12 plants) so that customers can buy their bedding plants in small quantities without root disturbance. Plastic packs are also available in the same basic form.

Apart from the break-up units, the role of all these boxes or trays is similar—seed sowing, rooting of cuttings and pricking off. Their respective merits culturally cause tremendous conflict of opinion; hygiene is a major advantage with plastic trays whereas the risk of disease carry-over

Square peat pots have the advantage of fitting neatly into ordinary seed boxes. Growth is excellent, and the seedlings suffer little or no root disturbance when planted out. The side of the box has been removed to show the roots of the marigolds beginning to grow through the sides of the peat pots. This is the moment to plant out.

in wooden boxes is very real, necessitating washing with a solution of 1:49 formaldehyde, or cresylic acid at 1:39, some weeks before use. Expanded polystyrene, due to its insulating properties, offers a warm home for the plant, but in some quarters the opinion is that plants do not thrive so readily in polystyrene as in plastic or wood; this is possibly because its porosity makes water application more tricky.

Plastic dome covers are designed to cover all sizes of plastic trays, forming very convenient mini-propagating cases, possibly an ideal arrangement for the gardener with limited propagating space in the greenhouse and needing to use a porch or even a light window in the home for additional space.

Fig 51

Seed sowing

Preparation

Where soil-containing compost is to be used in clay pots follow the filling procedure shown in Fig 51. With plastic pots it is

Another view of a seed-box filled with peat pots. Note how neatly they fit to give maximum productivity. This is still further increased by the very low failure rate on transplanting owing to the almost complete absence of root disturbance.

perhaps doubtful whether the layer of roughage is justified (except for very fine slow-germinating seeds) especially if a modern soilless mix is used. For boxes or containers it is doubtful whether any crocks are needed, as the admittance of air and moisture movement are more influenced by evenness of consolidation than anything else, provided the compost has a good texture.

Always use *warm* compost, firming it well with the fingers to the corners and then levelling off with a pot-firmer or the base of another pot or suitably sized box about $\frac{1}{2}$in below the pot or box level. Compartmentalised trays should be filled in the same general manner, although firming is more readily achieved by 'dumping'. The surface of the compost can be finished off with some light coloured fine sand, especially for very tiny seeds like lobelia or primula, as it not only enables the distribution of seeds to be observed but ensures intimate contact of seed on compost. Once again with special soilless seed composts this procedure may not be thought essential. A level surface on top of the receptacle is, however, necessary for fine seeds in all circumstances.

Prior to sowing, all compost-filled receptacles should be thoroughly watered with a fine rose and allowed to drain, during which interval labels should be prepared, showing plant species, variety and date of sowing. Plastic labels have almost entirely ousted wooden tallies, although there is a lot to be said for the cheapness of the latter on a short-term basis.

Sowing methods

Open the seed packet by tearing off a corner, shake the seed into a piece of paper and use the finger and thumb to distribute it evenly on the prepared compost—this can be difficult if the seed is very dust-like. Alternatively a folded piece of paper can be used as a spill and the seeds encouraged to come out evenly by gentle shaking. At what density to sow seeds depends a lot on circumstances; it is always better to err on the thin side than to sow so thickly that the little seedlings are overcrowded, a state of

affairs that leads to the encouragement of damping-off disease.

Fine seeds are not covered, merely being pressed into the top of the compost; most other seeds are covered with a little sifted compost, either scattered on with the fingers or worked through a fine ($\frac{1}{8}$–$\frac{1}{4}$in) riddle or sieve, a soup strainer being a useful item of equipment at amateur level. The depth of covering is related directly to the size of the seed. The covering can be gently firmed if thought necessary. When seeds are sown individually they are simply inserted into the receptacle by hand just below the surface. Pelleted and pilled seeds are sown *on* the surface.

Germination

Whether to follow the traditional practice and cover seeds first with a sheet of glass and then paper, or to leave the seeds on an open bench, perhaps with mist irrigation, or alternatively to place them in a germinating cabinet, is definitely a matter of personal choice and the facilities available. Germinating temperatures vary greatly, but as a general rule 65-75°F (18-24°C) is desirable day and night, although for more specific recommendations see cultural notes in Part II. In 90 per cent of cases the amateur gardener will use the glass and paper method to ensure humid conditions and avoid drying out, examining the seedlings regularly to observe signs of germination and wiping moisture from the glass. Where mist propagation is practised in boxes or receptacles such surveillance is not so necessary, but in a germinating cabinet (which is dark) constant vigilance is required. It is important, as soon as a major percentage of the seedlings *germinate,* to bring them into the light, otherwise etiolation occurs, which results in a badly weakened plant very prone to disease attack. At the same time care must be taken *not* to subject the little seedlings to excess sunlight, which can burn them up badly, and this means using temporary shading, blinds or green coloured polythene.

Watering

Whether watering is required before germination occurs depends much on species, coupled with temperature level and humidity of atmosphere. Drying out must not occur, and the practice of using capillary benches for germinating purposes has much in its favour in this respect, as applying water overhead can expose the seeds and leave them proud of the compost. Alternatively the receptacle can be immersed in a tray of water.

One reason why germinating cabinets are favoured in commercial circles is to avoid the watering problem, as the humidity in them is so high that watering is seldom, if ever, needed before germination occurs. Where mist units are used for germinating purposes it matters little whether the the seedling is exposed, as it is kept continually moist by the watering and damage by excessive exposure to the sun is unlikely.

Once seedlings are developing freely on the greenhouse bench in a position of good light they should be watered freely accord-ing to demands, avoiding over-watering and the provision of too humid an atmosphere which will encourage damping-off. Preventive measures for damping-off are described in the chapter on pests and diseases.

Difficulties

Under most circumstances and with seed of a non-temperamental nature, air, moisture and correct temperature will bring about germination in a specific number of days. Delay in germination may be caused by faulty seed or careless storing, or by the wrong germinating conditions for the species, especially in respect of temperature and light. Compost with poor structure, inhibiting the entry of oxygen, will literally stop the seed breathing, as indeed will saturation of the compost. Drying out could also be disastrous.

Some seeds have naturally hard testas (eg sweet peas) and some pre-soaking treatment can speed up germination—by chipping, rubbing with sandpaper, soaking

Germination of ipomea seeds in Jiffy strips. These strips are rows of preformed peat pots. One seed is sown to each pot, and when the time comes to transplant the pots are simply severed without disturbing the seedlings.

briefly in very hot water or in warm water for a long period or alternatively for a specified period in strong sulphuric acid (this requires precise reference to a botanical list). Sometimes a period of cold followed by warmth will bring about germination; hardy primulas for example can be sown and left outside over the winter, then brought in to germinate in the spring with ease. Such complications are, however, more the exception than the rule.

Seed sowing in frames and borders

What has been said about the sowing of seed in pots, pans or boxes applies generally in the case of sowing seeds in frames, the seed being sown in many cases in the actual ground, although it can be sown in receptacles; follow the same principles of shade for a few days and regular watering thereafter. No special conditions apply other than adequate soil preparation, checking its lime and nutrient content by analysis, a good firm seed bed and the avoidance of drying out. Seed can be sown in drills, or spaced out, or sown broadcast, as with brassicas, which can be merely scattered on the surface before either being covered with some riddled soil or pressed in with the back of a spade.

Weed control may be a problem in frames, necessitating sterilisation either with chemicals or by heat, although weedkillers such as paraquat can be used on the delayed seed bed technique, ie soil is prepared some weeks in advance of sowing and paraquat applied 2–3 days *after* sowing. Alternatively specific weedkillers such as CIPC can be applied.

The same general principles apply when sowing seeds direct in greenhouse borders.

Ancillary propagating equipment

Dibbers can be made with any convenient piece of stick 4–5in in length and pointed at one end, or plastic dibbers can be purchased. Dibbers are used for space-sowing seed; marking holes for the insertion of cuttings; for pricking off, making the indentation necessary to receive the little

plants; and either a dibber or tally can be used for easing young plants out of their pots or boxes.

A series of round or rectangular firmers with handles are invaluable where a lot of seed sowing is involved. Any handyman can make these up. A similar sort of item with nails or wooden pegs inserted is useful for pricking off on a large scale, being pressed into the prepared box to make the little holes to take the young plants (see Fig 52). A fine-rosed watering can is an essential, as also are some metal trays for immersing the trays or pots when water is to be given from below. Seed sowers made of plastic are also available, although many gardeners prefer to use their fingers. A professional gardener sowing many boxes of bedding plants every year will find a series of little measures extremely useful to measure the correct amount of seed per box. A series of fine sieves can be made from metal mesh material tacked on to wooden framework, or fine $\frac{1}{16}$, $\frac{1}{8}$ and $\frac{1}{4}$in riddles can be purchased. Sheets of glass of various sizes for covering boxes are essential, unless plastic dome covers are available for plastic trays. For removing cuttings from plants use either a *sharp* thin knife or razor blade, preferably one-sided for safety or in a special holder.

Pricking off procedures

It is essential to move seedlings on or prick them off when they are sown broadcast; those which are sown individually are left undisturbed, which apart from the

Fig 52

196

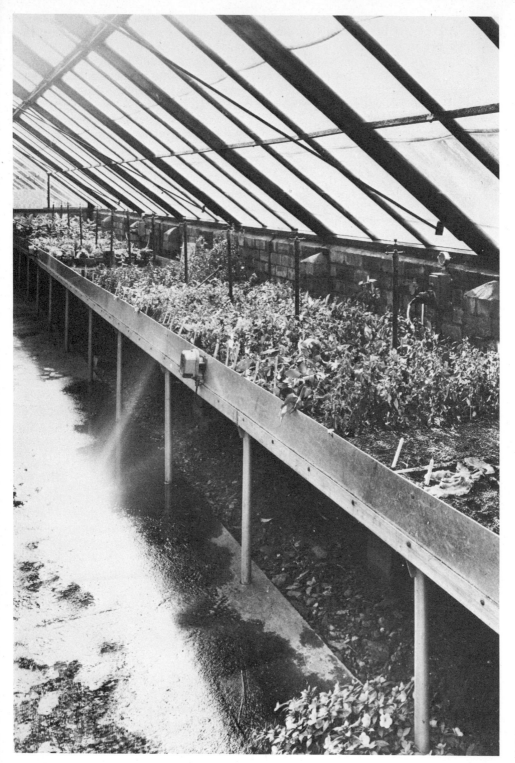

A greenhouse bench
designed for mist
propagation.

Fig 53

Boxes are generally used for pricking out, using a compost nutritionally acceptable for the time of year. For most bedding plants allow about forty-eight per standard tray. The little seedlings must not be planted too deeply and they should be firmed gently with the base of the dibber.

Rather close, humid conditions are given for a few days after pricking off the plants then being given good light and plenty of air, subsequent treatment depending on method of culture dictated by species. A period of hardening off or acclimatisation will be necessary for plants being moved to cooler quarters or out of doors, whereas permanently housed greenhouse plants will eventually be potted on, the same being true of plants being maintained in the greenhouse for stock supply purposes.

Propagation of ferns from spores
(See Fig 53).
Spore sowing involves the use of very well-crocked pots and a very fine compost, the compost being watered by immersion before the spores are pressed into the surface and covered with glass. Place in a saucer or water to retain moisture. The little plants which appear should be pricked off individually.

Labelling
Always label seed boxes, pots and so on, with either plastic or wooden labels, giving dates, species and variety.

saving in time, is in fact one of the major advantages of this technique. Pricking off involves very careful extraction of individual seedlings or groups of seedlings (in the case of lobelia) using a dibber or tally and avoiding serious damage to roots. The advantages of early pricking off were emphasised by the John Innes Horticultural Institute many years ago.

Chapter 18
Vegetative Propagation

Many plants propagate themselves vegetatively by means of crowns, runners, suckers, rhizomes, tubers, natural layering, and of course by bulbs and corms. We are concerned here not with natural but with 'artificial' methods of vegetative propagation, primarily the use of stem cuttings.

Inducing the sections of vegetative tissue taken from a plant to form roots is a technique with many advantages over seed propagation. Speed is one of them, so also is the production of a plant with identical characteristics to the parent (with certain exceptions). Obviously this has great advantages in propagation, as it enables good forms to be readily perpetuated. *Coleus blumei*, for example, is readily raised from seed and the resulting seedlings are generally varied and in many cases of interesting colour form. To sow seed selected from a desirable openly pollinated plant would most likely result in further variance, whereas cuttings taken and rooted will perpetuate the form and colour. These are commonly called 'clones'.

The main disadvantage of vegetative propagation concerns possible disease transmission. Some degree of selection must of course be constantly exercised by a vigorous process of roguing, as is necessary with dahlias propagated from cuttings arising from over-wintered tubers. While the F_1 seedlings of dahlias offer endless possibilities for bedding display work, cuttings are the only way of ensuring the fixed forms and disease transmission is therefore a major problem in both commercial and amateur circles. This is also true of chrysanthemums. The use of heat therapy to burn out virus infection and so enable only clean stock to be vegetatively propagated is referred to in a later chapter. The technique is one which amateurs may hesitate to use.

Botanical aspects of vegetative propagation

The ability of a plant to 'think' and pursue a deliberate course of planned action is still a matter of dispute in the botanical world. That a plant is without feelings and merely accepts its fate with stoicism is not accepted by some botanists, the most recent work in this direction being done in Russia. The fact remains, however, that the gardener, not the plant, must generally make the decision when and how to propagate, and at the same time try to interpret the optimum conditions for encouraging the portion of plant selected to become self-supporting as soon as possible. 'Wound shock' invariably arises when it is severed from its parent; it must be encouraged over the shock, and simultaneously persuaded to put out roots.

The first stage of propagation is when the cambium layer which exists between the phloem and the xylem in dicotyledonous plants forms a skin or callus over the wound. This is both to prevent loss of moisture and to protect against fungal and bacterial invasion. This cambium layer then stimulates either dormant buds or root primordia to form, both in the area of severance and further up the stem. It is interesting to note that while buds form stems above ground from external tissue, roots are formed from internal tissue. There must obviously be a subtle differentiation in root origin between different types and portions of plants. If, for example, one takes a cutting from a chrysanthemum stool or dahlia tuber well down near the root ('Irishman's cuttings') when there will no doubt be root initials present, then roots will develop externally. What significance this may have on the ultimate performance of the newly formed plant is a matter for hot debate in specialist exhibition circles, yet for the average gardener the theory of it all matters little, the important issue being the formation of roots. It must also be repeated that the role of the cambium is vital in most aspects of propagation (including grafting and budding) to bring about union between two sections of a plant.

Hygiene is important when removing a portion of plant from its parent, as also is the avoidance of jagged tears, so leaving tissue without a cambium layer to form a skin and protect itself against attack from weak pathogenic organisms. On the other hand, there is an increasing use of the snap-off technique of severing cuttings (avoiding any mechanical means other than those necessary to remove the stipules or leaves), this being practised almost universally in the nurseries of specialist chrysanthemum and pelargonium raisers. This is perhaps mainly a preventive measure against the spreading of disease, though it is also contended that the tissue is more severely wounded by mechanical means, whether it be with a knife or a razor blade, cells actually being dissected, whereas with snapping the cells break off at the cell walls. This raises the further interesting line of thought that the urge to recover from the shock of snapping off might be less than that experienced on mechanical removal.

Hormones or auxins

Hormones or auxins occur naturally in all living plants and are responsible for triggering off cell activity or chemical processes. They are chemical 'messengers' which encourage changes in activity without themselves becoming changed in nature. Their effect on growth behaviour is profound and they are conveyed rapidly around the plant according to the special demands necessitated by changing circumstances, of which the initiation of new roots on plant sections removed from the parent is a typical example. Should there be a shortage of hormones or auxins in the portion of plant removed from the parent, research work has shown that certain chemical substances will produce a res-

ponse similar to that produced by natural mones, and indeed may in fact be more effective than natural hormones in certain instances. Such materials are called growth regulators and are used for a wide range of purposes including weed control, growth suppression and, most important in the context of propagation, inducing new roots to form. How these hormones act on plants is complicated in the extreme, but obtaining the right response is largely a matter of using the correct material and the proper dilution at the right time.

While, generally speaking, the use of hormones speeds up the rooting process, this is not always the case, nor is it certain that the hormones will induce roots to form on difficult species. Experience over the years shows that an artificial hormone material is more useful on soft leafy material and at fairly high propagating temperatures in the 65–75°F (18–24°C) range. Solutions of the hormone can be used to immerse the base of the prepared cutting material for 18–24 hours; it is rinsed with water before insertion. The more popular method is to dip the wet base of the prepared cutting in a powder containing the hormone and this is perhaps more hygienic. Directions on the use of hormones are issued with the respective products and should be closely followed.

Types of stem cuttings

It is important that the selected cutting is in good physical condition, free from obvious pests and diseases and with sufficient reserves of food in the form of carbohydrates and proteins to sustain it until it is capable of separate existence and consequent vegetative increase in root, stem and leaf.

It has been stated over the years that soft cuttings are undesirable, this relating to their high ratio of nitrogen to carbohydrates, and while there is undoubtedly some foundation for such a belief, it would not appear to be wholly substantiated by the more modern methods of propagating practised on commercial holdings. Here soft, actively growing cuttings of chrysan-

200

themums and other plants are often preferred to those of a harder nature. There is obviously a difference between active growth in good light and lush softness, however, and the latter should generally be avoided as there are unlikely to be sufficient food reserves to sustain the tissue. Whether it is, in the light of modern technology, desirable to follow older practice and let stock plants intended for provision of cuttings become pot bound and harden their growth in any way by limited nitrogen application and other means is open to debate, it now being thought better to encourage more liberal growth. The age of material selected for cuttings varies, but as a general rule younger tissue contains a higher proportion of meristematic (actively dividing) cells.

There are three main types of stem cuttings—soft, semi-hard and hard, but in greenhouse culture we are more concerned with the soft or semi-hard group.

Soft cuttings

A great variety of greenhouse plants are raised from soft cuttings because the growth of many greenhouse plants is of a soft nature. Soft cuttings are, however, also taken from a vast number of outside plants herbaceous, alpine and shrub. As the name implies, the cuttings are selected from soft new growth which either arises from the base of the plant in the spring, eg basal cuttings from chrysanthemums, cuttings arising from dahlia tubers or from the new growth which frequently develops out of doors after a plant has completed flowering, as with pelargoniums. Plants can often be cut back to induce fresh new growth to develop, this being true of ericas and a great many more.

A mist propagating unit is virtually essential to the rooting of soft tip cuttings. Many plants that could not be rooted at all before the invention of mist propagation are now considered easy with its aid.

201

Removing soft cuttings from the plant involves first of all careful selection of balanced non-etiolated (not drawn or spindly) growth which snaps off cleanly, generally but not always below a node, which is the area from which leaves and buds arise and generally possessed of a wealth of meristematic cells. Many plants can be rooted very simply from internodal cuttings, but gardeners generally prefer to take cuttings below a node (see Fig 54) as their rooting conditions are not as sophisticated as those of the commercial grower; internodal cuttings could suffer a period of die-back and the risk of disease. Certainly with those plants having a soft or hollow stem, nodal cuttings are more reliable. Heels can be left on some plants to advantage (see Fig 55) as this exposes a larger cambium area and is very useful for a lot of soft wooded cuttings removed from shrubs such as deutzia, philadelphus and many more. While non-flowering section cuttings are desirable others can be used, although the flowering stem should be removed to avoid using up valuable reserves of food. The base of cuttings should be trimmed, removing stipules or other superfluous tissue which would merely rot if left.

The size of cuttings varies, but 2–5in is average. Lower leaves should removed, not only to reduce the transpiration area, but to avoid rotting. Where a shrub has very large leaves (eg hydrangea) it is permissible to reduce the leaf area by half or thereabouts, but a reasonable area of active leaf is essential ro the rooting process, as a soft shrub deprived of its leaves to the extreme tends to debilitate rather than produce root. Pipings of carnations are simply pulled out of a node and, after removing the lower leaves, inserted in the rooting medium (see Fig 56).

Rooting

Apart from some cacti and succulents, all cuttings should be placed in rooting mecium as soon as possible. Where rooting hormones are used, the cuttings should be immersed or dipped in this according to directions. Fungicidal waterings or dustings may be advisable, especially with soft

Fig 54   Fig 55

material in very bad weather to avoid ever present disease such as botrytis. The rooting period for soft cuttings can vary from 2–3 days for coleus, up to 3–4 weeks or even longer; the average is 10–21 days. A high success rate is usually possible in mist units, propagating cases or polythene tents.

The provision of a humid atmosphere is a basic essential for the successful rooting of all *soft stem* cuttings. This is achieved by the use of mist propagation units, propagating cases, plastic domes or white polythene tents or bags, the basic objective of these techniques being to reduce transpiration and enable the cutting to conserve its energies for the vital process of producing new roots. It is advisable to group cuttings, the quicker rooting species being kept apart from those that take longer. Quick-rooting dahlias, chrysanthemums and coleus should obviously not be grouped with conifers and heathers. Stating a precise rooting period for each species is difficult owing to varying conditions, but when possible an indication will be given

Fig 57

Fig 56

in the cultural notes. Downy leaved species tend to rot in too close an atmosphere such as that under polythene tents because of moisture collecting on the leaves, resulting in botrytis.

An open free-draining warm rooting medium is the prime requisite for maintaining cuttings turgid and in good condition for the quick formation of roots. They can readily be housed in boxes or benches of rooting media with bottom heat provided either by soil warming cables or mini-bore or under-bench heating. Many cuttings can be rooted, perhaps less quickly but with great success, under cooler conditions, either in a greenhouse or frame, heated or cold, or in white polythene tunnels.

The qualities of rooting media are fully discussed elsewhere and the importance of studying this subject in depth cannot be over-emphasised. In the most general terms mixtures of half peat and half sand are most frequently used for rooting a wide range of species. Preparation of the cuttings and insertion distances vary according to species; again in general most soft cuttings are inserted 1–2in apart (Fig 57).

Semi-hard cuttings
This term relates to material which has become partly lignified, or in other words has started to become woody, especially at the base. Propagation by means of semi-hard cuttings relates almost exclusively to the propagation of shrubs from July until September, a wide range of shrubs being propagated during this period with shoots carefully pulled off with a heel, which is trimmed of any surplus thin tissue obviously not containing any cambium cells. Rooting time depends much on the maturity of the tissue, although with many species 2–7 weeks is average, but also on temperature provided.

Hardwood cuttings
As the name implies, this mode of propagation involves the use of mature lignified wood and is a technique which has application both out of doors and under glass. It is

usual to select well-matured one-year-old growth of various lengths: up to 3–4ft long in the case of salix (willow); a more usual length is 8–12in, as for blackcurrants; but cuttings can also be very short, eg 2–3in in the case of roses. A heel of older wood is not only advantageous in some cases, but thought to be essential with many conifers, although once again with modern propagation methods views are changing in this direction. It is essential that each cutting has at least one live bud near its tip, and when the unripe tips of the shoots are removed care should be taken to leave the bud at the apex of the tip, otherwise die-back to the bud will occur with consequent risk of disease (see Fig 58). The base is trimmed below a node in the majority of cases. Buds may be left at the base of the cutting when a stool is required, as for blackcurrants; conversely where a leg is required, eg for red currants, the lower buds are removed, leaving only buds at the tip.

The etiolation of hardwood cuttings by earthing is thought to be desirable for many fruit trees, although more recent techniques concerned with storage of the normal cuttings in temperature controlled

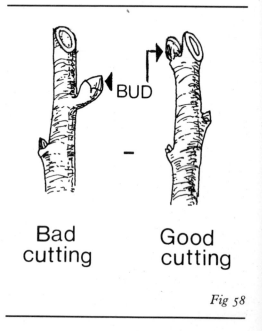

Bad
cutting

Good
cutting

Fig 58

Fig 59

bins have given highly successful results.

'Eyes' are hardwood cuttings with a section of stem on both sides of the node (Fig 59), as in vines, although they can readily be propagated from soft shoots also.

Hardwood cuttings are usually taken in the autumn when they may be inserted individually out of doors or in a cool greenhouse or, as with fruit cuttings, stored in heated bins until spring. It is interesting to note that while evergreen species of shrubs bear leaves deciduous species do not, and this would lead one to assume that only the leaf-bearing species would respond to a heated propagating case. Such is not always the case, however, and quite dramatic results have been obtained by inserting nearly dormant hardwood cuttings bereft of leaves into warm propagating benches, where under the influence of moisture and heat they have broken into growth and been rooted with ease (eg roses). Research is proceeding with the rooting of a great many other species of dormant hardwood cuttings under propagating house conditions and under white polythene.

Root cuttings

These are not commonly used for greenhouse plants, although many species of shrubs and border plants may conveniently be rooted in a frame or greenhouse. The method is to lay suitably sized portions of root (in the case of *Phlox paniculata* these are about $1\frac{1}{2}$–2in long) in a box of compost, covered by about $\frac{1}{2}$-$\frac{3}{4}$in of the same compost; but here again reference should be made to books relating to the propagation of shrubs, herbaceous plants and fruit trees. In the case of phlox root cuttings are used not only for convenience but to avoid the spread of eelworm. Root cuttings may sometimes not give rise to identical progeny.

Leaf and leaf petiole cuttings

The production of adventitious buds in the fleshy leaves of many plants is well known, the best example being *Begonia rex*, where the fleshy leaves, if cut at the main veins and pegged down with small pebbles or footing media in a propagating case, will invariably produce little plants at the points of incision. Leaf petioles of streptocarpus and saintpaulia are well known examples of greenhouse plants propagated by detaching the plant with the petioles, which are inserted fairly deeply in a rooting medium in pots or boxes. Streptocarpus leaves are often better reduced to half their size to avoid excess moisture loss. Many shrubs also lend themselves to this technique.

Leaf bud cuttings

This involves the use of a bud stem section with the cambium exposed either by removing a bud, as carried out for rose budding, or with a leaf left in the case of camellias, although both of these can be propagated by leaving the stem intact and making a cut at its base. In both cases the cuttings are inserted around the edge of a pot.

Meristem propagation

This is a technique used by specialist raisers whereby the tip of the growing plant involving the meristem is selected

205

Bottom-heat is essential
to the rooting of many
cuttings.

and grown in agar solution. It is thought that this area is free from fungal and virus infection.

Layering

This has not a great deal of application in greenhouse culture, although an excellent example is chlorophytum; the flower tips can be pegged to the ground (Fig 60). Layering can be applied, however, to a vast range of woody specimens grown in the greenhouse, when it is convenient to layer a stem into a pot of compost. Border carnations grown indoors are also typical of the layering technique, when stems are pegged down into compost after making a short elongated cut through the stem.

Air layering can also be carried out with plants such as ficus which become too tall, although it can also be applied to a number of species by removing a ring around the stem, dusting the wound with a hormone powder before wrapping moist sphagnum moss around the wound and covering this with a ring of polythene secured carefully top and bottom with rubber bands (see Fig 61). The polythene allows air to enter but prevents loss of moisture.

The practice of grafting under glass

The process of grafting involves the bringing together of the cambium layers of selected stocks and scions, there being several methods of achieving this, only a limited number of which have application under glass. Grafting is a more likely operation under glass commercially than in amateur spheres, although there is nothing to stop the gardener with specialised interests carrying it out successfully. If there is one vital clue to successful grafting in most of its forms, including budding, it is to appreciate the importance of a union of cambium layer, without which failure is inevitable.

Grafting under glass allows work to be carried on over a longer period, and as humid conditions can invariably be created, the normal protection and sealing of the

Fig 60

Fig 62

Fig 63

Fig 61

graft area is not essential.

Saddle grafting of rhododendrons

Perhaps the most usual operation is the saddle grafting of rhododendrons (Fig 62), when selected variety scions are grafted on to *R. ponticum* stocks. Stock and scion should be approximately of the same diameter, the stock being previously potted up (9–12in high) in a 5–6in pot and brought into the greenhouse from outside in January, February or March, and after a few days cut back to 1½-2in. By making a cut with a sharp knife an inverted V is formed, compensating cuts being made in a 3–4in four-leaf terminal bud-bearing section of the selected scion. After fitting the scion carefully in the stock, ensuring that at least one and preferably both sides of the respective cambiums correspond,

208

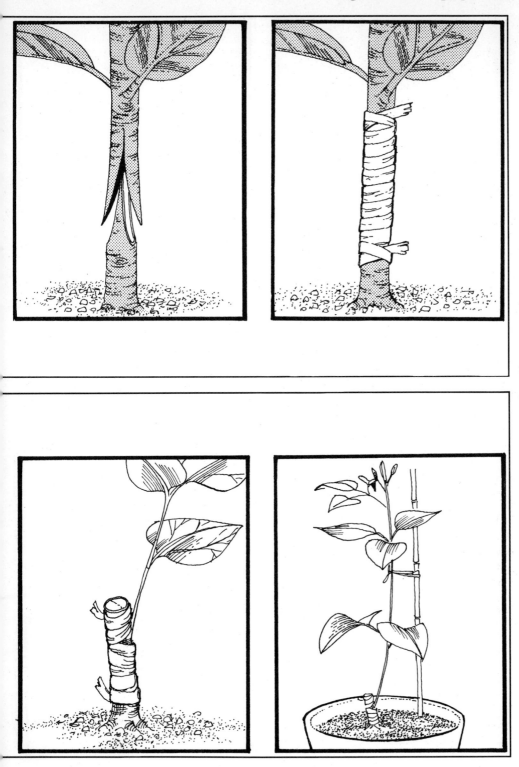

the union is bound up tightly with raffia (see Fig 62). They are then placed in a warm propagating case until a union is effected, when fresh vegetative development appears on the scion. Magnolias and fruit trees can be raised by this method also. Many rhododendrons previously saddle grafted are now rooted from cuttings.

Splice grafting is also practised under glass, especially with *Cytisus battandieri*, which is a weak grower on its own roots and is grafted on to a stock of common laburnum, potted up in the same way as rhododendrons and brought under glass. A splice graft is the same as a whip and tongue graft without the tongue, and simply involves two slanting cuts, it once again being imperative that one side of both stock and scion corresponds, before binding up with raffia. Roses and clematis (on *C. vitalba* stock) are also propagated in this way, although cleamtis are now frequently grown on their own roots. The method is to take soft shoots from a greenhouse-grown plant of the desired variety and make two scions from one but cutting the stem down the centre. Roots of *C. vitalba* raised from seed sown in the previous March are cut back to 2in above ground-level and a compensating 1in cut is made in the stock, with a lip, allowing the half stem of the variety to be fitted in and bound with raffia before placing in a closed propagating frame (see Fig 63).

Double forms of *Gysophila paniculata* are grafted on to seed-raised stocks of the single form, but in this case wedge-shaped stocks of the double form are inserted in split root stocks before being bound up with raffia (Fig 64). This is usually carried out during February or March. Here again this practice has tended to fall into disuse as double forms are now raised successfully on their own roots. Cacti also are grafted in this way.

Inarching or approach grafting is sometimes carried out under glass, when the stock and scions of roughly similar size and growth, and in pots, are bared of a 2in slip of bark and brought together by tying with raffia.

Conventional budding can be carried out under glass with roses and other species, although there is no great advantage in this other than perhaps speed for the specialist gardener or plant breeder (Fig 65).

Fig 65

Sources of propagating material

These are many and varied. With increased specialisation taking place in most spheres of greenhouse culture, there are many central sources of cuttings produced by specialist raisers under strict supervision (virus diseases and fungal disorders are readily distributed by vegetative propagation). Due to poor winter light in Britain, provision is also made for cutting material from the Mediterranean zone, particularly with chrysanthemums and carnations.

The constant stream of new varieties to replace worn out or deteriorating stocks of plants, more especially chrysanthemums and dahlias, necessitates constant reappraisal of the situation and the purchase of reliable new stock at fairly regular intervals, a lot depending on the intensity of culture. With specialised pot plants such as pelargoniums the same pattern prevails, and specialist producers of young plants retain stock plants under strict supervision; the same is true of specialist fruit tree or soft fruit producers.

Fig 64

A modern glass-to-ground
cedarwood greenhouse.
One of the most popular
models for the amateur.

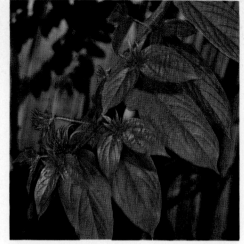

Quisqualis indica, the Ragoon creeper, a stunning greenhouse scandent shrub in much the same idiom as *Euphorbia pulcherrima*.

Hibiscus rosa-sinensis, a greenhouse shrub with huge flamboyant flowers in colours from yellow through orange to crimson.

Cascade chrysanthemum 'Sunrise'.

Adenium obesum, the
desert rose, a curious
succulent forming a
short, grossly swollen stem
and bearing its flowers at
the tips of quite thin
shoots.

Many crocus species make ideal plants for the alpine house. Some of the finest ones flower in mid winter when their flowers would be ruined by weather out of doors.

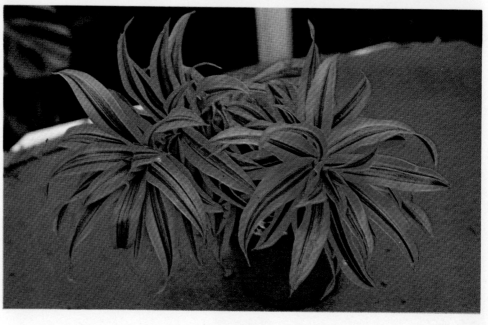

Pleome reflexa 'Song of India', a very fine variegated form of this slow-growing greenhouse shrub.

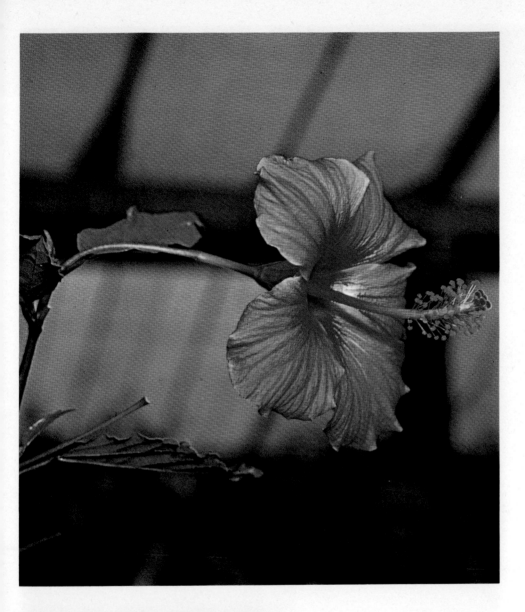

Hibiscus rosa-sinensis,
another form of this
delightful greenhouse
shrub. The flowers can
measure up to 8 inches
across.

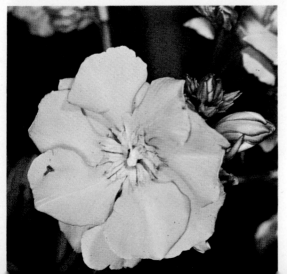

Nerium oleander, the
common oleander of
Mediterranean holiday
resorts, grown both for its
large colourful flowers and
for its delightful scent.

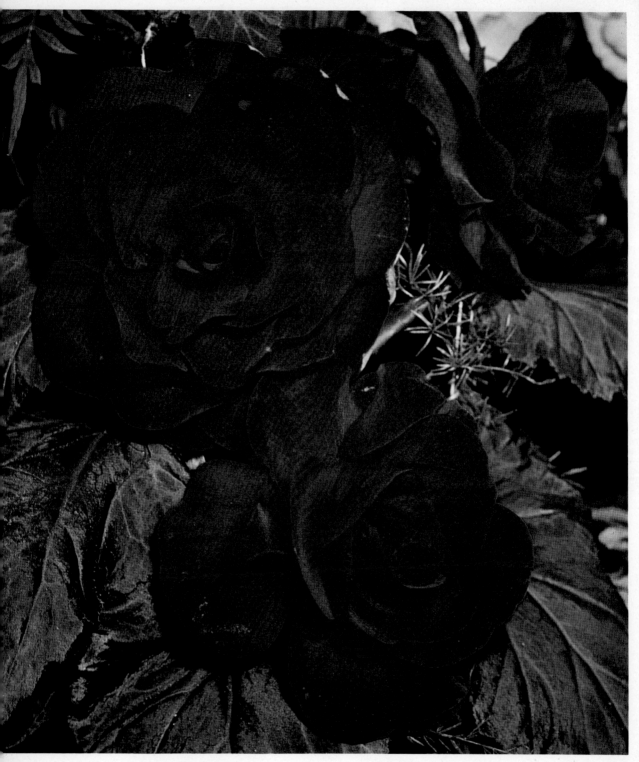

Begonia 'Firebrand', one of
the most brilliantly coloured
of all begonia cultivars.

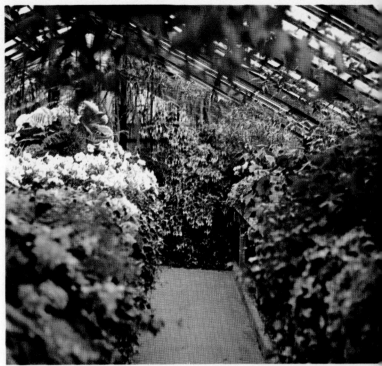

Allamanda cathartica, the
most spectacular of this
genus of scandent
greenhouse shrubs. It is
exceedingly poisonous in
all its parts.

A general view of a well-
managed greenhouse.

Another view of the same
greenhouse, showing the
broad, uncluttered path.

*Maranta leuconeura
kerchoveana*, a popular
foliage house and
greenhouse pot plant.

Brunfelsia calycina, a striking greenhouse shrub. Popularly known as the 'Yesterday, today and tomorrow bush' because the flowers open deep purple, fade to mauve the second day and white the third day, falling on the fourth.

Primula x kewensis, one of the most popular of all the primulas grown as flowering pot plants in the greenhouse. It is an ideal candidate for a soilless compost.

Coleus probably offer a wider range of coloured leaves than any other group of plants that can be grown in greenhouses. There are numerous named forms, and seedlings are always worth raising.

The alpine house, a general view. Note the solid staging designed to take the weight of the six inches of loose grit in which the plants are embedded in their pots.

Gloxinias and streptocarpus are both popular flowering greenhouse pot plants. The plant shown here, known as *Gloxinia* 'Saxon Court' is, in fact, an intergeneric hybrid between the two.

A greenhouse stocked with mainly flowering pot-plants. Though this may look effective, many of the plants are grown in a reserve house and only brought into the display house when in flower.

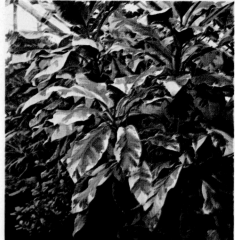

One of the boldest of variegated greenhouse shrubs, *Pisonia brunoniana* 'Variegata'.

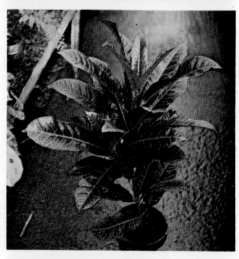

A splendid croton, *Codiaeum* 'Emperor William'. The broader the leaves of crotons the more tender they are. Narrow-leaved forms will withstand much cooler conditions.

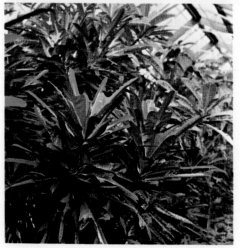

Another croton, *Codiaeum* 'Fred Sanders', another tender broad-leaved variety.

Above
An unnamed croton seedling with relatively narrow leaves. This is a fine bushy specimen, but plants need plenty of light if they are to branch.

Below
Codiaeum langii sport, a very striking plant. Avoid cutting crotons back in the hope of making them branch: unless plenty of charcoal powder is applied to the wound they may 'bleed' to death.

Zingiber officinale, whose roots provide ginger. The flowers are borne a little above the ground, with the leaves growing much taller. Needs plenty of room in the greenhouse border.

Begonia 'Mrs T. White'—a beautifully grown specimen.

Above
Philodendron erubescens 'Burgundy', the most colourful form of this plant. Though often grown as a house plant it seldom gives of its best except in the greenhouse.

Below
Lapageria rosea, one of the most beautiful of all greenhouse climbers. The waxy pink or white bells are six inches long and of tremendous substance. It does not require high temperatures.

Bougainvillea hybrida, a scandent tropical shrub ideal for training under the roof of the greenhouse. It needs careful pruning to keep it under control.

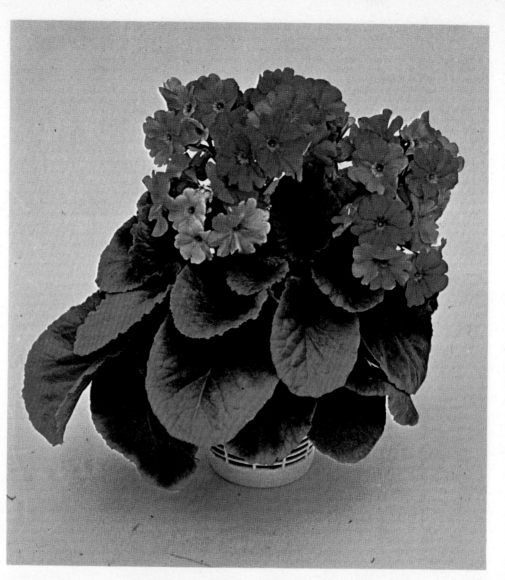

Primula obconica, an excellent pot plant for growing on in the greenhouse for home decoration when in flower.

Dwarf African marigolds can be grown on in the greenhouse until in flower before planting out, provided they are gradually and fully hardened.

Vine weevils *Otiorrhynchus
sulcatus* feeding on the
roots of *Cyclamen
persicum.*

Damping-off disease
Pythium spp. of lettuce
seedlings.

Spore pustules of Rust
Puccinina antirrhini
affecting antirrhinum stem
and leaves.

Galls *Exobasidium vaccinii* on azalea leaves. Though ugly, these are not fatal.

Below centre
Ray blight *Mycosphaerella ligulicola* affecting a chrysanthemum bloom.
Below bottom
Botrytis cinera infection of a carnation flower.

Distortion of a
chrysanthemum flower
due to the feeding activities
of capsid bugs *Lygus
rugulipennis*.

Scale insect infection of
aphelandra.

Part 2

On the Growing of Plants in Greenhouses

The reader is advised against considering these cultural notes in complete isolation. Reference should be made back to Part I where appropriate, especially to those chapters dealing with soil analysis, nutrition and growing media, and also to the book list at the end where specialist information is indicated.

For varieties the reader is urged to make full use of the current issues of the excellent catalogues published by the major seed houses and nursery firms, especially the firms whose names are acknowledged in the preface.

Chapter 19

The tomato, originally a small prostrate spreading plant from South America, belongs to the genus *Lycopersicon* and two distinct species, *L. esculentum* and *L. pimpinellifolium,* and several botanical varieties exist. The large-fruited tomato as we know it today still yearns for the high light conditions and warmth inherent in its make-up. Most crops of tomatoes are likely to be earlier and more successful in areas of good light in well-sited modern light-admitting greenhouses than they are in dull areas in greenhouses of poor design. For early crops the level of heating should also be sufficiently high and effectively distributed.

Nutritional standards for tomatoes

Tomatoes are greedy plants, especially when grown under glass and coerced into producing their maximum weight of fruit. It is generally accepted that for 50–60 tons per acre, which is 9–10lb of fruit per plant, the following nutrients are necessary!

	Amount per plant
800–1000lb potash (K_2O)	1oz
400–500lb nitrogen (N)	$\frac{1}{2}$oz
75–100lb phosphorus (P_2O_5)	$\frac{1}{8}$oz
110–130lb magnesium (MgO)	$\frac{1}{8}$oz
500–600lb calcium (CaO)	$\frac{1}{2}$oz

Allowing for loss through drainage and 'fixing' of phosphorus, especially in soil-based growing media, it is general to provide for about one-third of the plants' needs in the base dressing, this being made up to almost half by the nutrient reserves present in most soils or growing media, the remainder of the nutrients being supplied by liquid feeding or top dressing applications during the growing season. The calcium is supplied by adjustment of the pH figure. When border soils are intended for tomato culture it is advisable to have the soil analysed, the acceptable standards being as follows:

pH 6–6.5; 5.5–6 for soilless media

Nitrogen Owing to the extreme variability of the nitrogen figure and its presence in different forms and at different temperatures, ie as ammonium, nitrate, etc. this figure is not always available from soil laboratories, but when it is it should be stated as 'high' (100–150 ppm nitrate)

Phosphorus 50–60mg/100g P_2O_5 or 41–70 ppm P or index 5

Potash 60–80mg/100g K_2O or 500–700 ppm K or index 5

Soluble Salt figure pC 2.8–3, CF 15–10, Index 3–4

The nutrient levels of various composts used for tomato culture, ie John Innes Potting No 2 and soilless mixtures, are discussed in Chapter 15. A point of some importance which will be repeatedly stressed is the need to avoid high salt contents, especially at the propagating stage.

Deciding on cultural methods

The many and varied cultural methods for tomatoes which have been developed over the last decade tend to make a decision on any particular cultural method difficult. The main reason why so many methods have developed is to avoid soil sickness, persistent diseases such as deep-seated virus infection and brown root rot, and pests like the cyst-forming potato root eelworm. In addition, variation of cultural methods avoids most of the physiological disorders arising from monoculture.

Hydroponics Tomatoes can be grown successfully by this method, either on aggregate or in pure solution. The advantages and disadvantages are as for the above systems. (See note on new cultural techniques at end of this chapter.)

Comparison of cultural methods

Conventional border culture Plants grown in greenhouse borders.

For

Stable water and nutritional regime.
Generally speaking less water loss than
from containers, bales or troughs.
Excellent crops with *new* reliable soils.

Against

Seepage of water from outside may chill
soil. Control of water and nutrients
difficult as searching root system can develop
Soil slow and costly to warm up. Build-up
of pests, diseases, salts and plant acids.
Problems of excess vigour, especially when
soil sterilised by heat

Grafted plants in borders Standard varieties of tomatoes grafted on to root stocks with
inherent resistances.

For

Similar advantages to border culture in
respect of water regimes. Plants usually
grow well in unsterilised soil. Certain
varieties are now available with inherent
resistance to wilt disease

Against

As for border culture. Grafting is tedious
and costly, and requires extra propagating
space. Virus disease can readily be spread
during grafting, apart from which the
vigorous roots penetrate to virus infested
soil. Fruit can be later in developing. A
severe check to growth can occur if variety
root is removed on planting

Ring culture Plants are grown in 9in bottomless pots or other suitable 'rings', spaced
out on 4–6in layer of inert porous material (grit, ashes or gravel).

For

Only small quantities of clean or sterilised
media are required annually to ensure a
pest- and disease-free start at relatively low
cost. Growing media warms up quickly
and excellent vigour control can be
maintained. Ring culture successfully
overcomes deep-seated pest and disease
problems

Against

Feeding and watering are constant and
precise tasks; water loss is high, especially
in hot weather and early in the season
before roots are well developed in the
aggregate. The aggregate restricts border
use later for other crops, although
chrysanthemums in pots can be grown on
ring culture systems. Nutritional problems
can arise from the limited amount of
growing media in the ring

Straw bale culture Plants are set out on small ridges of soil or soilless media on 'heated'
straw bales.

For

An excellent warm start for plants with no
cold checks. Provides pest- and disease-
free conditions (provided clean compost is
used). A degree of CO_2
enrichment is provided by the
decomposing straw

Against

Large amounts of water are needed
initially and to keep the plants moist
throughout the season. Bales take up a lot
of room ('wads' can be used instead), are
costly in some areas, and there is a risk of
weedkiller contamination.

216

Plastic bags, peat troughs, polythene trenches, peat mattresses, bolsters, etc There are many variations of these methods, all involving limited quantities of growing media, renewed annually or biennially (and sometimes less often).

For	*Against*
Advantages similar to those for ring culture. Excellent control of growth can be exercised and crops of a high order achieved	Watering and feeding require great care to avoid build-up of salts. This is not the system for the occasional gardener, absent from home for long periods

Hydroponics Tomatoes can be grown successfully by this method, either on aggregate or in pure solution. The advantages and disadvantages are as for the above systems. (See note on new cultural techniques at end of this chapter.)

Planning for tomato growing

The two basic decisions which must be made concern the growing method and the timing of the crop, all other cultural aspects revolving around them. Given a new site on which a greenhouse is erected, where the soil by physical examination is of good structure and drainage, by laboratory analysis of acceptable nutritional status, and by eelworm determination found to be free of potato eelworm cysts containing live larvae, there is much to be said for using the existing soil. It should be borne in mind, however, that as the border soil becomes progressively more sick, sterilisation by either heat or chemicals will invariably be necessary if it is intended to continue border culture without grafting. Here again cost cannot be ignored, nor indeed can the practicability or otherwise of sterilisation. Where sterilisation or soil renewal is not feasible then the way is open for alternative cultural methods.

Crop schedules

A decision on timing needs careful assessment of all the factors: whether or not there is good natural light in the district concerned, the light-admitting qualities of the greenhouse, the efficiency of the heating system, whether or not one is prepared to pay the heating bill for early crops (remembering the availability of tomatoes all the year round from countries climatically more favourably placed). Some districts are known to be late maturing because of sun shut-off, exposure, industrial pollution, and so on. Conversely, the early cropping potential of favourable areas is also well known.

Early crop, no supplementary lighting

Propagation period	12–14 weeks
Sowing the seed	Mid/end November
Pricking off	End November/early December (8–12 days after sowing)
Spacing out	1st spacing early/mid-December (6–8in) 2nd spacing early/mid-January (12in) final spacing late January (15–16in if space available)
Planting out	1st–3rd week February (according to natural light levels)
Harvesting	Mid-March/early April

NOTE With later crops this time is considerably reduced, and there will be variation according to region and natural light level. As stated earlier, very early crops should not be attempted unless cultural facilities are excellent and light levels good.

Early crop, supplementary lighting

Propagation period	9–10 weeks
Sowing the seed	late November/early December
Pricking off	early/late December (after 8–12 days); light treatment then given for 17–21 days at 68°F (20°C) day 60°F (16°C) night according to growth rate or until spacing out the plants
Spacing out	As for the unlit crop, generally 2–3 times
Planting out	Variable; generally late January till early February. Earlier plantings are achieved because of benefits derived from supplementary lighting
Harvesting	Mid-March/mid-April, the effects of supplementary lighting depending greatly on area and type of season

Early crop, growing-room propagation

Propagation period	7–8 weeks
Sowing the seed	Mid-December
Pricking off	Late December (after 8–12 days), when light treatment (12–16 hours daily) at 78°F (26°C) 'day' 66°F (19°C) 'night' is given in the growing room for 14–21 days at 1,000 lumens until first truss is initiated. Small pots are required during light treatment, when thereafter the plants are potted up in 4¼in pots
Spacing out	6 × 6in in propagation house, when some supplementary lighting is beneficial (12–16 hours daily) for 7–10 days
Planting out	Late January/early February
Harvesting	Early March/early April (depending on natural light level of the area)

Second early crop, natural propagation

Propagation period	10–12 weeks (shorter if lights are used)
Sowing the seed	early/mid-December
Pricking off	late December/early January (after 10–14 days)
Spacing out	as for early crops
Planting out	end February/mid-March
Harvesting	Late April/early May

Mid-season crop

Propagation period	9–10 weeks (variable according to natural light level of the area)
Sowing the seed	late December/early January
Pricking off	mid-January (8–12 days after)
Spacing out	as before
Planting out	mid March/early April
Harvesting	early/mid-May

Late crop, in moderately heated greenhouse

Propagation period	8–9 weeks (or less)
Sowing the seed	from mid-February
Pricking off	late February
Spacing out	generally twice
Planting out	mid/late April
Harvesting	June

Later or cold crops, including follow-on crop

Propagating with heat, cold cropping in greenhouse. Mild heat in the greenhouse is, however, always advantageous, especially at night, to avoid high humidity.

Propagation period	6–7 weeks (8 in colder greenhouses)
Sowing the seed	early/mid March (in heat) until May for very late crops
Pricking off	late March/early April (in heat for early period) until May for very late crops; in the latter case potting can be into large pots
Spacing out	As for late crop
Planting out	early May/June
Harvesting	July/September

Propagation procedures

Many gardeners prefer to obtain their tomato plants from a nurseryman for a specific planting time, but there are those who prefer to raise their own, particularly when there are other propagating activities in progress. They should note that initiation of the first and second trusses within the plant takes place at a very early stage of development, long before the trusses are visible. The temperature and light intensity at which this initiation occurs is thought by some research workers and experienced growers to have a profound effect on the ability of the flower to produce fertile pollen and set. Temperature levels also have a considerable effect on the number of flowers on the truss. Satisfactory conditions in these respects must be provided to ensure the production of good plants.

While tomatoes can be propagated vegetatively from 4–5in cuttings rooted in a peat/sand mix at 65°F (18°C), it is not a practice which has enjoyed any great popularity, due to the risk of virus disease transmission, and also because of the expense of maintaining stock plants throughout the winter months. It is, however, a useful procedure for making up any loss later in the season, simply rooting strong side shoots as they are removed, particularly those from ground-level.

Seed sowing

Sowing can be carried out in a receptacle compatible with the scale of operations, a standard seed tray being suitable for 250–300 seeds and a 5–6in pot for about 50–60 seeds ($\frac{1}{4}$oz seed produces about 1,000 plants). Use John Innes seed compost, Levington, or peat/sand mixes, which are all suitable; or germinate seeds in a peat/sand mix with lime only added, using liquid feed as soon as germination occurs, thus avoiding possible ammonium damage and subsequent possible damping-off. Space sowing in strip pots, blocks, or in boxes is becoming very popular, especially prior to grafting, and is made simpler by the ready availability of pelleted or pilled seed.

The chosen receptacles are filled with suitably warmed compost, struck off level then pressed down to within $\frac{1}{4}$in of the top. The seed is broadcast thinly (2–3 per sq in) or in $\frac{1}{8}$in drills made with a piece of cardboard, before being covered lightly and gently firmed to keep, if possible, the seed coat below compost level during germination and so avoid the risk of virus infection which occurs when the seed leaves of one plant catch the outside of the seed coat of another. Pelleted seed is sown on the surface and kept moist by covering with polythene. Space sowing in the actual containers, according to some authorities, avoids the check which inevitably occurs during pricking off, but it is not always convenient. When grafting is to be carried out it is advisable to sow the seed of the root stock about 7–10 days before the variety, owing to the slower germination of the former (see Fig 66).

Shade boxes or pots, or cover with paper or black polythene (especially pelleted seed). Germination can also be carried out in a germinating cabinet. A germinating day/night temperature of 65°F (18°C) is now accepted as optimal to avoid the predominance of the short jointed nonproductive rogues or mules induced by higher temperatures.

Pricking off or potting

While there are differences of opinion on the need for early pricking off owing to possible coincidence with truss initiation, it is at present generally accepted that pricking off should take place within 8–12 days of sowing, before roots have developed to any extent. To maintain plants in good condition, especially for the early crop and more particularly if they are to be allowed to flower *before* planting, a pot size of $4\frac{1}{4}$in (or equivalent block size) is generally recommended. Pots may be of clay, plastic, peat or polythene. Blocks should be retained in trays or boxes to avoid disintegration, especially when wet. Dark coloured pots absorb solar radiation better (see also Chapter 17 on plastic versus clay pots).

The compost for potting is usually John

Young tomato plants in Jiffy strip peat pots. Tomatoes benefit more than most plants from being started in these peat pots since any damage to the roots can become a source of infection. When grown this way the entire pot and plant can simply be put straight into the final growing position without damage to the roots.

Innes No 1 or soilless media. Soilless media tend to give softer plants than those raised in soil-containing media. Less nitrogen would also seem to be required in poor light areas, especially for early raising. Where plants are raised under artificial lights on capillary watering systems, a very rough sand should be used to give good porosity. Whatever compost is selected, the salt content should not be excessively high, otherwise growth restriction can occur.

Handling seedlings

Except where space sown these are removed from the containers with a tally, carefully holding the leaf tip not the stem, and inserted into half-filled pots; the remaining compost is then pressed around the seedlings. Alternatively they can be inserted into dibber holes sufficiently deep to take the seedling without root restriction. The compost should be firmed by giving a sharp tap on a bench before the seedlings are lightly watered in. Seedlings can also be pricked off into boxes prior to grafting (12–24 per box) in which case the dibber method is used.

Place plants preferably on a slatted type bench with bottom heat, unless soil-warming benches are being utilised or propagating cases.

Temperature levels from pricking off to cropping

Generally speaking, higher temperatures under conditions of good light invariably increase rate of growth and reduce the number of flowers and therefore potential fruit on the bottom truss, although earlier ripening of the fruit is achieved. Conversely lower daytime temperatures will give larger bottom trusses but later development, and this could have some effect on the viability of the pollen. High night temperatures result in taller plants and low night temperatures in squat plants, often with leaves curled upwards; high daytime temperatures in low light intensity areas will induce leggy plants, simply because the plants cannot manufacture sufficient carbohydrates to sustain balanced growth. The following are the generally accepted temperature patterns in the UK for north and south respectively, positive day temperatures referring to recordings in a screened or at least sun-shaded thermometer.

Northern growers (latitude 54–58°N)

Stage	Night		Positive day		Ventilation commences at	
	°F	°C	°F	°C	°F	°C
1	56	13	68	20	74	23
2	56	13	68	20	74	23
3	56	13	68	20	74	23
4	62	17	64	18	68	20

Southern growers (latitude 50–54°N)

1	60	16	68	20	74	23
2	60	16	64	18	74	23
3	62	17	68	20	74	23
4	62	17	64	18	68	20

Stage 1 From pricking out the seedlings to visible appearance of the flower buds in the first truss

Stage 2 From first truss flower buds to anthesis (the opening of the first flower in that truss)

Stage 3 With the first blooms bursting into colour, the plants are planted out into borders or still in pots and the period extends to 4 weeks after picking the first ripe fruit

Stage 4 To end of cropping

Propagation periods involve stages 1 and 2, but generally speaking few gardeners would be able to adhere to the stated temperatures with the same precision as the sophisticated commercial grower, which makes the case for purchasing plants stronger. Compromise overall day/night temperatures in the order of 60°F (16°C) plus or minus a few degrees either way are now general in average gardening circles, ventilating at 70–74°F (21–23°C) under all circumstances.

General care of young plants

Reference back to the production programmes will show that spacing is an essential part of tomato propagation to ensure sturdy well-developed plants with the production of the bottom truss of fruit low down.

Watering should be carried out according to the container and the compost. All-peat composts require less water than more porous peat/sand or soil/sand mixes, peat and paper pots less water than clay or plastic pots, while soil blocks can dry out quickly unless kept close together initially. Peat and paper pots should be kept wider apart than plastic or clay pots to avoid their becoming soggy and disintegrating. It is essential that plants' water needs are gauged carefully, as either under- or over-watering can have serious consequences. Many gardeners use water at air temperature in preference to tap water, although research has shown that this makes little difference.

Whether to feed young plants or not depends much on the compost, although in general regular feeding is advisable to keep plants growing strongly, particularly in soilless mixes when regular feeding is most certainly always advisable, taking care to avoid the build-up of soluble salts. Either proprietary or self-formulated feeds may be used. Later propagated plants with their quicker development may not need such constant feeding, unless in soilless mixes.

221

Support with split canes will be required for tall plants which are allowed to flower before planting.

Constant attention to detail is essential for young plants, as any disorder can have serious long-term repercussions. The main points to look for are as follows:

Symptoms	Cause	Treatment
Pale green plants	Lack of light. Too high temperatures. Excess nitrogen	Drop day and night temperatures slightly, balance feeding
Very dark green plants Curling leaves. Shrivelled edges	High salt concentration. Too much feeding being given	Reduction in feeding. Flush out salts with plain water
Dark blue coloration of leaves. Stocky hard growth	Greenhouse too cold or affected by draughts	Check heating efficiency with maximum/minimum thermometer. Restrict draughts with polythene curtains
Seed leaves dead. Pale or stunted plants	Either of the above	Check growing conditions. Use liquid fertiliser at correct dilution
Spindly leggy growth. Shrivelling and burning of leaf tips	Too much heat caused by lack of ventilation. Dryness and overfeeding also contributory factors	Damp down frequently. Ventilate at 70°F (21°C). If no automatic ventilation, leave vents open during absence
Poor growth and colour with yellowing lower leaves despite regular feeding	Too much water	Give organic stimulant such as dried blood at 2oz/gal. Reduce watering
Wilting, debility or distortion, often associated with dark green coloration	Virus or fungal disease or pest attack	See later chapter for prevention and control of pests and diseases
Leaf mottling	Unbalanced fertiliser or shortage of trace elements	Check feed concentration. Possible weedkiller damage

Production of grafted tomato plants
Root stocks resistant to various maladies are used to overcome weaknesses in the desired variety. These are F_1 hybrids and are available as follows:

Fig 66

KNVF   Fusarium wilt, verticillium wilt, corky root and nematode resistance
KVF   Fusarium and verticillium wilt, corky root resistance
KN   Corky root and nematode resistance (root-knot eelworm, *not* potato eelworm)

Root stock is generally slower to germinate than the fruiting variety, and should be sown on average 7–10 days earlier. Root stock seed is sown as for the fruiting varieties in trays or in pots and pricked off into boxes at a density of 12–24 per box, the object being to raise sturdy easy-to-graft plants. Grafting is carried out when plants of both the fruiting variety and root stock are about 4–6in tall and $\frac{1}{8}$in thick, although for inexperienced gardeners the plants may be allowed to become larger.

After removing the seed leaves a downward sloping cut is made in the root stock $\frac{1}{2}$-$\frac{3}{4}$in long, and a corresponding upward cut is made in the fruiting variety, the tongues then being fitted together and bound up with lead strips or transparent adhesive tape, this being easier if two people are doing the work. The top leaves of the root stock above the graft are then removed and the two plants potted up in a $3\frac{1}{2}$–$4\frac{1}{4}$in pot. Union of the grafts will occur readily on an open bench if the plants are closely spaced, although they can be draped with a polythene 'tent' to ensure more humid conditions. Plants are given similar temperatures and treatment as previously stated (see again Fig 66).

When planting it is generally advisable for the root of the fruiting variety to be

223

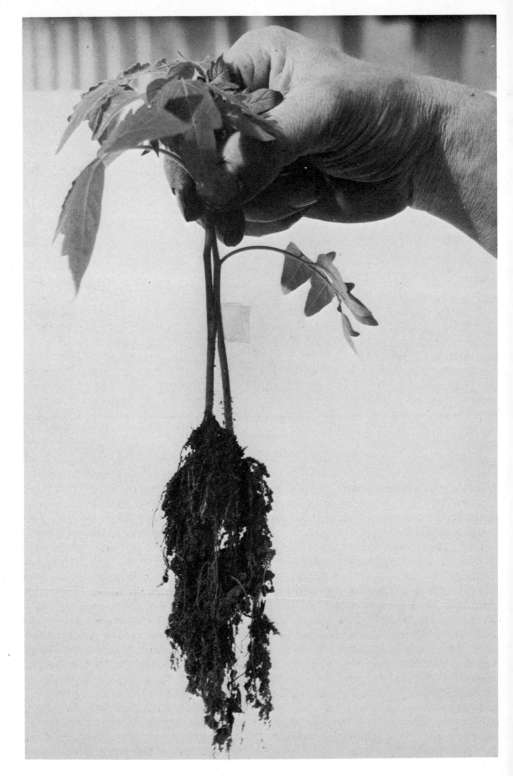

Grafting tomato plants.
This is a relatively easy
operation, and when
disease resistant stocks
are used with non-
disease resistant varieties
the mature plants are
virtually disease resistant.

224

removed to avoid the transmission of various diseases by the non-resistant variety root, although this can result in a severe check to the plants. In most cases the fruiting variety root seldom develops to any extent. Care should be taken to ensure the utmost hygiene during grafting, and it is advisable to dip the blade frequently in a solution of 2 per cent trisodium phosphate to avoid the spread of virus.

The time and trouble involved in grafting, or alternatively the high cost of purchasing plants at nearly twice the price of normal plants, must be weighed carefully against alternative cultural systems involving clean media.

Border culture—pre-planting preparations

No chances should be taken with border soil. It is advisable to have some form of analysis carried out, even if it is only a pH and potato eelworm check.

Borders should be cultivated carefully by digging, adding supplies of clean organic matter to condition the soil. Many of the troubles which occur when growing tomatoes in borders emanate not from any specific pest or disease or lack of nutrients but simply because of the poor physical condition of the soil. If good well-rotted farmyard manure is available, this should be used at 1cwt per 8–10sqyd, provided that the border has not been heat sterilised —this could cause excess nitrogen problems. Peat is especially reliable at 6–10lb per sqyd. Where sphagnum peat is used in quantity for conditioning tomato borders (or growing borders generally) it is wise to add extra lime, ie in addition to that shown to be necessary by soil analysis, generally 4–6oz per bushel of peat. Municipal composts can be used at rates of up to about one-fifth or one-sixth of the soil bulk, although on a long-term basis they can give rise to heavy metal build-up if used to excess.

Organic gardening enthusiasts will obviously wish to use 'properly made compost', and this will invariably result in fruit of excellent quality, although in my experience disease problems can develop in time, especially if something goes wrong with the compost-making system.

Soluble salt problems

A problem with tomato borders, especially if they are not new, is the build-up of soluble salts, and flooding may be necessary to flush these salts out. This should be carried out to the following levels

Border area	Heavy soil	Light soil
10 sq yd	80 gallons	40 gallons
20 ,,	160 ,,	80 ,,
30 ,,	240 ,,	120 ,,
40 ,,	320 ,,	160 ,,
80 ,,	640 ,,	320 ,,

Soil analysis will determine the need for flooding or otherwise, it being unnecessary to flood if the salt content falls within the normal level. Flooding should certainly be avoided if possible, as, apart from chilling the border, it can be detrimental to soil structure. In the majority of cases and where previous crops have been grown with adequate water supplies, it will merely be necessary to water the border to ensure that it is sufficiently moist at planting time. Larger quantities of water are best applied in mist form to minimise soil structure damage.

Application of lime

Lime will be necessary to adjust the pH to the 6–6.5 level, and should be lightly forked or watered in after even application. Either ground limestone or magnesian limestone can be used as required by analysis, lacking which information an 8–10oz per sqyd application will normally suffice. Direct contact between lime and any farmyard manure applied should be avoided by digging in the latter before applying lime to the surface.

Application of tomato bases

It is necessary to apply fertilisers as a pre-planting base dressing to provide a 'bank' or reserve of nutrients. Owing to differing circumstances, including whether the soil is heat-sterilised, chemically sterilised or new, there are several procedures:

Crop	Soil	Quantity per sq yd	Base type
Early and main crop tomatoes	Sterilised by heat	6oz 2–3oz 2–3oz	High potash base Sulphate of potash *Magnesium sulphate
Early and main	Chemically sterilised or unsterilised	6oz 3oz	Medium potash base *Magnesium sulphate
Late tomatoes (heated or cold grown)	Heat sterilised	6oz 3oz	High potash base *Magnesium sulphate
,,	Chemically sterilised or unsterilised	6oz 3oz	Medium potash base *Magnesium sulphate

* Do not apply magnesium sulphate if there is a high soluble salt problem and flooding is not practicable. Vigorous or weak varieties may necessitate modifications to these quantities, as will soil analysis. Following lettuce or other crops a high nitrogen base feed at 6oz per sq yd should be applied.

Base fertiliser	Nitrogen % N	Phosphorus % P_2O_5		Potash % K_2O
		Sol.	Insol.	
Standard	9.5	9	0.5	13.2
High potash	6	10	0.5	17.5
High nitrogen (seldom necessary)	12	5.5	0.5	6
John Innes base (use as high potash)	5.2	7	0.5	10

Base fertilisers are applied 7–10 days before planting and the border is then lightly forked and raked to be reasonably level and firm.

Pre-planting preparations for other cultural systems
Grafted plants are set out in prepared borders, sterilisation not normally being carried out unless there is a serious weed problem.
Ring culture It is necessary to take out the border soil, if any exists in the first case, and replace this with a 6–8in layer of inert aggregate which can be weathered ash, perlite, granite chips, coarse sand or gravel. This must be inert and free from chemical residues such as the sulphur

Fig 67

Polythene bag culture Large black polythene bags (medium gauge) with drainage holes (Fig 69), holding approximately half a bushel of a soilless media, are spread out on top of the border soil on a layer of polythene, or preferably on a layer of free-draining inert aggregate. Bolsters can also be used, these simply being bags of growing media which have the top sections removed to allow planting, drainage being provided by making slits in the sides of the bags. Boxes of soil are filled *in situ* at the appropriate distance apart, old apple or orange boxes frequently being used for this purpose on a short-term basis.

Trough and trench culture Troughs made up with pegs and wire to a 6–8in depth, or alternatively trenches set in the ground

Fig 68

which would be found in fresh ashes. The aggregate should be in an even layer with free drainage (Fig 68). The usual 'ring' is a whalehide pot (bituminised paper) of 9in diameter with or without a bottom. Plants are potted up in a warm greenhouse and grown on to a certain stage before setting out in the aggregate (if pots have bottoms). Rings are generally spaced out 20–24in apart and filled to within 2in of the top with the chosen compost, usually John Innes No 2. Soilless media can also be used, although in this case plants will require feeding much earlier than if grown in a good John Innes compost, of which about 12lb per 9in whalehide will be required.

with plastic drainage tiles running through them, are becoming popular for tomato culture in commercial circles. Soilless media is generally used. There are many variations on these systems, some of which involve the use of troughs made of concrete or expanded metal; in all cases the main criteria are the use of dependable soilless media and outlets for surplus mixture (Fig 70).

Polythene buckets (2 gallon size) with drainage holes are filled with soilless media, this system being perhaps most successful with lignite or peat/vermiculite media, or various other aggregates for hydroponic culture.

Peat mattress systems involve the use of whalehide pots on top of a 2–3in layer of peat in a shallow polythene trough, and Levington compost has been used with

Fig 70

some success for this system in recent years. The method, however, has been employed for many years among commercial growers with pest and disease problems. Many growers merely place whalehide pots on top of the existing border soil, a practice which should be attempted only when border soils are not sick (Fig 67).

Straw bale culture

Deep-seated virus infection or eelworm problems led initially to the development of this system based on the old 'hot bed' and using the beneficial aspects of composted straw and the production of CO_2. Wheat straw is preferable to oat or barley straw, as it is harder textured and does not decompose so quickly. Straw bales do, however, take up a lot of room and alternatively 8–10in wads may be used, particularly where height is limited. The straw is first of all saturated with water over a period of several days in a greenhouse temperature of about 50°F (10°C), the heating system being put into operation if the weather is cold. After soaking, the fertiliser (see below) is added to the 40–60lb bales and flushed in with more water. In recent years it has been found that a shorter period and smaller quantities of fertiliser are required for the fermentation process than were once thought necessary. Quantities of fertiliser required to induce fermentation vary with the weight of the bales, but the following average quantities for a 50–60lb bale provide a good guide

Fig 69

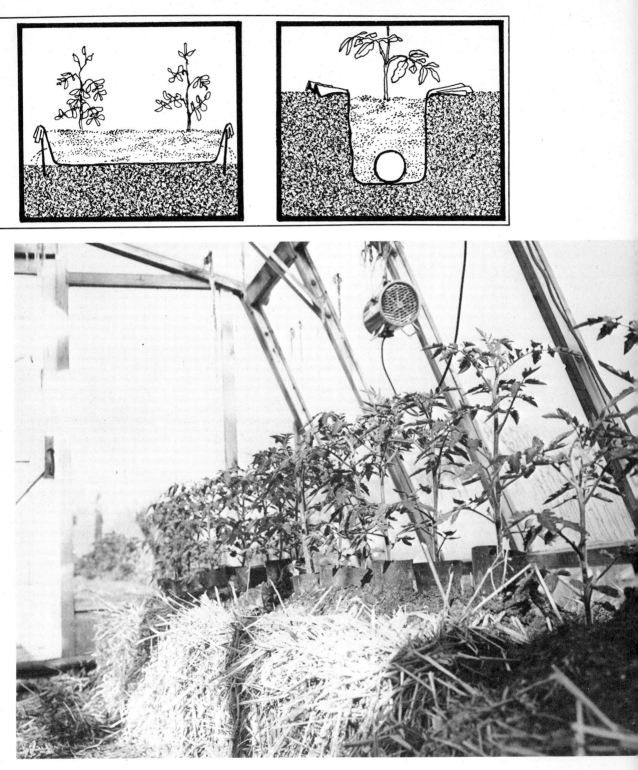

Straw bale culture of tomatoes. This is one of the most popular methods of growing tomatoes, and is fully described in the text.

(*pro rata* for wads). For each bale apply: 1lb ammonium nitrate-lime (Nitro-Chalk or similar); 6oz triple superphosphates; 6oz magnesium sulphate; 12oz potassium nitrate; 3oz ferrous sulphate.

Some gardeners still favour the older practice of a longer decomposition period. This involves ammonium nitrate-lime applied at the rate of 1½lb per bale after the straw is wet, followed by a further 1lb per bale in 3–4 days, and followed 3–4 days later by the quantities of fertiliser given above, but reducing the ammonium nitrate-

lime to ¾lb. As an alternative 1½lb compound fertiliser can be used for the final dressing in addition to the ¾lb ammonium nitrate-lime.

After the full application of the nutrients a shallow ridge of compost (of low nutrient status) is run along the top of the bales. The temperature of the bales in the centre will reach about 110–130°F (43–54°C) and when the temperature drops to about 100°F (38°C) planting can take place, although this is not a vital matter as the plants seem to respond to the heat generated. It is usual to set out three plants per bale, angled and subsequently trained obliquely so that they are not unduly congested, as they will be if planted and trained straight up.

Planting

As the main source of light in the northern hemisphere is southerly, it is advisable to plant in rows running north-south to avoid restriction of light, or alternatively to plant on the square system. Commercial planting distances allow between 13,000 and 14,000 plants (or more) per acre, but for all practical purposes in smaller greenhouses it is usual to allow about 4sq ft of border or trough per plant for the *total area* of the greenhouse (see Fig 71) which means about 18 × 18 or 26 × 14in or thereabouts. Spacing is not a vital matter, but close planting is not generally advised, as while it may seem at first sight to guarantee a larger crop, the reverse is often the case, as it restricts air movement and encourages disease. For ring and straw bale culture see relevant notes in section above.

Whatever system of culture is involved, the planting of tomatoes *must not take place* until a temperature of 56–57°F (14°C) can be achieved in the growing medium at a 5–6in depth, as checked by a soil thermometer. With this must go the proviso that light levels must be suitably high, a matter for adjustment in relation to the selected cultural programme. Heating systems must obviously be operating sufficiently in advance of planting time for the necessary temperature level to be achieved, showing the benefit of well-designed systems capable of imparting radiation warmth to the soil in addition to raising the air temperature to the level stated.

Where very early crops are involved, special care must be exercised; it is folly to plant automatically on a certain date every year, when the soil may still be cold. Early crops are planted in good light areas with efficient heating systems from late January to mid-February onwards, although for the majority of amateur gardeners with a fair level of heat, mid-March to mid-April is the most usual time, waiting until April or May for crops grown without heat.

Plants should ideally be 12–14in high at planting, with the first truss of flowers fully developed and showing colour on one or two blooms for the early plantings, so that the developing fruit will act as a brake on rank vegetative development, especially in rich media. For planting in borders, holes are taken out at the appropriate distance apart with a trowel or planting tool a few days before actually planting, to allow the soil at the sides and base of the hole to be

Fig 71

warmed by solar radiation and air currents. Plants are then set out with reasonable firmness, the seed leaves an inch or so above soil-level. Previously watered plants in clay or plastic pots should be carefully removed without undue disturbance, by tapping them out on a hard surface; paper or peat pots and blocks can be planted intact and can be left on the surface to root gradually. Should plants be unduly leggy, perhaps because planting is delayed by another crop such as lettuce, they can be layered by setting the plants on their sides.

With other systems of culture the same general procedure should be followed, taking care to check planting distances.

Successful establishment

The first task of the young tomato plant is to establish itself successfully, and to achieve this the roots must develop out from the root ball into the growing medium. Where the growing medium is too wet and cold, air will be excluded and the production of new roots inhibited to the extent that they may die back and become infected with weak pathogens. The young plant will often put out new surface adventitious roots in an effort to survive, but it is inevitable that a checked plant will eventually collapse. A dry growing medium will also hinder root development, as also will a heavy concentration of soluble salts

Ideally, therefore, the growing medium should be rendered compatible with the production of new roots in respect of temperature, moisture and soluble salt content. Soil temperature and moisture content are issues which can readily be checked whereas soluble salt concentration cannot (without a salt meter), although troubles in this direction should not arise if preliminary soil analysis is followed by careful base fertiliser application. With formulated growing media it is essential that these be obtained from a reliable source or correctly mixed. If, on the other hand, a plant is able to develop new roots with great rapidity, especially in a heat sterilised soil rich in nitrogen and ammonia, it can rush into non-productive vegetative growth.

Air temperature should also be at the desirable level, it being especially important that night temperatures do not drop excessively in relation to day temperatures. High humidity encouraged by frequent damping down and avoidance of too early ventilation will also assist with the establishment of plants. In completely cold greenhouses (with no heating), establishment of plants can be very difficult, particularly during periods when cold nights are followed by hot days. But when environmental control equipment is available to regulate temperature and humidity within fine limits, successful establishment is relatively easy.

Early watering procedure

A summary of watering procedure for young plants is as follows:

Cultural system	First waterings of plants	Moisture state of growing medium	Humidity of atmosphere
Border, including grafted plants	Minimal waterings in area of root ball to prevent wilting	Keep merely moist by damping	Damp frequently with fine rose overhead, especially in mid-morning
Ring	Adequate and frequent watering of root ball	Also give light waterings to whole growing medium to prevent drying out	Dry atmosphere usually prevails, making very frequent damping necessary

Straw bale	Daily or twice daily to keep whole growing medium ridge moist	Use hose or overhead sprays to keep bales wet	The atmosphere is usually sufficiently moist due to bales being kept wet, but damp down also if necessary
Polythene bag, trough, bolster and trench culture	Only minimal watering in area of root ball required	Provided they are sufficiently damp at planting time, peat-based media usually retain moisture content well	Damp down as for border culture
Peat mattress	A compromise of treatment between ring and bag culture. Light ball waterings only	As above, but ensure that the small amount of growing medium in ring does not dry out	A sufficiently high humidity is generally maintained if peat mattress is moist, but damp down on bright days
Container systems	Treat as for border culture where soil-based media is used. For soilless media the same care should be taken as for bags	No further watering will generally be necessary for large bulks of growing medium, apart from damping until plants are established	Frequent damping down, especially for raised box systems

Support, training and pruning

There are several ways of supporting tomato plants—tying to tall canes, or better still by the use of 3–5 ply fillis, Italian hemp or polypropylene twine (the last mentioned in many ways being preferable to string), tied in a loose knot above the cotyledons but under the lower leaves, and secured to a sufficiently strong horizontal wire 6–8ft above ground-level, and firmly secured to the structure (fully laden tomato plants are extremely heavy). The plants are carefully twisted clockwise round the twine as they grow. Netting and plant wires are often used for oblique and layering systems of training (Fig 72). Training methods are extremely varied, and may be summarised as follows:

Vertical training (A) Plants are stopped on reaching horizontal wires on short-term cultural systems. On long-term crops plants are arched over wires (A2).

V-training (B) Plants are trained out obliquely and alternately in different directions. Useful with straw bales where plants are set closely together.

S-hook system (C) This involves the use of 16 gauge S-hooks set 14in apart, plants being supported so many hooks along and dropped a hook as the season progresses, thus being progressively layered obliquely at an angle of 30–35°. Wires or hooks should be used to prevent bottom truss trailing on growing medium. At ends of row plants are turned on to next row (C2).

Layering (D) Initially trained vertically, plants on their strings are detached before reaching the horizontal wire, and dropped to an angle of 30°, usually when lower trusses are picked. Layering in all its forms

233

Fig 72

allows greater stem lengths at a convenient height.

Lateral training (E) The plants are trained obliquely at a 35–40° angle, wide mesh or polypropylene netting being a useful supporting medium. Tie plants on to netting with loops of string or wire/paper clips. Lower plants as season progresses. Interlocking hooks or similar devices can also be used.

Choice of any particular training system will depend on length of growing season, type of greenhouse, and whether there is adequate ventilation to avoid the problem of disease which frequently occurs in systems other than vertical, due to restriction of air movement.

Pruning Side shoots are removed when small and the lower leaves when they start to yellow, indicating that they have served their purpose. Opinions differ on the severity of de-leafing, but generally speaking defoliation up to the ripening truss is sufficient to allow free circulation of air. Leaves are best removed when the plant is turgid, with a quick up-and-down movement, although a knife can be used, making sure that no snags are left. Plants are generally stopped at a certain height, both to facilitate their handling and to restrict unproductive development of foliage at a time when flowers are unlikely to set and form fruit.

Watering and feeding during the season

The amount of water and the method of applying nutrients to the plant vary greatly according to cultural methods and

234

the medium involved. As plants grow larger they obviously make greater demands on both water and nutrients.

Assessment of water requirement

Visual determination is perhaps the most widely practised method. Tensiometers are useful for small scale growers and can either be related to a water requirement table, or state whether the soil is wet, medium or dry. An evaporimeter is a simple piece of apparatus which, by reference to tables, enables the evaporation loss of the plants and the amount of water necessary to compensate for it to be calculated. More sophisticated equipment indicates water requirement in relation to light intensity.

The following figures apply to the

Training tomatoes. The natural habit of the tomato is to flop around on the ground. Training is essential if healthy plants are to be maintained and good crops produced.

235

quantity of water required over 24 hours by plants with a canopy of leaves and about 3ft tall, no allowance being made for loss by drainage or surface evaporation:

Weather pattern	Water requirement by plant for full 24hr day in temperate climates
Very dull/cloudy and dull most of the day	$\frac{1}{4}-\frac{1}{2}$ pint
Dull/overcast most of the day	$\frac{1}{2}-\frac{3}{4}$,,
Fairly sunny/cloudy with bright periods	$1\frac{1}{4}-1\frac{1}{2}$,,
Sunny/only occasional cloud	$2-2\frac{1}{4}$,,
Very sunny/sky clear and sunny all day	$3-3\frac{1}{4}$,,

Taking an average of about 2 gallons per week from April to September—about 22 weeks—this gives a total of 44 gallons per plant, not counting water lost in drainage and evaporation. For ring culture, polythene bags or straw bales, very considerable amounts extra to the above may be required. To calculate the amount of water delivered by a hosepipe, spray lines or other means, check the amount delivered per minute and then calculate how much water will be applied in a certain time. In a small greenhouse with a hose running at 2 gallons per minute, one merely needs to water for 20 minutes to deliver 40 gallons of water—common practice with about 40 border grown plants in an average greenhouse.

Mulching is a useful technique for preventing surface evaporation of moisture in border growing, using either granulated peat or short straw, taking care to add about 4–5oz of ground limestone per bushel to offset the acidity of sphagnum peat.

Judging whether plants are over- or under-supplied with water can be difficult due to nutritional complications, but over-watered plants will usually tend to go lighter in colour with a yellowing of the bottom leaves due to the exclusion of air from the growing medium and the inability of the plant to extract nutrients from it, particularly nitrogen. Apart from wilting, under-watered plants go dark green and become hard or brittle; there can also be scorching of the foliage and dry set. It is important to note also that if the growing medium becomes dry its salt content rises, making it still more difficult for the plant to obtain water and nutrients.

Feeding

There is a considerable difference of opinion on whether constant or intermittent feeding is more successful, not only for tomatoes but for all crops. Ideally a plant with a constant and easily obtainable supply of nutrients and in a well prepared border soil of good physical structure containing slow-release nutrients may well enjoy excellent growth without the need for constant feeding. Conversely, soilless media have not the ability to store up nutrients in the same way as soil, and plants given only plain water will quickly become starved looking, as indicated by small pale-coloured leaves. Much of the success of tomato growing lies in being able to balance the quantities of nitrogen and potash the plant requires. Excess of nitrogen will result in lush over-vigorous growth, while shortage will give rise to thin hard stems, with yellowing of bottom leaves in severe cases. Excess of potash will produce hard squat plants with very curly leaves, whereas shortage usually allows the nitrogen content of the soil to predominate, with symptoms of excess nitrogen developing. Constant application of liquid feeds, which can be either self-formulated or proprietary, is essential, applying the feeds in nitrogen/potash ratio according to the needs of the plant, the same practice being followed with solid fertilisers.

It is usual to apply high potash early in the season, more balanced feeds later,

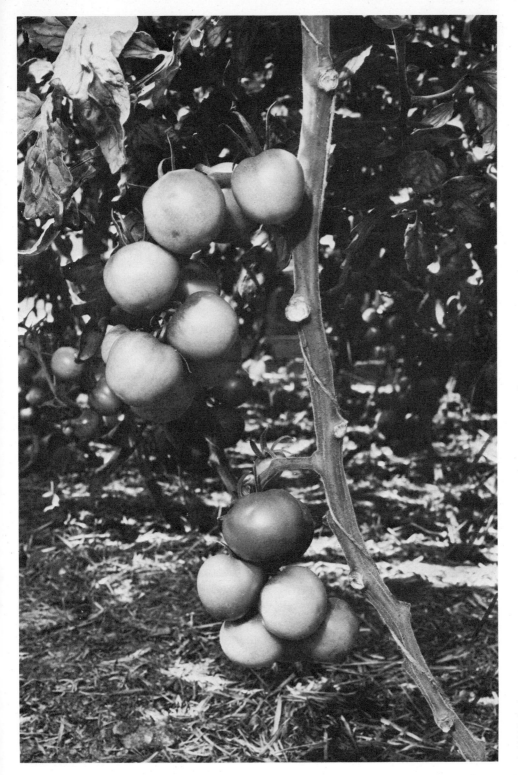

Well-grown trusses of tomatoes ready for picking. Note that the plant has been defoliated to encourage ripening of the trusses.

237

finishing in many cases with high nitrogen feeds.

Composition of feeds (oz/gal)				Nutrient (% weight/vol)	
K_2O to N ratio	Potas- sium nit- rate	Urea or	Ammo- nium nit- rate	K_2O	N
3:1 (high potash)	24	—	—	6.7	2.1
2:1 (standard)	24	5	6	6.7	3.4
1:1 (high nitrogen)	24	16	21	6.7	6.7

NOTE: This is the stock solution prepared by careful mixing in warm water. It is diluted to 1:200, generally with a calibrated dilutor. When using a watering can the solution is 1 fluid ounce of the stock solution in $1\frac{1}{4}$ gallons of water.

It is impossible to predict with any degree of certainty the amount of nitrogen required by plants, owing to variable drainage loss, vigour of plants, temperature levels and many other factors.

Care must always be taken *not* to apply either concentrated liquid or solid feeds to dry plants, as this will not only result in a rapid rise in salt concentration, but may physically damage the roots or necks of the plants due to the caustic nature of many fertilisers. When applying fertiliser in solid form, care should be taken to avoid 'swirling' by the use of a hosepipe, which can give rise to high concentrations in localised areas.

Foliar feeding is an extremely useful method of feeding plants, and tomatoes are no exception, but it is important to avoid the application of these feeds in hot sun, and to adhere strictly to recommended distribution rates.

Cultural systems other than border culture may require some modification to ball watering and feeding methods, es-

pecially where limited quantities of soilless media are involved. In containers constant liquid feeding can frequently result in a build-up of salt concentration and give rise to 'black bottom' due to low water availability or temporary deficiency in calcium caused by high salt concentrations. It is necessary to flush out with plain water on one or two occasions.

Straw bale culture may give rise to problems, a shortage of nitrogen frequently occurring early in the season due to its 'locking up' by the straw decomposition process. Later on there may be excess supply, necessitating extra potash at a time of year when the reverse is more usual.

Fruit picking
This should be carried out with care, removing the fruit by snapping the stem, leaving the calyx on the tomato. Fruit should not be left under a hot sun, as it quickly goes soft and deteriorates. When *wholesale* marketing of fruit is intended, it is usually picked fairly green and must be graded according to accepted standards.

Amounts of fruit picked vary from 6–15lb (or more). A good average is around 10lb. A material called 'Ethrel-E' is now used to ripen green fruit on the plant at the end of the season.

Removal of plants
At the close of the season the top of the plant is cut off 9–12in from ground-level and the rest removed with as much of the root as possible, necessitating in some cases the watering of the growing medium. Both foliage and roots should be deposited as far away from the greenhouse as possible. It is also sound practice to examine roots and estimate the degree of pest and disease attack, after which the greenhouse is then thoroughly cleaned by burning sulphur at 1lb per 1,000cuft, or by other means (see Chapter 32).

New cultural techniques for tomatoes
In the early 1970s much interest has centred around hydroponic systems, in aggregate or pure nutrient solution, either

in plastic mouldings or in polythene tubing or troughs. Production-line methods are beginning to develop, including two or three crops per year on a concentrated basis from a succession of plants taken only to the first or second truss stages.

Single and double truss cropping

A square area of cropping in a greenhouse is able to produce a certain number of pounds per year on conventional cropping. If taking the plant to ten or more trusses gives a yield of, say, 3lb per sq ft, it should be possible to improve this by setting the plants closely together and obtaining

$\frac{3}{4}$–1lb from each. Allowing a succession of crops per year there is scope for enormous yields.

Gardeners wishing to experiment with this technique in borders should set out the plants at 10–14in apart each way, supporting them with canes or netting and allowing two trusses to form. Under this method, however, there could be problems with soil sterilisation, and poor light may limit the number of crops per year to two instead of three.

Carbon dioxide (CO_2) enrichment

There has been in recent years much

A fine truss of one of the yellow varieties of tomato being grown under glass.

Tomato stem showing side-shoot which should be removed.

publicity about accelerating the growth of plants under glass by supplementing the natural complement of carbon dioxide gas in the atmosphere. In the case of tomatoes three-fold enrichment is carried out from half an hour after sunrise until one hour before sunset. Specific equipment is obtainable for the purpose, the amount of CO_2 supplied for a given period being measured by weight, not volume. Burning paraffin, propane, dry ice or liquid CO_2 are the various methods used, the requirement for tomatoes being 100–130lb for propagation and 700–800lb for the growing period per 1,000sq ft.

Coloured varieties
Most varieties grown by amateur gardeners and commercial growers conform to a fairly standard type but there is great variation in stem colour and hairiness, leaf shape and colour, plant habit and vigour, flower and fruit colour. The fruit colour types have a particular attraction, pale lemon, pink, yellow, tangerine, chartreuse, red with golden stripes, or brown with green stripes adding a superb rainbow effect to any salad and much appreciated by floral art enthusiasts. Most important, they are delicious to eat. Information and seeds can be obtained from Practical Plant Genetics, 18 Harsfold Road, Rustington, Littlehampton, Sussex, England.

See Chapter 32 for tomato disorders and pests, and current catalogues for varieties.

Chapter 20

Cucumbers, Melons & Peppers

The cucumber

Cucumis sativus is frequently grown commercially, like the tomato, in a single cordon, but is unlikely to be so treated by the majority of gardeners. The following method of culture will be found satisfactory on either a large or small scale.

Early crops should only be attempted in areas of good natural light and in a well-constructed greenhouse of good design. Cucumbers are lovers of warmth, demanding a minimum of 66°F (19°C) for optimum production, although they will produce worthwhile crops on a smaller scale at lower temperatures. Cucumbers are frequently grown on an amateur scale as a follow-on short-season drop subsequent to general propagating activities when the outside temperature levels are sufficiently high to avoid the high cost of heating necessary for early crops.

Programme of production

Earliest crops

Propagation period About 8 weeks

Sow seed From late October in very good light areas until December in poor light areas

Potting on 7–10 days after germination (or sooner)

Planting from mid-December until the end of February

Cropping February/March until September

Mid-season crop

Propagation period 6–7 weeks

Sow seed throughout January

Potting on 7–8 days after germination (sooner if necessary)

Planting throughout March

Cropping February/March until September

Mid-season crop

Propagation period 6–7 weeks

Sow seed throughout January

Potting on 7–8 days after germination (sooner if necessary)

Planting throughout March

Cropping March–April onwards

Late crop

Propagation period 4–5 weeks

Sow seed February–March

Potting on 2–5 days later

Planting April (until May for frames)

Cropping April–October

Seed sowing and germination

It is essential to observe almost clinical hygiene throughout the propagation stage of cucumbers, since they are extremely susceptible to infection by weak parasitic diseases. Good light is highly desirable for cucumber propagation, which means thoroughly clean glass to admit maximum light.

The compost for seed sowing should be absolutely clean, porous and free-draining, necessitating the use of coarse grit to give good aeration. All materials should be sterilised.

It is now general practice to sow the seeds (about 700 per oz) individually in paper tubes or peat pots and plant up in 4½–5in pots when large enough, this avoiding root disturbance and damage. On a larger scale seeds can be sown in seed trays, 40–48 per box, for potting direct into 4½–5in peat or paper pots thereafter.

Use plump seeds only (flat ones being discarded) and cover with ½in layer of compost. It matters little whether the seeds are placed flat, on their sides, or with the pointed end downwards; a convenient method for the amateur is to push them into the compost with the finger and thumb.

A temperature of 80°F (27°C) to ensure quick and even germination is desirable, although lower temperatures, down to 70°F (21°C), will give fair although more erratic results. Lower temperatures than this tend to give patchy germination, a lot depending on variety. Once sown, the seeds are covered with black polythene or paper and glass. Germination usually occurs with viable seed in about two days at higher temperatures and in up to four days at lower temperatures. Immediately the cotyledon appears the little plants should be given maximum light. Germinating cabinets can be used. A practice still followed by some gardeners is to germinate seeds in between thick blotting paper kept thoroughly soaked in a shallow tray, at a temperature of 80°F (27°C), the seedlings being potted up with tweezers immediately.

NOTE: Root stock *Cucubita ficifolia* is available for grafting varieties on to, and imparts resistance to wilt disease. Grafting procedure is similar to that described for tomatoes.

Treatment of young plants
The potting sequence varies, but the following is a summary of the accepted procedure.

Box sown plants	Potted in 3in pots 7–10 days after germination in winter, or 2–5 days in spring. After 10–14 days the plants are potted on in $4\frac{1}{2}$–5in pots
Small pot sown	After 10–14 days potted in $4\frac{1}{2}$–5in pots
Large pot sown	This method is used for late sowing and avoids all re-potting

Some gardeners sow the seed direct into 6–7in pots to enable the plants to be housed for a longer period in propagating temperatures. The temperature during the propagating stage (excluding germination) should be 70°F (21°C) day, 66°F (18°C) night, ventilating at 80°F (26°C).

Composts for potting
John Innes No 1 in winter and up to John Innes No 2 in spring is usual, although peat or peat/sand mixes can be equally satisfactory. Plants must be handled with extreme care, the compost being firmed up only loosely. Plants are put closely together to begin with, and finally spaced out to 12 × 12in. They are ready for setting out when the roots are sufficiently developed to avoid disintegration of the root ball. Open benches have been shown to be more successful than solid benches for cucumber propagation.

Feeding
Plants may require feeding in John Innes compost, particularly towards the end of the propagating period; with soilless mixes feeding is essential, using either proprietary feeds or home-made feeds at a dilution rate of 1 : 400 (not 1 : 200 as for tomatoes).

Artificial illumination
The need to use supplementary lighting depends on time of year and natural light levels. When conditions are poor, cucumbers with their very large leaves will respond reasonably well to artificial light, which may shorten the propagation period considerably.

Specification for supplementary lighting
HLRG mercury fluorescent reflector lamps 2.5ft above bench, 4ft apart. Alternatively MBFR/U lamps suspended 3ft above bench at 4ft apart can be used. Both types of lamp can either be permanently fixed or on a sliding rail to allow batch treatment. Either type will cover 200 seedlings. Fluorescent tubes can also be used but are not as efficient as the other lamps. Lighting period should not be in excess of 17 hours in each 24, the plants having 7 hours of darkness daily over a period of 14–20 days. (In experimental work plants treated for longer have responded well.) A 12 hour lighting cycle, the lights being changed at 10.00 hours and 22.00 hours, gives both batches their share of supplementary lights. The plants are placed under the lights when the seed leaves or cotyledons are fully open.

Enrichment with carbon dioxide

There is insufficient evidence to show that CO_2 enrichment is of great assistance during the propagation period, although it can certainly be experimented with, particularly in areas of good light.

Preparation of beds

Cucumbers are most successfully grown in beds raised above the ground soil level, as this ensures good drainage and soil aeration.

For commercial growing soil sterilisation by one or other of the methods discussed in Chapter 14 will be necessary, while on a smaller scale special beds or straw bales will be used and the need for sterilisation diminishes. Whatever soil is used must be sterilised or clean, there being much to be said for a good loam derived from stacked turf put through a $\frac{1}{4}$in riddle.

Beds must be made up on an area of perfect drainage, which may involve the incorporation of very coarse sand or gravel through the border soil below the selected bed area. The farmyard manure selected should preferably be from a farm where the animals are straw bedded, avoiding if possible manure containing wood shavings or peat, particularly the former. The first layer of manure is spread on the ground 6in deep and about 20–24in wide, followed by 4in of soil; further layers of manure and soil are added. The beds should be about 20in high with straight sides and a flat top. The beds are prepared about 2 weeks ahead of planting and watered for 7–10 days before planting, to induce fermentation and rapid release of ammonia. The temperature of the beds will rise quickly and planting can commence when it has fallen to about 80–90°F (27–32°C).

Straw bales and wads

The procedure for straw bale fermentation is very similar to that described for tomatoes. Many gardeners thoroughly soak the bales over a period of around 3 weeks or so before the intended planting date, applying $1\frac{1}{2}$lb of ammonium nitrate lime after the straw is wet, followed by another 1lb in 3 days and a further $1\frac{1}{2}$lb of a complete slow-release trace-element-containing fertiliser, the above being quantities for normal 50–60lb bales. Cucumbers appear more susceptible to salt damage than tomatoes, necessitating caution when ammonium nitrate lime is applied, although owing to the varying nature of the straw, plants can suffer from nitrogen deficiency when insufficient nitrogen has been applied during the fermentation process. At all events, the fertiliser applications are watered in lightly. A check should be kept on the temperature of the bales, planting commencing when the temperature of the inside of the bales has dropped to about 80–90°F (27–32°C).

Straw wads 8–10in wide can be used, applying the fertiliser *pro rata* to the total quantity of straw used.

Isolated beds

Several systems are involved here, the main criteria being to isolate the beds from pests and diseases contained in the greenhouse border by using large clay pots, 9in whale-hide pots, or conveniently designed boxes. But good aeration and drainage are necessary or fungal diseases may quickly attack.

Planting

Cucumber plants are ready for planting when 12–15in high with eight to ten leaves formed, although smaller plants are often set out with great success, especially for later planting. The actual planting procedure is to set about 18–24in apart directly into soil–manure beds, with a trowel, making sure each is firmly set with no air pockets. If the root ball is a little 'proud' of the bed, this often helps to avoid fungal disorders at the plant's neck. No plant which shows the least evidence of disease should be planted under any circumstances. Always water the plants well before knocking them out of their pots, unless they are in peat or paper pots when the whole pot is planted. Where straw bales are being used, run a ridge of clean soil and peat 5–6in deep on top of the bales, or better still peat plus lime at 5–6oz ground limestone per bushel, as this avoids the possibility of disease introduction when using unsterilised soil.

After planting the plants are initially watered in and the greenhouse kept humid for a few days. When it is seen that the roots have started to run, general watering can commence.

Greenhouse temperatures should ideally be 70°F (21°C) day and 66°F (19°C) night, ventilating at 80°F (27°C) for the first 8–9 weeks of cropping. Thereafter temperatures are reduced to 66°F (19°C) day and 62°F (17°C) night, ventilating at 75°F (24°C) to ensure good quality and colour. It is important to avoid cold draughts.

Training systems

Some planning is obviously necessary before planting to ensure that means of adequately supporting the plants exists. Indeed the actual placement of the beds or bales will depend almost entirely on the training system adopted. Broadly speaking there are three basic ways of training: (1) arch training, (2) oblique cordons and (3) vertical cordons. The method chosen must relate not only to the size of green-house but to the number of plants being grown. In many amateur-sized green-houses one row of arch-trained or single cordons will invariably suffice, vertical cordon systems being more suitable where other crops such as tomatoes are being grown in the greenhouse. Where arch training is adopted it will be necessary to erect a framework of wood and wire on which the plants are arched (Fig 73).

Vertical and oblique systems are more likely to interest the smaller scale grower. Basically all that is involved is having a strong wire horizontally above or at an oblique angle to the plants in a similar manner to that employed when growing tomatoes. The plants are bent over to give 'slack' before securing fillis or polypropylene twine around the neck of the plants in a non-slip loop. They are then twisted around the string as for tomatoes, removing all the laterals which first appear, then allowing short laterals to form, followed by longer laterals higher up the plant. This is to avoid spoilage of fruit from trailing on the beds. Male flowers are removed to

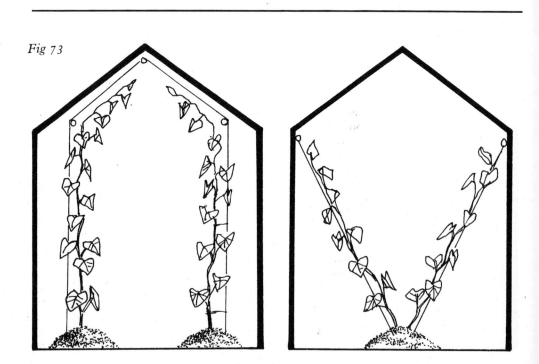

Fig 73

244

avoid pollination, allowing a reasonable quantity of female cucumbers to develop. Failure to remove the male flowers may result in fertilised and malformed fruits. The use of all-female cucumbers has helped enormously to alleviate this chore.

Seasonal feeding and general culture
Cucumbers require regular watering, a regular supply of nutrients and good environmental control if they are to be a highly successful or economically viable crop. Constant visual assessment of the nutrient situation is necessary. For short-season crops grown in properly made up beds supplementary feeding may not be needed. Guidance on this matter can be forthcoming from having an analysis made of the soil used for the soil/manure bed. A pH of 6.5 is the aim, with phosphate and potash figures at index 3 (see soil analysis, Chapter 13). The use of nitrogen as Nitram or Nitro-Chalk (or other form of ammonium nitrate lime) at approximately 1oz per sqyd run of bed about 6 weeks after planting is fairly standard practice for long-season crops. Alternatively 18oz of ammonium nitrate may be dissolved in 1 gallon of water and applied at a dilution of 1 in 200. Potash can be applied by giving sulphate of potash at 1oz per sqyd at intervals of 4 weeks, commencing 8 weeks after planting. Alternatively use a complete proprietary liquid feed at 2–3 week intervals or, if self-formulating the feeds, concentrate on high nitrogen feeds early in the season, changing to high potash feeds later. The plants themselves should give a good indication of their requirements. If thin and hard, nitrogen is required; if gross and over-vigorous, potash is required. A nicely balanced growth should be kept as such by a good balanced nutrient approach.

CO_2 enrichment later in the season
This has been shown to be beneficial in specialised situations, particularly later in the season, but it should be noted that considerable natural enrichment takes place from the decomposing beds or straw bales and for all normal purposes it is doubtful whether the use of artificial enrichment would be economically justified, the exception being a late planted crop to crop into the winter.

Necking up
This practice is useful for promoting the development of surface adventitious roots, later in the season using soil or peat (plus 5–6oz ground limestone) in a mulch 6–8in deep.

Shading will not normally be necessary with a healthy crop.

Mulching
This involves the application of composted farmyard manure when the white roots are seen on the surface of the beds. It is a practice not without risk, however, as ammonia gas can cause irrevocable damage if released from too fresh manure. It is better, therefore, to store the manure out of doors for a few days before bringing it into the greenhouse to be spread on the beds and well damped in. The manure should be kept away from the main stem to avoid stem rot. The number of mulches given depends on the length of season, but

usually two or three will suffice. The use of only one, or at the most two mulches of straw is a useful and often more acceptable alternative. The value of mulching, apart from providing a source of nutrient in the case of FYM, is to prevent 'capping' of the beds when they lose porosity and fail to absorb water freely.

Watering

Fairly large quantities of water will be required initially, keeping the beds moist after planting by twice or thrice weekly dampings. Then after 3 or 4 weeks a heavy watering is given once a week in combination with damping of the beds two or three times a week in hot weather. Methods of watering can involve spraylines, drip irrigation, or hosepipes, and the amounts of water to apply, in very broad terms, are about two to three times the quantity of water required by tomatoes in borders and up to twice as much more than tomatoes grown on straw bales. The amount of water given to the beds is usually sufficient to maintain a humid enough atmosphere without resorting to the frequent damping down once thought to be essential with cucumbers, since disease is associated with constant high humidity. It will be noted that cucumbers can readily be fitted in with a crop of tomatoes, with largely similar temperature and humidity requirements.

Picking the crop

Carefully pick cucumbers by cutting the supporting stalk. It is usual to harvest every 4–5 days. Fruit should be kept reasonably cool after detaching from the plant. Compulsory grading standards apply for cucumbers if they are offered for sale in *wholesale* markets and details of the gradings can be obtained from any marketing officer or horticultural adviser. Cucumbers are usually packed in cardboard flats in 10s, 12s, 14s, 16s or more, well covered with paper.

Frame culture

Cucumbers make a useful frame crop, usually being planted following lettuce during April or May, according to district, when all risk of frost is past (see frame varieties in catalogues). While it is possible to make up hot beds this is seldom practicable; soil warming cables are frequently used to give sufficient warmth to allow early planting or quicker development.

It is frequent practice merely to take out holes 12in wide and 9in deep, replacing the soil with equal parts of well-rotted stable manure and good garden soil. Alternatively use well-dug soil dressed with 3–4oz per sq yd of fertiliser. Either one or two plants 8–10in high can be set out per frame sash, the single plant in the centre or the two plants at diagonally opposite corners.

A coat of whitewash should be put on the glass over the planting station to assist establishment, especially if weather is hot, and the tops should be pinched out when the little plants start to grow quickly. The resulting side shoots are turned out either to the four corners or to the sides, no further pruning being carried out until fruits are well formed. Male flowers should be carefully removed and the plants carefully watered and ventilated. Straw may be laid on the ground to keep fruit from rotting on the soil. Considerable yields can be achieved with comparatively little attention.

For later crops seeds can be sown direct into the frame, using two seeds at each station and selecting the stronger plant.

Cucumbers may also be grown under cloches, being planted out 2–3ft apart in late May or June.

See Chapter 32 for pests, diseases and physiological troubles.

The melon

Cucumis melo is closely related to the cucumber, requiring for its cultivation a hot arid atmosphere with at least 60°F (16°C), and it is happier at temperatures well above this. It is not therefore a commercially profitable crop in temperate climates when imported melons from warm countries are available at reasonable prices all the year round. However, on a smaller scale, melons are grown following general propagating activities and also make an excellent frame crop. There are many varieties in the catalogues outside the usual range, eg among the canteloupes, which can be produced as delicacies.

Cultural programme
in greenhouses

Seed sown	March–April
Planted	April–May
Harvested	July–August–September

In frames

Seed sown	March–April in greenhouses
Planted in frame	April–May
Harvested	August–September

Seed sowing

Sow seeds either on their side or end in 3¼–4in pots of clay, plastic or peat, using JI potting compost No 1 or soilless compost of high nutrient level. Germination occurs best at 65–70°F (18–21°C) in a propagating case, it being advisable, as with cucumbers, to ensure a brisk germination in astringent conditions as the young plants are extremely disease prone.

Preparations for planting

The older method of cultivation for the early crop was to make up a hot bed with farmyard manure, preferably in the greenhouse border (underbench heating generally being necessary) and leave it over a period of days to allow dispersal of ammonia, not always very practical in a mixed culture greenhouse. More usually these days, and in particular with a warm greenhouse, good riddled loam is used with a small proportion (one-fifth to one-sixth part) of well-rotted farmyard manure. Alternatively leaf-mould or peat can be used. Where a hot bed is used the soil mixture is placed on top of the bed after it has cooled down a little and the ammonia dispersed. John Innes No 2 compost can be used instead of the soil/manure mix with reasonable success. The placement of the bed must be in relation to a trellis or other means of support and depends on the length of the season and level of management. While a continuous bed 12–18in high takes a lot of soil, it is more retentive of moisture than the mounds 10–12in high, frequently recommended, which dry out all too quickly during absence on business.

The young melon plants grow strongly in good light, being supported if necessary with a short cane and planted out (like cucumbers) slightly proud of the soil at 2½ft apart when the soil mix is sufficiently warm, preferably 65–68°F (18–20°C). The plants are well watered in. If possible the greenhouse should be kept warm and made more humid by limited ventilation for a few days, though melons can cope with some departure from the rules.

Constant watering is necessary, especially when rapid growth is seen. The leading shoot should be trained up the supporting trellis before pinching out the growing tip, which encourages the development of the side shoots which bear the flowers. Some restriction in side-shoot growth will be necessary to avoid a clutter of leaves, bearing in mind that it will only be necessary to leave a small number of female flowers, pinching side shoots out a leaf or so beyond the selected female flower. The unisexual nature of melons necessitates manual pollination by removing the male flowers and placing them into the open centre of the female flowers, which can be readily recognised by the swelling behind the petals. It is important to do this when the sun is shining and to pollinate five to six flowers on each plant simultaneously, otherwise there will be varying development and size, although this to a degree may be desirable on smaller scale culture.

Top dressing with soil, plus the use of liquid fertilisers, are the main cultural requirements. Avoid saturation of the soil, which appears to predispose to disease, especially at the neck of the plant. To prevent stem collapse some gardeners use broken pots as a shield against moisture. A moist growing atmosphere is frequently advised but is not now in favour as it provides ideal conditions for many diseases to flourish.

Support for the plant
Fruit must be individually tied in to the trellis or supported by small nets. There will be on average 5–6 melons per plant, it being unwise to allow any more to develop.

When the fruit begins to change colour this is a sign that it is ripening, at which time water quantities are reduced and, if possible, freer ventilation given, the fruit being carefully detached with scissors when ripe.

Culture in frames
The cultivation of melons in frames is basically similar to their cultivation in greenhouses, it being better to remove the soil at the planting station and replace it with a suitable compost or soil/manure mix. Normally only one plant per Dutch light frame is allowed, being conveniently planted in the middle of the sash, generally at a time of year when lettuces have been harvested, preferably in May or June. After setting out young plants, whitewash the glass to give shade to prevent the plants wilting particularly in hot weather. The top of each plant is pinched out when the young plants are 6in high to encourage early side shoot development. This results in bushy plants which produce sufficient flowers, generally 5–6, to pollinate as before, observing the same general procedure.

Watering and feeding requirements are the same as for greenhouse culture, ensuring adequate supplies of moisture and reasonably free ventilation during hot weather. As for cucumbers, a layer of straw on the soil helps to prevent deterioration of fruit.

Vegetable marrows and courgettes
(Cucurbita pepo ovifera)
Members of the cucumber family, the vegetable marrows are becoming much more popular as a greenhouse crop, some listed varieties having been specially bred for forcing either in frames, cloches or greenhouses, the fruit produced being known as *courgettes*. They are raised in a similar manner to cucumbers by sowing the seed singly in pots from January on-

wards, depending on whether heat is to be used for their culture; February sowing in heat being advisable for culture under relatively cool conditions. The plants are grown to planting stage in 4–5in pots in JIP2 or similar, being fed if necessary to encourage vigorous growth. They are planted 2–3ft apart in either heaps of soil plus well-rotted farmyard manure, or holes in the ground filled with this mixture. If too vigorous growth is noted, the pollination of blooms may not be achieved despite assistance by hand pollination (as for melons). The leading shoots should be pinched out to encourage side growth, which in time is also pinched out and side growth restricted to reasonable levels.

Vegetable marrows need cool, slow, but frost-free growth, and do not lend themselves to short-season culture. For the amateur gardener with limited growing space it may be better to raise the plants initially under glass and grow in frames or cloches out of doors. Sow seed in February for planting in frames during April–May;

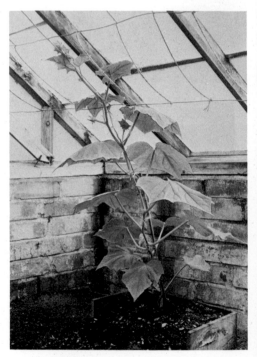

The training of marrows through string netting. This method of training has many advantages, the chief of which are avoidance of damage by soil-surface pests, and of misshapen vegetables due to resting on the ground.

248

for outdoor growing sow seed in March for planting outside in late May or June when all risk of frost is past.

Peppers)*Capsicum annuum* var. *grossum)*
Peppers, like tomatoes, belong to the order solanaceae and their culture is in many ways similar. Indeed a number of nurserymen previously specialising in tomatoes have become interested in the commercial production of peppers. Several varieties are offered, most of them prolific and several resistant to tomato mosaic virus (see Chapter 32).
Cultural details
Seed is sown, as for tomatoes, in John Innes seed compost or soilless equivalents

Vegetable marrows make an excellent greenhouse crop, being generally more tender and succulent than fruits grown out of doors.

Exotic desert fruits like melons can be grown to perfection in the greenhouse.

from January onwards, being germinated at 65°F (18.3°C) and covered by paper or glass. Seedlings are pricked off into 4¼in pots in John Innes potting No 1 or soilless equivalents and given good light and temperatures of a similar regime to that given to tomatoes, their training also being similar. They are frequently planted up singly in 8–9in pots using John Innes No 2 or soilless compost, although in the latter case liquid feeding must be commenced earlier. Alternatively they can be grown like tomatoes after similar soil preparation. Support is usually with canes and string, the plants achieving a height of about 3–5ft.

Aubergines (*Solanum melongena*)
These 'egg plants' also belong to the Solanaceae. Sow seed in February/March, following the instructions for peppers above. They do, however, require cooler growing conditions than either tomatoes or peppers otherwise they do not set too well.

Chapter 21

Other Vegetables under Glass

Lettuce in greenhouses and frames

The lettuce *Lactuca sativa* is increasing in importance as a greenhouse crop since the breeding of short-day varieties has made year-round production possible. The quality of greenhouse lettuce, furthermore, is better than that of lettuce grown out of doors and it needs only relatively cool conditions for cultivation.

Lettuce thrives in a fairly rich soil, pH 6–6.5, of fairly high nutritional status-potash and phosphate index 4 and high nitrogen levels. It is particularly suscep-tible to high salt concentration and grows best in a moist regime. Lettuce culture in a greenhouse is almost entirely confined to growing in borders, although on an ama-teur scale pots may be used. It requires *relatively* high light intensity, and light levels during the winter months in many areas are too low for entirely successful growing.

Production programme

The following provisional programme is subject to considerable variation according to region and natural light levels:

Seed sowing in greenhouses or frames	Planting under glass	Cutting	Comments
August	September	Nov–December	Can be difficult in poor light areas
10–20 September	Mid-October	Dec–January	
Late Sept–October	Oct–November	Feb–March	Growing room propagation can considerably reduce propagation period
Nov–December	Dec–January	March–April	
January	February*	April–May	
February	March*	May	
February*			
Can be planted outside March–April in soil blocks or grown in greenhouse			
March–July*	April–August*	May–October	

* do not require heat

Seed sowing procedure

For many years it was standard practice to sow lettuce in standard seed trays at the rate of 300–500 per tray in either John Innes or a soilless seed compost (low nutrient for winter, high nutrient for spring/summer), but there is now much interest in individual sowing of pelleted or split pill seed in soil or peat blocks, the block making and sowing being carried out mechanically on a large scale. Small peat pots can also be used to good advan-tage for space sowing. Alternatively seed can be sown direct in greenhouse borders or frames. There are 16,000 lettuce seeds per oz and the germination percentage is usually fairly high; 10/64–12/64 grading pelleted seed contains approximately 6,000 per lb. Figures given for seeds per lb are usually rounded to nearest 1,000.

When sowing seed fill boxes (or pots), strike off level, then firm up with a board. Scatter seed on thinly and cover lightly before firming in. Water with a fine rose and place seed either in a germinating cabinet or cover with black polythene. Pelleted or pilled seed should be sown individually in the selected container, watered in, and covered with polythene. These germinate more evenly in high humidity with plenty of air and moisture, germination frequently being delayed by covering the seed too deeply. There is increased interest in space sowing pelleted seed directly into borders, singly or doubly at 8×8in intervals, or at 4×4in, thinning out. Firm and thorough preparation is essential.

Germination occurs under a wide range of temperatures, although 55–60°F (13–16°C) is the optimum. Good light levels must be given to seedlings as soon as they germinate, otherwise they become etiolated and drawn.

To avoid damage to roots prick off before too large, either directly into prepared borders or into small peat pots or peat blocks when direct sowing into these is not practised in the first case. The soil for peat or paper pots should be of John Innes Potting No 1 nutrient level, and the same is true of peat or soil block composts.

The use of growing rooms

The use of growing rooms in the raising of plants considerably shortens the propagating period, and is increasingly practised. Seed is sown normally and germinated either in a germinating cabinet or a warm greenhouse in stacked boxes. As soon as the seedlings have germinated they are placed under lights at 500 lumens and given *continuous* 24 hour light at a temperature of 68°F (20°C) for 5 days, before being pricked off into blocks and given continuous 24 hour light for 10 days at 500 lumens. They are watered and fed regularly when in the growing room and develop very rapidly, being ready for planting 3 weeks after sowing. Alternatively 1,000 lumens can be given on a double batch system (12 hour lighting in each 24hours)

for 5–6 days more or less according to development.

Space sowing techniques are also readily adaptable to growing room conditions. It is difficult to quote exact techniques for growing rooms as they tend to be the subject of frequent modification, but the basic principle is quite clear; to raise plants on a programmed basis (and a planned cropping scheme) irrespective of weather conditions, utilising 'waste heat' from the lights to warm the growing room or whatever other erection is being used. Carbon dioxide enrichment is beneficial in growing rooms at 2–3 fold rate (600–900 or 1,000 ppm).

Preparation of borders

Greenhouse borders should be analysed to check the nutrient level with particular reference to the pH figure, the greenhouse thoroughly washed down and consideration given to whether sterilisation in any of its forms is necessary. Lettuce, while prone to certain fungal maladies, does not make a soil sick, particularly if grown as a single crop and then followed by tomatoes. For successive cropping, however, some sterilisation would inevitably be needed, there being much use made of the sheet steaming technique in commercial circles. Chemical sterilisation in one or other of its forms will also be effective since, apart from the incidence of fungal disease, weeds can be very troublesome with this closely grown crop, chickweed being a particular menace, although chlorpropham (CIPC) weedkiller has been used with some success in this instance under glass.

Lettuces are frequently grown before a tomato crop and therefore the soil treatment is complementary to both crops. If *clean* FYM is available this should be dug in at 1cwt per 8–9sq yd, care being taken that the FYM does not introduce weeds (alternatively sterilise the soil thereafter, flooding after heat sterilisation to reduce the salt content to around pC 3–3.1, index 2). Base feeds in the order of 1–2oz per sq yd of hoof and horn meal and 4–5oz per sq yd of a medium potash fertiliser are general, although when soil is found on

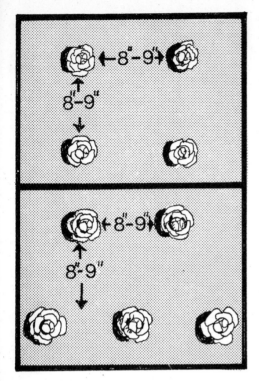

Fig 74

analysis to be well supplied with phosphate and potash (index 4), apply only the hoof and horn meal, particularly if FYM has also been applied.

Borders should be well forked and raked to a reasonable tilth, being of a moisture content where the surface only dries out after a few days but plenty of moisture is available at lower depths. If this is not the case, borders will require a light watering or alternatively the plants should be well watered in after planting.

As a preventive against root rot quinto-zene dust is applied evenly a day or two before planting, being raked well into the surface.

Planting

The soil should be warmed to 50–52°F (10–11°C), which may mean turning the heating on a week or so before planting in the winter months. Spacing is important for hearting and health; 8 × 8in square or staggered is general, give or take a little for size and growing habit of varieties. Use a dibber when planting from a seed box,

checking for brown discoloration indicative of disease. Plants in peat pots or blocks should be planted with a trowel, or on a larger scale by a mechanical planter which indents the soil. Water the plants in lightly with a fine rose on a hosepipe, or spray-lines (Fig 74).

Temperature patterns

Lettuces respond to low night (45–48°F/ 7–9°C, or lower) and slightly higher day temperatures (55–60°F/13–16°C), especially when carbon dioxide enrichment is being carried out—approximately 140–150 lb CO_2 per 1,000sq ft being required for the winter crop from half an hour after sunrise to one and a half hours before sunset for approximately 4–5 weeks. Continuous daytime carbon dioxide enrichment is only feasible during the lower temperature winter months when no ventilation is necessary, and day temperatures tend to reach 65°F (18°C).

Some of the hardier varieties will tolerate reasonably low temperatures. The rule should be to select a variety suitable for the likely environment, or else to adhere to the temperature recommendations for a particular variety.

Light intensity is also an important factor to bear in mind: the net effect of too high a temperature under poor light being non-hearting, apart from physiological troubles such as tip burn of the leaves.

Watering and ventilation

Better lettuce is produced in high moisture regimes. Where soil is of a retentive nature and water tables high, it may be unnecessary to water lettuce at all, but in general watering commences when the lettuces have a leaf spread of 2–3in, an average application overall being about 5 gallons per square yard. Too heavy dampings or overhead sprayings should be avoided as this encourages fungal diseases. Two dustings of dicloran or benlate are generally given during the season, especially in dull, wet areas with a high risk of botrytis during the winter months.

Ventilation is important in preventing excessively high day temperatures, particularly following upon a relatively cold

Lettuces are one of the easiest of greenhouse crops. They can be had in good heart in mid-winter and are especially useful as they can be intercropped with tomatoes.

night. Rapid fluctuation of temperature causes tip burn. Ventilation should be given at the 65°F (18°C) level.

Harvesting
Lettuces are cut when they have achieved a reasonable size. This varies from 12–13 weeks down to 6 weeks for the later spring crop. The use of growing rooms shortens the period. Begin cutting early to prevent wastage.

Varieties
Basically there are two main types—the tight hearted light coloured 5B type and the big darker Dutch lettuces which are looser. Select varieties suitable to environment and time of year, ie short day lettuces for the dull winter months, and note resistances offered in the catalogues with

reference to local conditions (see chapter on diseases and pests).

Mustard and cress
Both outside mustard *(Bromica juncea)* and greenhouse cress *(Lepidium sativum)* are annuals belonging to the Cruciferae, grown as a salad crop for the young leaves. Success lies in a brief growing period under conditions of good light. Either sow thickly on well-prepared soil and cover with damp sacks until germination, or sow in boxes or punnets of compost, soak, and cover with black polythene. The seedlings are ready for cutting in 10–14 days or less, according to heat level and time of year. Weeds are the main problem. Soil should be sterilised, pH of about 6.5, and the

254

compost selected should be of a reasonable nutritional standard, index 3 for phosphate and potash levels and a high level of nitrogen.

French beans

The French bean *(Phaseolus vulgaris)* is a mouth-watering delicacy which can be grown to tender perfection in a greenhouse, whereas out of doors cropping can be severely restricted in a poor summer.

Dwarf French beans may be grown in large pots, either clay or whalehide. The pots are half filled with John Innes No 2 potting (or similar nutrient level) compost; 4–5 seeds are put in each 8in pot and 5–6 seeds in each 9–10in pot, and top dressed with more soil when they have made 6–8in of growth. Support is achieved by using beech twigs.

Climbing French beans are best grown in well-prepared greenhouse borders, 12–18in apart in rows 5–6ft apart, or alternatively given 18–20in apart each way in a square system. Seeds may be sown directly into the border, but are better germinated in small peat pots for planting out during April. Support is by cane or twine, the growth being 'twisted' in, in much the same way as for tomatoes, although the tips may have to be tied in. If frequently sprayed with water, kept warm and given free ventilation on sunny days, they generally grow vigorously and produce remarkably heavy crops of very tender pots. The plants should merely be kept within reasonable limits by training. This is a crop which can give a surprisingly high return for a modest area.

See Chapter 32 for pests and diseases of beans.

Forced vegetables

In addition to the vegetables so far discussed, there are others which are forced in greenhouses:

Seakale *(Crambe maritima)*

This plant, which is found wild in maritime districts of Europe, is grown for the blanched shoots which are produced in heat and darkness during winter and spring. A batch of plants is raised initially by sowing seed out of doors in April in deeply dug soil enriched with manure. Seed is sown thinly in drills 1in deep and 12in apart and seedlings thinned to 6in apart. Plants are kept well hoed and free from weeds and left undisturbed until the following February or March, when they are lifted and planted about 2½ft apart each way in a well-prepared site. The plants are prevented from forming a flowering stem by cutting off the crown of each plant when planting just below soil level. The plants are restricted to one stem and the foliage allowed to die down before lifting for forcing in the autumn.

When lifting plants for forcing, trim off all but the central root and pack closely, either in soil under the staging or in boxes of good soil. If given a temperature of 45–50°F (7–10°C), plenty of water and complete darkness, succulent blanched shoots will be produced.

The side shoots or root cuttings are stored in batches for planting the following February or March, it being important to make a straight cut at the top and a slanting cut at the base. They are set out vertically in well prepared soil in dibber holes 15–18 in apart in rows 2ft apart with the *top* (straight cut) of the cutting just below the soil surface, again limiting each plant to one strong shoot. These plants will provide a supply of forcing roots, the same rotation as previously described being carried out in the autumn.

The blanched shoots are ready for use when 6in or so long. Once the roots have been forced they are destroyed after removing any suitably sized sections of root to reserve as a further source of cuttings.

Rhubarb *(Rheum rhaponticum)*

Early forced rhubarb is a commercial crop of some significance. It is forced in dark heated sheds at 50–55°F (10–13°C), usually fan ventilated to avoid the risk of fungal and bacterial diseases (see Chapter 32). On an amateur or professional scale it is first of all necessary to build up a stock of two- to three-year-old rhubarb crowns.

Propagation Commercial practice is to divide established crowns, this being quicker and more dependable than propagation from seed. Each section must bear one or more terminal buds, these being planted in well-cultivated soil with a pH of 5.5–6.0, phosphate and potash index 2, on a 3–4ft square-planting system. Large areas are pre-treated with a simazine based weedkiller at 2lb (active ingredient) per acre. Vigorous growth is encouraged by dressing with nitrogen at 2–3cwt per acre ($1–1\frac{1}{2}$oz per sq yd).

Preparation for forcing Forcing crowns are those which have been established for at least two years. They are ploughed, dug or forked out of the ground and allowed to become frosted. A points system is used to determine the optimum time for housing the various varieties. To install the necessary soil thermometer make a vertical hole 4in deep with a cane the same diameter as the bulb. Insert the thermometer so that the bulb is in direct contact with the soil with the graduated part of the stem lying horizontally along the surface. Fill the hole gently with sifted soil, disturbing the soil as little as possible. Leave the thermometer in position *undisturbed* until the end of the season and do not cover with a box for protection. The temperature should be read every day at 9 am (10 am before British Summer Time ends). Any readings above 49°F (9°C) are ignored. All readings below are subtracted from this base of 49°F (9°C) and the daily differences added up: these are the 'cold units'. By 1972 three varieties had been tested at Stockbridge House, Yorkshire, and the optimum stage for lifting from the field was found to be:

Timperley Early	200 cold units	
Prince Albert	300	,,
Victoria	520	,,

Forcing The lifted crowns are placed in forcing sheds or in boxes under the greenhouse staging, packed tightly together with soil or peat to fill up the spaces and cover the crowns. If given warmth and moisture and *complete* darkness, blanched shoots will be formed according to the temperature level. After forcing the crowns are discarded.

Asparagus

There is not a great deal of interest commercially in forcing *Asparagus officinalis*, a member of the Lilaceae. But it is worth while lifting a few plants to produce succulent early shoots. Make up a hot bed out of manure and old leaves in a corner of the greenhouse; rapid fermentation should take place. When the temperature has dropped, put a thin layer of soil or peat over the manure and pack in the asparagus plants tightly before covering with a further layer of soil or peat.

Alternatively they may be planted up in the greenhouse border, or in boxes of soil, in December/January, and early shoots will be produced according to the temperature level provided. After harvesting the plants are generally destroyed.

Chicory

Known botanically as *Cichorium intybus*, this vegetable is grown for its leafy blanched shoots in the winter months. Seed is sown out of doors in May (in the UK) in well-prepared soil $\frac{1}{2}$in deep in rows 15in apart, being thinned out to 8–9in apart.

The plants are kept clean by hosing and are lifted in the autumn, the tops cut off and stored between layers of fine sand in lines in a dry place or at the foot of a dry wall. The roots are lifted in as required and packed tightly together in boxes with some soil between them. If kept moist, dark and at a temperature of 55°F (12.8°C) shoots will be ready for cutting in 3–4 weeks, or longer at lower temperatures.

A useful place is beneath suitable draped greenhouse staging, providing a succession of blanched shoots which can be forced every fortnight.

Mint *and* parsley

Plants can be lifted into the greenhouse to continue growth during the winter. Parsley

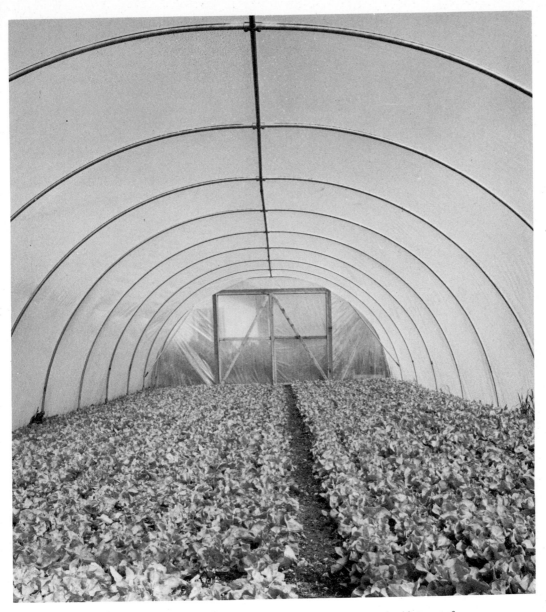

A wide range of
vegetables can be
cultivated under glass or
commercially under
polythene structures.
Lettuces are probably
the most popular such
crop.

257

should be in 6–8in pots; mint should be planted closely in deep boxes of good loamy soil, when with warmth and moisture new shoot will form. Parsley pots are also popular.

Other vegetables
A number of outdoor vegetables can also be grown in cold or heated greenhouses where they will be ready for harvesting a great deal earlier, eg beetroot, carrots (special forcing varieties), onions, peas, radish, spinach, turnip. Give adequate watering and free ventilation during the spring months. All require fertile soil, pH 6–6.5 and potash and phosphate index 2–4. Beetroot and turnip do not stand frost.

Many vegetables can be started off under glass for eventual growing outside, eg early brussels sprouts, early cabbage, early cauliflower, sweet, corn, leeks and parsley in addition to those already mentioned. Seed is best sown in peat pots, Jiffy 7s or peat blocks and germinated at 55–60°F (13–15.6°C) before hardening off for planting out.

Chapter 22

The grape vine (*Vitis vinifera*)

Ideally vines should be planted in a specially prepared border either inside or just outside the greenhouse, the stem being led in just above ground level and the roots able to spread freely and derive benefit from rainfall. Culture in large pots or tubs 12in or more in diameter may be an excellent arrangement for the smaller greenhouse.

Preparation of vine borders

A vigorous vine will demand a section of greenhouse border at least 3–4ft wide and 6–8ft long with a prepared soil depth of 2ft or more. It would be folly to try to grow a vine in a diminutive structure.

The preparation of a vine border in traditional pattern is exacting in the extreme demanding (1) complete removal of the soil to a full depth of 2ft 6in, (2) a 6in layer of rubble or broken brick with drainage (it is sometimes advisable to dig much deeper and arrange for an *in situ* sump of rubble), (3) a layer of inverted turves, (4) a mixture of 5 parts good sifted loam, 1 part mortar rubble (if not procurable broken brick will suffice), 1 part decayed manure, and any wood ash which may be available, (5) 2–4oz of bone meal per sqyd and, if mortar rubble was not used, $\frac{1}{2}$–$\frac{3}{4}$lb ground limestone per sqyd. This compost was used over generations; it may not be practicable now. Good soil plus a little manure can be used instead, so long as good drainage is provided. JIP2 compost is used when planting in large pots or other containers.

When placing the roots out of doors the same procedure should ideally be followed for the make-up of the bed, but the same compromise may have to be made, with attention again to drainage. The philosophy that the carcass of a dead animal forms a good foundation for a vine may well have its merits, although it is a practice seldom acceptable.

Propagation and planting

Vines are frequently bought as young roots, although they can readily be propagated from 2in 'eyes' taken in late winter and put in a pot with the 'eye' at soil level. Also layers, 3 bud stems, or young growths. Given heat, young plants are ready for setting out in June or July of the following year.

Dormant vines are usually planted between October and early February, anything from 5–10ft apart according to the system of training employed. For a single cordon 5ft apart will suffice, but one vine is usually sufficient for the amateur greenhouse. If the greenhouse is oriented with the ridge running north–south it would be advisable to plant the vine in the centre or to one side of the north end. This will allow the vine to travel along the one sloping roof and, provided it is ruthlessly restricted, still allow the culture of other crops. A better arrangement can be made if the greenhouse is oriented east–west, when the vine could then be trained along the north sloping roof, or planted on the north side and largely confined to this to avoid the restriction of light from the southerly aspect (ie if in the northern hemisphere). Where the whole greenhouse can be devoted to the culture of the vine then the centre at the end away from the door is as convenient a location as any. In lean-to structures it is usual to train vines on the glass side.

Support is usually provided by a series of wires run horizontally 8–10in apart through wire eyes screwed into the astragals (glazing bars). Alternatively, mesh materials can be used. With an alloy house it will be necessary to make a wooden framework.

Planting

The vine, self-raised or bought, is taken out of its pot and the roots opened up or disentangled, it not being advisable to leave them in a compact ball. It is then planted into container or border by spreading out the roots well, setting not too deeply, watering in and, after a good firming, mulching the surface of the soil with peat or well-rotted farmyard manure. When the root is planted out of doors it will be necessary to remove a brick or two, or a section of glass or wood, keeping the opening to a minimum and covering one root and wrapping the stem with sacking and filling any air space with straw and sacking.

Pruning and training

Dormant vines *must* be cut back to 4 or 5ft after planting; a young growing vine planted in summer is cut back to two buds after planting. Strong growth should invariably result, encouraged by plentiful watering and spraying the young leaves and stems. In the small greenhouse there is much to

Fig 75

be said for allowing only one main rod, but vine rods are very accommodating and at any stage the decision can be altered and another 'main' growth allowed to develop.

In the winter subsequent to planting, *new growth* on the main rod or rods is cut back to 3 or 4ft and any lateral shoots to two plump base buds which can readily be found if searched for, although not obvious.

Annual pruning follows the same general pattern of cutting back a proportion of new growth, although there will come a time when this cannot be achieved and the vine has to be restricted according to space available.

The number of laterals must be determined at a fairly early stage, it generally being convenient to have a lateral running off about every 2ft of rod. It is also important to decide in which direction the shoots are to be allowed to form; if the main rod is run along under the ridge of the greenhouse the laterals can be tied down one side to the gutter, or the other way round (Fig 75).

It is general practice to allow the vine to become established over two or three years before any fruit is allowed to form, but in the restricted conditions of amateur greenhouses it would seem futile to carry out this practice, it being more desirable to restrict the vigour by early cropping or any other means, always provided of course that the vine has at least enough root system to sustain growth. After cutting back the laterals to two plump buds, two shoots are allowed to form each spring; the stronger and preferably the one bearing a bunch of embryo fruit is selected, the other being removed completely. This procedure is followed (spread out over a period to avoid shock) at each lateral growth point until in the end the single, double or treble rod is left with a number of single laterals growing out in one or both directions.

The laterals are gradually pulled in to the supporting wire or mesh material and tied, progressively shortening the string used. The tip of each lateral should be nipped off at the second leaf past the

260

Training a vine under glass. This is how the vine should look immediately after pruning.

bunch of grapes, or if no grapes, as with a young vine, the lateral is stopped at about the seventh leaf. Sub-laterals formed after stopping are restricted to one leaf or so, although this is not critical. No system of pruning is rigid; it must be adapted to circumstances and space.

Cultural treatment

Early vines will start into growth by January or February in the greenhouse if there is sufficient heat. With unheated greenhouses growth will start later. Water is applied to the roots, and the vents are shut a little to encourage a humid atmosphere, while the rods may be syringed well with plain water. In order to get an even break of buds it may be necessary to arch the leading shoots over by untying the rod from its support, but with younger vines this is seldom necessary. When the flowers appear the greenhouse should, if possible, be kept drier, ceasing syringeing and avoiding damping down. Pollination and fertilisation generally occur readily, but it may be necessary to tap the rod or dust the flowers with a little cotton wool on the end of a cane.

Vines should never be allowed to dry out. Borders should be watered with a fine rose, keeping the surface moderately moist, and a good thick mulch of peat will assist in this direction. Vines growing in pots or boxes must be watered regularly, indeed this is one of the main disadvantages of growing them in this manner.

About 55°F (12.8°C) is satisfactory for flowering, and for rapid swelling of the berries the ideal is 65°F (18.3°C) day and about 60°F (15.6°C) at night. Feed with weak liquid manure at this stage. During ripening plenty of air should be given to avoid botrytis. Vines will resent sudden temperature changes just as much as any other crop, and can react very positively by 'shanking', when the skins of the berries shrivel or the berries 'scald'. Ideally a little air should be left on at night always, particularly when the berries are ripening.

Thinning and harvesting

The thinning of grapes is most important. A start should be made when the berries are about the size of peas, using special vine scissors and leaving the berries about half an inch apart. Success at shows depends much on the shape of a bunch of grapes and a little practical experience goes further than pages of description. A few weeks after thinning the rapidly swelling berries appear to stop growing, this being because they are stoning, and ideally the temperature should be dropped a little during this period. It is important not to allow too many bunches of grapes to remain on a vine, about 1lb per foot of rod being usual. The bunches will ripen according to variety, temperature and season, and should be harvested when ready; in a cold greenhouse in a northerly latitude there can be difficulty in fully ripening the grapes of some varieties such as 'Black Hamburg'.

Winter pruning follows the sequence described previously and should be carried out annually when the vine is dormant. After pruning lift all dead leaves and rubbish and then rub all loose bark from the main rod of the vine and paint with a strong solution of malathion, or other general insecticide avoiding the buds otherwise they can be damaged. This procedure is to kill off over-wintering pests.

The border should be given a good top dressing of well-rotted farmyard manure annually, and in addition a dressing of 3–4oz per sq yd of a good balanced general fertiliser as growth commences.

Varieties

For heated greenhouses: Alicante (black), Black Muscat, Gros Colmar (black), Lady Downes (black), Madresfield Court (black), Muscat of Alexander (white), White Frontigman.

For cold or cool greenhouses: Black Hamburg, Buckland Sweetwater (white), Fosters Seedling (white), Forbes Seedling (white), Gros Maroc (black), Reine Olga (reddish).

For pests, diseases and physiological disorders see Chapter 32.

The cultivation of peaches and nectarines

Peaches and nectarines are types of *Prunus persica*, the difference between them lying in the felt-like skin of the former and the smooth skin of the latter. Like the vine, the peach and the nectarine pose problems for cultivation in small greenhouses. It is asking too much to expect a vigorous bush to perform well under severe restriction, and gardeners would be well advised to consider these problems before embarking too enthusiastically on their cultivation. An alternative may well be to grow them in small pots.

Traditionally peaches are grown on the wall of a south-facing lean-to, a practice which fits in well with vines being grown against the glass. Alternatively the peaches can be grown against the glass (12–15in from it) and a vine run along the ridge from the end. To do real justice to a peach, a wall height of 10–11ft will be necessary, with commensurate height for the glass portion. They can be excellently grown in a span-roofed structure on an alternate staggered arrangement where more than one bush is grown, and a greenhouse with a width of 10–12ft and 8–9ft high will give reasonable room for development (Fig 76).

Greenhouses may be cold or heated. Adequate roof and side ventilation is important. Supporting wires should be run 9–10in apart in vine eyes 3–4in from the wall or 9–10in from the glass, or some other support provided.

Production programme

Heat given December/January—fruit harvested June

No heat—fruit harvested July/August/September according to variety

Preparations for planting

The long-term nature of a peach or nectarine demands a thorough approach to border preparation. When the soil is initially of good quality and drainage is in no way impeded, it will suffice to work through a reasonable quantity of broken rubble and well-rotted manure or compost to an area of 6 × 3ft per tree. Peat is now frequently used in quantity for soil improvement and

in this case lime should be applied at 4–5oz per bushel of peat to offset its acidity and in addition at approximately 1lb or more per sq yd of border, according to analysis, to bring the pH up to about 6.5, with a phosphate and potash index of between 2 and 3. Where the soil is completely unsuitable excavate to a depth of 2–2½ft for the area of 6 × 3ft referred to above. Fill up with a good layer of rubble through which is mixed any *clean* garden rubbish available, along with a liberal application of bonemeal and basic slag. Once again a good John Innes type compost (JIP1) will suffice, but the magnitude of the task shows the need to think in terms of improvement rather than substitution if at all possible. The roots of peaches and nectarines in modern greenhouses will invariably gain access to the outside soil and it may be necessary to improve the outside area concerned.

A heavy mulch of well rotted farmyard manure should be spread over the surface sufficiently long before planting to allow a degree of drying out yet keep the mixture moist.

Fig 76

Planting

On delivery from the nursery the tree should have its roots spread out in a wide shallow hole, after removing any roots damaged in transit. Deep planting is not advisable, 2–3in of soil over the top roots being all that is required. Leave a space of 4–5in against the wall or the side of the greenhouse. Water in thoroughly. Tie branches loosely to support wires or trellis framework; these are finally spaced out and secured after pruning and before growth starts in the spring. If trees are bought with a well-developed fan shape, the main branches should in the first pruning be cut back to about half their length to encourage the development of new side shoots, as peaches and nectarines *fruit on the previous year's new wood* and a constant supply of this is necessary to keep the tree productive. The training of a young plant requires more detailed information than can be given here.

It is important that from the time growth commences there should be a plentiful supply of moisture, otherwise a newly planted tree will draw on reserves of sap and possibly collapse and die back completely.

Flowering, pollination and setting fruit

Blooms will be produced very early in the season, being formed while there is very little leaf growth. Pollination must be assisted by tapping the branches and dusting the open blooms with a rabbit's tail or cotton wool on a cane, keeping the air dry and the house relatively cool at 45–50°F (7.2–10°C)—if this is not made impossible by other activities. If it is, then the peach or nectarine must take 'pot luck' and there may be very erratic setting and fruit production.

Much can be done to encourage growth and good setting by syringeing or hosing with a *fine* rose early in the morning of a day which promises to be bright, this being a practice which should be persevered with until fruit is well formed. Dryness of atmosphere will also induce red spider attack.

After it is seen that tiny fruits have set,

the temperature may be gradually increased to 65–70°F (18.3–21.1°C) by day and 55–60°F (12.8–15.6°C) by night, emulating the conditions experienced in out-of-doors culture later in the season. Vents should be shut down early at night to conserve heat as much as possible.

Thinning of fruit

Thinning to avoid over-cropping is generally done first to a limited extent after the tiny fruits are set, then later to about one fruit per square foot, or roughly one fruit per shoot, this taking place over a period when the fruits are the size of small walnuts ($\frac{1}{2}$–$\frac{3}{4}$in). Remove with scissors to avoid tearing the bark. During this second thinning period high or erratic temperatures must be avoided, or a large fall of fruit may be induced.

Summer pruning

Surplus growth must be rubbed out (gradually, to avoid shock) throughout the season when an inch or so long, except during the flowering period, the object being to rub out *all* buds growing outward, leaving only two or three well placed to replace the shoots presently bearing fruit. Failure to remove surplus shoots and loosely tie in the remaining young growth will result in a forest of growth and a completely unmanageable tree.

Harvesting

As the fruit ripens it should be allowed the full benefit of the sun by tying aside any growths that shade it. When picking the fruit handle it very carefully, especially peaches which bruise very easily.

After the fruit is gathered, frequent hosing of the foliage should be carried out and full ventilation given, along with plenty of water at the roots to coincide with the mild autumn rains they would receive out of doors. The application of very diluted liquid manure is also advisable to strengthen the shoots and buds for next year.

Winter pruning

When leaf fall is complete the tree should be carefully pruned, cutting out suitable old shoots which have borne fruit and tying in well-placed new shoots. There must obviously be compromise here, eg a fair proportion of old shoots must be left because of new shoots coming from them. As the tree grows pruning becomes more exacting, and gardeners are again reminded that they should not enter into the growing of peaches or nectarines unless they are prepared to give the detailed attention necessary.

Root pruning

Where trees are over-vigorous and non-productive it may be necessary to carry out root pruning by completely lifting trees up to 5 or 6 years old, cutting off strong tap and coarse lateral roots and replanting. This is carried out in the dormant period.

Nutrition

Each January or February give a total dressing per tree of 7–8oz of a good compound trace-element-containing fertiliser, scattered evenly over the ground for a reasonable area out from the tree. Each autumn after the fruit is gathered apply $\frac{1}{2}$–$\frac{3}{4}$lb of hydrated or 1lb of ground limestone per sq yd. Over-vigorous trees should not be too liberally fed. Weak trees can be fed more generously to the extent of applying stimulants during the growing season or giving additional nitrogen as in sulphate of ammonia in February at 1–2oz per sq yd.

Varieties

White fleshed and yellow fleshed peaches and nectarines are available, fruiting according to level of heat and variety from June to the end of September.

For pests, diseases and physiological disorders see Chapter 32.

Figs

The fruit of the fig *Ficus carica* does not ripen fully outside in northerly latitudes except in favoured sheltered situations, but under glass two or even three crops of fruit can be achieved per year.

Planting

Avoid any greenhouse area likely to be in shade. The sunny wall of a lean-to structure is ideal.

It is best if borders are excavated to a depth of about 3ft and some concrete or corrugated iron put down, followed by a 6in layer of broken brick, on top of which is placed good leafy loam with some mortar rubble worked through. The purpose of sealing off the bottom is to prevent downward growing roots which can result in rank unproductive growth. Really deep digging will generally suffice, broken concrete slabs being laid down in the process. Allow plenty of room, 12ft or more for each fig (unless of course they are grown in pots).

Fan-trained trees 3–4 years old are generally purchased, and planted either in autumn or late winter according to the level of heat; late winter is suitable for colder growing conditions. Trees are trained out in fan form on suitable wires or trellis, the bottom 12in from ground level being kept clear of all growth. Congested branches should be thinned out before planting.

Seasonal culture

Figs respond to regular watering, a steadily rising temperature from December onwards, starting at 55°F (12.8°C) and reaching 65°F (18.3°C). Humidity should be maintained by regular spraying with clean water. The figs will grow at a rate commensurate with prevailing temperatures, and cooler growing is the more usual procedure in these days of high fuel costs. When fruit is seen to be well formed and ripening, freer ventilation should be given where possible. A second crop can be achieved in a reasonably cool greenhouse by cutting away older shoots to allow development of new shoots to bear the next crop. This practice is repeated after the second crop has been picked, leaving a fair balance of well-spaced shoots—and this is the whole essence of pruning procedure. In addition some shoots should be rubbed out in spring and summer and lateral shoots stopped at the fifth or sixth leaf from the base. Once again the aim should be to avoid overcrowding.

Regular watering coupled with the application of weak liquid manure should keep the figs growing healthily, as they are greedy plants.

Over-cropping is the main cause of failure, especially on young trees, and some restriction of fruiting should always be aimed at.

Culture in pots

The culture of figs in pots follows the same general pattern as all pot-grown fruit, the essence of success being to stop young lateral shoots at 4 or 5 leaves in summer, then cut out over-crowded wood in winter and, most important, avoid over-cropping.

Propagation

Figs are propagated by seed, layering, budding or grafting, layering being a ready way of getting a new young bush by pegging down a suitably placed shoot into the top of a pot and by mulching it to induce roots to form. Budding and grafting are also useful techniques.

Varieties Brown Turkey, White Marseilles, Negro Largo, Bourjassotte Grise, White Ischia, Black Ischia.

For pests, diseases and physiological disorders see Chapter 32.

Strawberries

Strawberries are native to Europe in small-fruited forms, *Fragaria vesca* and several others. The cultivation of large-fruited strawberries is attributed to the introduction of *F. virginiana* from North America in the seventeenth century, the first British raised large-fruited variety being Keen's 'Imperial' by Marshall Keen in 1806.

General culture

Much research has gone into the techniques of growing strawberries successfully under glass, as they are a high value crop. It is highly important in the first place that runners be selected only from plants of the highest quality and as free as possible from all strawberry ailments, virus and eelworm in particular. Every effort must be made to get young runners established in their forcing grounds as soon as possible. Mobile structures are frequently used in Holland for early strawberry culture and the young newly rooted runners are planted out in their respective plots directly they are severed from the parent plant and irrigated until they are growing strongly. For mobile greenhouse culture the plants are planted at 10 × 10 or 12 × 12in or thereabouts in 4ft 6in beds, the greenhouse being pushed over the plots in December or January. The Belgians plant at the same density in slightly raised beds 4ft 6in–5ft and 2–3ft apart in a static greenhouse in autumn. Black polythene mulch with lay-flat irrigation underneath the polythene is invariably used, and irrigation is again relied upon to prevent any set back.

Much more use is now being made of whalehide or peat pots to establish plants in, the plants being brought into the greenhouse in January, and this is a practice likely to appeal to the gardener. On a still smaller scale the young rooted runners are potted into 5–6in pots after severing from the parent plant, using John Innes No 2 compost.

A vernalisation period is thought essential for strawberries in order to initiate flower buds, and is brought about by periods of lower temperatures. In small scale growing the pots are left outside until late December, being protected from severe frost by straw or other means. The necessary vernalisation period is completed by the time they are lifted into the greenhouse or covered. The plants are kept cool for 3–4 weeks and then heat is applied to coax them gradually into growth. Flowers will form according to the temperature level given, generally in February or March, during which time the flowers should be dusted with a rabbit's tail or cotton wool to assist pollination. Strawberries are, in the main, self-fertile, but at that time of year and in the environment of a greenhouse there will be few, if any, pollinating insects, though high temperatures will encourage bees if a hive is placed in or near the greenhouse. If kept well watered and given weak liquid feeding the plants can be encouraged to produce fruit by April or May, considerably earlier than out of doors. At lower heat levels they will still crop much earlier than out of doors. Commercially they are only grown for one year in greenhouses, new 'maidens' being planted annually, although two-year-old plants can be lifted when dormant and can perform extremely well.

Cold frame culture

Strawberries can also be grown most successfully in cold frames, the runners being established in July or August at 10 × 10in, the sashes being put on during late January or February. Drying out is the risk in frames, resulting in small malformed fruits. When possible the sashes should be left off during the day in the flowering period to allow entry of insects for pollination, or this can be done artificially by dusting the flowers, a practice essential with early flowering in heated frames. The plants can be left in frames for two or three years, but kept well cleaned of runners. When strawberries are grown under cloches or polythene tunnels the same general procedure is followed, although once again the plants can be left for a few years.

Environmental control

Environmental control is particularly important with strawberries grown in greenhouses, frames, cloches or tunnels, and it may be necessary to take preventive measures in wet humid areas by spraying with fungicides. Support for the fruit by wires or other means will help by preventing fruit/soil contact. Strawberries in greenhouses respond to low intensity artificial lighting at 9–10W per sqyd given during the night for 2–3 hours, this encouraging earlier flowering.

Cold storage for runners

The putting of runners into cold storage will allow planting in June and July for autumn cropping under glass, or alternatively the early establishment of plants in pots in May, deblossoming by removing flowers and bringing well-established plants into the greenhouse in January. If when runners are lifted they are tied in bundles of 25 or 50 and stored long-term in 38mu gauge polythene bags at 28–30°F (−2 to −1°C), this allows planting out over a period and provides for successional cropping.

Varieties Note that Gorella is especially good for early forcing and is one of the main varieties grown in continental Europe for this purpose. Royal Sovereign tends to be susceptible to botrytis under glass. Redgauntlet (early) and Talisman (late) can both be double cropped in a good year.

For pests, diseases and physiological disorders see Chapter 32.

Fruit growing in pots

The growing of fruit in pots is a very old practice which has tended to fall out of favour in recent years. The full range of fruits may be grown including apricots, apples, pears, cherries, plums, peaches, vines, figs, nectarines, citrus fruits, strawberries and so on. No great demand on space is made and greenhouse space is available for other activities at various times of the year. The growing of fruit in pots allows the production of limited quantities of superlative quality fruit in areas which may be so bleak and exposed that outdoor culture is impossible. It is also useful for the production of fruit for the show bench.

Only greenhouses of good design and well situated to receive full sunlight should be considered: a greenhouse partially shaded by a vigorous peach or vine is not really suitable, although if it is a lean-to structure and a peach is grown on the rear wall, pots may certainly be grown in the front portion. Fruit in pots is an interesting and tempting subject for the conservatory that is also used for recreation. It is not generally necessary to think in terms of artificial heat, except perhaps the very minimum in the coldest areas. The pots are placed on the greenhouse floor—soil, ashes or concrete—and frequently on bricks to prevent supplementary rooting.

Type of bush

A restricted growing habit is essential, which involves the use or training of specially shaped trees grown on dwarfing rootstocks obtained from a reliable nurseryman. The skilled gardener can start with a 'maiden' (one year grafted) on a

267

dwarf root stock and shape the tree, but it is generally better to buy specially shaped trees from a nurseryman, and better still if the bushes are already established in pots, three years old, and well furnished with buds so that fruiting can start immediately. With maidens it takes time to build up the framework before fruiting commences.

Cultural procedure

Delivery of trees is best taken in the autumn at dormancy or leaf fall, when they are potted up into 9in pots. It is unwise to put a small bush into a large pot of 10–12in diameter, as the secret of success with pot-grown trees is root restriction, though as the trees get older they may eventually graduate to 10–12in or even larger pots. The pots used should be very sturdy and have drainage holes in the sides as well as in the base. Only the heaviest gauge plastic pots should be used, it being necessary in some cases to put one inside the other to impart sufficient strength, boring holes in the sides with an electric drill. If new clay pots are used they must be soaked well before use, and all pots must be scrupulously cleaned by washing. All pots are given a deep layer of drainage in the form of broken pots or pebbles over which is put a layer of coarse peat or coarsely shredded peat.

Much is made of the need for a good turf-based compost derived from stacked turf and it is unlikely that this can be bettered by any of the modern composts. Through the loam for apples and pears should be mixed one-third part of very well rotted farmyard manure or well-made, reliable garden compost. For apricots, peaches, nectarines and figs avoid the farmyard manure but add bonemeal and lime at 4oz and 2oz per bushel respectively. The compost should be well mixed and under cover for a few weeks before use, finally adding some coarse bonemeal plus a liberal scattering of ground limestone. The compost should be sufficiently moist, rendering it so by watering if necessary.

Shorten all vigorous lateral and downward growing roots before potting up with great care, packing the compost in with a potting stick in layers until it is 1in below the rim of the pot.

After potting the trees must be well watered and placed in a sheltered situation at the foot of a sunny wall, the pots of 'hardy' trees being plunged to their rims in good soil or ashes or alternatively protected with straw or peat to avoid damage by freezing, care being taken that they are not waterlogged. Hardy trees—apples, pears, plums and cherries – can remain out of doors until the buds begin to swell; apricots, peaches, nectarines, vines, figs and citrus fruits are better brought into the greenhouse immediately after potting, being given plenty of room and ventilation.

Seasonal treatment

While the culture of fruit in pots demands considerable care and attention to detail, it is remarkable what can be achieved by regular watering and feeding; indeed, because of the limited root area the importance of this cannot be over-stressed. It is also essential that free ventilation should be given in the morning and excessively high temperatures avoided, particularly during the initial period of stoning in the case of peaches and nectarines. Assistance with pollination of all trees is desirable, using a rabbit's tail or cotton wool.

Regular syringeing is essential to encourage healthy growth of leaves and to discourage attacks of red spider, which can have a disastrous effect. Feeding with liquid manure should be practised after the fruits are set, once fortnightly at first, increasing the applications to once weekly later. As soon as the trees are in full growth a top dressing of equal parts of well rotted farmyard manure and soil should be given and moulded up round the edge of the pots, raising their height several inches to allow watering. Due to the limited root area, the importance of regular watering and feeding cannot be over-stressed.

Pruning and fruit thinning

In spring and summer there should be reduction of new growth. With apples and pears lateral growths should be pinched back to about 4–5in or less, leaving only

Many fruits like the cherries shown here, as well as apples, pears and plums, can be grown successfully in the greenhouse, where heavier crops would generally be produced than on plants grown out of doors.

269

a proportion of them in the case of apples otherwise the tree will become a tangled mat of growth. Peaches and nectarines, which fruit on new wood, should have well-placed shoots selected and allowed to make reasonable growth before having the tips pinched out. Some thinning of fruit will be necessary, leaving only one fruit per cluster on apples and pears and thinning plums out singly every 2–3in or more, while peaches and nectarines should only be allowed to form one fruit per 9sq in of tree. Figs should only have their shoots thinned. Apples and pears can be taken out of doors when the fruit is ripening and the pot plunged in soil for safety and conservation of moisture. Wind damage can be avoided by securing each fruit with raffia to a convenient branch.

After fruiting, all types of trees are ripened off by placing out of doors, carrying out any re-potting in October along similar lines to those already described. Annual re-potting, while not necessary, is advisable in many cases, moving vigorous trees to a slightly larger pot. Again, the hardy trees can remain out of doors in a sheltered spot but the rest should be brought into the greenhouse.

Pruning is carried out by reducing the laterals in apples, pears and plums to within two or three buds of the base, and on trees such as peaches, which fruit on new wood, leaving only a proportion of well-placed sturdy shoots to bear next year's crop.

Specific pest and disease control is best (see Chapter 32); there is generally no need for the routine practices necessary with crops out of doors.

Chapter 23

Bedding Plant Production

Many types of plants are grown as 'summer bedders' for planting in the period April–June. Greenhouse production considerably shortens the propagation period, especially where germination is under mist or in cabinets, followed by the use of either growing rooms or supplementary lighting.

The majority of bedders are seed raised; others are propagated by cuttings or division.

Cuttings are taken in August/September/October before and during plant lifting at the end of the summer bedding season, or in spring from over-wintered plants, or from over-wintered tubers in the case of dahlias. Autumn rooting can take place in either cool greenhouses or cold frames; lush growth is not desirable as plants tend to become too large before the spring—keep very much on the dry side. Early spring rooting can be carried out at higher temperatures and the plants kept growing strongly. Plenty of light and as free ventilation as possible within the limits of the weather should be the rule for all over-wintered plants. Dahlias, begonias and other tender plants are of course over-wintered in heated greenhouses or in the case of tubers in a mulch of peat in frost-free cellars.

There is much to be said for using Jiffy 7s for the rooting of all cuttings as they sustain the plants for a considerable period before potting on is necessary.

Seed sowing procedures for bedding plants are on traditional lines (see Chapter 17). Damping off disease is frequently encountered with bedding plants especially when sterilised soil forms part of the compost with the resultant release of ammonia. Antirrhinums and lobelia are particularly prone to damping off.

Pricking off is required at an early stage in the development of seed sown bedding plants to avoid tangled roots and etiolation. Break-up containers are useful as root disturbance is avoided at planting. Nutrition is important with the use of soilless media; many bedding plants will suffer acutely from starvation if diluted liquid feeds are not given regularly.

Acclimatisation through a period of progressively cooler temperatures is necessary. Normally plants are placed out in frames in April, depending on the region; less water is given and ventilation gradually increased. Feeding with diluted liquid fertiliser may be necessary to sustain growth, but not to the extent of inducing lushness.

For pests, diseases and physiological disorders see Chapter 32.

The tuberous begonias are among the most exotic of plants that can either be grown in the greenhouse or started in the greenhouse for bedding out in summer.

Name and type	Propagation and time of germination	Germination temperature category
*These plants are usually grown as pot plants.		
*_Ageratum houstonianum (A. mexicanum)._ Annual. F₁ hybrid and 'straight'	Seed in Feb/March. Sown on surface. 3 weeks	65–70°F (18.3–21.1°C)
Anchusa capensis. Annual variety	Seed in Feb. 2–3 weeks	65–75°F (18.3–23.9°C)
*Antirrhinum. Perennial treated as half-hardy annual. Many F₁ hybrids available	Seed in Feb. 10–21 days	65–75°F (18.3–23.9°C)
Aster _Callistephus chinensis._ Tender annual	Seed in March. 2–3 weeks	65–75°F (18.3–23.9°C)
*Begonia, fibrous, _B. semperflorens._ Half-hardy perennial treated as annual	Seed Dec–March for smaller plants. Sow thinly on surface. Apply liquid feeding after germination. 2–3 weeks	65–75°F (18.3–23.9°C)
*Begonia, tuberous, _B._ × _tuberhybrida._ Half-hardy perennial	Seed in Nov Dec. By division of tubers after starting them into growth. By planting tubers dormant. Short-day plants and may need supplementary light and day length control	65–75°F (18.3–23.9°C)
*Calceolaria _C. integrifolia, C. rugosa_ and others. Half-hardy perennials treated as annuals. F₁ hybrids available	Herbaceous types from cuttings in autumn or spring. Seed Nov–Jan. 2–3 weeks	65–75°F (18.3–23.9°C). Grow cool 48–50°F (8.9–10°C)
C. gracilis. Annual	Sow March/April. 2–3 weeks	65–75°F (18.3–23.9°C)
Carnation _Dianthus caryophyllus_ Annuals, including 'Chabaud' *Perennials	Annuals sown Jan–Feb. 2–3 weeks Cuttings or layering in summer. Seed in spring. Do not flower well until following year	70°F (21.1°C)
Chrysanthemum _C. carinatum._ Annual	Seed in Feb/March. 2–4 weeks	65–75°F (18.3–23.9°C) Grow cool
*_C. leucanthemum._ Perennial. (See also Chapter 26)	Seed in Feb/March or later. 2 weeks	65°F (18.3°C) Grow cool
Chrysanthemum parthenium (Matricaria capensis). Perennial	Seed in Feb. Cuttings in spring. 2–3 weeks	65–75°F (18.3–23.9°C)

Colour	Height	Distance apart and main role	Seed per oz (approx)
Blue shades	4–9in	6–8in. Edging	200,000
Blue	8in	6–8in. Edging or low display	1,200
Various shades, pinks, whites, reds	12–24in	12–14in. Mass display	177,000 (cover seed tray with polythene bag or domes)
Various	8–24in	10–12in. Mass display	12,000 (wilt resistant varieties available)
Wide range of colours. Some with dark leaves	6–12in or more	6–12in. Mass display	2,000,000
Extremely large range of colours and flower form	9–12in	9–12in. Mass display	15,000 per 1/128oz
Red, yellow, orange, scarlet and crimson	10–18in	10–12in. Mass display	550,000
Yellow	18in	9–10in. Mass display	
Various	10–14in	10–12in. Edging	14,000
Various	12–18in		
Various. Singles and doubles	18–24in	12–18in. Mass display, cut blooms	10,000
White	12in	9–10in. A 'dot' plant	20,000
Yellow and white	8–12in	6–9in. For dwarf beds	150,000

Name and type	Propagation and time of germination	Germination temperature category
Cleome spinosa (C. pungens). Annual	Seed in Feb/March. Resents root disturbance. 2 weeks	65–75°F (18.3–23.9°C)
Cosmos. Tender annual *Cosmea bipinnata*	Seed in Feb/March. 1–2 weeks	65–75°F (18.3–23.9°C)
Dahlia variabilis. Tender perennial. Hybrids	Seed in Feb/March. Cuttings Feb/March or plant tubers direct either dormant or started into growth. Will stand no frost. 2–3 weeks	65–75°F (18.3–23.9°C)
Dianthus 'Nana Giganteus'. Annual. F$_1$ hybrids	Sow Sept for the types requiring long season of growth (eg 'Queen of Hearts'). Other types sow March	65–75°F (18.3–23.9°C)
D. chinensis (D. sinensis). Perennial	Sow in Sept or earlier out of doors. Can also be sown in Feb	65–75°F (18.3–23.9°C)
Dimorphotheca aurantiaca. Annual	Seed in Feb/March. 2–3 weeks	65–75°F (18.3–23.9°C)
Dorotheanthus bellidiformis (Mesembryanthemum criniflorum) (Livingstone daisy). Half-hardy annual	Seed in Feb/March. 2–3 weeks	65–75°F (18.3–23.9°C)
Gazania splendens. Perennial. Hybrids	Seed in Jan/Feb. 3 weeks	60°F (15.6°C)
Gladiolus species and hybrids. Perennials	Corms planted direct or started in heat prior to planting outside in May	58–60°F (14.4–15.6°C) or lower
Heliotropium aborescens (H. peruvianum). Tender perennial	Seed in Feb/March or cuttings in spring. 2–3 weeks	65–75°F (18.3–23.9°C)
Impatiens wallerana (I. hostii, petersiana, sultani). Tender annuals and perennials. F$_1$ hybrids (Balsam)	Sow from early March. Cutting at any time, but for bedding out March. 3–4 weeks. High humidity essential (fungicidal dust also advised). Sow direct	70–75°F (21.1–23.9°C)
Kochia scoparia (burning bush), cv. *'childsii'* (compact), var. *'trichophylla'*. Tender annuals	Seed Feb/March. 1–2 weeks	65–75°F (18.3–23.9°C)

Colour	Height	Distance apart and main role	Seed per oz
Pink	36in	18in	12,500
Various	36in	12–18in. Background for borders. Cut flowers	5,000
Wide range of colour and flower form. Singles and doubles	Dwarf seedlings 12–18in. Other varieties 24–72in	12–36in. Dwarf seedlings for edging or mass display. Mixed varieties for cut bloom and exhibition	3,000
Scarlet and mixed	6–12in	6–10in. Excellent mass display, especially 'Queen of Hearts' types	20,000
Carmine, pink, salmon, white	4–6in	6in	28,000
Various	12in	6–9in. Good for sunny banking. Flowers close at night	10,000
Various	Creeping	12in. Ideal for sunny bankings. Flowers open in sun	110,000
Various. Daisy-like flowers	9in	6–9in. Flowers open and close with temperature change	12,000
Wide range of colours	18–48in	10–12in	Corms bought by count
Blue and mauve	15–18in	10–12in	50,000
Pink, orange, white, red shades	12–18in	Mass display for formal bedding	60,000 (variable)
Lovely foliage	12–15in, 24in	Best used as 'dot' plants or background to bed	30,000

African marigolds (which actually come from Mexico) germinate readily and can be planted out at flowering size if grown in peat pots.

DIRECT STRUCK CUTTINGS
THREE WEEKS

Pelargoniums can be grown from a cutting to give a full season's flowering in a single year.

Name and type	Propagation and time of germination	Germination temperature category
Lobelia erinus. Annual	Dec–mid March thinly on surface. Plant out in clumps	65–75°F (18.3–23.9°C)
L. cardinalis and *L. fulgens.* Perennials	Cuttings in autumn or spring	65–75°F (18.3–23.9°C)
Lobularia maritima (Alyssum maritimum) and var. *benthamii.* Annual	Seed in Feb/March. 2 weeks	65–75°F (18.3–23.9°C)
*Marigold (American) *Tagetes erecta.* Tender annual. F₁ hybrid (name changed from African marigold 1970)	Sow March. 1–2 weeks	65–75°F (18.3–23.9°C)
Marigold (French) *Tagetes patula.* Tender annual	Seed in Feb/March. 1–2 weeks	65–75°F (18.3–23.9°C)
Mimulus cupreus cultivars. Perennial	Seed in Feb/March. 2–3 weeks	65–75°F (18.3–23.9°C)
Nemesia. Tender annual	Seed in Feb/March. Avoid check to growth by pricking off early. 2–3 weeks	65–75°F (18.3–23.9°C)
Nicotiana alata (N. affinis var. *grandiflora.* Tender annual	Seed in March. 1–2 weeks	65–75°F (18.3–23.9°C)
Pansy *Viola tricolor.* Hybrids and F₁ hybrids. Perennial	Seed in Dec/Jan until March. 2–3 weeks	65–75°F (18·3–23.9°C)
*Pelargonium × hortorum ('Geranium'). F₁ and F₂ hybrids; P. zonale is one of the parents. Tender perennial.	Cuttings in autumn and spring. Seed in Jan/Feb direct into Jiffy 7s or similar. Use dwarfing agent Cycocel to keep dwarf. 2–3 weeks	70–75°F (21.1–23.9°C)
Penstemon × gloxinioides. Half-hardy perennial. Hybrids	Seed in Dec/Jan. Cuttings autumn/spring. 2–3 weeks	65–75°F (18.3–23.9°C)
Petunia × hybrida. Tender annual. F₁ hybrid	Seed Feb–March. Not covered. Germinate cool. 1–2 weeks	65–75°F (18.3–23.9°C)
Phlox drummondii. Tender annual	Seed Feb–April. 2–3 weeks	55–65°F (12.8–18.3°C)
Polygonum capitatum. Tender perennial	Seed Feb–April. 2 weeks	65–70°F (18.3–21.1°C)
Poppy, Iceland, *Papaver nudicaule.* Perennial	Seed Jan/Feb. 2 weeks	55–60°F (12.8–15.6°C) Grow cool
Portulaca (sun rose). Tender annual	Seed in Feb/March. 2–3 weeks	65–75°F (18.3–23.9°C)

Colour	Height	Distance part and main role	Seed per oz
Blue, red, white. Compact and bushy forms	4–9in	6–9in	800,000
Blue grey foliage	24–36in	'Dot' plants	
White and pink	4–6in	6–8in. Edging	80,000
Gold, orange, yellow	12–36in	12–14in. Formal bedding	8,000
Orange, red, yellow shades	6–12in	6–9in. Edging	10,000
Reds, pinks, yellows	12–15in	10–12in. Showy beds	600,000
Various bright shades	9–12in	9–12in. Edging	100,000
Pink, white, yellow	10–48in	Dot plants or background. Cut flowers	250,000
Various colours. Selfs or mixed shades	6–8in	10–12in. Edging	20,000
Carefree seedlings pink, salmon, red, scarlet, white. Sprinter, scarlet	9–18in	10–12in	5,000
Scarlet and carmine shades	30in	12–14in. Mass display	55,000
Brilliant stabs of red, scarlet, pink and white	10–12in	9–10in. Mass display	200,000
Pink, yellow, scarlet	6–12in	9–10in. Mass display or edging	14,000
Pink	Trailing	6–8in. Used for window boxes or tubs	35,000
Bright shades	18in	9–10in. Mass display	175,000
Various	6in	6–8in. Edging	280,000

Name and type	Propagation and time of germination	Germination temperature category
*Salpiglossis. Tender annual. F₁ and F₂ hybrids	Seed in Feb/March. 2 weeks	65–75°F (18.3–23.9°C)
*Salvia. Tender annual S. patens. Perennial	Seed Feb–April. Cuttings Feb–April. 2–3 weeks Cuttings in Feb	65–75°F (18.3–23.9°C) 65–75°F (18.3–23.9°C)
Scabiosa atropurpurea (scabious). Annual	Seed Feb/Mar. 2–3 weeks	65–75°F (18.3–23.9°C)
Senecio cineraria (S. bicolor, Cineraria maritima). Half-hardy perennial	Cuttings in autumn/spring. Seed Jan–Feb. 2–3 weeks	65–75°F (18.3–23.9°C)
Statice Limonium sinuatum, and L. bonduellii. Annuals	Seed Feb–March. 2–3 weeks	65–75°F (18.3–23.9°C)
Stocks: Mathiola incana (Ten-week). Annual and biennial 'Beauty of Nice'	Seed in Feb/March. 2 weeks	65–75°F (18.3–23.9°C) then lower to 55°F (12.8°C). Drop to 50°F (10°C) to selected double light leaved plants 65–75°F (18.3–23.9°C)
Tagetes tenuifolia pumila. Tender annual	Seed Feb–March. 1–2 weeks	65–75°F (18.3–23.9°C)
*Verbena × hybrida. Perennials	Seed in Feb/March. 3–4 weeks	65–75°F (18.3–23.9°C) Grow cool
Viola cornuta cultivars	Seed Dec. till March. 2–3 weeks	65–75°F
*Zinnia elegans and other species. Annuals	Sow seed direct in small pots or containers. 1–2 weeks. March	65–75°F (18.3–23.9°C) then 60°F (15.6°C)

Verbena, another half-hardy annual that needs to be started in the greenhouse for summer bedding.

Colour	Height	Distance apart and main role	Seed per oz
Blue, brown, lavender, scarlet	24in	10–12in. Mass bedding	125,000
Scarlet	6–12in	10–12in. Mixed mass bedding	7,500
Blue	18–24in	12–14in	
Wide range of colours	42–48in	12–18in. Background plant for borders	4,500
Silver foliage	12–24in	Dot plant	85,000
White, blue, yellow	18–24in	12in. Cut flowers for drying	350
White, red, blue, rose	10–12in	10–12in. Mass bedding	16,000
White, red, blue, rose	15–18in	12–14in	
Yellow, golden orange	8in	6–8in	35,000
Scarlet shades	10–12in	6–9in. Good edging plant	10,000
Blue, yellow, purple	4–8in	6–9in. Edging or inter-planting	25,000
Wide range of colours	12–24in	Excellent for mass display and for cut bloom	2,500–4,000

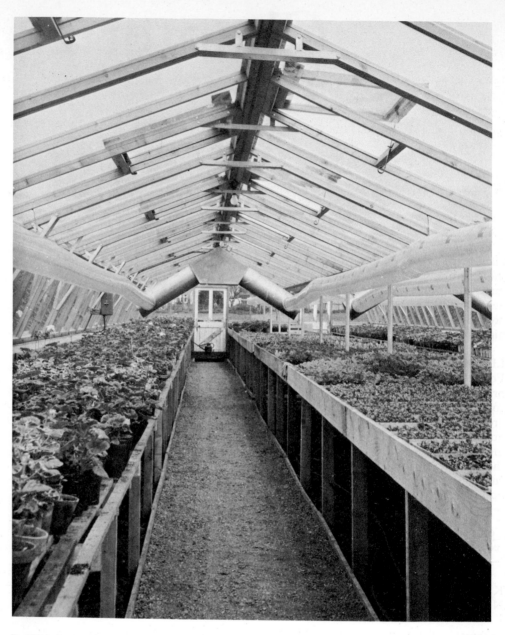

Bedding plant production
carried out on a
commercial scale.
Similar benching and
heating arrangements can
be applied to smaller
greenhouses.

Chapter 24

Pot plants & Shrubs

Nothing can equal the light-admitting greenhouse for the culture of top-quality pot plants, especially the flowering kinds. Greenhouses should be drip-free or rendered so by sealing strip or other means, benched (preferably in tiers), and with full facilities for watering, shading, ventilating, potting and storing.

Propagation methods are specific to the plant being grown and details are given in the cultural notes. Examine all plant material for pest and disease and take any necessary measures before placing in the greenhouse. General hygiene must be of a high order.

Liquid feeding

For seed sowing, vegetative propagation, pricking off and potting, the respective composts are listed in Chapter 15. Actively growing plants generally need additional nutrients, depending on size of pot, leaching due to water requirements, and whether or not the plant is a gross feeder. In Chapter 15 some formulae are given for liquid feeds, but the self-mixed formula is repeated here for convenience.

Composition of feeds (oz/gal)				Nutrient (% weight/vol)
K_2O to N ratio	Potassium nitrate	Urea or	Ammonium nitrate	K_2O N
3:1 (high potash)	24	—	—	6.7–2.1
2:1 (standard)	24	5	6	6.7–3.4
*1:1 (high nitrogen)	24	16	21	6.7–6.7

*1 in 300 (1 fl oz to 15 pints)
*1 in 400 (1 fl oz to $2\frac{1}{2}$ gall)

This is the stock solution prepared by careful mixing in warm water; it is diluted to 1 in 200 generally with a calibrated dilutor (for pot plants this can be 1 in 300 or 400 where desired). When using a watering-can the dilution (1 in 200) is 1 fluid ounce of the stock solution in $1\frac{1}{4}$ gallons of water. The object is to vary the nitrogen/potash ratio to achieve the balance of growth required: high nitrogen for leaf growth, high potash for soft plants when more flowers and less leaf is the aim, and standard potash/nitrogen when balanced growth is exhibited and it is decided to sustain this. Time of year and region can confuse the issue as far as nutrient balance is concerned, plants grown in northerly latitudes generally requiring lower nitrogen feeds, especially during the duller months.

Artificial illumination

Supplementary lighting adds to the quality or intensity of natural light and is useful in the duller months for those light-demanding plants which tend to become debilitated. Day length manipulation is used mainly to induce earlier flowering (or to delay it). These matters are discussed in Chapter 10, and interested gardeners should consult advisers on the appropriate electricity boards who will give details of the latest lighting techniques and their application to pot plant culture.

Half-hardy annuals as pot plants

In addition to the plants listed in the following tables, a number of half-hardy annuals are highly suitable as pot plants and are becoming popular. These are indicated by an asterisk in the previous bedding plant table, and the best varieties for pot growing are listed in seedsmen's catalogues, a wealth of new varieties being produced annually for this purpose. All are sown in the early part of the year in a high temperature (75°F/23.9°C) and pricked off (except balsam) into Jiffy 7s or peat pots for flowering in 3½–4in pots or larger. Most require pinching out to induce bushy growth, but their culture is simple.

For pests, diseases and physiological disorders see Chapter 32.

Aloe striata, something of a rarity but one of the most striking of all the aloes in cultivation.

Flowering Pot Plants

Type and main varieties	Approx height	General description and characteristics	Flowering period
Abutilon × hybridum	12–18in	Attractive flowers and foliage	Summer
Achimenes grandiflora	6–9in	White, pink and blue flowers. Excellent in hanging baskets	Summer
Aechmea *fasciata* (pink) *fulgens* (scarlet and black) *lindenii* (yellow and red) *mariae-reginae* (red and pink) *veitchii* (scarlet)	12in	Leaves from funnel-shaped rosettes which hold water. Flowers have very colourful bracts	May–Aug
Agapanthus praecox subsp. *orientalis* (blue) and *orientalis* 'Alba' (white)	2–3ft	Bulbous plants for pots or borders	Summer
Aloe *humilis* (grey leaved) and vars *striata* (leaves striped) *variegata* (partridge-breasted aloe)	10–12in	Succulents with thick tapering leaves. *A. variegata* spiky variegated leaves with red fleshy stem. Not difficult but requires attention to detail	Summer
Anthurium *Andreanum* *scherzerianum* *crystallinum*	18in	A specialist plant. Cylindrical flowers on large colourful spathe. Cut flowers. *A. crystallinum* a foliage plant. Spathes small	Long period

Propagation method	Pot size and compost	General cultural details
Cuttings in spring. Also seed in spring. 65–75°F (18–24°C)	5–6in. JIP2	Grow cool, 55°F night (12.8°C)
Rhizomes (tubers) in March/April. 5 or 6 to each. Also seed in spring. 65–75°F (18–24°C)	5in. Peaty soil	55°F (12.8°C) night. Support with twigs
Suckers removed at base of plant and potted	6in with side drainage. Peat/ leaf mould or soilless plus broken brick	Minimum of 50–55°F (10–12.8°C). Plenty of moisture. Water little in winter. Avoid draughts
Division in March. Seed in spring. Germinate at 65–75°F (18–24°C)	6–7in or borders. JIP1	Free drainage necessary. Water liberally in summer
Seed in April (may not be true due to hybridisation), or cuttings taken as suckers from base of plant in summer	5–6in. JIP1 plus extra drainage	Free drainage is essential. Keep dry in winter or plants will rot. Water sparingly in summer. Give plenty of sun. Minimum of 55°F (12.8°C)
Seed in summer. Germinate at 70–75°F (21–24°C), 150 per seed tray pressed into surface, or division of old plants early in year	3in then 5in pots. Compost open. pH 5.5	Grown at minimum night temperature of 65°F (18°C). Water sparingly in dull cold weather and shade. For flowering raise temperature to 70–75°F (21–24°C)

Agapanthus praecox subspecies *orientalis,* formerly known variously as *A. umbellatus* or *A. orientalis,* one of glories of the greenhouse. The plants shown here are growing out of doors in an exceptionally mild position. They make excellent plants for tubs, being overwintered in the greenhouse.

Begonia 'Jenny Bisivine', one of the most delicately coloured of all the large-flowered cultivars, white and palest pink.

Type and main varieties	Approx height	General description and characteristics	Flowering period
Aphelandra squarrosa var *louisae* (zebra plant) 'Brockfield' 'Silver Beauty'	12in	Dark green leaves with conspicuous white markings along the veins. Yellow flowers. Careful culture needed	May–Nov
Arum lily (see *Zantedeschia aethiopica*)			
Asclepias curassavica (blood flower)	1½–3ft	Purple-red and orange-red flowers followed by unusual fruit. Fairly easy to grow	Summer
Astilbe × arendsii Popular vars: 'Fanal' (dark red, bronze foliage) 'Gladstone' (white) 'Koblenz' (carmine) 'Montgomery' (deep crimson)	2–2½ft	Simple to grow	Spring
Azalea indica (Japanese azalea), correctly *Rhododendron indicum*. Many vars *A. obtusa*, correctly *R. obtusum*	12–18in	Mass of flowers on attractive foliage. Excellent for decoration in greenhouse or home. *Not* hardy. Attention to detail required	Dec–April
Begonia × cheimantha 'Gloire de Lorraine' *B. × hiemalis* 'Optima'	6–12in	Make colourful pot plants for greenhouse and home decoration. Easy to grow if kept fairly cool	Autumn–winter
Begonia coccinea, 'President Carnot' *fuchsioides manicata metallica nitida (B. minor) haageana*	Various	A wide range of mainly large-leaved begonias which can be grown as shrubs or large pot plants, having ornamental leaves and attractive flowers. Simple to grow in the right environment	Large part of year
Begonia semperflorens (fibrous begonia) New vars constantly produced incl F₁ hybrids	6–12in	Excellent for summer decoration. Relatively simple to grow	Summer–autumn

284

Propagation method	Pot size and compost	General cultural details
Cuttings 4–6in in bottom heat (14–21 days) at 75°F (24°C) in peat plus sand. Leaf bud cuttings also	3½in pots, JIP1, then 5in pots, JIP1	Give heat at 65°F (18°C). Liberal watering and high nitrogen feeding
Seed in spring. Division and half-ripe cuttings	7–8in. JIP1 or 2	Minimum of 60°F (15.6°C). To obtain bushy plants pinch out tips of shoots
Seed in spring for planting outdoors or division in Sept–Oct for indoor planting	5–6in. JIP1	For forcing, give initial period of 28 days or longer at 42°F (6°C). 6 days at 85°F (29.4°C) then force from end Oct at 60–85°F (16–29°C). May be grown colder, but later
Cuttings from strong shoots in June–July. Rooted in peat/sand	Cuttings in 3in pots, then 5–7in or larger. Peat compost	Pot at 50°F (10°C) and raise gradually to 65°F (18.3°C). After flowering remove spent blooms. Re-pot and encourage growth, shortening long branches. Plunge out of doors in shady position in July and keep feeding
Leaf and stem cuttings Jan–May at 70°F (21°C) from stock plants. Give lighting to encourage vegetative growth. Leaf cuttings from Oct to Dec rooted at 65°F (18°C).	3in then 5in. JIP1. Keep compost slightly acid	Grow at 60°F (15.6°C). Give shade in spring and summer and feed regularly. Reduce temperature to 55°F(12.6°C) when in flower. Do not grow too hot or they become vegetative
Root readily from cuttings 5–6in long in peat/sand during spring and summer	3in then 5–6in and upwards JIP2	Very tolerant of a wide range of conditions, but prefer some shade from really hot sun, otherwise leaves may 'burn'
Seed on top of compost. 15,000 seeds per 1/128oz. Germinate at 70°F (21°C). Can be pricked off in groups initially for individual potting from Oct-Feb	3½in then 4½in or larger. JIP2	Minimum 60°F (15.6°C) night temperature. Supplementary lighting helps germination

Camellia japonica, though perfectly hardy, often has its flowers damaged by frost or rain when grown out of doors. Perfect flowers can be obtained when grown under glass, and this is particularly true of the modern American *Camellia japonica* cultivars which are slightly more tender than the Japanese and European cultivars.

Type and main varieties	Approx height	General description and characteristics	Flowering period
Begonia × tuberhybrida (tuberous)	12–15in	Delightful large-flowered pot plants, especially for the show enthusiast. Pendulous form excellent for hanging baskets. Fairly straightforward culture	Summer–autumn
Beloperone guttata (shrimp plant)	9–12in or taller	Very unusual and attractive flower for the warm greenhouse, but does not tolerate neglect	Large part of year. Best in summer/autumn
Billbergia *bakeri* *iridifolia* *nutans* *speciosa*	18in	Unusual flowers and leaves, with red, green and lilac shoots. Relatively straightforward	Late winter but always attractive
Bouvardia × hybrida (many excellent vars in scarlet, salmon and pink)	12–15in	Low-growing greenhouse shrub, having very attractive waxy heads of flowers	Winter
Browallia speciosa 'Major'	18in	Star-like blue flowers (there is a white form)	According to sowing date
Brunfelsia calycina and other spp	2–3ft	Low-growing greenhouse shrub with purple flowers in clusters	Summer
Cacti (see Chapter 28)			
Calceolaria × herbeohybrida 'Multiflora Nana' and many excellent cultivars incl F₁ hybrids	12–18in	Magnificent pouch-like flowers for greenhouse decoration. Can be tricky to bring to full glory, but does well with care in cool conditions	Spring–Sept
Camellia japonica	18–24in	Camellias are hardy and grown as shrubs in many areas. Simple to grow as pot plants	Feb–Mar

Propagation method	Pot size and compost	General cultural details
Seed in February at 65–70°F (18–21°C) for normal varieties. Start tubers growing Feb–Mar. Divide into sections in March, leaving a strong shoot, and pot	3in then 5 or 6in. JIP1	Grow at 60°F (15.6°C). Give shade in spring and summer and feed regularly while flowering in cool atmosphere
Cuttings from young shoots in summer rooted in peat/sand at 65°F (18°C), cutting back plant if necessary to provide these	3in then 5 or 6in. JIP2	Resents over-watering (yellows leaves) and grows best in well-heated environment
By suckers which develop from base	3–6in. JIP1	Keep cool at 50°F (10°C) in winter
Cuttings of young shoots 4in long in late spring in propagating case	5–6in. JIP1	Cut back hard after flowering and pinch new shoots until August. Minimum temperature of 50–55°F (10–12.8°C)
Sow seed in March for summer flowering, July for winter and spring. 110,000 seeds per oz	3in then 5–6in pots. JIP1	Light shade in summer. Grow fairly cool. Do not over-feed or over-water. Requires support with twigs
Cuttings of half-ripe shoots in June or July in propagating case	5–6in. JIP1	Re-pot after flowering. Keep on dry side Oct–Feb. Water and feed freely March onwards. Pinch out young branches to keep bushy. Minimum of 50°F (10°C)
Sow seed pressed into surface or covered with sand to facilitate sowing in July/August for next March/April, or Oct for May. Germinate at 65–75°F (18–24°C). 20,000 seeds per 1/32oz	3in or Jiffy 7s then 5 or 7in by Oct. JIP2	Must be grown cool for good hard maturing and bushy plants. Can be left in cold frame until autumn, at about 55°F (13°C). Reduce water in winter, but keep well fed after growth starts in February
By leaf bud cuttings in March	6–8in. Lime-free JIP1	Keep cool and do not over-water

Type and main varieties	Approx height	General description and characteristics	Flowering period
Campanula isophylla 'Alba' and 'Mayi'	5–6in	Pendulous. Attractive little plants for pot culture or hanging baskets. Blue or white flowers. 'Mayi' has Variegated leaves	May–Oct
Campanula pyramidalis	5ft	Excellent show plant for the exclusive greenhouse	Summer
Canna indica and hybrids (Indian Shot)	12–18in	Brilliant coloured flowers. Easy to grow	June–Aug
Capsicum annuum	10–12in	Grown for their decorative fruit. Not the easiest plants due to their dislike of variable conditions	Fruit in autumn–winter
Carnations (see Chapter 25)			
Celosia argentea var. *cristata* (cockscomb) var. *plumosa*	12–15in	Colourful plumes of flowers in red and gold. Cockscomb has fluted flowers, var. *plumosa* has spikes of flowers. Fairly straightforward	May–Sept
Ceropegia woodii	Trailing	Fleshy leaves and purple flowers	Summer
Chorizema ilicifolium	15–18in	In native habitat in Australia grow to 10ft or more, but adapted for pot culture or greenhouse border in Britain. Graceful red flower-bearing branches	Summer
Chrysanthemums in pots (see Chapter 26)			
Cineraria cruenta, correctly *Senecio cruentus* 'Grandiflora', 'Multiflora', 'Multiflora Nana'	15–18in	Showy pot plants for home and greenhouse, especially where heat levels are low	Mar–June
Citrus spp (oranges, lemons, grapefruit and tangerines)	Will grow tall if space allows	Showy leaves and fragrant flowers. Ideal for large tubs or pots in amateur greenhouse or conservatory	Spring

Celosia, one of the most popular of flowering pot plants for the greenhouse and the home.

Propagation method	Pot size and compost	General cultural details
By cuttings taken in August or Feb/March from cut-back plants inserted round the edge of 5in pots	Singly in 3½in pots or several in larger pot. JIP2.	Very adaptable plants which can be grown with ease. Require regular watering
Seed in June, transferred to open ground for potting up in October	8–9in or border border	Will readily grow in cool greenhouses with little trouble
Jan–June, nick seed to induce germination. Put in small pots for planting outdoors in summer. Division of existing roots in spring	Flowering plants in 8–10in pots. JIP2	Easily grown plants requiring the minimum of attention. They go dormant in winter and can be stored dry
Seed in February sown thinly and potted up when very small	3½in. JIP1	Grow at 60–65°F (16–18°C). Pinch hard for bushy growth. Shade to prevent scorch. Spray overhead to encourage setting and feed when fruit forms
Seed in Feb/March in JIP1	3in pots with JIP1 then 5–6in and JIP2	Must be kept growing constantly, with no ckecks, at not less than 55°F (12.8°C) at night. Keep cooler and drier when flowers are formed. Over-watering can rot stems
Cuttings in April/May	5–6in. JIP2	Grow at not less than 55°F (12.8°C)
By seed in pots or cuttings with a heel in August when they root readily in fairly cool conditions	3in then 5–6in. JIP2	Plant in loamy soil. Minimum of 45°F (7°C). Prune by shortening shoots after flowering by one-third. Plunge out of doors after flowering. Re-pot every second or third year
Seed May–September in JI seed compost at 60°F (16°C). 150,000 seeds per oz	3½in then 5–6in. JIP1	Grow cool giving adequate ventilation, especially during dull weather. Give dilute liquid feed adding some Epsom Salts occasionally
Seed in spring or at various times	Move up pot size. Very rich compost—JIP3	Grow cool and give plenty of air; never allow drying out. Small fruits may be formed

289

Type and main varieties	Approx height	General description and characteristics	Flowering period
Clivia miniata Many excellent hybrids	12–18in	A highly coloured bulbous plant with strap-like leaves for long-term pot culture. Gives little trouble	Spring
Columnea gloriosa	Trailing or supported	Usually for hanging baskets but can be grown in pots at edge of staging or trained up a stake. Brilliant racemes of flowers	Summer
Crassula coccinea (see *Rochea*)			
Cuphea ignea (cigar flower)	6–10in	Tubular cigar-shaped scarlet and black flowers with white tip	Summer
Cyclamen persicum	9–12in	One of the best-known Christmas pot plants but can be in flower at other periods by varying sowing dates, particularly with early compact strains. Many different forms available including early compact strains, standard strains and mixtures	Winter
Cytisus canariensis ('Genista' of florists)	12–18in	Shrubs, but frequently grown in pots where they make attractive plants	Spring
Daphne odora 'Aureomarginata'	12–18in	Exquisite perfume, easy to grow. All the daphnes can be grown in pots successfully	March
Dipladenia boliviensis D. × hybrida 'Rosacea' sanderi splendens	Climbing or trailing	Large rose-shaped flowers with yellow throat (Award of Merit RHS). Can be grown either as greenhouse shrub or pot plant. Easy	Summer

Cyclamen species flower from September till May and all through the bleakest months of the winter if grown in a frost free greenhouse.

290

Propagation method	Pot size and compost	General cultural details
Seed in propagating case, but usually division of existing plants	Usually in 7–9in pots in JIP2	Responds well to slow-acting fertiliser such as bonemeal. Re-pot every 4–5 years
By cuttings in spring–early summer, taking tips of shoots; rooted in propagating case in peat/sand	3in and JIP1, then hanging baskets or 7in pots	Keep moderately cool in summer and water very sparingly in winter
Seed in March (100 per tray)	3in then 5in. JIP1	Pinch out to form bushy plant. Keep cool
Soak seed in water 24 hours. Sow thinly in JI seed compost, 60–65°F (16–18°C). Sow July/Aug to flower following autumn; Oct/Nov for smaller plants (in 5–6in pots) the following autumn; Jan/Feb to flower in 4–4½in pots in Dec. Feb/Mar in 3½–4in pots to flower December. Corms can be potted up in August or earlier if available	At second leaf stage into trays (40 per box) in JIP1. In Apr into 3½in in JIP2, then 5–6in or larger with JIP2 or 3 (no liquid feeding required in 3)	After pricking, give 65°F (18°C) for a few days, then a steady 60°F (15.6°C) until established. Shade in summer if necessary. Ventilate freely. Feed regularly and try to keep temperatures at 50–55°F (10–13°C) to induce more flowers to form. Remove bloom which forms periodically. Water carefully, *avoiding the corms*, and water less in winter
Firm cuttings in summer after flowering, in peat/sand	3½in in JIP1 then 5in in JIP2	Requires little more than regular watering and some shading. A succession of young plants necessary to maintain attractive appearance
Cuttings in propagating case in spring or layer for other types. Grafting may also be carried out	5–6in. JIP2	Keep outside for most of the year, bring in during the winter. Re-potting may be necessary after cutting back
Cuttings 1–2in long with two leaves in propagating case in November	3in JIP1	Grow at a minimum of 55°F (12.8°C). As house plant requires trellis for training. Water and feed freely in summer. Keep dry in winter

Type and main varieties	Approx height	General description and characteristics	Flowering period

Echeveria
  derenbergii
  harmsii
  Worfield Wonder
	9–18in	Rosettes of leaves with tubular red, yellow, or white flowers on arching spikes. Easy to grow	Spring–summer

Epacris
  impressa (red and white)
  longiflora (white-tipped crimson flowers)
	3–5ft	Delightful Australian shrubs which lend themselves to pot culture in frost-free greenhouses. Tubular bi-coloured flowers	Winter

Erica (heath)
  canaliculata (white)
  gracilis (pink)
  gracilis 'Alba' (white)
  hyemalis   (pink)
  × *willmorei*
	12–18in	'Typical' heathers but with larger more colourful flowers. A 'fickle' plant which requires more care than the average gardener is prepared to bestow	Winter

Eucharis grandiflora	12–16in	White scented flowers. Lily-like leaves. Easy	Spring
Eucomis punctata *(E. comosa)*	2ft	12in greenish-yellow spikes with fairly long leaves. Easy	Summer
Euphorbia pulcherrima (Poinsettia) (many excellent vars with red or white bracts)	1–4ft	Grown for coloured bracts (leaves) which surround insignificant flowers. A most popular Christmas plant. A plant for the fastidious gardener if it is to be grown to perfection	Winter or other period by day-length manipulation

Exacum
  affine
  macranthum
	9–12in or more	Violet-blue flowers with yellow stamens. Scented. Straightforward to grow	Summer

Felicia amelloides (blue marguerite)	12–18in or higher	Blue daisy-like flower. Easy	Summer
Francoa ramosa (Bridal wreath)	12–15in	White flowers on long slender stems. Easy	Spring/summer

Propagation method	Pot size and compost	General cultural details
Seeds in spring or summer. Cuttings of side shoots in April–August. Offsets.	3½in, flower in 5–6in. JIP1	Minimum of 45°F (7°C). Water sparingly in winter, but less so in spring. Do not water crowns of plants.
Cuttings 1–1½in in July– August in propagating case	3½in then 5–6in. JIP2	Minimum of 45–50°F (7–10°C). Pinch out growing points to form bushy plant. Cut back hard in spring then re-pot. Plunge out of doors in summer and bring in during September
Cuttings Nov–Jan in acid peat (3 parts peat/1 part sand), at 60–65°F (16–18°C). Root in 4–6 weeks. No rooting powder advisable	3½–5in. JIP1 but substituting flowers of sulphur for lime	After the propagation period keep cool [55°F (12.8°C)], shading all summer, giving liquid feeding, sulphate of ammonia at ⅛oz per gallon until July. Take into greenhouses in September and give gentle heat
Plant bulbs in autumn and early spring	6in JIP1	A simple plant to grow. Likes shade. Min. temp. 50°F (7°C)
Plant bulbs or offsets in March	6in. JIP1	Will grow well as long as it is kept frost free
Cuttings from 'rested' plants in July–August under mist or in propagating case. Singly in peat pots or Jiffy 7s	Singly in 4½in, or 3 plants in 5–6in or larger. JIP1 plus extra peat	Grow at minimum of 60°F (15.6°C). Size of plant produced will be related to time of taking cuttings. Never allow to dry out. Liquid feeding every 7–10 days. Pinch out leading shoot. High temperature will assist with colouring of bracts. Dwarfing compound ('Cycocel') can be used
Seed in Feb/March	3½in then 5in and 3 or 4 plants per pot. JIP2	Give plenty of water and some shade. Support needed. A simple little plant to grow
Seed in March/April at 50°F (10°C)	3½in then 5in or 6in. JIP1	May not bloom until second year. Keep frost free
Seed in March and thereafter divide plants each March/April. Also cuttings, March	3½in then 5in or 6in. JIP1	Keep almost dry in winter but frost free. Water freely in summer and give liquid feeding

Type and main varieties	Approx height	General description and characteristics	Flowering period
Fuchsia (lady's eardrop) A vast range of species, varieties and hybrids	9–18in or higher	Scarcely needs description, being one of the most popular greenhouse plants. Membership of the British Fuchsia Society is available for enthusiasts. Not difficult to grow but demands attention to watering, shading and ventilation	Summer/ autumn/ winter
'Geranium' (botanically, *Pelargonium*). Zonal pelargoniums, regal pelargoniums, ivy-leaved, scented. Many excellent varieties have been produced in the late 60s and early 70s, including 'Irenes' from the USA and from seed the F_1 'Carefree', 'Sprinter' and F_2 'Fleuriste'	Various, around 12–18in	Too well known to need much description. One of the simplest plants to grow, provided they are not over-watered, especially if in peat-based composts	Zonals at all times. Regals in summer
Gesneria, correctly *Rechsteineria* species	6–10in	Large clusters of tubular flowers. Fairly simple to grow	Summer
Gloriosa (glory lily) *rothschildiana superba*	Climber	Large climbing plant with lily-like flowers of orange, red or yellow, with swept back petals. Flowers in summer	Spring– summer
Gloxinia speciosa, correctly *Sinningia speciosa*	9–12in	Excellent showy pot plant but subject to damage unless handled carefully. Leaves mark and bruise easily	Summer
Haemanthus albiflos (white) *coccineus katherinae* (red) *multiflorus*	1–3ft	Bulbous plant for cool greenhouse culture. Relatively simple to grow	Summer

Propagation method	Pot size and compost	General cultural details
Cuttings from Feb onwards from stock plants which have been rested and started into growth in Dec/Jan at 60°F (15.6°C). Small cuttings only in peat/sand in close atmosphere. Insert cuttings around edge of pot, with polythene bag covering	Peat pots or Jiffy 7s, then into 5–6in pots. Older plants can be in very large pots. JIP2	Grow hot at a steady 60°F (15.6°C). Keep potting light (compost *not* rammed). Water sparingly to begin with then more generously. Give liquid feeding when roots fill pot. Pinch out tips of shoots to encourage side shoots. Shade when necessary
Cuttings from stock plants in Jiffy 7s or peat pots from August to April, or at any time for zonals. Cuttings 2½–3in in length, preferably *nodal*. Root well at 65°F (18.3°C) with bottom heat. Seed sown in Jan/Feb	3½in then 5–7in pots according to size of plant involved. JIP1	Easy to grow but does not like to be over-watered, especially in winter. Grow fairly cool throughout. Liquid feeding desirable using balanced ratio 1:1:1. If nitrogen shortage evident extra nitrogen may be given. Use 'Cycocel' dwarfing compound, especially for 'Carefree' and 'Sprinter'
Sow seed in January, pressed into surface and covered with polythene. Cuttings from young shoots in spring or tubers in February, singly in small pots or in groups in larger pots	3½in then 5in pots. JIP1	Minimum winter temperature of 55°F (12.8°C). Tubers dried off in winter for potting in February
Grown from tubers planted in March singly in 6–7in pots in JIP2. They can be increased by offshoots in spring and by sowing seed in March	See propagation	Climbs by means of tendrils and must have a winter temperature of not less than 55°F (12.8°C). Dig out tubers for winter
Seed in February at 70°F (21°C) on surface. Start tubers in March–April. Leaf cuttings in summer. Cuttings in spring	3½in then 5in. JIP1	Minimum of 50°F (10°C). Shading essential. Water with care, only syringeing during hot weather. Feed as buds open. Dry off after flowering for re-potting in March/April
Pot in March/April or leave undisturbed for several years. Detach offsets at planting time	5–6in or larger. JIP1	Simple plants to grow. Rest after flowering

Type and main varieties	Approx height	General description and characteristics	Flowering period
Hedychium gardnerianum (ginger lily)	2–6ft	Tall spikes of dense yellow flowers in summer. Requires space	Summer
Heliotropium arborescens (*H. peruvianum*) (Heliotrope)	1–3ft or more	Lavender and purple, also white. Slightly scented. A simple plant to grow	Summer
Hippeastrum (popularly but wrongly called amaryllis)	2–3ft	Bulbous plants of great beauty. Not difficult to grow	Summer
Hydrangea macrophylla (*H. hortensis*) in a wide range of cultivars	1–2ft or more	Excellent plant for pots but needs careful cultivation for shapely plants. Definitely for the specialist	Spring–summer
Hymenocallis narcissiflora (*H. cala-thina*) *speciosa*	18–24in	Bulbous plants, strap-shaped leaves, white silver striped flowers on long stems. Simple to grow	Spring
Impatiens wallerana (*I. hostii, sultani, peter-siana*) (busy Lizzie) F₁ hybrids	9–18in or higher	One of the best-known pot plants. Easy to grow in a number of ways. Self and bi-coloured blooms	Summer/ autumn over a long period

Propagation method	Pot size and compost	General cultural details
By division of rhizomes in spring. Use JIP1 or similar		Almost hardy plants which will grow in good garden soil in tubs or borders. Water and feed regularly in summer. Dry out in winter. Re-pot in March if necessary after cutting back
Seeds in Feb/March at 65–75°F (18.3–23.9°C). Cuttings in spring	3½in or Jiffy 7s then 5–6in. JIP1	Old plants can be retained for re-potting every few years
Pot up bulbs in Nov–Feb in JIP1 or similar	5in. JIP1	Easy plants to grow in variable conditions. Re-pot every 3 years
Internodal stem cuttings between February and May (non-flowering shoots) in peat/sand	3in pots. JIP2 for pink vars. For blues add extra peat to JIP1, less lime plus ½lb per bushel of aluminium sulphate	Requires 'stopping' to produce bushy plant, then careful watering. Grows well at 55–60°F (12.8–15.6°C). Stand outside in shade for summer. Support with canes July and bring into greenhouse in Sept/Oct for gradual forcing from Dec onwards. Keep nitrogen and phosphate levels low during feeding. Use iron sequestrine if foliage turns white (due to too alkaline a soil). For blue vars use blueing compound, 1oz aluminium sulphate in 2 gal water at fortnightly intervals. Shading is generally needed
Pot up bulbs or offsets in autumn or early in the year when growth is seen to be starting	6–7in. JIP1	Cheerful plants for the frost-free greenhouse. Some other types of hymenocallis require more heat but in the main are very adaptable and require re-potting only every 3 or 4 years. Rest after flowering
Sow seed to give succession plants. On surface of JIP1 or soilless. Cover with polythene. If given 70–75°F (21.1–23.9°C) it will germinate quickly. Remove polythene on germination. Cuttings root easily in Jiffy 7s or pots of peat/sand compost	3½in or Jiffy 7s, flowering in 4, 5, 6in or larger. JIP1	Keep well watered. Pinch to ensure bushy plants. Give some shade from hot sun

Type and main varieties	Approx height	General description and characteristics
Ixia (corn lily) Usually obtainable as mixed hybrids *I. viridiflora*	15–18in	Easy and showy plants with grassy leaves and spikes of pink, red, white or blue flowers Startling blue-green with a blackish centre
Ixora *chinensis* (red to yellow) *coccinea* (red) *griffithiana (I. congesta)* (red and yellow) many hybrids and cultivars	3–4ft	May be grown as shrubs or in a large pot. Strong evergreen foliage and attractive flowers. Easy
Jacobinia *carnea* (pink) *coccinea* (red) and others	2–3ft	Excellent and very attractive plants for greenhouse and home. Can be tricky
Kalanchoe *blossfeldiana*	8–10in	Brilliant display of red flowers in summer. Requires attention
Kohleria eriantha *(I. soloma erianthum)*	18–24in or more	Attractive veins and spotted leaves with orange, red, white flowers. Easy
Lachenalia aloides (Cape cowslip) 'Burnham Gold' 'Nelsonii' (yellow) Many modern varieties	12–18in	Bulbous plants with spikes of cowslip flowers. Excellent for hanging baskets. Easy to grow
Lilium *longiflorum* *tigrinum* and others	18in	Becoming very popular as pot plants, either being forced or allowed to flower naturally. A specialist crop demanding attention to detail
Limonium *suworowii* *profusum*	12–15in	Purple and white flower in spikes
Marguerite *Chrysanthemum* *frutescens* (white) *coronarium* (yellow)	18–20in	An attractive pot plant. Useful for cut flowers. Easy

Flowering period	Propagation method	Pot size and compost	General cultural details
May/June	Bulbs in 5in pots in September	5in. JIP1	Simple to grow. Keep out of doors like other bulbs until Christmas when they can then be forced gently. Support may be needed
Summer	Cuttings of firm shoots in spring and summer	8–9in. JIP2	Needs warmth to grow well. Prune into shape in February. Keep dry in winter
Late summer–winter	Cuttings in July every second year to keep a supply of young plants raised in peat/sand in propagating case	6–8in. JIP2	Prune back after flowering. Keep at not less than 55–60°F (12.8–15.6°C). Water and feed well in summer. Water sparingly in winter or spring after flowering
Winter	Seed sown in March in JIS at 65–70°F (18.3–21.1°C). Cuttings in March	Seed trays or small pots JIP1. Mid-June into 4½in JIP2	A plant sensitive to day length. Grow at 60–65°F (15.6–18.3°C). Shade to give short days (see Chrysanthemums, Chapter 26) in July or early Aug from 16.30 to 08.00 hrs for 24 days
Summer–autumn	Propagate from tubers	5–6in. JIP1	Grows well in warm humid atmosphere. Not difficult to cultivate in moist greenhouse
Spring	Pot up 4 or 5 bulbs in 5in pot in August. Seed in March	5in. JIP1. 3½in	Bulbs dried off after flowering for re-potting. Cool atmosphere. Need plenty of light in winter when growing or they become too vegetative
Spring	Bulbs are stored at low temperatures 33–35°F (0.6–1.7°C) to enable them to flower early	5in pot, 1in below surface. JIP1	Flowers according to temperature level; 60–70°F (15.6–21°C) is average. Prone to leaf scorching. Use calcium nitrate at ½oz per gallon to offset this
Summer	Seed in Feb–Mar at 65°F (18.3°C). *L. profusum* from cuttings in summer	Small pots, then 3in, then 5in. JIP1	Grow at minimum of 45°F (7.2°C). A relatively straight-forward plant
Summer	Cuttings Aug/Jan. Seed in February	3in then 5–6in. JIP1	Simple to grow; requires merely the protection of a greenhouse to flower profusely. Over-feeding makes plants too tall

Type and main varieties	Approx height	General description and characteristics	Flowering period
Medinilla magnifica	3–4ft	Handsome greenhouse shrubby plant. Large leathery leaves with pink flowers. Easy	Summer
'Mesembryanthemum' *Lampranthus* *aureus* (yellow) *blandus roseus* (pink) *coccineus* (scarlet) *haworthii (Erepsia haworthii)* (magenta)	12–14in	Excellent and colourful plants for pot culture. Can be used outside. Simple plants to grow	Summer
Mimulus glutinosus (aurantiacus) (monkey flower)	18–24in	Very showy and easy to grow	Spring–summer
Myrtus comunis (myrtle)	As pruned	Beautiful foliage and scented flowers useful in floral art. Easy to grow in large pots or borders	Spring–summer
Nerine *bowdenii*, several varieties *samiensis* and hybrids	18in	Showy bulbous plants with scented white and pink flowers. Simple to grow, but may not flower each year	Sept–Oct
Nerium oleander (oleander)	Up to 6ft	Bushy plants which will become large if allowed to. Pink, white, crimson, purple or yellow flowers, single or double	Spring–summer
Ornithogalum (chincherinchee) *arabicum* *lacteum* *thyrsoides*	18–24in	Bulbous plants. Spikes of white flowers	Spring–early summer
Oxalis *bowiei* (purple) *deppei* (red)	6–9in	Excellent plants for pots or baskets. Easy to grow	Spring
Polianthes tuberosa (tuberose)	18in	Bulbous plants. Lovely spikes of white single or double flowers. Very strongly scented. Easy	Summer

Propagation method	Pot size and compost	General cultural details
Half-ripe shoots with heel in November. Bottom heat essential	3in then 6in. JIP2	Minimum of 55–50°F (12.8–15.6°C). Re-pot in February. Water well. Shading necessary to start off. Water and feed frequently in summer; keep dry in winter
Cuttings after flowering	3½in then 5–6in. JIP1	Keep frost-free for winter. Never over-water, especially in winter
Cuttings in summer	3in then 5in. JIP1	To keep dwarf cut-back each February and pinch shoots in summer
Cuttings late spring and summer	Start in small size then pot up gradually. JIP2	Must be grown cool in greenhouse
By offsets and bulbs potted up in July, 3 bulbs in a 6in pot and 1 bulb in a 3in pot	3 or 6in. JIP2	Re-pot only every few years as they do well if pot-bound. They like resting in the spring and early summer. Water and feed well during growing period and top dress pot with fresh compost
Firm ripe cuttings 3–6in long in summer	3½in then 7–8in or larger. JIP2	Prune shoots back one-third after flowering. Rub out shoots at base of flower buds. Can be put outside in summer but keep well watered (stand pots in water). Water sparingly in winter
Seed in spring–summer. Give 60°F (15.6°C). Division in October	3in then 5in. JIP1	Must be in well crocked pots. Re-pot each spring as new leaves expand
Pot up 4 or 5 tubers in 5in pot in autumn	5in. JIP2	Put in pots for forcing about February then bring into greenhouse. Dry off and re-pot in autumn
Pot up bulbs in succession in Jan–Feb, singly or in threes. Usual to buy bulbs annually	5–6in. JIP2	Keep cool to encourage rooting then force into flower at brisk temperatures

Type and main varieties	Approx height	General description and characteristics	Flowering period
Polyanthus *Primula vulgaris, P. elatior* A wonderful range of vars	9–10in	Wonderful as pot plants since the introduction of the 'Royal Pacific' strains. Very easy to grow	Dec–Feb
Primula kewensis malacoides obconica sinensis	12in	*P. obconica* the most popular. A delightful and long flowering pot plant. Good house plant at light window. Some people allergic to them	Spring–summer
Rehmannia angulata elata	3–4ft	Foxglove-like pink or purple flowers	June
Richardia (arum lily—see *Zantedeschia*)			
Rochea coccinea (*Crassula coccinea*)	9–12in	Attractive plants with red scented flowers. Very easy to grow	Summer
Roses (see also Chapter 25) Dwarf types	16–18in	Many varieties can be grown in advance of outside flowering	Spring–summer
Saintpaulia ionantha (African violet)	8–10in	Excellent pot plant for the home. Many delightful shades of blue and pink, also white F_1 hybrids now available	Various
Salpiglossis sinuata	12–14in (dwarf type) up to 3ft	Beautifully shaped flowers. Can be tricky	Summer, autumn–spring

Propagation method	Pot size and compost	General cultural details
Seed in March–June, pressed into the surface. Cover with clear polythene and give 60–70°F (15.6–21.1°C)	3½, 4 or 5in. JIP1	Respond well to *cool* growing and regular watering. Give shade from direct sunlight in cool greenhouse. Or keep in pots outside in cold frames for lifting in during December. Use 2:2:1 liquid feeding
Seed thinly in May–June. Germinates at 65–70°F (18.3–21.1°C)	3½in then 5in. JIP2 with pH 5.5–5.8	Grow cool and keep well watered, potting only lightly. Reduce watering during winter. Apply iron sequestrine if leaves go white
Seed in June/July at 60°F (15.6°C) or by cuttings from basal shoots after flowering. Root cuttings can also be taken	3in then 7in. JIP2	Frost-free conditions only. Treat as biennial. Raise cool and light in greenhouse in winter. Feed and water well when flowers form
Cuttings in spring and summer. Select from terminal shoots if rooting in peat/sand, at 60–65°F (15.6–18.3°C) round edge pot	3in then 5in. JIP1	Cool greenhouse conditions. Keep dry in winter. Must be well dressed
Buy in plants and pot up dwarf growing varieties	5–7in. JIP1	Keep as cool as possible. Pay strict attention to pest and disease control
Seed in Aug/Sept at 70–75°F (21.1–23.9°C) in JIS plus extra peat (can be sown any time to flower 6 months later). Leaf petiol cuttings with petiols inserted in sandy compost at 70°F (21.1°C); lift plants and pot separately	3½in. JIP1	Grow at 65°F (18.3°C). Water from below to avoid leaf marking. Give shade. Feed when plant becomes pot bound each year
Sow seed in July–Sept in JIP1	4in then 6in. JIP2	Can be difficult to prevent damping off. Overwinter in small pots and pot up to 6in in February, giving a minimum of 50°F (10°C). Pinch out leading stem to give bushy plant. Do not overwater in winter

Type and main varieties	Approx height	General description and characteristics	Flowering period
Salvia	9–12in	Chiefly grown as a bedding plant but becoming popular as a pot plant	Summer–autumn
Saxifraga stolonifera (mother of thousands)	12–16in	Excellent for hanging baskets or staging. White flowers on graceful stems.	Spring–summer
Schizanthus (butterfly flower or poor man's orchid)	18–24in	One of the showiest spring greenhouse plants. Not difficult, but temperamental	Spring
Schlumbergera truncata (*Zygocactus truncatus*) (Christmas cactus)	Pendulous	A well-known winter flowering plant. Simple to grow	Winter
Solanum capsicastrum pseudocapsicum	12–14in	Grown for its decorative red berries	Winter
Spathiphyllum Spathiphyllum	18–24in	White spathes. Cultivation similar to Zantedeschia (arum), which see	
Strelitzia reginae (Bird of paradise flower)	3–4ft	Unusual and worth growing on the wall of a greenhouse for its flowers like tropical birds' heads	Spring–summer
Streptocarpus Many complex hybrids	3–4ft but dwarf types 15in	Trumpet-shaped flowers of blue, white, pink, red or salmon. Simple to grow	Summer
Tillandsia lindeniana	15in	Epiphytic plants. Interesting foliage and very attractive flowers. For the specialist	Summer
Torenia fournieri	12in	Lilac with yellow throat. Attractive, late-flowering easy-to-grow plants	Summer–autumn

Propagation method	Pot size and compost	General cultural details
Sow seed from mid-February to May or later. Seed must be germinated at 70–75°F (21.1–23.9°C)	3½in Jiffy 7s then 5in. JIP2	Give a growing temperature of 55–60°F (12.8–15.6°C). Too low temperatures and excess watering will yellow the leaves
Increase by runners any time	3½in then 5in. JIP1	Keep cool and in well-watered pots. Can be grown out of doors in mild areas
Sown August until January in 65°F (18.3°C). Grow 3 in a pot for best effect	3½in then 6in or 7in. JIP1	Likes cool steady growth, planty of light, pinching to make bushy and support with split canes. Water sparingly in winter, generously in spring
Propagates with ease from stems rooted any time	3–6in. JIP1	Water sparingly in summer. Give light feeding from Oct onwards
Like tomatoes. Seed in January and February thinly at 150 per tray at 65°F (18.3°C). Also from cuttings, in propagating cases	2⅛in or Jiffy 7s then 3½in, JIP1 plus ¾oz magnesium sulphate. For 5in pots JIP2 plus magnesium sulphate	Needs plenty of light for sturdy growth. Pinch to keep bushy. Stand in frame in summer. Syringe frequently during flowering in July–Sept to induce good setting. Avoid over-watering. Feed with 1 : 1 : 1 after berries are set
Division in spring	6in. JIP2	Plenty of sun and adequate water in spring and summer. Never below 50°F (10°C)
Seed in Feb–Mar at 65°F (18.3°C) and again in July. Leaf cuttings in August will also root	JIP2	Grow cool, not less than 45°F (7.2°C). Begin watering in March and feed from April. Encourage to flower again following year by removing old flower stems
By suckers which develop at the base of plant	Orchid type compost (see Chapter 30)	Minimum of 55°F (12.8°C). Requires warmth and humidity to thrive
Seed in March/April. Pot up 3 plants per 6in pot	6in. JIP2	Requires some shade like begonias. Support necessary with twigs

Type and main varieties	Approx height	General description and characteristics	Flowering period
Trachelium caeruleum	18in	Rather like a gypsophila only more floriferous	Summer
Tulbaghia pulchella	12–18in	Bulbous plants with blue heads of flowers	Summer
Vallota speciosa (Scarborough lily)	18–24in	Mass of bright red or pink flowers at top of short stem. Excellent greenhouse or house plant	Summer
Veltheimia bractata (*V. viridifolia*)	12–18in	Bulbous plant like small red-hot pokers. Simple to grow	Early spring
Zantedeschia aethiopica (arum lily) *angustiloba elliottiana* and dwarfer varieties	2–3ft	A well known plant with its white trumpet flowers	Spring

Foliage Pot Plants

Type and variety	Description	Height
Acalypha wilkesiana	Large olive green leaves with a broad margin of carmine	18–24in
Acorus gramineus 'Variegatus'	Green and cream variegated grass-like leaves	8–10in
Aglaonema commutatum	Interesting dark green leaves banded with chevron-like silvery markings	12–18in
Ampelopsis brevipedunculata	Attractive three-lobed leaves like fronds	Climbing
Araucaria excelsa (Norfolk Island pine)	Pale green branches in tiers, reminiscent of a Christmas tree	12–24in
Aspidistra elatior often mistakenly referred to as *A. lurida*	Too familiar to need description. 'Variegata' has cream-striped leaves	18–24in
Begonia masoniana	Has black angular markings on the leaves, hence the common name Iron Cross begonia	12–24in

Propagation method	Pot size and compost	General cultural details
Seed in July in frames out of doors	7in. JIP2	Best treated as a biennial. Keep frost-free through the winter, then water and feed liberally
Pot up in March/April. Propagation by detaching offsets	5–6in	A simple plant to grow. Rest in winter
Pot up deeply in early summer, one per pot. Can be propagated from offsets which form at base	5–6in. JIP2	Hates disturbance; leave 3 years in same pot. Feed when growth starts. Very little heat required. Some shade beneficial in May/June
Pot up in September. Small bulbs appearing at base form a means of propagation	5–6in. JIP2	Frost-free conditions. Do not need potting every year
Divide up in July/August after flowering	7–8in. JIP1 plus one-third part of rotted FYM	A great favourite with the floral art enthusiast, but not popular with gardeners because it introduces green fly. Dry off after flowering

Propagation	Culture
Half-ripened shoots taken in the summer. Heat is necessary in the propagator	JIP2 with extra peat. Syringe with tepid water in summer
By division of the tufts in the spring	JIP1. Cool conditions. Also thrives out of doors. Loves wet conditions as these are aquatic plants
By division of the roots in March into small pots	3 parts loam, 1 part peat, 1 part sharp sand. JIP2
Cuttings of soft shoots in summer	Ordinary soil
By seed or cuttings in propagating case	Ordinary soil; is nearly hardy
By division when re-potting	Likes shade. Stand out of doors in summer. JIP2
Leaf or stem cuttings any time in propagating case. Also by leaf or a portion of it with the underside veins cut at 1in intervals, placed flat on a sandy compost	JIP1. Slow-growing and requires more heat than other begonias. Needs some shade

Type and variety	Description	Height
Begonia rex hybrids and other foliage types	Variegated foliage, many colours	12–24in
Caladium × hortulanum (hybrids of *C. bicolor* *C. humboldtii*	Variegated red, cream and green leaves, very attractive Small green leaves with translucent white mottling	12in
Chlorophytum comosum '*Variegatum*' (spider plant)	One of the best-known house plants with its variegated striped leaves	12–18in
Cissus antarctica (kangaroo vine)	Toothed leaves of a shiny dark green colour. Excellent for covering an area	12–18in
Cissus rhombifolia (natal vine)	A vigorous plant that climbs by tendrils. Leaves brownish and some-what hairy, but mature to a dark shiny green	Climbing
Coleus blumei	Nettle-like leaves, in a wide range of variegated colour forms	12–18in
Collinia elegans (*Chamaedorea elegans*) (stove plant)	Slender stems and graceful leaves	8–10ft
Cordyline terminalis various cultivars	Leaves 12in long and 4in broad tapering to a point, red-pink with dark green featherings on either side, or variegated red, cream or purple	18in
Croton, correctly *Codiaeum variegatum* and cultivars	Brightly coloured foliage in a wide range of shapes and colours	12–24in
Cyperus alternifolius (umbrella grass)	Umbrella-like clusters of leaf-like bracts on top of stiff green stems	18–24in
Dieffenbachia maculata (dumbcane)	Dark green leaves with white markings	12–24in
Dizygotheca elegantissima (*Aralia elegantissima*)	Beautiful palmate leaves, reddish at first, then dark green	24–36in
Dracaena Dracaena	Variegated or coloured foliage	18in
Elettaria cardamomum	Interesting plant. Member of the ginger family. Attractive dark green foliage and smells of cinnamon	12in
Euonymus radicans variegata, a form of *E. fortunei*	A creeping plant with silvery green variegations	6–8in

Propagation	Culture
as above	Water sparingly in winter. JIP1 or 2. Shade from strong sun
Leaves die down in winter. Tubers should be stored in the pots at temperatures not below 55°F (12.8°C)	Repot tubers in March at 65°F (18.3°C) minimum in coarse peaty mixture
Layer from small plantlets which form on flower heads	Useful and easy to grow. Rich soil and much water. JIP2
Leaf buds or terminal cuttings	Staking is necessary. Needs light but not in the sun. JIP1 or 2
By cuttings of hard new growth placed in water	This plant will tolerate most conditions but not excessive sunshine
By seed. Also by cuttings rooted in propagating case in spring	Shade from strong sun. Keep well watered. Feed regularly. JIP1 or 2
By seeds in March 1 in deep in pots after soaking for a day or two. Requires high temperatures to germinate 85°F (29.4°C)	Do not expose to sun. Minimum of 65°F (18.3°C). JIP1
Seed in March at 85°F (29.4°C). Main stems cut to 1 in lengths inserted horizontally in sandy soil. March/Apr temperature 75–80°F (23.9–26.7°C)	Needs a rich soil containing much peat. Water well in growing season. JIP2 plus extra peat
Cuttings with at least 6–7 leaves, also leaf bud cuttings. Both in propagating case	Give full light and keep cool. Shade only in full sun. Tricky but worth while. Minimum of 55°F (12.8°C) in winter
Division in March or April, or use tips of shoots	JIP1 or 2. Give shade
Terminal and stem cuttings, the latter with two buds horizontally. Both in propagating case	A fairly easy plant to grow. JIP1
Root cuttings in March. Seeds sown in March	JIP1. 65–70°F (18.3–21.1°C). Ample supply of water
Stem and leaf bud cuttings in propagating case	Shade from bright sunlight. High humidity necessary. JIP2
By division any time	Do not expose to full sun. Give plenty of warmth and moisture. JIP2
By stem or leaf cuttings or by pegging down runners. Also by division	Good soil, leafy and light. JIP1 or 2

Type and variety	Description	Height
× *Fatshedera lizei* (fat-headed Lizzie), hybrid *Fatsia* × *Hedera*	Large shiny green leaves. Satisfactory foliage plant. Variegated form also exists	18–24in
Fatsia japonica (rice-paper plant)	Large glossy green lobed leaves	18–24in
Ficus *benjamina*	Lax leaves and branches that give it a 'weeping' form	24in
elastica (India-rubber plant)	Erect plant, shiny leaves	12–24in
pumila	Creeping or climbing	
Fittonia *verschaffeltii*	Semi-trailing with red-veined dark green leaves	6–12in
var *argyroneura*	Leaves green with white veins	
Grevillea robusta (silk oak)	Grown as a tree in Australia; makes an attractive pot plant with bronze-green leaves	12–24in
Gynura aurantiaca	Dark green leaves with red or purple hairs	24–36in
Hedera (ivy) *canariensis* *helix* many cultivars	Good house plants. 'Chicago', 'Evan', 'Glacier', 'Little Diamond' have beautifully variegated leaves	Climbing
Helxine soleirolii (*Soleirolia soleirolii*) (mind your own business)	Low growing plant with trailing stems and tiny leaves	Trailing
Hoffmannia *refulgens* *roezlii*	Noted for their colourful foliage, the leaves having a curious quilted effect, deep green tinged with coppery red	12in
Maranta (prayer plant) *leuconeura* and var *kerchoveana*	Apple-green leaves with purple markings turning brown with maturity	6–8in
Microcoelum weddelianum (*Cocos weddeliana*)	Leaves feather-shaped	12–24in
Monstera deliciosa	The leaves are a glossy dark green of a leathery texture with slightly bizarre perforations	Climbing
Neoregelia carolinae	Bromeliads with ornamental leaves. Green with coloured markings. 'Tricolor' has cream stripes	9–12in
Nepenthes species (pitcher plant)	Grown for their coloured insectivorous pitchers	Climbing

Propagation	Culture
Terminal and leaf bud cuttings in propagating case. Half peat/half sand	Must be supported and shaded from bright sun. JIP1
From seed or cuttings taken in the spring	Copious watering and regular feeding. JIP1
Leaf bud and terminal cuttings in propagating case	Requires more water than the rubber plant Not the easiest of plants to grow. Water regularly but sparingly. JIP1
From cuttings of firm young shoots taken in spring, rooted with bottom heat	Good soil and a warm, moist atmosphere. JIP1
From seed sown in early spring, also cuttings with heels of old wood attached	Prune off points of shoots occasionally to induce bushy growth. JIP2
By cuttings taken in the spring	Give as much light as possible, but not direct sun. JIP1
By cuttings taken in the spring. A tip cutting 2–4in long will root in water or sandy soil	Resents over-watering in winter and care should be taken not to over-pot. JIP1
By division in spring	Any soil. Can be a nuisance if allowed to develop
By cuttings of young growth in sandy soil in propagating case with brisk bottom heat	A coarse soil mixture of peat, sand and loam should be satisfactory at all stages of growth
By division of tubers in February or March, also by leaf cuttings in moist heat	Rich soil and feed during summer. Re-pot each year. Water abundantly March–September. JIP2
Seed 1in deep in light soil, temperature 85°F (29.4°C). At any time	Minimum temperature 50°F (10°C). Must not stand in draught. JIP1
Seed or cuttings and requires a high temperature—a task for the professional	Water freely March–October. Syringe twice daily. JIP1
From seed or offsets. A temperature of 70°F (21.1°C) is needed	Use potting compost, peat, leaf-mould, or sphagnum moss. Best if they are not over-potted
3–6in one-year-old shoots in spring and summer	Orchid-type compost

Type and variety	Description	Height
Nephthytis 'Emerald Gem'	This plant is light green not emerald, in spite of its name, and has a variegated effect	Climbing
Oplismenus hirtellus 'Variegatus'	A member of the grass family with 1–3in pointed leaves, white with green midrib	8in
Pandanus veitchii (screw-pine)	These palm-like plants have spiny dark green leaves with silver margins	12–18in
Pellionia repens (*P. daveauana*)	A creeping plant. Dark bronze leaves irregular grey-green centres	
Peperomia argyreia (*P. sandersii*)	Thick smooth leaf, almost round but tapers to a sharp point. Dark green and silver in colour	3–6in
Peperomia griseo-argentea (*P. hederifolia*) (pepper elder)	Small heart-shaped leaves that have a metallic grey appearance	3–6in
Philodendron erubescens 'Burgundy' (sweetheart plant)	Slow growing climber with arrow-shaped leathery leaves, coppery when young, later dark green with reddish-purple stems	Climber
Pilea cadierei (aluminium plant)	A very attractive plant with embossed silvery markings on the foliage	12–18in
Rhiphidophora aurea (*Scindapsus aureus*) (ivy arum)	Heart-shaped leaves. Dark green with heavily marked cream variegations	12–18in
Ricinus communis (castor oil plant) 'Gibsonii' 'Sanguineus'	A shrubby plant with green palmate leaves Bronze leaves Reddish-purple leaves	12–18in
Sansevieria trifasciata (mother-in-law's tongue) 'Laurentii'	Sword-like twisted leaves rising vertically from the soil. Grey and grey mottled Leaves yellow-variegated	3–4ft
Saxifraga stolonifera (*S. sannentosa*) (mother of thousands)	Roundish variegated leaves. Graceful stems of white flowers	12in
Schefflera actinophylla	A slow growing but eventually a large plant, each leaflet may reach a length of 10in. Leaflets radiate around the stalk	12–18in
Sedum sieboldii	Yellow blotch in the centre of rounded green leaf	8in

Propagation	Culture
Stem cuttings, any time	Can be trained to a cane, but better still to a cork bark or wire cylinder filled with moss kept damp for the aerial roots. A rich compost and plenty of feeding in the summer are required
From stem cuttings	Needs good winter light, warmth and good soil. JIP2
By suckers with some heat	Good winter warmth, plenty of water in summer and acid leafy soil
Propagation is easy from cuttings	Considerable care in winter with regard to temperature and watering. JIP1
Cut a leaf in half and insert the cut surface about $\frac{1}{2}$in deep in a rooting medium with bottom heat	Requires careful watering. Temperature in winter must remain above 50°F (10°C)
By leaf cuttings in the spring. Leaf complete with stalk is inserted vertically 1in deep in rooting medium	Requires careful watering. Temperature should remain above 50°F (10°C). JIP1
Terminal cuttings, leaf bud cuttings rooted in a temp. of 70°F (21.1°C)	Rich leafy soil needed. Min. temp. 55–60°F (12.8–15.6°C)
Propagation is easy from cuttings	Shade from bright sun. Rich soil and plenty of water in summer
By root division in Feb/March in peat, sphagnum moss, sand or a little charcoal	Water with care and keep temperature above 50°F (10°C) in a light situation. Must be stopped occasionally. JIP1
Seed in February	Plenty of light required for good plants
'Laurentii' has to be increased from suckers to retain the variegated leaves. Others can be propagated by leaf cuttings in May–August	Rich soil with plenty of grit and very sparing watering. Needs winter warmth
By detaching runners, any time	Grow cool. JIP1
Cuttings in spring	Feed regularly in growing season. Benefits by yearly potting on until in a fairly large pot. JIP2
Propagate by short cuttings which root easily	Dies down in winter so must be kept dry. Restarts in February

Type and variety	Description	Height
Selaginella species	Green or variegated, evergreen. Creeping or erect	4–6in
Sparmannia africana	The house lime produces pale green, translucent, hairy leaves	18–24in
Tetrastigma voinierianum	A vigorous climbing plant with five-lobed slightly flaccid-looking leaves	Climbing
Tradescantia species (Wandering Jew/Sailor etc)	The leaves are variegated with silvery-white or yellow streaks, sometimes purple tinged. Some with downy leaves	Trailing
Vriesia splendens	The leaves, forming an upright rosette, are dull green with purplish-brown transverse bands	12–18in

Greenhouse shrubs

Many of the greenhouse shrubs can also be grown in large pots or tubs and quite a few of the smaller or restricted shrubs have already been described as flowering pot plants. In nearly all cases the necessary space for development is more important than adherence to a strict regime.

The soil for growing greenhouse shrubs need not be of a very high nutritional standard, but it should be in good physical condition. To this end deep cultivation and sometimes excavation of the existing soil may be necessary, especially where shrubs are being grown in borders against walls or on the floor of a conservatory or other largely glass erection. Saturation of the growing media by seepage of water from outside is a very frequent cause of failure, lack of moisture being less of a problem than might be imagined, as many shrubs send down roots to a fair depth, often well outside the greenhouse or conservatory. Generally speaking soil to JIP1

Shrubs for the Greenhouse or Conservatory

Name	Description	Temperature category
Abutilon (flowering maple)	Summer flowering	Min winter temp of 50°F (10°C)
megapotamicum	Green and yellow leaves; yellow and scarlet flowers	
striatum 'Thompsonii'	Green and yellow leaves, orange flowers	
'Savitzii'	Smaller leaves, variegated with white	
vitifolium	Large leaves, blue flowers	
and many others		
Acacia	All grown for their beautiful catkins and at their best against a wall, although can be grown as shrubs or trees if space permits	Minimum of 45°F (7.2°C)
armata		
dealbata (mimosa wattle)		
drummondii		
longifolia		
riceana		

Propagation	Culture
Cuttings 3in long in peat at a temperature of 80°F (26.7°C)	Equal parts peat and sphagnum moss. Shade from sun
Roots readily from cuttings. It may be cut back severely	Does best in warm conditions and in smallish pot
Leaf bud or terminal cuttings	Feed during the growing season but do not over-water at any time
Old plants should be replaced regularly by rooting cuttings in 3in pots with JIP1	An ideal plant for the edge of the greenhouse staging
By offsets inserted in small pots of sandy peat. Temperature 75–85°F (23.9–29.4°C)	Require warm conditions but not full sun during summer

or 2 standard should be aimed at.

Support and pruning

Support for climbing or clinging shrubs is provided either by longitudinal wires or plastic or wooden trellis. Shrubs grown in relatively cramped conditions will certainly require pruning. Broadly speaking shrubs either form flowers on new wood of the current or previous year's growth, or on spurs emanating from older portions of wood. It is important therefore to ascertain the flowering mechanism and prune accordingly. In many cases, however, such a specific approach is not necessary and pruning merely to keep the shrub within limits and well shaped is all that is required.

Temperature levels

Few gardeners maintain a greenhouse exclusively for the well-being of shrubs and it is therefore a case of first of all selecting a suitable shrub for the intended temperature level for the main greenhouse activity (see table which follows).

Propagation	Cultural data
Cuttings at almost any time of year. Side shoots with heel are best inserted in propagating case	Prune back to two or three branches from the base, merely shortening shoots of pot-grown species by half. Train against a wall or support
Seeds in spring and summer, specially 'chipped'. Cuttings in July of semi-woody heeled side shoots	Cut young plants back one-third and side shoots similarly. Prune annually by thinning out weaker shoots and cutting back side branches. Keep well watered and feed when actively growing

Name	Description	Temperature category
Allamanda cathartica var *hendersonii*	Evergreen climber with a feast of yellow flowers over a period in summer. Will cover a large area if allowed to	Minimum of 50°F (10°C)
Anemopaegma (formerly *Tecoma* or *Bignonia*) (trumpet flower)	An excellent evergreen climbing shrub with beautiful yellow flowers in September	Minimum of 45°F (7.2°C)
Araucaria excelsa (monkey puzzle, Norfolk Island pine)	Grown as evergreen pot plant for its attractive leaves	Cool culture, being quite hardy
Aristolochia elegans and other species (calico flower, Dutchman's pipe)	Climbing plant which will cover the roof of a greenhouse or conservatory with curious but pleasing dull white flowers mottled with purple in August	Minimum of 55–60°F (12.8–15.6°C)
Bougainvillea *glabra* (rose) *spectabilis* (lilac rose) 'Lindleyana' 'Mrs Butt' (rose) 'Mrs Louis Wathen' (reddish orange)	One of the showiest greenhouse climbers bearing brightly coloured bracts. Evergreen. Idealy for a sunny corner in a conservatory	Minimum of 50°F (10°C)
Bouvardia × *hybrida* Many excellent varieties in scarlet, salmon and pink	Dwarf greenhouse shrub, 12–15in, having very attractive waxy flower heads in winter	Minimum of 50–55°F (10–12.8°C)
Brunfelsia *B. calycina* and others	Low-growing evergreen greenhouse shrub 2–3ft with purple flowers in clusters in summer	Minimum of 50°F (10°C)
Callistemon citrinus 'Splendens' (bottle brush tree)	One of the best known of greenhouse shrubs. Evergreen. Flowers in April–June, the interest being in the stamens, not the petals	Minimum of 40–45°F (4.4–7.2°C)
Camellia japonica varieties, and hybrids, especially *C.* × *Williamsii Donation* (*C. japonica* × *C. saluenensis*)	As shrubs must be given space to grow properly on their own or against a wall. Flowers in winter and spring, the showiest of all evergreen greenhouse shrubs	Minimum of 40–45°F (4.4–7.2°C)
Cassia corymbosa	Excellent for training on a wall or trellis. Beautiful bouquets of yellow flowers in late summer	Minimum of 40–45°F (4.4–7.2°C)

Propagration	Cultural data
3in cuttings in March rooted in frames or inside a mist unit. Plant up in 5in pots, put them into benches or borders of good soil	Prune back previous summer's growth to 2–3 buds in February. Water freely in summer, sparingly in winter
By seed if available but generally by three-jointed cuttings in summer, planted up into 5in pots when rooted for eventual planting out in well-prepared borders	Cut back side branches after flowering to 1–3ft of all wood on main branches. Trim back to 10–12in apart. Remove all weak or superfluous growth in spring. Requires regular feeding
Propagates easily by cuttings in Aug or Sept in warm propagating case. Does best in a loamy compost (JIP2 plus peat). Grow in 5–6in pots	Must be kept frost free. Re-pot if necessary in Feb. Feed regularly in summer
Root from cuttings taken in June or July in propagating case. Grow in tubs or borders in good garden soil. Seed can be sown in March	Cut back in Feb if too vigorous. Keep frost free
4in half-ripe cuttings in Aug in propagating case. Pot up in 3in then 5in pots, preparatory to planting out	Prepare 2 × 2ft planting area of good soil plus peat with perfect drainage for planting in autumn. Prune back previous summer's growth to within two buds of base in Feb. Can also be grown in pots.
Cuttings of young shoots 4in long in late spring in propagating case. Pot up in 5 or 6in pots in JIP1.	Cut back hard after flowering and pinch new shoots until Aug
Cuttings of half-ripe shoots in June or July in propagating case. Pot on when rooted in 5–6in pots in JIP1	Re-pot after flowering. Keep on dry side from October till Feb. Water and feed freely from March onwards. Pinch out young branches to keep bushy. Can also be grown as pot plant.
Seed in April. Cuttings in Aug in propagating case	Fairly hardy. Can be pot grown but at their best in well-prepared greenhouse border with good garden soil. Cut back strong shoots by half and weak shoots by two-thirds after flowering. Water sparingly in winter
Seeds at any time for distinct species. Grafting of several varieties on to *C. Japonica* in spring or cuttings from young shoots in July-Aug in propagating case	Fairly hardy, they thrive in frost-free conditions. Prune into shape after flowering and avoid either excess moisture or dryness (resulting in botrytis or bud drop). Grow as cool and airy as other greenhouse activities allow
Cuttings of young shoots in propagating case in early summer	Grow in frost-free conditions for best results. Prune by cutting back previous year's growth in Feb

317

Name	Description	Temperature Category
Cestrum aurantiacum and other excellent species	Very useful semi-climber for the greenhouse or conservatory	Minimum of 40°F (4.4°C)
Chorizema ilicifolium (red)	In their native Australia these evergreen shrubs grow to 10ft or more. Adapted for pot culture in Britain with their graceful flower-bearing branches	Minimum of 45°F (7.2°C)
Clerodendrum (glory bower) *splendens* (scarlet) *Thomsoniae* (crimson and white) *speciosissimum* (syn. *C. fallax*) (scarlet)	Climbing shrub with very showy flowers for large greenhouses or conservatories. Needs support and very well heated environment. Flowers in summer	Minimum winter temperature of 60°F (15.6°C)
Clianthus *formosus (C. dampieri, C. speciosus)* (glory pea) *puniceus* (parrot's bill)	A most striking shrub with very showy red flowers growing 3–6ft against a wall. Can thrive out of doors, but does well in a cold greenhouse. Fowers May–June	40–45°F (4.4–7.2°C)
Cobea scandens (cup and saucer vine)	An excellent and popular climber for greenhouse or conservatory, but can be too boisterous for a small area. Has Caterbury Bell type blooms from May to October. May also be used for balconies	50–55°F (10–12.8°C)
Crossandra infundibuliformis (C. undulifolia)	An excellent and showy plant for pots or borders. Flowers in summer	Minimum of 55°F (12.8°C)
Datura *cornigera* (angel's trumpet) (white) *sanguinea* (orange-red)	A plant with large coarse foliage and flowers 7–8in long. Grown usually in large tubs or 12in pots to flower in summer	Minimum of 45°F (7.2°C)
Doxantha capreolata (glory flower), previously known as Bignonia	Vigorously growing evergreen climber with yellow and red trumpet flowers against glass or wall of greenhouse or conservatory, reaching up to the roof. Flowers in spring and summer	Minimum of 40–45°F (4.4–7.2°C)

Propagation	Cultural data
Cuttings of young wood in Aug in propagating case in JIP1. Pot on for planting out	Can be grown in large pots but happier in good soil in a wall border. Trim young plants lightly and older plants harder by cutting side shoots to a few buds in late winter. To keep bushy pinch shoots
By seed in pots or cuttings with heel in Aug, when they root readily in fairly cool conditions	Plant in loamy soil. Shorten shoots by one-third after flowering, then plunge out of doors. Re-pot every second or third year. Can also be grown in greenhouse border
Seed in March at 65°F (18.3°C) and gradually move up to 7in pots using JIP3. Cuttings in spring and Aug rooted in propagating case. Also by root cuttings and suckers in some cases	Trim back branches in spring. Plants need plenty of light and resent over-watering
Seed in spring or summer. For *C. formosus* by grafting on to seedlings of *Colutea arborescens*: insert wedge-shaped section of clianthus in a slit in colutea, bind with soft wool and insert in propagation case. *C. puniceus* can be raised from cuttings on its own roots. Pot up in 6–7in pots	Gives little trouble if grown cool and frost-free either in pots or in tubs
Seed in February–March. Pot on, using good garden soil	Simple to grow. Merely requires branches cut back to 2 buds (like a vine) in Feb or March, and occasional restriction when it gets out of hand. A succession of new plants from seed is often less trouble
Seed or cuttings in March. Pot into 3in then 5in pots	Best to raise new plants from seed or cuttings annually. Shorten main shoots to keep bushy
Cuttings in spring in pots or open beds or propagating case in JIP1	Can be a large and vigorous shrub requiring pruning back. Pot up young plants frequently. Water little in winter, but water and feed copiously in summer
Cuttings of short shoots in bottom heat in peat/sand. Potted on into good garden soil	A bushy shrub relatively easy to grow in large tubs or greenhouse borders. Do not over-water in winter

Name	Description	Temperature category
Gardenia jasminoides (Cape jasmine) and double form 'Florida' *nitida* *thunbergia*	Small compact evergreen shrubs up to 3ft tall with large white single and double flowers in summer, and later if heads are removed	Not less than 55–60°F (12.8–15.6°C)
Hibiscus species (rose mallow)	A beautiful shrub with magnificent flowers in summer. Will grow to 6ft	Minimum of 55–60°F (12.8–15.6°C) in moist atmosphere
Hoya (wax plant) *Bella* *carnosa*	An excellent and dependable greenhouse climbing plant which produces masses of waxy pink flowers in early summer	Minimum of 55–60°F (12.8–15.6°C). *H. carnosa* the hardier
Humea elegans (incense plant)	Scented and ornamental leaves. Grows 4–5ft tall with droopy reddish flowers in late summer	Minimum of 45–50°F (7.2–10°C)
Iochroma coccineum (scarlet) *fuchsioides* (orange scarlet) *grandiflorum* (purple)	Shrubs which grow to 6ft and produce flowers in autumn	Minimum of 40–45°F (4.4–7.2°C)
Ipomoea (pharbitis, morning glory) *learii* (perennial) *tricolor* (annual)	Annual and perennial rapidly climbing plants for the greenhouse	Grows well at 55–60°F (12.8–15.6°C)
Jasminum (jasmine) *angulare* (white) *mesnyi* (*J. primulinum*) (yellow) *polyanthum* (white, pink in bud) and other species	Excellent greenhouse shrub for growing against a wall. Most are very fragrant and flower early in the year	Minimum of 45°F (7.2°C)
Lagerstroemia indica (crape-myrtle) and cultivars	Summer flowering shrub of various colours. Grown in large tub or pot or well-drained borders	Minimum of 45°F (7.2°C)
Lantana camara and cultivars	Flowers form in flattish heads, pink orange or yellow. Form big bush up to 6ft or can be kept small in pots. Evergreen. Summer flowering	Minimum of 45°F (7.2°C)
Lapageria rosea (Chilean bellflower)	One of the best-known greenhouse twining shrubs with its evergreen leaves and bell-like pink flowers. Summer flowering	Minimum of 45–50°F (7.2–10°C)

Propagation	Cultural data
Cuttings of young shoots 3in in length in peat/sand in March with bottom heat. Pot into 3in, 5in and then 7in pots for flowering, using JIP2	Must be 'coddled' by bench warming until established. A succession of young plants should be raised as bush goes straggly. Pinch shoots of young growth to induce side-shoot formation
Shoots 3in long on bottom heat in March, but may be slow	Given warmth, a fairly simple shrub to grow, shoots being cut back by about half in Jan or Feb. Pinch out to give a bushy plant
By layering of shoots in pots or by cuttings in spring and summer. Use JIP1 or good garden soil	At its best rambling from good soil in a greenhouse border but could be grown in large pots or tubs, being re-potted every 3/4 years
Sow seed in summer and pot up into 5–6in pots with JIP1 once small pots are full of root, then into 7 or 8in pots in spring with JIP2	Do not over-water in winter. Support needed, along with regular feeding and watering in spring and summer
Cuttings in summer. Pot up into 9–10in pots with JIP3, or put in greenhouse borders	Must be kept frost-free. Water very little in winter. Support needed
Seed in March for annual species. Seed in March or cuttings in summer for perennials. Best planted in greenhouse border in good soil of JIP2 standard	Perennial type, must be kept frost-free but dry. Requires adequate support with string or trellis
Cuttings in summer, potted on when rooted and then planted either in large pots or in borders. JIP1 or 2 standard	Simple shrub to grow. Cut back after flowering. Merely requires to be frost-free. If in pots stand out for summer
Cuttings of young shoots in March–April in JIP1. Grow on in soil of JIP2 standard	Prune back hard in Feb. If in pot stand out for summer period. Keep dry in winter.
Cuttings in spring, or seed in Feb–March in propagating case	Cool greenhouse subjects. Pinch out shoots to keep dwarf if necessary. Prune in winter by cutting back shoots hard
Layering in spring and summer is best method of propagation. JIP2 standard	Do best in specially made-up beds as they like a free root run. Top dress each spring with new soil

Name	Description	Temperature category
Manettia *bicolor* (red and yellow) *inflata* (same with less yellow)	Climbing shrubs for warm greenhouses with lovely tubular flowers in summer	Minimum of 55–60°F (12.8–15.6°C)
Metrosideros (closely related to *Callistemon*) *diffusa* (crimson) *excelsa* (crimson) *robusta* (scarlet)	*M. diffusa* is an evergreen climber and *M. robusta* and *excelsa* are trees. The large stamens of the flowers are the main attraction in spring	Minimum of 45°F (7.2°C)
Passiflora (passion flower) *P. caerulea* and others requiring more heat of which *P. antioquiensis* (red) is popular	Frequently grown in greenhouses or conservatories because of unusual flowers. Vigorous climbers and need room. Flower over a long period in summer	Minimum of 45°F (7.2°C)
Pelargonium spp	Although dealt with under Pot Plants, pelargoniums make excellent greenhouse shrubs in large pots or borders	Minimum of 45°F (7.2°C)
Petrea volubilis (purple wreath) (lilac blue)	Large twining shrub not suitable for a small greenhouse. Beautiful and showy flowers April–May	Minimum of 45°F (7.2°C)
Plumbago (climbing leadwort) *capensis* (blue) *rosea* (red)	Climbing or trailing plants for walls. Copious flowers in late summer	Minimum of 45°F (7.2°C)
Rhodochiton atrosanguineum	Perennial climber for warm greenhouses; up to 10ft tall with reddish-purple flowers in summer. Leaves heart-shaped	Minimum of 45°F (7.2°C)
Sparmannia africana (African hemp)	Large plant with large leaves and white flowers with purple-tipped stamens	Minimum of 40°F (4.4°C)
Stephanotis floribunda (Madagascar jasmine)	One of the best greenhouse climbers for perfume and beauty. White flowers in summer. Evergreen. Can be grown in small pots	Minimum of 50°F (10°C) but cool airy conditions
Streptosolen jamesonii	A climbing shrub for pots or borders. Orange flowers in June and July. Can grow to 6ft or more in large pot	Minimum of 45–50°F (7.2–10°C)
Trachelospermum jasminoides (Chinese jasmine)	White scented flowers from June to August	Minimum of 40°F (4.4°C)

Propagation	Cultural data
Cuttings in May–June. Pot up 2 or 3 plants together in 6–7in pot in JIP2	Must have good warmth and need a fair bit of room. Trim into shape after flowering
Seed in April. Cuttings in Aug	Frost-free greenhouse. In borders or large pots in good garden soil. Trim into shape after flowering
Cuttings with heel in bottom heat in spring and summer, although node cuttings will also grow. Seed in spring	Cool growing conditions for *P. caerulea*. *P. antioquiensis* needs more heat. Keep dry in winter and cut back fairly hard after flowering
Cuttings rooted any time. Plant up in tubs, or borders in JIP1 or 2	Will not stand frost. Trim to shape occasionally. Useful as a source of cuttings
Cuttings 2in long in spring/summer. Soil of JIP3 standard	Grow in borders of good soil only where there is sufficient room for development. Cut back weak branches in Feb
Cuttings in spring or early summer	Can be grown either in tubs or borders. Prune back when desired in Feb, cutting back shoots by a third to a half once established (before this merely shorten slightly in Feb)
Can be treated as annual, raising from seed sown each spring. Pot up 6 or 7in pot or border of JIP2 standard	Uncomplicated plant to grow for the summer period
Cuttings in spring and summer with bottom heat	Cut back previous year's shoots to within 1–2in of base
Cuttings in spring. Pot up in large pots or plant in border	Cut out weak shoots and shorten main shoots in Feb. Discard plants if they get too straggly
Cuttings in summer in bottom heat	Cut back plants in Feb after resting
Cuttings in propagating case in summer or layering any time. Pot up or plant in borders to JIP3 standard	Almost hardy but give heat in frost-free greenhouse in cooler areas. Prune back in winter and stake shrubs in summer

The Passion flower,
Passiflora caerulea, is one
of the most spectacular
of all climbing
greenhouse shrubs.

Chapter 25

The rose as a flower crop

The growing of roses under glass is becoming increasingly popular, not only commercially but in amateur spheres with particular emphasis on floral art material or exhibition (see varieties for forcing in rose growers' catalogues). They tend now to be treated as a short-term crop, the bushes being forced to produce up to five flushes per year, and replaced after two or three years according to their performance.

The amateur gardener, however, may merely concern himself with a few bushes in 9–10in pots to provide blooms in advance of those grown outside, and for a longer period into the autumn (the Royal National Rose Society has a recommended list).

Ideally roses thrive best in light airy conditions in a well-ventilated greenhouse with a minimum temperature of 50–55°F (10–12.8°C). The soil, of good texture and porosity, should have a pH of 6.5 (too far above this can lead to deficiency problems) and a phosphate/potash index of 3–4. Much use is now made of complete trace-element-containing fertilisers such as Vitax Q4 at 6oz per sqyd in addition to farmyard manure at 1cwt per 6/10sqyd. Good drainage is essential, which means thorough cultivation if borders are to be used, and the free use of crocks in pots.

Roses are grown commercially 'on the flat' in borders 4–5ft wide, planting distances being 10–12in each way. Budded roses are generally best on an *R. canina* stock, while grafted roses are best on *R. inermis*. Planting time should be in November/December for budded roses, grafted roses being planted in the spring. Planting should be firm, and the same is true with potting.

Growth should be commenced slowly in January/February with 45°F (7.2°C), rising gradually over 14–21 days to 55°F (12.8°C). Higher temperatures will obviously prevail during the summer months, but excessively high temperatures should be avoided by free use of ventilators. Regular watering, preferably by low level irrigation systems, or on a small scale by hose (with a fine rose) is essential, avoiding saturation or excessive dryness.

Budded roses when planted should be pruned back to 4–5in from ground level and main shoots pinched when they develop to encourage lower growth when approximately at the 5-fivers stage (5 leaflets). There should ideally be some selection and thinning of shoots and a degree of disbudding is necessary with hybrid teas.

Following each flush of growth a straight form of nitrogen should be given—Nitro-Chalk, Nitram or urea formaldehyde, at normal application rates and watered in. Pest and disease control is particularly important, using sulphur if necessary for mildew on a continuous basis (see Chapter 32).

Potted roses can be rested by plunging in ashes out of doors in October, being pruned and brought into the greenhouse in February/March for the production of early blooms. Liquid feeding should be given. Roses should be pruned lightly between flushes.

The culture of carnations

The carnation, like any other crop, reacts unfavourably to monocultural practices, diseases becoming established in border soils which are virtually impossible to eradicate. Border culture should only be considered, therefore, where the soil is 'new'; subsequently isolated beds of one form or another are necessary, and in amateur spheres this includes pot culture. Raised beds can be constructed of precast concrete, sheet or corrugated asbestos;

Carnations grow far
better in the greenhouse
than out of doors, and a
far wider range of
varieties can be grown
this way.

ground or surface beds are best prepared on a concrete base with wood sides and ends; and for small-scale culture sunken beds can be constructed cheaply by using polythene sides and base, providing outlets for surplus moisture by drainage tiles or slits in the base. Some form of sterilisation will be necessary for all beds.

Carnations on a long-term basis require support, this being best provided by the use of strong metal supports at the ends of the bed, using wires, cross battens and coarse string or alternatively neeting. For pot culture, support is provided by canes and string.

Growing media and nutrition

Carnations make large demands on nutrients and soils should be adjusted following soil analysis as follows:

pH   6.5 at planting time (lower for peat composts—see Chapter 13)
Nitrogen   High (50–150 ppm nitrate), a difficult figure to adjust
Phosphorus and potash   Index 3–5
Magnesium   Index 4
Soluble salt   Index 2–3

Such nutrient levels are met by using John Innes No 2 potting compost or equivalent soilless mixes. When the existing soil is being used, and subsequent to adjustment of the pH following analysis, a normal base application is 1–4oz superphosphates, 2–6oz sulphate of potash, approximately 2–4oz magnesium sulphate, and between 1 and 2oz hoof and horn according to the time of year and soil analysis. The higher nitrogen dressing is given at times of the year when water requirement is low in winter or early spring and liquid feeding is therefore not practical. Compound base fertilisers can be used at rates of up to 8–9oz per sq yd, there being virtue in selecting one with a trace element content. Reduce applications if analysis merits it. Hydroponic systems have much application in carnation culture.

Propagation

The commercial practice in the UK and Europe generally is to buy in high-quality tested cuttings from specialist raisers. There are some excellent sources of supply open to the amateur grower, and arrangements can sometimes be made to obtain small quantities of cuttings from specialist nurserymen. Gardeners or growers anxious for detailed information on stock build-up are referred to the *Ministry of Agriculture Bulletin No 151* in which the subject is discussed in some detail. This bulletin also deals with the effective storage of cuttings at $32°F \pm \frac{1}{2}°F$ ($0°C \pm \frac{1}{2}°C$), a technique which assists the rooting process. Research has shown that cuttings taken from flowering plants seldom show the same vigour as cuttings taken from stock plants used solely for the purpose.

Dip cuttings in hormone rooting powder or soak overnight in a diluted solution (alpha napthalene acetic acid formulations give best results). Insert in porous rooting medium (pH 7 being desirable; see also Chapter 18) at a density of 50–70 per sq ft, which is fully 1in apart each way. Give good light and bottom heat, either by soil warming cables, under-bench or mini-bore pipes, in the region of 70–72°F (21.1–22.2°C) for ten days after cutting insertion, when thereafter temperatures are reduced to 62–65°F (16.7–18.3°C) as a weaning measure. Rooting should take place in 18–21 days. Smaller scale propagation can readily be carried out in seed boxes with plastic domes, and mist benches, if available, are also helpful, especially from March to September. No more watering should be carried out than is needed to prevent wilting, since too much watering encourages fungal diseases. There is no advantage in leaving the cuttings after rooting, as this merely results in a greater check when potted.

Programme of production

Carnations can be planted at any time of the year and will start flowering according to the light intensity, heat level and other factors. The following are the advantages of planting in different months:

January planting   Cuttings rooted in good light areas will, if left unstopped, produce the first flush of flowers by April/May, and the first lateral flowers in June. Stopping the plants by nipping out the centre stem will delay flowering by 2–3 weeks.

April/early May Cuttings planted in April/early May and stopped once will flower in late August/September. A second stop will enable the plant to give greater continuity of flowers into late autumn.

June Most gardeners will find that summer plantings suit them best, stopping the plants to take the first flowers in winter, after which there tends to be a shortage of flowers until about July and August the second year.

Autumn planting The worst time, as the young plants will have difficulty in developing in the diminishing light and may fall prey to fungal disorders if environmental control is not of a very high order. The first blooms will not appear until the following spring.

Growers and professional gardeners will obviously need to study planting times from an economic angle.

Plant spacing

Average planting distances are 8 × 8in in a square planting system. Closer planting up to 5 × 4in gives an earlier yield but generally increases disease potential. For pot growing, three plants per 9in pot is average.

Water requirements

Plants are set out in relatively damp soil or media and should merely be watered in and thereafter watered according to their needs, which will vary enormously according to whether plants are in raised, sunken, or ground beds, or in pots. In commercial spheres water requirements are related to the readings taken from evaporimeters and determined in the UK by Ministry of Agriculture centres. These, and tensiometers, can be used on a small scale with some success.

Stopping and disbudding

Stopping refers to the removal of the terminal growth to encourage lateral bud development; it also delays flowering. The *single stop* is the removal of the first small pair of leaves, the plant being bent over until it snaps off cleanly. Raising the night temperature to 60°F (15.6°C) for 2–3

weeks after stopping, and more frequent damping, encourages lateral growth development. In general, from a single stop about five buds will be produced.

A *stop and a half* relates to a supplementary stopping of some of the subsequent laterals. Commercially this is done to delay flower production over a poor price period. It can also be done for flower show timing. Where no stopping is carried out the plant is allowed to form its terminal buds and flower early, a practice which may well suit the amateur. It is used as a means of avoiding glut periods.

Disbudding of stems down to the one terminal bud is necessary weekly in summer and every two to three weeks in winter (see Figs 77 and 78).

Seasonal feeding

Supplementary feeding is usually necessary soon after planting carnations, this either being applied dry and flushed into the soil or growing media, or applied in liquid form through an irrigation system or a rose on the end of a hosepipe. The dry feed generally used is 3 parts by weight of dried blood (or 2 parts sulphate of ammonia) and 1 part sulphate of potash applied at 2oz per sqyd at 12–14 day intervals. Very considerable research has been carried out in the whole sphere of carnation nutrition at the Glasshouse Crops Research Institute at Littlehampton in Sussex and elsewhere, and generally speaking equal parts of nitrogen and potash (K_2O) throughout give the best results. Reference back to Chapter 15 shows a range of nutrients in this category, it being important to avoid too high concentrations which can quickly result in salt build-up.

Gardeners using pots may also find it inadvisable to feed too lavishly and there is much to be said for erring on the side of safety, since feeding can always be increased but it is not so easy to remove excess nutrients.

Temperatures

Accepted regimes now appear to be a night temperature of 50°F (10°C) raised to 54°F (12.2°C) from March to October and a

Fig 77

Fig 78

positive day temperature of 60°F (15.6°C) with ventilation coming into operation at not more than 70°F (21.1°C), although it is doubtful if such precision is possible in small greenhouses.

Lighting

Research findings indicate that periods of long days or continuous lighting hasten the inducement of flower buds. Lighting is applied from dusk to dawn using tungsten filament lamps, with 150 watt bulbs at 12–15ft centres, 5ft higher than the growing point of the plant, for 14 days in summer up to 45 days in winter.

Young shoots remain vegetative until they have formed 5–7 pairs of expanding leaves, after which in forming another 5–6 pairs of leaves a flower bud develops. This means that from April onwards in the United Kingdom and countries of similar latitude plants have 12–14 pairs of leaves to the flower bud, but if the shoot reaches 5–7 pairs of leaves when days are short (ie after September) it will grow up to 22 pairs of leaves before flowering in the spring. Dusk to dawn lighting will induce all the plants in the 5–7 pairs of leaves category to produce flower buds despite the short days. The whole technique of lighting carnations is still the subject of considerable research, but the general implications are quite clear.

Carbon dioxide enrichment

This is still not a precise technique, but research workers claim that an improvement in the quality of cut flowers is achieved by two- or three-fold carbon dioxide enrichment, especially during the winter period.

Varieties

There is a countless number of varieties demanding constant reappraisal, but in general terms the Sim sports have achieved most popularity in terms of cropping potential.

Foliage and Flower Crops from Seed under Glass

A number of perennials and annuals are grown for cut flower production, decorative purposes and floral art, in greenhouses. Culture is usually straightforward and involves sowing seed and pricking off as described under Bedding Plant Production

Type	Seed sowing	Temperature category
Antirrhinum F_1 greenhouse hybrids	October	Germinate at 65–75°F (18.3–23.9°C). Grow on at 60°F (15.6°C)
Asparagus plumosus, correctly *A. setaceus* *A. sprengeri*, correctly *A. densiflorus*	Sow March–April for outdoor planting the following spring. Soak seed for 48 hours	Germinate at 70–80°F (21.1–26.7°C). Grow on at 60°F (15.6°C)
Gerbera jamesonii	Sow seed in Feb/March. Prick off the small plants into Jiffy 7s	Germinate at 65–70°F (18.3–21.1°C). Grow at 60°F (15.6°C)
Matthiola incana (stock)	Sow mid-Oct–Dec. Prick out Jan–Feb in cool greenhouse	Germinate at 60°F (15.6°C) then lower to 50°F (10°C) for production of light leaved doubles
Zinnia elegans and cultivars, double flowered	Sow dressed seed (captan) in March–April in individual small pots. Alternatively prick out 4–5 days after germination	Germinate at 70–75°F (21.1–23.9°C) and grow on at 60°F (15.6°C)

Planting distance	Flowering period	Comments
12 × 12in in well-prepared soil of greenhouse border	March–May	Excellent for cut blooms
Can be planted out in greenhouse 12in apart	For foliage	Useful for flower arranging
Plant out in well-prepared land 12 × 12in	Continuous, more productive in winter	An easy plant to grow. Requires fairly cool conditions. Excellent for floral art
Plant 6 × 8in in well-prepared bed, pH 6.5. Wider apart for 'Giant Excelsior' strain	April–May	An excellent crop for early cut flowers
10–12in apart in well-prepared border preferably dressed with fungicide (Alisan or Butrylex)	Summer	Avoid too high humidity at any stage to offset botrytis

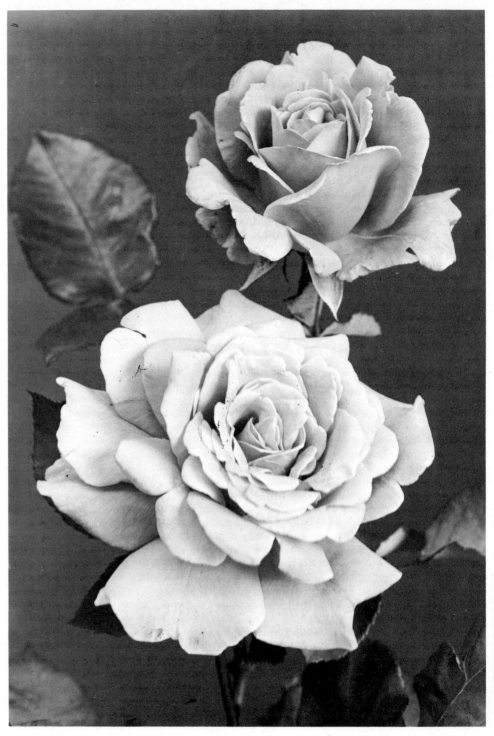

Roses can be grown with
outstanding success
under greenhouse
conditions. One of the
advantages of growing
them in greenhouses is
that it is easier to control
the incidence of disease.

332

Chapter 26

Chrysanthemums

Terminals   Crown buds

Fig 79

Terms used in chrysanthemum culture (Fig 79 and Fig 80.)

Bud sport   One shoot produces flowers of a different colour or shape from those on the rest of the plant. It is a vegetative mutation due to spontaneous genetic change and the sport can be perpetuated by cuttings from the shoot.

Break bud   A chrysanthemum plant grown naturally develops a single stem in the first instance and then produces a flower bud at its tip at varying heights according to variety. This is called the break bud because leafy shoots break into growth immediately below to form a branched plant. While the break bud is usually imperfect, it is satisfactory in the case of late rooted cuttings grown on single stems and many large-flowered exhibition varieties.

Natural break   The formation of the bud restricts the extension of the main shoot and further growth of shoots takes place when the buds in the axils of the leaves

Fig 80

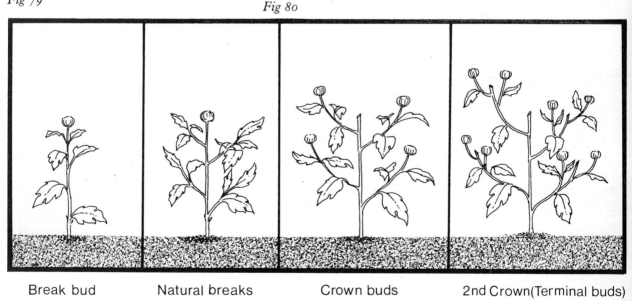

Break bud   Natural breaks   Crown buds   2nd Crown (Terminal buds)

below the break bud develop. This process and the shoots that form are collectively called the natural break.

Crown buds (see Fig 79). These shoots, if left to grow, will in time produce a crown flower bud at their tips, below which further leafy shoots will be produced which will again in time form a second crown bud. First crown buds, if left, will produce flowers, or if removed by 'stopping' will allow the second crown buds to develop. First crown buds invariably give fuller flowers than second crown buds though very full flowering varieties are often better on second crowns.

Terminal buds (see Fig 79). When a shoot which arises from a leaf axil ends in a cluster of flower buds (not a bud with a cluster of leafy shoots) the central bud is known as the terminal bud.

Stopping   The removal of the growing point to induce a shoot or a number of shoots to develop lower down on the plant than would be the case if it were left to grow naturally. Varieties differ in the forming of breaks, some producing natural breaks too freely. The number can be reduced by pinching out the top of the plant before the breaks appear. If on the other hand there are not sufficient breaks, it may be necessary to stop subsequent tips to the branches to form more.

Disbudding   This is the careful removal of flower buds which form around the terminal bud, this bud being said to be 'taken'. If the buds are all allowed to form this is called a spray, whereas the single flower per stem is called a standard.

The main forms of chrysanthemum culture

1. *Earlies out of doors*   Propagation in greenhouses or frames in the early part of the year for planting and flowering out of doors in borders (early flowering types).

2 *Protected flowering*   Propagation in greenhouses or frames in the early part of the year for planting out of doors in borders to flower in autumn under the protection of sashes, mobile greenhouses or plastic structures.

334

A fine display of chrysanthemums.

3 *Pot culture* Propagation in greenhouses in the early part of the year for planting in pots which can be lifted indoors for flowering, or left outdoors in the case of earlies. Not to be confused with intensive culture of pot chrysanthemums which is dealt with in a separate section at the end of this chapter.

4 *Lifters* Propagation in greenhouses in early part of the year for growing in borders out of doors, for lifting into greenhouses for flowering (lifters).

5 *Semi-direct planting* Late propagation in greenhouses, or purchase of late-struck cuttings, for growing in frames or protected areas (preferably in peat pots to avoid checks). These are then lifted into greenhouse for continued vegetative growth and flowering.

6 *Direct planting* Planting direct in greenhouses to flower in natural season, this including (a) earlies under glass and (b) late-struck cuttings during July and August. Cuttings can be self-propagated in the case of earlies but are more usually bought in for direct planting in July or August.

7 *Spot cropping* The same as (6) but, by day length manipulation, grown for a specific period out of natural season.

6 *Year-round culture* This, using bought-in cuttings, involves day length manipulation with artificial lighting or shortening by shading.

Types of chrysanthemum
Flower form
1 Incurved—where the majority of the petals turn inwards to form a ball-shaped flower
2 Incurving—the same, but flowers are of a looser habit
3 Reflexing—where petals turn outwards or have a drooping habit
4 Singles—which have a ring of petals; up to five rings for exhibition
5 Large exhibition chrysanthemums—which have enormous flowers of incurving, incurved or reflexing habit
6 Other types, including Spiders, Rayonnante, Anemone, in the early, mid- and late-flowering groups
7 Sprays—for cut flower production or in pots (frequently called American sprays)

Charm chrysanthemums are started anew from cuttings taken each February. They flower in October, and the flowers are produced so freely that they completely hide the foliage.

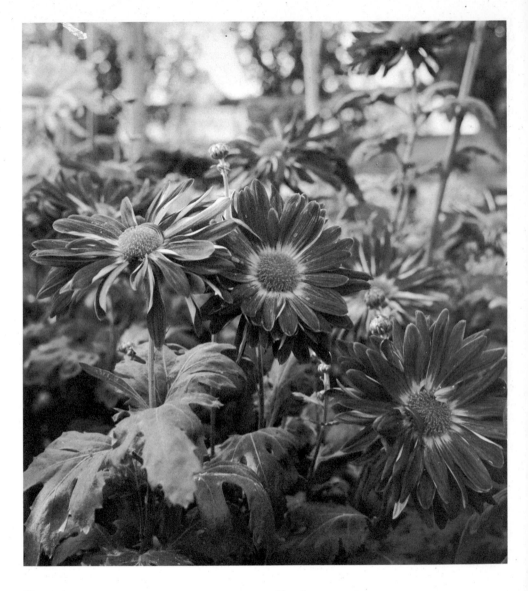

Chrysanthemum
'Crimson Glory', a very
fine single.

Further groupings

For indoor culture, natural season, spot cropping or year-round culture, varieties are categorised as tall, medium or short. Still further grouping relates to temperature requirements during bud initiation periods, requiring reference to specialist catalogues. For direct planting and year-round culture chrysanthemums are categorised in response groups, according to the number of weeks from bud initiation to flowering under inside conditions.

The photoperiodic nature of chrysanthemums

Most chrystanthemums (apart from non-photoperiodic earlies and some 'mids' which successfully initiate their flower buds in long days) will only initiate their flower buds when the day length is less than about 12–14 hours. Equal day and night length occurs on about 21 March and 21 September. It follows therefore that for natural season cropping it is necessary to plant sufficiently in advance of bud initiation to ensure sufficient vegetative development beforehand, a matter which will be referred to in more detail later. Because of this photoperiodicity, chrysanthemums react very positively to the artificial stimulus of shading to make artificially short days, or lengthening with low intensity light to give artificially long days. Response groups indicate when the chrysanthemum will flower from bud initiation, and cropping can be organised accordingly.

Lighting equipment

This involves the use of 100W tungsten clear filament lamps. For beds 4ft wide tungsten rubber sheathed or polychloroprene cables are suspended 4–5ft above the centre of the bed. The 100W lamps are spaced 6ft apart (or 60W 4ft apart) in special lampholders made of neoprene with waterproof connection to the cable. *The importance of this cannot be overemphasised.* Very careful wiring is required; preferably the system should be professionally installed. It may be incessary to increase the amount of light in winter in very poor light areas.

The period of light necessary will be 2 hours in April, May, August and September, 3–4 hours in October, November, February and March, and 5 hours in December–January. It is usual (and also cheapest) to give light in the middle of the night to ensure that the dark periods do not exceed 7 hours. Cyclic lighting (3 minutes on, 9 minutes off) has been found effective, although it is not a technique which appears to have been widely developed. It is obvious that a time clock is an advantage for the operation of the lights. From March to September shading with 38mu dense black polythene sheeting or other dense material is necessary to simulate short days, usually from 18.00 hours until 07.00 hours. This is achieved by putting the polythene over metal hoops or by block arrangement. Support both in beds out of doors and in greenhouse borders is by means of strained nylon netting.

Cultural programmes: (relating to latitudes 50–58°N)

Definition of crop	Propagating time	Planting or potting in frames	Planting or spacing out of doors or in greenhouse	Stopping (may be once or twice)	Flowering time	Temperature
1 Outdoor crop— earlies	Feb–Mar	Mar– April	Late April– May	May– June	July– Sept	Prop at 60–65°F (15.6–18.3°C) and grow cool as above
2 Flowering with protection	Feb–Mar	Mar– April	Late April– mid-May	May– June	Aug–Oct or later	as above

Definition of crop	Propagating time	Planting or potting in frames	Planting or spacing out of doors or in greenhouse	Stopping (may be once or twice)	Flowering time	Temperature
3 Pot-grown for flowering out of doors with protection or lifting into greenhouse	Feb–Mar	April–May	Late April–mid-May	May–June	Aug–Oct or later	as above
*Pot-grown** large exhibition types	Dec–Jan	Feb–April	April–May	March–May	Oct–Jan	as above
4 Lifters	Feb–March	Feb–April	April–May	May–June	Sept–Nov or later	as above
5 Natural season (semi-direct)	Cuttings bought in or rooted	End June 6 × 6in or 4½in peat pots	Planted in greenhouse 9 × 9in at end of August	3rd week July	Oct–Dec	Minimum of 55°F (12.8°C) (especially during bud initiation)
6 Natural season—direct planting, single stem	Plants normally purchased		10–15 Aug at 5 × 5in (4,300 per 1,000sq ft)	Not stopped	December	56°F (13.3°C) for 6 weeks then 50°F (10°C) minimum
as above, two stem	Plants normally purchased		Last week July, at 7 × 8in (1,950 per 1,000sq ft)	10–14 days after planting	December	as above
as above, three stem	Plants normally purchased		2nd week July at 9 × 9in (1,330 per 1,000sq ft)	4th week July	December	as above
7 Direct planted—early flowering crop	December or purchased		Late Jan–Feb 10 × 12in (1,330 per 1,000sq ft)	Mid-end Feb reducing stems to 4 per plant when growing strongly	According to variety but around June	Minimum night temp 45°F (7.2°C)

8 *Spot cropping***

Date planted	Spacing	Lighting	Shading	Flowering	Temperature
6 January	5 × 5in	6 Jan–14 Feb	20 March–bud colour	Early May	60°F (15.6°C)
20 May	5 × 5in	Nil	8 June–bud colour	Mid-December	as above
28 August	5 × 5in	28 Aug–27 Sept	Nil	Mid–April	as above

* Although not normally practised, later planting can be carried out for two crops.
** These dates are merely approximate and can be varied considerably.

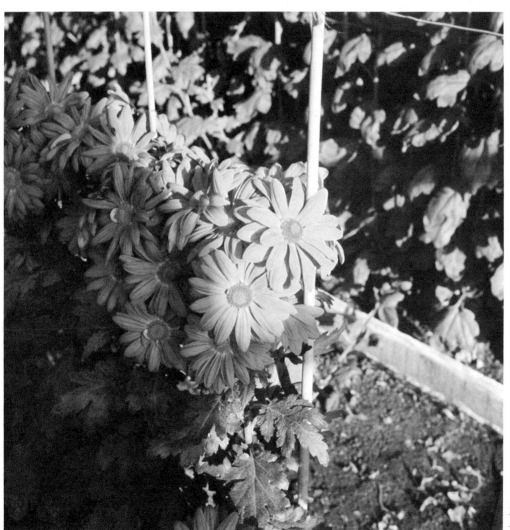

Spray chrysanthemum
'Tuneful'—a stunning
vivid orange single.

339

Year-round cropping

This requires exact programming on a week-by-week basis by specialist cutting suppliers, following the necessary shading and lighting pattern and basically the same cultural, spot cropping or direct planting procedures. Difficulty can be experienced in poorer light areas if considering year-round cropping, especially during the dullest months of the year.

IMPORTANT NOTE A technique which is finding favour is to root cuttings in $2\frac{1}{2}$in peat pots or small pots and take them to the 12 leaf stage under glass, giving supplementary lighting if necessary during poor light periods and 'short days' immediately on planting out in the greenhouse border. This technique obviously has application not only in year-round cropping and direct planting.

Cultural procedures

Where propagation material is being retained, it is important that this be selected carefully. Hot water treatment of the stock may be desirable for eelworm control before the stools are boxed up with good clean compost, when cuttings will freely form with warmth and moisture. It is important not to induce growth too early, particularly in the case of earlies which often grow better from a shorter period of growth. Initial growths from stools are in any case of poor habit and should be removed and discarded.

Rooting and planting of cuttings

Whether cuttings are prepared below a joint or node or merely snapped off is a matter for individual choice, although cuttings below a node are more desirable for amateurs who will often have a lower level of heating with consequent slower rooting. Cuttings are taken $2-2\frac{1}{2}$in long, trimming off the lower leaves and dipping the base of the cuttings in rooting hormone if this is thought necessary before inserting them $\frac{1}{2}-\frac{3}{4}$in deep and $1-1\frac{1}{2}$in apart in seed trays or, on a smaller scale, in pots, in a mixture of equal parts peat and sand or for later propagation in John Innes No 1. Jiffy 7s may also be used with success.

Cuttings are well watered-in and given bench heat to 55–65°F (12.8–18.3°C) level. Rooting will take place within 7–21 days. Various techniques are practised to induce quicker rooting: mist propagation, polythene bags over pots or boxes, plastic dome covers. Too high humidity can lead to damping off problems.

When rooted, as confirmed by a freshening of the top growth, or visible evidence of root formation (in Jiffy 7s), cuttings can either be potted into 3in clay, plastic or peat pots, using John Innes No 1 or a soilless equivalent or, where applicable, planted out 5 × 5in apart in well-prepared soil in frames. Plants should be potted or planted firmly. Early flowering varieties which are rooted in January/February may have to be boxed up in boxes containing JI No 1 and kept in the greenhouse until the danger of frost is past and they can be put into frames. Alternatively, frames can be protected from frost by the installation of electrical tubular heaters (preferably controlled by a thermostat) which will maintain the air temperature above freezing point.

Stopping

Stopping is usually carried out when 6–9in growth has been made (up to 15in with some varieties) and the bottom buds are seen to be breaking naturally (ie anticipating the natural break). It is achieved by the removal of the whole top of the main stem, without removing the first fully developed leaf. With programmed crops under glass it is unnecessary to be so exact, the tips of the main shoots being stopped in a routine manner 10–14 days after planting. Stopping should not coincide with planting or potting. After stopping it is usual to thin down the number of remaining shoots (generally 3–5) according to purpose and of course variety, although one or two extra shoots should be allowed to compensate for breakages.

Time of stopping can be critical, especially when showing is involved and it should be noted that varieties which produce the best flowers on second crown buds (having fewer petals or being ball shaped) will require a second stop, which means, in general terms, stopping varieties to be flowered on their first crown buds (and therefore stopped only once) 14–21 days *later* than those to be flowered on second crown buds, which will be stopped for a second time after an interval of 4–6 weeks, whether in borders or pots. The first stop will, in many cases, be while the plants are in frames or small pots.

Sometimes the break bud develops before the plant has produced sufficient laterals for flowering requirements, and to offset this the top two or three laterals should be stopped by carefully removing their terminal buds before they reach an appreciable size, allowing them to produce second crown flowers which will generally flower about the same time as lower placed laterals or first crown flowers.

Some large exhibition varieties may require stopping 14–20 days earlier than

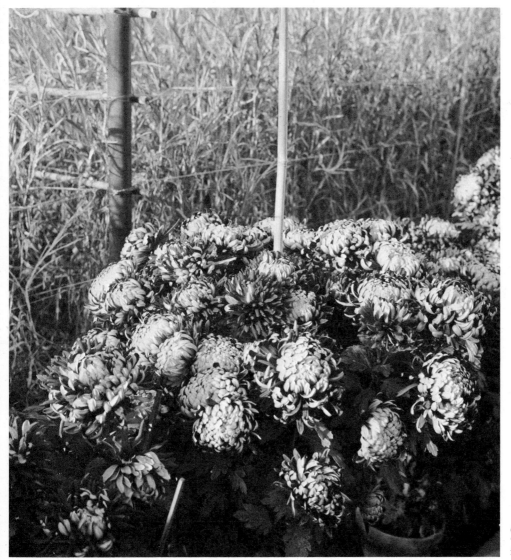

Chrysanthemum 'Cochineal', one of the famous Poitevin strain.

the appearance of the natural break warrants in order to ensure time for the development of a full flower. Conversely, varieties which produce over-full flowers are improved by stopping on the natural break and allowing free development of the upper laterals, removing the lower ones. There can be no general rules, and top exhibitors generally achieve results because they have learned by experience what to do and what not to do.

Outdoor planting

This will apply to earlies, lifters and to chrysanthemums being grown under protected cultivation. Ground must be well prepared with a pH of 6.5, phosphate and potash index 4 or slightly higher, magnesium index 2, and salt concentration index 4. A base feed of 4–6oz per sq yd using one of balanced proportions is usually applied before planting out of doors, but some guidance from analysis is always useful. Planting distances are usually 12 × 12in or 12 × 14in in beds 4ft wide, although for lifters more space is generally given between the rows to allow easier lifting. Support will be necessary by canes or stout nets, although for lifters nets are obviously not suitable.

Pot-grown chrysanthemums

Plants in 3in pots are moved to 5in pots once the roots are well through the ball, this being ascertained by holding the pot upside down and allowing the root ball to drop into the hand. John Innes No 2 potting compost is invariably used, with plenty of roughage in the bottom of the pot, the plants being well firmed-up. Final potting into 8 or 9in pots is carried out when once again the roots are well through the 5in pots, this time using John Innes No 3 or special compost, roughage and a potting stick to ram the soil in firmly, as uneven potting affects water retention and nutrient release.

One of the main requirements of the growing of chrysanthemums in pots is to have a compost with a high fibrous content which assists the retention of moisture and provides improved feeding for the roots. Most exhibitors try to maintain a stack of loam for this purpose (see Chapter 15 for method).

After final potting, three strong canes 4–5in apart are inserted around the edge of the pot and the plants initially supported by strong twine around the canes, later tying the number of shoots left individually to each cane. Pots are placed close-up against each other for a few days to give them some protection, then placed in a line 6in apart, usually on gravel or ash paths not recently weedkiller-treated, especially if the usual weedkiller used is with sodium chlorate which can last up to 2 years in the surface of the soil. The paths must be absolutely level, a spirit level being used to check this if necessary. At least one cane per plant must be tied to a strong wire or fence.

Plants must be fed and watered regularly and the pots given an occasional turn to prevent rooting into base, although it has now been established that a considerable amount of moisture is pulled up from the base.

(Chrysanthemums can of course be grown on the ring culture system in much the same way as tomatoes; see Chapter 19.)

Disbudding and lateral removing

Any generalisation on disbudding procedure is impossible owing to the differing cultural methods involved. It is usual, however, where single stem or standards are being grown as opposed to sprays (year-round or spot cropping) to reduce to all but the central or terminal bud in the absence of individual preference to the contrary. With spray varieties being grown either direct or semi-direct it is usual to remove the terminal bud to give a better shape of spray, and in addition some stopping of the lower side shoots may be carried out. Lower laterals must also be removed.

Watering and feeding

Regular watering and feeding with liquid or solid fertiliser is essential on a regular basis for all chrysanthemums, whether growing out of doors or in pots. Trickle irrigation systems are extremely useful for the watering of large pots. Medium nitrogen liquid feeding should be practised unless growth is too hard, when high nitrogen is necessary, or too soft, when less nitrogen is necessary. The following is a summary largely for greenhouse grown chrysanthemums, but it is broadly applicable also to conventional pot culture.

Liquid feeds

Crop description	Stock solution oz/gal		Dilution 1–400 = 1 fl oz in 2½ gallons 1–300 = 1 fl oz in 15 pints
	Potassium nitrate	Ammonium Nitrate	
Direct planted—summer	24	21 or 16oz urea	* High nitrogen ** 1 in 400
Pots—summer up to bud			
Direct planted—winter	24	6 or 5oz urea	Medium nitrogen 1 in 400
Pots—summer after budded			
Pots—winter	24	6 or 5oz urea	Medium nitrogen 1 in 300

*or proprietary feeds at same nitrogen/potash ratios, or as reccomended by suppliers
**Feed strength may be varied according to circumstances

Lifting in
Plants in pots are better safely housed in September–early October before any frost occurs, this being particularly important with plants with good bud development. Before housing, the plants and pots should be laid carefully on their sides and given a thorough drenching with a suitable insecticide and a mildew specific. They should then be allowed to dry off before being taken into the greenhouse *pot* first to avoid damage to the breaks. Space about 18in apart each way.

Keep the greenhouse fully ventilated for a few weeks to let the plants sweat; heat is then given to the 45–50°F (7.2–10°C) level. Watering and feeding must be continued with, it being usual in the latter case to concentrate more on potash to limit growth and encourage better flower colour, although there can be no hard and fast rules in this case. Mildew can quickly establish itself under conditions which are too humid, so also can botrytis which causes spotting on the blooms, particularly of white varieties. Pest control should also be given regular consideration.

Lifters
Before lifting in plants, greenhouse borders which have previously grown tomatoes are given a good forking and, while fertilisers are usually unnecessary, some ground limestone at 4–6oz per sqyd is advisable to adjust the pH to the 6.5 level. Plants are lifted with a sharp spade, it frequently being advisable to cut around the root area a week or two beforehand. Whether plants can be lifted with a good root ball depends on soil type, this being difficult with light soils, especially if dry. Growing in plastic or wire baskets is sometimes practised to avoid disintegra-

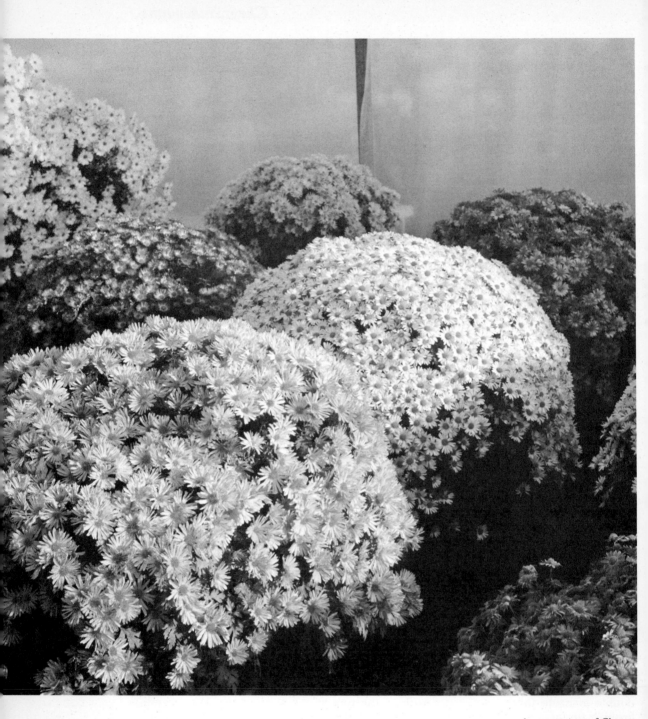

An assortment of Charm
chrysanthemums. Each
great dome-shaped show
of flower comes from a
single cutting taken
afresh each year.

344

tion of the root ball, while at the same time achieving a measure of root restriction. Plants being lifted must be handled very carefully otherwise side shoots can be broken off, particularly with brittle varieties, eg 'Loveliness'. Planting in the greenhouse is usually close, 6–9in apart in rows 12–18in apart, and thoroughly soaked-in. The greenhouse is kept cool by ventilation and, while some wilting is unavoidable, the plants usually recover fairly quickly and start growing again when heat is given to the 45–50°F (7.2–10°C) level, the same precautions being carried out against mildew and botrytis as described for pot-grown plants. Feeding is stopped when the buds are showing colour.

The canes invariably used as supports for lifters are of course lifted in along with the plants.

Direct planting techniques (for late-struck cuttings, early planting, spot cropping and year-round planting)
Direct planting is often thought to be a very complicated procedure, whereas in fact it can be a lot simpler and less demanding in care and attention than conventional culture. The only difficulty is in obtaining the necessary cuttings in the small quantities desired, as few specialist suppliers are willing to supply less than 50 of each variety.

It is possible to take and root cuttings at the normal period of the year in February or March and plant them out in greenhouse borders or frames at 9 × 9in; these, if stopped once or twice again, will serve as a source of late cuttings which if necessary can be rooted again and the same procedure followed.

Mid-season varieties
This involves planting from mid-June until mid-August as per the programme already outlined, selecting the single, double or triple stem crops. Beds in the greenhouse approximately 4ft wide must be put in good physical condition by the liberal addition of peat and adjustment of the pH to 6.5, phosphate index 5, potash index 4, and magnesium index 3–4. This

can usually be achieved by the application of a standard base dressing at 4oz per sq yd or 2 parts hoof and horn, 2 parts super-phosphates, and 1 part sulphate of potash and 1 part magnesium sulphate, leaving out the hoof and horn if liquid feeding is to be practised from the outset. Spacings are according to the table previously given. It is important not only to space the plants exactly, but grade out the cuttings so that the smaller ones are placed on the outside of the beds. They are planted firmly and evenly and watered in.

The same procedure is followed for spot or year-round culture.
Seasonal culture for direct planting
It is usual to keep plants more humid for a few days after planting to help them to re-establish themselves. Support by means of stretched 6in nylon netting is essential at an early stage of development, raised gradually on posts as the plants grow. Regular, even watering, coupled with temperature control to the level stated in the programme should be the aim, with the object of achieving 55–60°F (12.8–15.6°C), especially during the latter part of September and early October when buds are being formed. Feeding programmes are similar to those discussed earlier.

The flowering period will be as outlined in the programme, either summer for early flowering or October–December for autumn natural season cropping, with flowering at other times according to the programme followed. It cannot be emphasised too strongly that while the culture of natural season direct planters is relatively straightforward, specialist and year-round cropping requires tremendous precision, particularly where quality is important, and a highly specialised approach to cropping and strict planning is necessary.
Semi-direct
The timing for this is stated in chrysanthemum-growing programme 5. Nutrition from an early stage is important to encourage sufficient vegetative growth during the outdoor period, and liquid feeding

from the outset may be necessary.

Where plants are put into peat pots, these should be 4¼in and John Innes No 2 or its soilless equivalent used, the plants being placed in rows 6 × 6in apart on a layer of peat and mulched well with peat in order to reduce watering needs. Alternatively the plants can be planted up 6 × 6in apart in good soil with a pH of 6.5 and the standard stated for outdoor planting.

Growth must not be too soft otherwise breakage readily occurs through wind and when planting: wind protection in one form or another must be provided, and considerable care must be exercised when handling the plants. Very careful watering is necessary to avoid checks.

The plants should be lifted into a more comfortable environment before the third week of September at the latest, unless the weather is very mild or temporary cover can be laid on. It is not desirable that budding should coincide with lifting and planting, but when the plants are indoors too soon they tend to make insufficient vegetative growth and to flower on stems that are far too short.

Stopping is carried out as per the respective programmes, unless for single stem or standard crops which are grown on the break bud.

Pest and disease prevention measures and control should be given constant attention.

Sterilisation of borders

Where spot or year-round cropping is practised then soil sterilisation, usually by the sheet method (Chapter 14), is imperative. For natural season cropping following tomatoes, experience shows that where the soil is of an acceptable standard nutritionally (generally speaking, if it is acceptable for tomatoes it will be suitable for chrysanthemums) the soil sterilisation carried out for the tomatoes will suffice for the following crop of chrysanthemums in that year. There can, however, obviously be no generalisation.

More recently raised beds or sunken polythene-lined beds filled with soilless media have been used successfully for chrysanthemum culture.

Showing chrysanthemums

Most people who take the growing of chrysanthemums seriously will sooner or later gravitate towards exhibiting them, either at their local shows or at national level. Any properly run show in Britain will conduct its chrysanthemum business in accordance with the rules of the National Chrysanthemum Society and the Society's publications *Code of Rules for Judging Chrysanthemums* and *Exhibiting and Judging* should be read by all intending exhibitors.

Ash Base system for earlies

This method has become popular with exhibitors for the housing of rooted cuttings before planting out. It reduces the attention required and may also give better plants in the end. A frame is prepared with a base of 4–6in of coarse ashes firmed well. On top of this ash base a 3in layer of JI No 3 compost is laid into which the rooted cuttings are planted about 5 × 5in each way. The compost should not be too dry and an initial watering may be given to settle the plants in. Thereafter water is withheld for 10–14 days (a light overhead spray being given if the plants wilt excessively) so that the plants send out roots in search of moisture and a good root system is built up. When they are well established and growing strongly, water may be applied liberally and the good drainage conditions ensure that no waterlogging occurs. The plants revel in the cool root conditions and growth is rapid. Supplementary liquid feeding may be given as the plants reach the end of their time in the frame, and normal spraying precautions against pests should be taken. In most cases the plants will be stopped in the frame. Air should be admitted progressively and, weather conditions permitting, the frame lights should be removed altogether in the later stages so that the plants are hardened off before planting out. The plants can be lifted with a small hand fork and if the system has been operated correctly it will be found that the massive root systems have used up practically all the compost in the frame.

B-Nine

Some chrysanthemum cultivars have a natural habit of growth which makes them rather taller than is desirable, especially when they have to be housed in greenhouses. Other varieties tend to have a rather long unsightly neck below the bloom, a condition aggravated when grown under frames or covers which draw them up to the light. A chemical solution containing 5 per cent of the ingredient N-Dimethylaminosuccinamic acid plus a wetter, commonly known as B-Nine, is of considerable assistance to the exhibiting chrysanthemum grower in alleviating these conditions. It works not by checking the growth of the plant, but by inducing lateral rather than longitudinal expansion of the cells. The result is a stockier, dwarfer plant, with stronger stems and shorter internodes. Normal dilution is 1:40 (1 tablespoon to 1 pint water) and is applied as a fine spray from a plastic (not metal) sprayer on to the top 6in of foliage to run-off point. Two or three applications may be given at any stage considered desirable but it is advisable to make the final application not later than 14 days before the bud is taken. In addition to restricting the height of certain cultivars it is also useful to control the height of plants at certain stages where they are tending to become drawn, eg in poor light conditions or in frames prior to planting out.

Pot chrysanthemums

The intensive culture of pot chrysanthemums is practised commercially on a large scale in Britain and Europe generally. It must not be confused with the culture of conventional chrysanthemums in pots since the varieties grown for year-round pot work have been specially bred for this purpose. The categories 'tall', 'medium' and 'short' are further divided into response groups of 9, 10 and 11 weeks, this referring to the time from bud initiation to flowering under a minimum temperature

of 60°F (15.6°C). Under the less precise conditions which frequently exist in smaller greenhouses, temperatures frequently fall below this level, resulting in delays to flowering. Conversely, should the weather be abnormally mild in the autumn or spring, flowering may be advanced. In order to maintain production on a year-round basis, day length manipulation by shading and lighting is necessary. The poor winter light in many northerly areas makes successful winter culture difficult and results in plants of etiolated growth and in flowers of low petal number. In general, few professional or amateur gardeners are much concerned with year-round culture, tending to confine their activities to natural season flowering.

Controlled flowering

Short-day varieties of pot chrysanthemums initiate their flower buds in day lengths of 12 hours, which means that *short-day varieties will not require artificial short days by shading between 21 September and 21 March*. Conversely, long days allow vegetative development before the short day period, and this is provided by lighting when the natural day length is less than 12 hours.

As with cut flower chrysanthemums, it is important to remember that for each week the plant is exposed to long days, a week must be added to the time taken to produce the plant in flower, eg an 11 week response plant given 2 weeks of 'long' days will not flower for 11 + 2 = 13 weeks.

The selection of varieties for pot culture is particularly important, as techniques require modification accordingly.

Tall varieties   These grow too tall for pots if allowed to develop naturally and require treatment with dwarfing chemicals. As stem length is unduly increased by long day treatment, they are therefore given short day treatment immediately after potting.

Medium varieties   Normally speaking, one week of long day treatment is given to these varieties after potting, although in good conditions this week of long days is generally unnecessary in spring and autumn.

Short varieties   Three weeks of long days in winter, two weeks in autumn and spring and one week in summer is the normal treatment, with the exception of vigorous varieties such as 'Neptune' which do not need any long day treatment in summer and can be given short days immediately after potting. When these varieties are grown at a time of year when day length is longer than 12 hours they are usually allowed to grow naturally for one or two weeks before being given short days but, on the other hand, if the day length is less than 12 hours artificial light can be used to give artificial long days.

Cultural details

Cuttings from specialist raisers are again desirable, having a special advantage in their uniformity of size for pot work. Amateur gardeners will once again find it difficult to obtain small quantities of cuttings and will need to contact a commercial grower or an amateur chrysanthemum specialist. On a limited scale, plants can be kept as a source of cuttings provided they are kept vegetative by long days.

Pot size and compost
Pot chrysanthemums are commercially grown five or six rooted cuttings to a $5\frac{1}{2}$in deep pan. Alternatively three cuttings can be put in a $4\frac{1}{2}$in deep pan, and one cutting in a $3\frac{1}{2}$in pot. Plastic pans or pots are invariably used.

Either a compost of JIP2 standard or a soilless equivalent can be used. Standard composts often give rise to trouble as their nitrogen level may be too high for the poor light conditions in northerly latitudes during the autumn and winter months, giving rise to lanky, unproductive growth. Many growers and gardeners could achieve much greater success by selecting a compost of lower nutrient level and liquid feeding from the outset, modifying the feed according to the growth exhibited. In general terms, higher nitrogen feeds are given in the summer than in the winter, irrespective of region, reducing the nitro-

gen level in winter commensurate with light levels.

Planting
Pots are loosely filled to within $\frac{1}{4}-\frac{1}{2}$in of the rim and firmed by dumping on a hard surface. Plants are then set into dibber holes at equal depth and equal spacing around the edge of the pots, with the base of the plant just below the surface of the compost. Cuttings with larger roots may require larger planting holes to allow entry of the root without damage. Cuttings should be watered in and the pots kept close together for a week or two, spacing the pots at 12 × 12in thereafter to allow sufficient room for uninhibited growth.

Pinching
The soft tip of the growing plant is generally removed two weeks after planting, except for single plants in $3\frac{1}{2}$in pots, when earlier pinching (7–10 days) is advisable to encourage a lower break. Single stem plants of certain varieties can be grown, being later disbudded so that only the terminal bud remains on each stem, extra plants being required in the centre of each pot in this case.

Disbudding
While many varieties will make good plants with no disbudding, there are exceptions of which the 'Princess Anne' varieties are notable. Plants grown singly in $3\frac{1}{2}$in pots are not disbudded at all, it obviously being an advantage to have as large a number of flowers as possible.

Dwarfing treatments
Phosfon is a dwarfing agent which is mixed in powder form with the compost for all tall varieties, generally speaking about $\frac{3}{4}-1\frac{1}{2}$oz per bushel according to variety, although makers' recommendations must be closely followed in respect of quantities for different varieties. Delays to flowering have been induced following the use of Phosphon. B-Nine, a liquid form of growth restrictant, can be sprayed on the plants 2–4 weeks after pinching when the resultant break shoots are $\frac{1}{2}$in or so in length and it is used at the rate of 8fl oz per gallon of water, the same distribution rate for all varieties. B-Nine may not be suffi-

Chrysanthemums are the second most widely grown of all greenhouse plants, only tomatoes being more popular.

349

ciently dwarfing for some very tall varieties.

Natural season culture
Many gardeners will be interested mainly in natural season culture, in which case either medium or short varieties are potted in the first week of September to allow two weeks or so of long days before 21 Sep-tember when bud initiation is naturally induced. Assuming bud initiation in late September/early October, varieties will flower during December, although much will depend on temperature and other factors such as the application of Phosfon, etc.

For pests, diseases and physiological disorders see Chapter 32.

Chapter 27

Anemones

Although mainly grown as an outdoor crop, anemones lend themselves to protected cropping in cool greenhouses, frames or polythene structures. Single anemones of the De Caen type are usually in demand, and many excellent colour selections have been made available, eg Hollandia (scarlet, very large flowers), His Excellency (scarlet), Sylphide (magenta), Mr Fokker (blue violet), The Bride (white). Bulbs of the double St Brigid type are available but produce fewer flowers than the singles, especially in winter, and the best varieties are: The Governor (scarlet), Lord Lieutenant (blue), The Admiral (magenta). French doubles are also available, although they are rarely grown for the production of cut flowers.

Anemone corms (tuberous rhizomes) are bought either as pointed pittens or the flatter buttons and are available in various sizes from 1–2cm up to 5–6cm. The 2–3cm size is usually grown commercially, flowering on average 12–13 weeks after planting. Larger sized corms may flower earlier but tend to fade out soon, and conversely smaller corms take longer to flower.

Anemones may also be propagated from seed, but this tends to be a long-term (although highly interesting) process.

Cultural details

Anemone corms must have frost protection. They will thrive in most well cultivated soils with a fairly high lime content (pH 6.5–7). The phosphate and potash index should be 2–3, and the soil conditioned with farmyard manure at 1cwt per 6–8sq yd.

Plant 4in apart in rows 12–15in apart, and cover with 2–3in of soil. If corms are planted in early July under glass or plastic, flowering will begin towards the end of September, be at its peak in December and

may well continue into March. Planting at the end of July or early August will give later flowering.

The soil should ideally be in a moist condition early in the development of growth. Reduce watering very considerably during the winter or it will certainly encourage disease. There is no need for high temperatures which will in fact merely spoil the flowers by 'blowing' them.

Freesias

The freesia belongs to the Iris family and is a native of South Africa. The main species is *F. refracta* 'Alba' (white), and in recent years this, together with *F. armstrongii* (red), *F. aurea* and *F. leitchlinii*, has been used for considerable hybridisation to produce better coloured and more prolific strains, especially the tetraploid and triploid strains (the usual freesia being a diploid).

The culture of freesias from seed

Sow April–early June for flowering September–spring. Freesia seed can be erratic to germinate and a variety of methods are used for 'chitting': soak for 2–4 days in water at 70°F (21.1°C); mixing with damp peat or vermiculite for a similar period at the same temperature, until the seed shows signs of growth; or in the case of slow germinating tetraploid seed, rubbing it between sandpaper before soaking for 24 hours. Darkness is necessary for germination in all cases, the seed being planted $\frac{1}{2}$in deep as soon as germination occurs. Later sowings can be made $\frac{1}{8}$–$\frac{1}{4}$in deep, directly into containers out of doors, covering with $\frac{1}{2}$–1in layer of peat to give moist darkness; 9in whalehide pots, 1 × 1in spacing, and JIP1 are suitable.

After germination plants will require 55–60°F (12.8–15.6°C) but cool moist growing conditions after the seeds have

(*excluding those already dealt with in plant lists)

developed are essential to keep growth sturdy. Containers should be placed on a sheet of polythene or hard slabbing and may be stacked fairly closely together as convenient. Some shelter from wind should be provided. Regular watering should be the rule, plus balanced liquid feeding every 10–14 days to keep growth vigorous, without producing excess soft foliage which flops about. Excessive watering should be avoided, not only to offset fungal disorders, but to avoid leaching out nutrients.

The crop should be brought into the greenhouse in September. The night temperature should not exceed 55°F (12.8°C) in September/October and March/April; drop to 50°F (10°C) from November to February. Excessive temperatures will result in unproductive growth. Support will be necessary either by netting or twigs.

Production from corms

Basically similar to production from seed, but spacing up to 3 × 3in and planting to 2in depth in JIP1. Normally corms are planted in spring to flower in the autumn, but see *Ministry of Agriculture Bulletin No 197* for details of storing for year-round production.

After flowering, growth should be encouraged for two months to allow development of the corms, which should then be lifted, dried and stored for two weeks at a temperature of 70°F (21.1°C), though flowering is improved if they can be stored at 86°F (30°C) for ten weeks in an electrically controlled heat treatment chamber. The corms from seed-raised plants can of course also be stored.

Hyacinths

Bulbs are imported from the Netherlands where their culture is a specialised task, especially when required for forcing. It is of interest to note that the two main methods of hyacinth propagation are cross-cutting and scooping. Cross-cutting involves three cuts over the base of the bulb deep enough to inactivate the main bud, bearing in mind that the hyacinth bulb, in common with all true bulbs, is a flower in embryo surrounded by leaves. Scooping is carried out with a special knife, the object once again being to destroy the main bud, yet cut the base of the scale leaves. After either process, the bulbs are placed in a room where the environment can be controlled to a fine limit in respect of both temperature and humidity until young bulbs are formed in the cut section at the base of the bulb. Parent bulbs, complete with these young bulbs, are planted in the autumn, generally in November, when they will eventually develop to the selected size after a process of lifting and replanting.

Bulb preparation

Hyacinth bulbs bought for early flowering have been 'prepared', this being a physiological process which affects the development of the flower bud. Bulbs intended for December flowering are lifted in June and stored at 86°F (30°C), gradually reduced to 78°F (25.6°C) during a period of 4–5 weeks, and thereafter to between 73–68°F (22.8–20°C) according to variety until the flower is completely developed inside the bulb when the temperature is lowered to 63°F (17.2°C). This treatment varies according to the intended time of flowering. Occasionally there are bad batches of bulbs which fail to flower well.

Bulbs are purchased according to size, from 18–19cm down to 14–15cm, and the price is usually commensurate with size, although in many cases smaller bulbs will flower better than large ones simply because the large flower of top sized bulbs is difficult to support and tricky to handle.

When bulbs come from the supplier they should be unpacked immediately and kept at between 55–60°F (12.8–15.6°C) or preferably cooler, as this will accelerate growth by assisting with the rooting process.

Planting

Hyacinths require little in the way of nutrition, as all the strength necessary is already contained in the flowers and scale leaves. Physical condition of the planting medium is, however, important. Sand and peat or peat alone are the usual choices, it being important in both cases to ensure that sufficient lime is added to bring the pH up to above 6. When bowls without drainage are used, peat and lime (shell) plus some charcoal (bulb fibre) is frequently used, a medium which tends to keep sweeter than soil-containing media. The chosen medium should be reasonably moist and should not have been used for bulbs before.

All containers, whether boxes, pots or bowls, should be at least 4–5in deep. Place the bulbs in with the nose showing when they are to be grown to the flowering stage on benches or pots; leave them half-covered for easier lifting if they are to be potted up in bowls after forcing. Spacing of the bulbs will vary according to whether they are being grown to maturity in pots or boxes or for forcing. Space out an inch or so apart if growing to maturity, while for forcing they can be packed fairly tight. They should be firmed in moderately. Some gardeners prefer to plant hyacinths in a double layer so that they will have a solid mass of flowers.

Note that for Christmas flowering, bulbs are planted in September; for January flowering in October; up to November for February flowering. When unprepared bulbs are grown for still later flowering planting in October is normal.

Root development

The prime requisites for bulbs after planting are coolness and moisture, during which period they develop sufficient roots to sustain them for flowering. The commercial grower frequently lays out his boxes on a flat surface out of doors and covers them with a thick (10–12in) layer of straw which is kept moist, the bulbs being kept cool by the principle of loss of heat on evaporation. On a small scale a good layer of peat, sand or even well-weathered ashes will suffice. Dark cupboards, sheds or cellars may also be used, it being remembered that a cool moist atmosphere of 48–50°F (9–10°C) is the ideal. Occasional watering may be necessary to achieve this (Fig 81).

Forcing

Bulbs are brought into warmer tempera-

Fig 81

tures when the shoots are about 1½–2in long with the flower bud well through the neck of the bulb. Long shoots result in weak flowers. For the first 10–12 days semi-darkness is desirable, which in a greenhouse will necessitate shading with paper or other material. Shading will induce the flower bud to extend without extensive leaf development. Temperatures of 65°F (18.3°C) initially, raised to 73°F (22.8°C) are ideal; on a small scale much can be done in a heated propagating case to save costs. Excess bottom heat should be avoided and, when benches have heating pipes underneath, a thick layer of peat should be put on the bench to prevent rapid drying out. Bulbs are kept well watered and not exposed to excessive sunlight, but care must be taken not to pour too much water on to the neck of the bulb as this will encourage the development of botrytis. Light spraying helps to keep a humid atmosphere and reduces watering needs. Temperatures should be lowered gradually as flowers begin to open.

For 'natural' growing the bulbs are taken out of the 'plunge' or dark area and merely given normal greenhouse temperatures, or taken into the home. The same philosophy of shade for a period should, however, be adopted for best results.

Commercially bulbs are lifted when in flower and planted up in decorative bowls.

Forcing in light-excluded structures

When bulbs are forced in light-excluded structures they are given temperatures of 75°F (23.9°C) until the flowers begin to open, dropping to 70°F (21.1°C) until

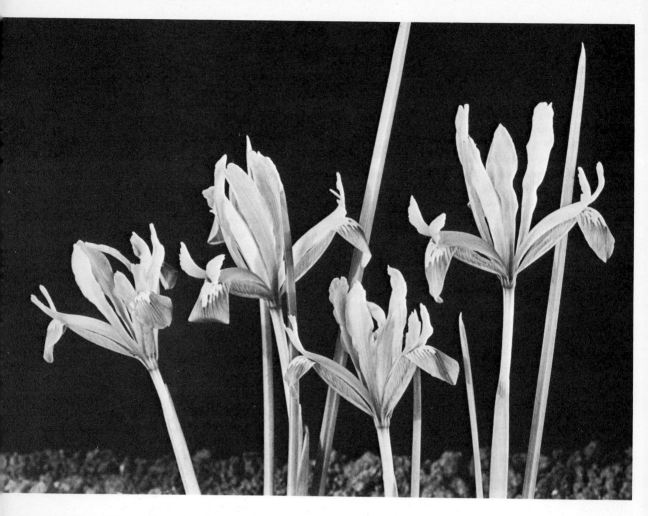

Iris reticulata 'Cantab', an outstanding variety with bright Cambridge-blue flowers, ideal for growing in the alpine house.

colour is showing and finally to 65°F (18.3°C) to complete the process. The level of lighting necessary is 100W/sq yd operated for 12 hours in each 24.

Iris

In the last few years the growing of irises under glass has become a major greenhouse crop, particularly as with preparation they can be induced to flower for a major part of the year. Of the numerous species, the main varieties for greenhouse growing have been selected from the Xiphium and Xiphiodes groups which are natives of the Mediterranean zone.

The embryo bud contained in the iris bulb is incompletely developed when the bulbs are lifted, and the development of the bud continues under cool storage at 48°F (8.9°C) or planted in cool soil.

Bulbs for forcing should usually be from 10cm upwards, uniform in size and should not have produced flowers the previous season. Out of season flowering of suitable varieties can be achieved by a combination of heating and cooling, this procedure being generally carried out by the supplier.

Main timings

'Wedgwood' varieties and sports Planting: end October–mid-February. Flowering: January–April (treated bulbs flower earlier)

All other varieties Planting: November–

354

January. Flowering: mid-January–early April

Retarded bulbs Plant outdoors in beds or greenhouse borders March–August. Flowering: July–early October or later under cover

Iris danfordiae (yellow) and I. reticulata (blue) are grown in pots, planting early in the year to flower in spring, 3–4 bulbs per 6in pot.

Cultural procedures

Irises can be grown either in boxes, pots or borders, in all cases with sufficient depth of soil (4–5in) to accommodate the root system. Any good garden soil with good texture and a pH of 6, and reasonably well supplied with nutrients, will suffice. The addition of peat is frequently necessary to improve soil texture. For forcing, plant very shallowly about 3in apart; for slower growing plant deeper, 2–3in. For planting between May and August mulch the ground with damp peat to keep soil temperatures as cool as possible.

It is usually recommended that for 'Wedgwood' and its sports 56–59°F (13.3–15°C) should be given for the first two weeks, maintaining or slightly raising the temperature at night to 64°F (17.8°C) to advance flowering. For other varieties give 52–54°F (11.1–12.2°C) for first two weeks, up to 56°F (13.3°C) for smaller bulbs (7–8 and 8–9cm). Coolness and ventilation is the general rule to avoid gross production of foliage and possible 'blindness' (when the flowers do not form). Support may be needed with nets or canes.

Lily of the valley *(Convallaria majalis)*
These are produced from imported 'pips', generally from Germany. Of the three grades available, only three-year or two-year top grade pips should be used. For very early flowering it is necessary to retard the pips from 10–12 weeks at 28–25°F (—4°C-—2°C) treating them as bulbs, thawing them out in a warm bowl of water at 80°F (26.7°C) for 12–15 hours. The retarding will generally have been carried out before purchase.

Forcing procedure
The pips should have their roots trimmed down to 3in before planting in 5in deep boxes or in a bed of similar depth, using a mixture of peat and sand. They are spaced 1–2in apart, being covered finally by a layer of damp peat. Complete darkness is necessary for the initial forcing process for 10–12 days, which will necessitate the use of a shaded greenhouse bench (using black polythene covers) or a shed. Bottom heat to the 70°F (21.1°C) level is necessary, and this can readily be provided by soil warming cables, with an air temperature of 60°F (15.6°C) for the first three days, 70°F (21.1°C) for the following three days and 80°F (26.7°C) for the remainder of the forcing period. The pips are thoroughly watered-in on planting and watered again in 10–12 days. When shoots appear in 10–12 days the shading is removed. When they are 12in long artificial light is given, to provide 16 hours of light and 8 hours of complete darkness until the flowers are ready for cutting. The lighting can be achieved by 100W tungsten filament lamps at 1 per sqyd, 2ft above the beds. Too strong a light or light given too soon will restrict stem height. Temperatures are reduced when cutting commences.

Muscari
Muscari armeniacum or grape hyacinths are useful flowers for greenhouse culture, both in bowls and for cut bloom. Specially prepared bulbs for early flowering can be obtained, although in gardening circles the late flowering of unprepared bulbs is usually more acceptable.

For forcing the bulbs are planted in 3–4in deep boxes in September–October, plunged out of doors for a period, and then brought into the greenhouse to flower. More usually, however, they are planted 1in apart in pots or boxes and kept cool (40–45°F) (4.4–7.2°C) for eight weeks or longer, when they are brought into flower in a moderately warm greenhouse.

Narcissus
For early flowering, pre-cooled bulbs

(double nosed I, II and III are generally used for forcing) are purchased, these having been given four days of heat at 93°F (33°C), followed by 63°F (17.2°C) for one or two weeks, then cool stored at 45°F (7.2°C) until planting. Bulbs for later flowering are given 63°F (17.2°C) till the flower is complete in the bulb, then stored at 48°F (8.9°C). Variations in temperature treatment are also used to influence flower size.

Planting in borders

Bulbs can be grown either directly in borders, or planted in boxes, bowls or pots. Any good soil with a pH of about 6 and a reasonable nutrient content will suffice. Planting direct into greenhouse borders is done in October, in rows 6in apart, the bulbs spaced 2–3in apart in the rows. Water in well and cover with straw. Keep as cool as possible by ventilating for 6–7 weeks, then raise temperatures in steps of 5–10°F (2.6–5.5°C) to around 65°F (18.3°C). Keep bulbs well watered, about 15 gallons per sq yd being necessary.

Planting in boxes

Push the bulbs into deep (5–6in) boxes of clean soil which has not grown bulbs before, pH adjusted to 6.25, leaving the bulbs with their noses clear. Cover with a

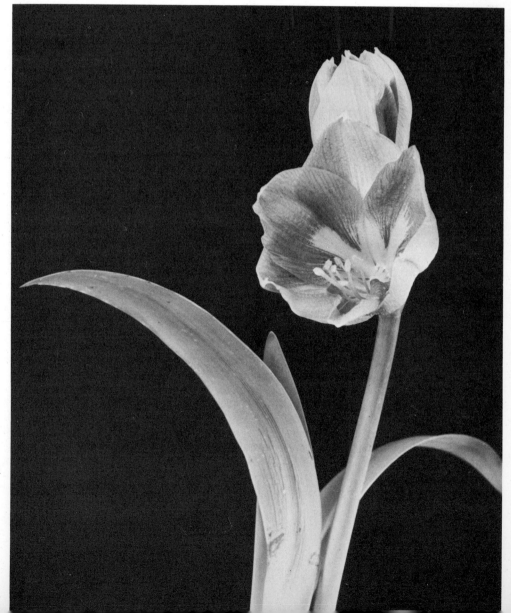

Vallota speciosa, the Scarborough lily, one of the most colourful of autumn-flowering greenhouse or house plants. Does equally well in pots or in the green-house border.

layer of sand or other material to act as a barrier between the soil or peat which will be used to cover them in a plunge out of doors to a minimum depth of 6in. This is generally achieved in the first week of October and adequate watering should be given to induce lower temperatures (by evaporation) down to about 45°F (7.2°C).

Boxes are brought into the greenhouse from the middle of November until February according to variety, when flowers are clear of the neck of the bulb and there is good root development, and not before (suppliers' catalogues should always be consulted for housing dates). Minimum heat is given for 7–10 days, the temperature gradually being raised to 65°F (18.3°C). Water the boxes as necessary and make sure that they get all the light they need, otherwise the leaves will become gross. Support may be provided with netting or broken canes and string.

Bowls or pots of bulbs should be treated in the same way, strict attention being paid to watering and the amount of light given. Bulbs for later flowering should be left longer in the plunge and given lower temperatures in the greenhouse or home.

Forcing under artificial light
This is carried out in the same way as described for tulips (below) although in general it is better to have higher light levels and lower temperatures (60°F) (15.6°C), taking 4–6 weeks on average for the bulbs to flower.

Pests, diseases and troubles Narcissi are not difficult to grow, but they can suffer from a number of troubles (see Chapter 32).

Ranunculus

There are three main groups: French, Persian and Turban, and Turkey or paeony-flowering, of which the last mentioned are increasingly grown as outdoor crops in mild districts. They also lend themselves to protected cropping, as this ensures better flower quality.

Planting times can vary from June and July for autumn flowering with cloche or mobile greenhouse protection, until Sep-tember for February to May flowering in the greenhouse. Ranunculus can also be planted in well prepared soil in March/April with the cover of a mobile green-house, to flower out of doors in the summer. The roots are planted with their claws downwards, 6in apart and 1–2in deep, and after flowering the tuberous roots are lifted and dried for future planting. They can also be grown in deep boxes or pots, but care must be taken that they do not dry out.

Schizostylis (Kaffir lily)

Schizostylis coccinea, a native of South Africa, and its two main varieties, 'Miss Hegarty' (early) and 'Viscountess Byng' (late), are tender bulbs grown on a limited scale in the greenhouse. They are propa-gated by division in spring when 3–4 shooted clumps should be put in 9–10in pots with JIP1 or 2. Given plenty of water they will flower in the winter months.

Sparaxis

These South African plants, *S. grandiflora* and *S. tricola*, are planted in November in greenhouse borders, 4in apart and 4in deep, in good soil, where they will flower in the spring.

Tulips

A wide range of tulips is grown both for bowl culture and for cut flower production in boxes or greenhouse borders. The flowering times of a tulip and the ability to force it to flower early depends on a range of temperature treatments best left to the suppliers, as wrong treatment will result in the production of deformed flowers. In recent years specially prepared bulbs called 5° tulips have been used to a large extent for cut flower production in green-houses.

5° tulips
Initially for two weeks the soil or growing medium must be kept cool, in the region of 50–55°F (10–12.8°C). 5° bulbs of a 12cm size are generally planted direct into green-house borders with a pH of 6.5 to 7 during the first week of November in rows 6in apart, the bulbs being 2in apart, with the

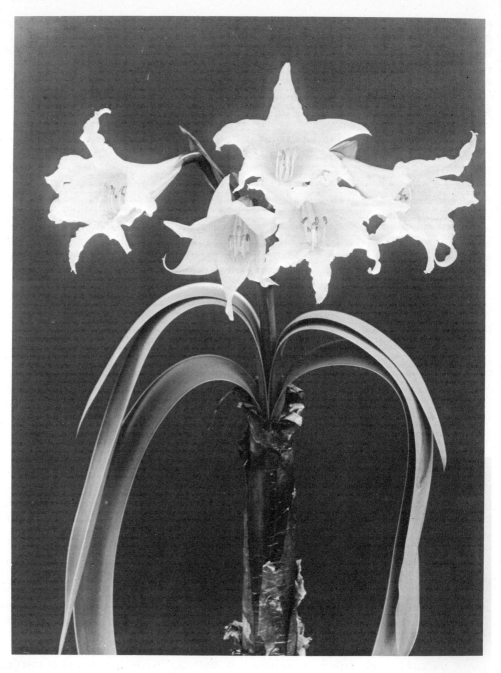

Hippeastrum procerum,
the blue hippeastrum,
something of a rarity and
one of the most exotic
bulbous plants that can
be grown in the
greenhouse.

top of the bulb ⅜in below soil level. It is
usual to grow in beds for easier management. After planting, the beds are thoroughly watered, not only to settle the soil
but also to reduce temperature, but waterlogging should be avoided. Heat is given

after 2 weeks, up to 64°F (17.8°C) air
temperature, and at this temperature
flowering occurs. For later flowering a
lower soil temperature, 51–52°F (10.6–
11.1°C), is necessary for two weeks, then
raise air temperature to about 50°F

358

(15.0°C), a procedure which will keep flower quality high. Ventilation should, however, be given to avoid excess humidity and possible spread of botrytis.

Pre-cooled tulips

These are usually grown in boxes, the bulbs being planted in early October according to their size (generally 11–12cm or larger) from 6 × 11 (66) up to 13 × 7 (91). Boxes should be 3–4in deep, clean and provided with adequate drainage. Soil should be of good texture with a pH of 6.5–7 and should not have been used for bulbs beforehand. Fill to within 1in of the top and press the bulbs into the surface, adding more soil to leave the nose of the bulbs exposed. A layer of sand or ash is then put on top of the boxes to form a barrier between bulbs and plunge soil.

Boxes are then stacked in rows out of doors and covered with a layer of 6in sand or peat, and straw in addition on top of this. The watering of the straw subsequently induces the cool conditions necessary by evaporation. Fungal dusts (quintozene) are useful *before* the bulbs are covered by the soil.

After being in the plunge for a minimum period of 6 weeks, bulbs are brought into the greenhouse when the flower bud is clear of the neck of the bulb (as can be determined by examination) and there is good root growth, the temperature then being raised gradually to 70°F (21.1°C). They should be given shading by newspapers or other means to draw the flower up, or alternatively by putting them under benches. Temperatures are dropped as buds show colour.

Bulbs can be brought into the greenhouse in succession to flower over a period, flowering commencing in mid-December. It is important, however, to pay attention to the programming provided by the supplier. Uncooled bulbs are given the same general treatment for flowering from January till March.

Pot culture

Bulbs being grown for pot display are generally of dwarfer varieties of early singles and doubles. They are planted up closely and fairly firmly in pots or bowls of various sizes, either in bulb fibre or clean soil in early October with the nose of the

Narcissi are among the most popular of bulbs for forcing in greenhouses. They can be had in flower months before they would bloom out of doors, and the flowers will get spoiled by neither frost nor rain.

359

bulb exposed. The bulbs may be plunged into a deep layer of soil or peat and put into a dark cupboard and after the necessary 6 week period brought into the greenhouse or a warm room where once again *shade is essential* to begin with. At all times where bulbs are being grown in boxes or pots, adequate water supplies should be maintained, but never to the extent of spotting the blooms by careless over-application. Gardeners frequently find that gross foliage and weak flowers result, this being due in the first case to an insufficiently cool rooting period, and latterly to excess temperatures applied too quickly.

There are many variations of tulip culture, including the use of mobile greenhouses, when the bulbs planted out of doors can be brought forward to flower earlier than the outdoor crop by covering in March or earlier.

Forcing under artificial light
A very successful technique is the use of artificial light at 100W per sq yd and 12–14 in above the top of the bulbs for 12 hours in each 24 at 65°F (18.3°C) to start with, dropping to 60°F (15.6°C) when buds show colour.

Varieties
A classified list of tulip names, which contains all varieties of tulips in cultivation, is available from the Royal General Dutch Bulbgrowers Society and from the Royal Horticultural Society, Vincent Square, London.

Catalogues provided by specialist bulb suppliers list all bulbs available for flowering at various times and for different purposes.

For pests, diseases and physiological disorders see Chapter 32.

Chapter 28

Cacti

Over the past few years cacti and other succulent plants have become increasingly popular. In the centrally heated conservatory and home they make ideal subjects and revel in the dry air. Their stylised shapes are remarkably in keeping with modern architecture. And all the old wives' tales about flowering only once in seven years have been exploded.

There are certainly many species of cacti that do not flower until they reach a considerable size, but equally so there are many that flower profusely as very small plants. Once plants do reach flowering size they should flower regularly every year providing they are well looked after.

In the wilds, cacti are found growing in a wide variety of conditions and climates. Those growing high up in the Andes of South America are covered by snow in winter. Some are epiphytic and grow in humus trapped in the crooks of trees—these are known as orchid cacti and are very popular as house plants because of their exceptionally large and colourful flowers. The majority of cacti, however, are found in naturally arid conditions such as exist in many parts of South America, Mexico and California.

A great many succulent plants are wrongly called cacti, simply because they have spines or thorns. A true cactus can always be identified by the way in which the spines grow, with clusters of several spines arising from central points along the ribs or on tubercles. These central points are known as areoles, and any plant that does not have them is not strictly speaking a cactus, although amongst these succulent plants there are many interesting and bizarre forms. There is one plant that grows like a string of beads, and another that has hairy flowers smelling of decayed meat to attract the horseflies that pollinate it. There are also the 'living stones', plants that grow in the very hot dry deserts of South Africa and have taken on the semblance of small pebbles to prevent themselves from being eaten by animals.

Cacti and succulents will thrive in any dry atmosphere—on a greenhouse bench, conservatory bench, or indoor gardens of various designs, the pattern being set by the cactus houses of many botanical gardens, that in Kew Gardens near London being an outstanding example.

Cultivation
Potting
Purchased cacti will probably be in a tiny pot that does not allow sufficient development room for new roots. Ideally re-potting should be done in late autumn or early spring when the plants are semi-dormant, though they do not seem to suffer from being moved carefully during the summer.

The potting compost should allow free drainage of water, otherwise the plants will quickly rot. A mixture of equal parts of good loam and gritty sand is suitable for desert cacti. Succulents need to be kept slightly damper than cacti so one part of peat should be added to this mix for them. Epiphytic cacti need a compost rich in humus, and 2 parts peat, 2 of leafmould and 1 of loam is ideal. Purchased John Innes composts are acceptable provided extra sand is added. Re-potting long-spined cacti may seem a formidable task, but if a piece of twisted paper is wrapped round the middle of the plant leaving a 'handle', the job is made much easier. Once in a reasonable sized pot, eg 3½in for globular varieties, further re-potting should be in the same size, being simply a replacement of exhausted compost. Flowering ability is adversely affected by too large a pot. Bowls or indoor gardens should be planted with the tallest plants at the back, low growing plants in the centre, and trailing plants hanging over the front and sides, finished off perhaps with a layer of flint chippings or small pebbles between the plants.

Watering

As with most other types of plants, water-ing should be done when needed rather than on a regular weekly or fortnightly basis. The amount of water required varies from nothing during the winter to a maximum at the height of summer of a good soaking when the compost is dry. After the winter rest watering should begin very gradually in warm weather around March or April. When the plants have started growing strongly the amount of water is

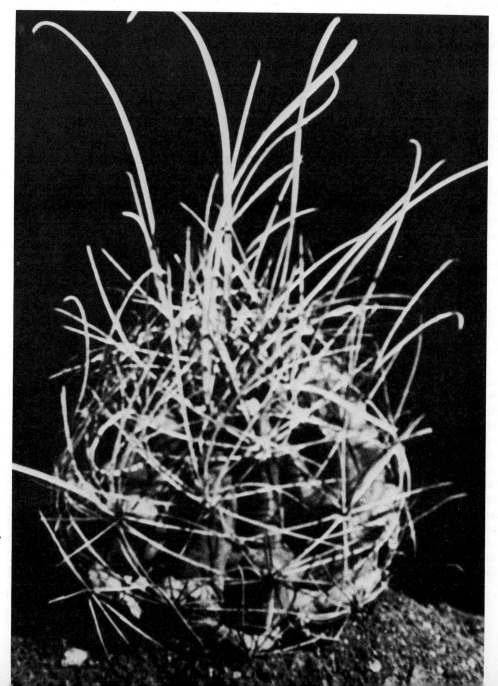

Ferocactus longihamatus, a popular little cactus with colourful reflexed spines.

increased until midsummer, after which it is gradually reduced until by September they are getting very little. By October no more water is given until the following spring unless conditions are exceptionally hot.

Feeding

It is not really necessary to feed cacti as long as they are re-potted occasionally to provide new soil for them. After flowering, however, a couple of waterings with very diluted liquid fertiliser does help to get the plants back into peak condition.

Ventilation

Despite the fact that they live in hot climates, cacti need plenty of fresh air. In a greenhouse give ventilation even on sunny days in winter and to leave both ventilators and door wide open at the height of summer, provided the range of other plants being grown allows this.

Heating

Through many varieties of cactus in the wild are covered by snow in the winter, they do not in damp temperate climates dry out before the cold weather as they do in their native lands. So, if exposed to frost, the water inside the plant will freeze, resulting in the death of the plant, and for this reason cacti should be kept at a minimum temperature of 40–45°F (4.4–7.2°C) throughout the winter. Some of the more exotic succulent plants and the epiphytic cacti need to be kept at 55–60°F (12.8–15.6°C). This means that unless expense is no object warmth-loving cacti are better lifted into the dwelling house over the winter.

Propagation

Basically there are four methods of propagating cacti: by dividing up old plants, taking cuttings, raising from seed or by grafting.

Division

This is the easiest way of propagating, as the offshoot has its own roots before it is detached from the parent plant. Unfortunately not very many types of cacti produce offshoots, and those that do are not perhaps the most interesting. The best time for detaching offshoots is in the early spring, as the young plant has the longest possible time to establish itself before the winter resting period.

Cuttings

Most cacti and succulents can be propagated quickly and easily by cuttings, but there are some difficult varieties which tend to rot before they produce roots. Before taking cuttings from a favourite plant one should consider whether this will leave ugly calloused stumps. Cuttings should ideally be taken in late spring, though they may be taken until quite late in the year providing bottom heat is available. It is best to take cuttings at a joint in the case of *Opuntia* species (prickly pear) but with tall upright types which do not make joints, 3 or 4in cut from the top of the stem will make a good cutting. Let them dry on a shelf for a day or two before attempting to root them in seed trays, pots of pure sand, or half peat and half sand.

Seed

Cacti can also be grown from seed. Mixed packets are available from most garden shops, but several firms deal in packets of single named varieties. The easiest way of building up a large collection quickly and inexpensively is indeed from seed. Some varieties will flower within two or three years of being raised from seed, but the majority take a great deal longer. Cactus seeds are very easy to germinate, the main problem being to keep them alive after they have germinated. Scatter the seeds over the surface of a pan or box of peaty compost, stand it in a few inches of water, and put a sheet of glass over the top. With efficient heat germination generally occurs within a month. Both before and after germination watering must be controlled so that the soil is never dry, or conversely waterlogged. The glass is then removed and the young cactus plants, which are very slow growing, can remain in the pan for a year before pricking out.

Grafting

Grafting is a rather specialised technique. It is used to speed the growth rate of slow-growing varieties by grafting them on to a

Cereus senilis, the old man cactus, a grafted plant. Grafting cacti is relatively easy, and the process is fully explained in the text.

vigorous root system of another species or culture. Grafting is often done by specialist cactus nurseries to enable them to produce saleable sized plants more quickly. Plants which are forced in this way often bear little resemblance to the same variety grown on its own roots. Spines especially do not seem so strong on grafted plants. One advantage of grafting is that plants flower earlier than they otherwise would. The stock which provides the root part of the graft is generally one of the faster growing *Cereus* group, chosen with a stem the same diameter as the scion. The top is cut off the stock leaving about an inch above soil level; the top of the scion is removed and the two surfaces joined as quickly as possible to prevent drying out. The two parts are held together either by a cactus or spine pin or an elastic band running under the base of the pot and over the top of the scion. The graft should be kept in a warm dry place until the two parts have united, taking care that no drips enter the cut when watering, which invariably starts rotting. Grafts usually take 4–6 weeks to unite and can be made at any time of year when both stock and scion are growing vigorously.

Varieties

Prickly pear types Many of these have short bristly spines that come away easily in the fingers. Whilst not poisonous, they are difficult to remove and cause severe irritation. Very few of these plants flower at the sort of size suitable for the home and are grown mainly for their attractive pads. *Opuntia ficus-indica* is the plant cultivated in parts of the world for its edible fruit, and is the true 'prickly pear'. The pads are large, up to 18in long, and have short spines.

Opuntia microdasys albispina has small dark green pads with pure white bristles at the areoles, giving the plant a spotted appearance.

Opuntia salmiana is a relatively dwarf-growing type which flowers freely even as a small plant. The flowers are pale yellow and measure about half an inch across.

Cacti grown for spines and hair

Echinocactus grusonii makes a large plant, covered in long golden spines.

Espostoa lanata is covered with long white hair which completely overhangs the spines.

Ferocactus wislizeni has long hooked spines, is very slow growing and will not flower until it is very old indeed.

Myrtillocactus geometricans is a very fast-growing variety with very short black spines and a pale blue/green stem covered with a powdery 'bloom' that comes off if the plant is handled too much.

Oreocereus trollii is another hairy variety but it also has very long bright red spines growing out through the hair.

Free-flowering cacti

Aporocactus flagelliformis is commonly known as rat's-tail cactus because of its long thin stems that trail over the edge of the pot. In early spring the whole plant is covered with large red flowers, and for these to be seen at best advantage the plant can be grown in a hanging basket.

Echinopsis eyresii produces masses of off-sets, so is very easy to propagate. If a large clump is allowed to build up the mother plant will flower regularly.

Rebutia miniscula is a very small plant, no more than 3in across even when fully grown. In time it will produce a great many offshoots and so build up a large clump. It is one of the most free-flowering cacti and will flower within two years of being grown from seed.

Stenocactus multicostatus is unusual in that it has wavy ribs. This plant too will flower when quite young.

Epiphytes, the orchid cacti

These plants are quite unlike the desert cacti in appearance, having flattened leaves like stems with no spines. When not in flower they are relatively uninteresting, but are well worth growing for the flowers alone, which are several inches in diameter

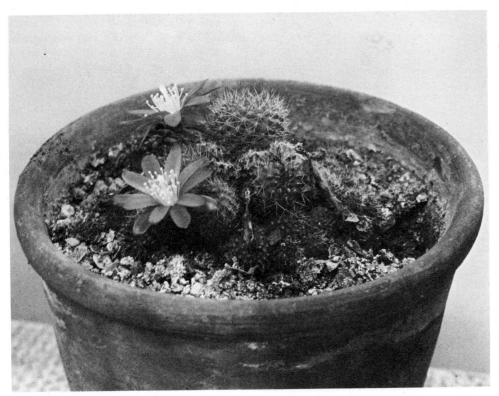

A well-grown pan of rebutia. Most rebutias have very brightly coloured flowers, usually oranges and reds, and flower freely.

and come in shades of red and orange, also white. Some are scented. There are not many natural varieties of epiphyllums, but a great many hybrids have been raised, especially as florists' plants.

Succulent plants

Echeveria derenbergii makes a rosette of pale blue leaves with pink edges. The small yellow flowers appear at the tip of a long stem from the middle of the rosette.

Lithops bella is just one of hundreds of types of stone plants. Individual plants measure about half an inch across and in time build up large clumps. In this particular variety the leaves are brownish-yellow with brown indented markings and white daisy-like flowers.

Sanseveria trifasciata laurentii is the popular mother-in-law's tongue plant. The long narrow leaves are dark green, mottled with light green and edged with yellow.

Senecio herreianus, known as the string of beads plant, is a creeping plant with globular leaves resembling miniature gooseberries.

Stapelia grandiflora consists of short thin angular stems. The flowers are very spectacular, measure 6ib across, are covered in hairs and smell of decaying meat.

Any of the plants in this list are also quite suitable for growing in the home and present no problems in cultivation. As one becomes more interested in cactus growing one comes across varieties that are rather more exacting in their requirements and need special greenhouse conditions. Such varieties are not usually available from florists but have to be obtained from cactus nurseries.

Chapter 29

Ferns

Accommodation requirements

There are something in the region of 9,000 fern species, growing throughout the world. The pleasure from growing them is immense, for though they do not produce exotic flowers they more than compensate for this by their grace, soothing colours and diversity of form. They can be divided roughly into five groups for the purpose of their cultural and accommodation requirements: the tropical group, the temperate group, the filmy ferns, and the epiphytic group and the hardy group.

The tropical group

Many of these are fascinating subjects that will grow fairly easily under greenhouse conditions. The temperature range must be maintained around the 70°F (21°C) level, dropping during the winter months to 67–68°F (20°C) to eliminate the risk of etiolation through the effects of poor light and excessive temperature.

The glasshouse used must be equipped with some means by which it can be shaded during the summer from direct sunlight. Heating is best achieved by hot water, through small-bore piping. Hot air heating is not suitable for fern culture, as this dries the atmosphere considerably, and the all-important relative humidity level drops too low. Humidity is one of the most important factors to consider when cultivating ferns. The use of the capillary bench system raises the atmospheric humidity level quite considerably, while also allowing the plants to take up water themselves, thus saving both time and effort. Not all ferns respond favourably to this method of culture, many requiring a very free-draining compost or growing medium. However, a simple system of benching with a shingle, gravel or ash layer 2–3in thick, on which the containers and plants are stood, is still a very satisfactory way of housing the plants. The floor and benching, if of the last type, should be kept moist by damping with a can or hose two or three times per day, more damping being necessary in the summer than winter months.

Ventilation will hardly be required, and should be applied with extreme caution if at all. A little air if and when the temperature reaches 85–90°F (29–32°C) could be given, but the humidity level must be watched and the young growth not allowed to flag badly.

If space and conditions allow, one can landscape an area of the greenhouse and plant out selected ferns to give a more natural appearance. Some of the larger species, eg tree ferns, which include the Cyatheas, lend themselves to landscape work, and can be underplanted with other species, eg *Blechnum*, *Tectaria* or *Nephrolepis*, to give a pleasing effect. This is a way of saving labour, as such a planted area will hold plenty of moisture and watering need not be carried out so frequently.

Suggested subjects *Nephrolepis* spp and cultivars, eg *N. cordifolia, N. exaltata, N. davallodes; Pityrogramma* spp (the gold and silver ferns); *Adiantum tenerum, A. raddianum.*

The temperate group

This next largest group contains many very pleasing plants, and indeed some from high-altitude tropical regions also. The cool-temperate fern house requires the same general refinements as does the tropical. Blinds must be provided and an efficient heating system is necessary, although the temperature here is kept at about 50–55°F (10–13°C) during the night and up to 65°F (18°C) during the day, above which ventilation must be applied. Being a cooler house, the humidity level is not so critical and is easier to maintain. Plants may be grown in containers on benching, or in a landscaped area. It is possible to incorporate the two methods in one house, using the specimens from the staging as they become larger to replace old plants, or fill gaps in the landscaped section.

Many of the Pteris are good specimens for such a house. *P. cretica* and its cultivars, *P. longifolia* and *P. vittata* are all fast-growing plants. *P. altissima* and *P. tremula* provide larger specimens attaining 2–4ft in height. These can all be raised easily from spores. Also suggested: *Cyrtomium falcatum, C. fortunei, C. caryotideum;* the spleenworts *Asplenium bulbiferum, A. mayii.*

The filmy ferns

This is possibly the most interesting of the fern groups. The plants are usually quite small and, as the name suggests, very delicate, much of the fronds being only one cell layer thick, giving the appearance of a thin film of tissue. They are exciting to grow, and some could be accommodated in the cool temperate house if grown in a closed case or frame (there are one or two designs on the market which would prove very suitable). One may, however, experience difficulty in obtaining material of these plants, due to their scarcity. A number are natives of New Zealand and they are all members of the family Hymenophyllaceae.

Humidity is particularly important for the filmy ferns. They require to be grown in a moisture-laden atmosphere, although not liking their feet in waterlogged conditions. They will not take full sunlight either, so must be partially shaded on all but the dullest days. A house devoted entirely to the culture of these plants need only be fitted with enough pipe heating to exclude frost. It must have good ventilation to enable it to be kept cool, but not to lower the atmospheric moisture-level. The proven method is to have a double opaque glass roof, with the ventilation applied between the glass layers.

There are some filmy ferns which originate from tropical environments, and these would require much higher temperatures.

A collection of ferns suitable for growing in the greenhouse. Genera shown include Asplenium, Adiantum, Nephrolepis and Athyrium.

Suggested subjects *Hymenophyllum demissum, H. wilsonii; Trichomanes venosum.*

The hardy fern group

This last group comprises the hardy and slightly tender species. They are natives of the colder parts of the globe, including Britain, and have to tolerate frost during part of the year, but need protection during the winter as much from excessive dampness as from cold. They may be housed in a cold greenhouse or cold frame, with some method of protection against the worst frosts.

These plants must have a dormant period in which to build up reserves, and most form a resting crown of young fronds tightly packed around the centre growing part of the plant. Water should be withheld during the winter, or applied only if the compost becomes quite dry. In this way slight frost will not damage the resting crowns.

Suggested subjects *Phyllitis scolopendrium; Adiantum venustum; Polystichum tsus-simense.*

The epiphytic group

The cultural needs of this group are discussed fully below.

General Fern Culture

A basic general compost for most terrestrial ferns consists of: 3 parts by volume moss peat, 1 part by volume loam, 1 part by volume coarse sand. The peat need only be put through a $\frac{3}{4}$in sieve to eliminate the very large lumps. The loam should be passed through a $\frac{1}{4}$in riddle and sterilised, preferably by steam. No fertilisers need be added to this mixture, as when the plants have fully permeated their allotted compost with roots, a liquid feed can be used to give added nutrient. To this compost, 'pea' gravel or granite chippings can be added for the temperate group of ferns. This gives sharper drainage, so necessary during wet or cold spells.

The epiphytic group requires a free-draining compost that will retain sufficient moisture without becoming waterlogged and sour. A large number of these epi-

368

phytic plants are in the family Polypodia-ceae. They respond well to the following compost: 3 parts by volume moss peat, 2 parts by volume fibrous bracken peat, 2 parts by volume sphagnum moss, 1 part by volume charcoal, 1 part by volume leaf-mould or bark chippings.

The majority of ferns object to being over-potted, ie given a large quantity of soil to root in, so it is usual to pot on in small stages, giving only one increase in pot size (eg ½in) at a time. There are exceptions to this, however, and a strong-growing plant during the spring and summer months will take a larger move without setback. When repotting, care should be taken not to damage the root ball, as this may cause the fronds to wilt and desiccate as a result. Some types produce a short rootstock and, when repotting, this ought to be partly covered by the new compost. Examples of this type of growth are to be found in *Pteris* species, eg *P. altissima, P. pacifica, P. tripartita*. Others produce a creeping rhizome or rootstock which must not be buried deeply, but kept at soil level and given adequate room to spread over the soil surface.

When potting, one must be guided for drainage not only by the system used but by the plants themselves. With capillary benching no crocking is the general rule: one is aiming at a good contact between bench and compost. However, certain fern species appear to become over-wet with this method, and it is preferable to revert to the old system of crocking and placing rough peat over this, before adding the prepared compost and potting.

Propagation

The quickest way of increasing one's stock is by vegetative propagation. Not all ferns lend themselves to this, however, but many may be so treated.

Bulbils

Quite a number of the ferns produce bulbils on their mature fronds. In many cases, the frond or part of it with the bulbils attached can be removed, pegged down on to a peat/sand growing medium, and placed in a propagating case for rooting to begin. When the plantlets have become established, they can be removed from the frame, separated and potted into general compost, thereby taking about 18 months to become mature plants. Examples of species that can be propagated in this way are: *Asplenium bulbiferum, A. viviparum, Diplazium proliferum, Tectaria incisa* (viviparous var.).

Rhizomes

The great majority of epiphytic ferns colonise new areas by means of rhizomes. These can be separated from the parent plant, preferably with a quantity of root intact, and attached by wire pegs to the medium on which they are to be grown, or tied to cork bark or other material if being grown in a truly epiphytic manner. It is not necessary to place it in a propagating case, unless the piece is small or weak, or a shy plant to establish, eg *Oleandra* spp, *Pyrrosia* spp, *Microgramma* spp. Rhizome propagation works very well for *Phlebodium aureum, Drynaria sparsisora*, species of *Davallia* in general, and some members of the genus *Polypodium*.

Root buds

The best known group which exhibits this feature are the platyceriums, or stag's-horn ferns. Not all the platyceriums produce root buds, but a number including *P. stemmaria, P. bifurcatum* and *P. alcicorne* do so quite readily. When the young plantlets resulting from these adventitious buds have produced their sterile 'nest' frond, they may be removed and potted into a 2½in pot, or placed immediately on to a piece of cork bark, on which has been placed a small cushion of sphagnum moss and osmunda fibre to accommodate their roots. Eventually they may be transferred to a larger pot or board, or even planted on a rock area to grow to maturity.

Diplazium esculentum produces a mass of young plantlets around the parent, and, if grown in a container, these can be cut out with some root and soil, potted singly, and will quickly make mature specimens.

Division

This method of propagation can be applied to many species and groups, usually rhizomatous. All that is needed is to slice up the plants. In this way a pan of, say, *Dennstaedtia* or *Drynaria* can be divided into halves or quarters, provided sufficient young growth is left in each section. The sections can now be potted or panned into a container of appropriate size and allowed to settle down and colonise their new home. No initial establishment treatment is necessary.

Spores

Anyone who has become interested in fern growing will sooner or later want to try to raise plants from spores. These are tiny dust-like bodies, which can be compared loosely to the seed of higher plants. The spores germinate to form prothalli, small and usually scale-like. The prothallus is the sexual stage in the life-cycle of ferns, where fertilisation takes place. The frond- and spore-bearing fern-plant grows up from the prothallus.

Raising from spores

The best time of year for sowing is roughly from March to June inclusive. It may be carried out later than this if need be, as the life of some spores is very short and it is possibly better to sow than to store for a long period. There are a number of different methods for raising plants from spores. The following gives good results, provided one pays attention to hygiene.

1 Sterilise sufficient pots for the number of items to be sown. Clay pots are preferable.
2 Fill to within $\frac{1}{2}$in of the lip with compost which should contain the following parts by bulk (each part should be sterilised to 180°F, preferably by steam) screened through a $\frac{1}{8}$in sieve: 3 parts moss peat, 1 part loam, 1 part sand. Put one crock (piece of clay pot) over the drainage hole, to stop the compost falling through. After filling, firm slightly with a firming tool (cut a circle of plywood to the required diameter and affix a handle to it).
3 Write labels for subjects to be sown. Plastic T-shaped labels are best, as they allow the covers to sit neatly on the pot rims.
4 After the pots have been prepared, water thoroughly with boiling water, which can be applied through a metal can with fine rose attachment.
5 Immediately (4) has been completed cover the pots with glass covers (convex watch-glasses are best, but plastic or glass petri dishes can be used; failing this, squares of ordinary glass will suffice).
6 The spore-bearing material, which has been previously collected and dried to allow the spore-cases to dehisce or break open in the packet, may now be sown. One pot is sown at a time, and the glass or plastic cover replaced as soon as sowing is complete. Only a thin dusting of spores is necessary to give the best results. Heavy sowing will cause overcrowding of the prothalli, often resulting in male gametes only being produced. Thus fertilisation cannot be achieved as early as is desirable and fungal infection is more likely to occur.
7 The sown pots are now placed in plastic watertight trays. A solution of potassium permanganate is poured into the trays to a depth of $\frac{1}{2}$–$\frac{3}{4}$in, to suppress any algal and fungal growth. To make up this solution, enough permanganate crystals are added to a gallon of water to produce a deep mauve colour. The plastic trays should be kept topped up with the solution as needed. The depth of solution in the trays should not exceed 1in; more would cause waterlogging of the compost in the pots.

The trays can now be put in the greenhouse, and kept under the staging in partially subdued light, and if possible raised above the ground by some method. This reduces water splashes and prevents water from the dampening process from entering the trays and contaminating the permanganate solution. A green flush of growth will be noticed in some pots after 4–5 weeks. Speed of germination depends on the temperature in which the pots are placed: 65–70°F (18–21°C) for the tropical subjects and around 60°F (15°C) for the temperate ones is adequate. This is the stage when fertilisation takes place, and as a result the sporophytes (young plants) will start to appear. The plants must now receive more light, and so can be moved on to the benches, but still kept in the trays, to absorb water from beneath. As the sporophytes develop, the covers on the pots may be gradually removed, and eventually the young plants 'patched off' into shallow trays, pans or small pots, depending on the quantity of plants needed. It is better to include three or so plantlets in each group

or patch, placing nine or so patches per 4in pan. With the tree ferns, eg *Dicksonia* spp, *Cibotium* spp, *Cyathea* spp, a single plant should be selected, as a strong single-stemmed specimen is required. When the patches have filled their allotted space they may be potted on. Each group can now be placed in a 2in pot, containing the general compost mixture, except for epiphytic plants, which require a more open growing medium (see above under General Fern Culture). As the plants develop, potting on can continue in stages until a pot about 5in diameter has been reached. By this time

Ferns are ideal plants to grow in a shaded greenhouse. If grown in a normally sited greenhouse particular care would need to be taken in providing shade for them.

the majority of ferns will be producing spore-bearing fronds, thus completing their life cycle.

Fern ailments

Due to the delicate nature of most ferns, one has to be most careful in selecting chemicals or other methods of control for pests and diseases. A good growing environment, producing strong plants, will do much to reduce the incidence of fungal or insect attack.

Scale insects These can be a considerable nuisance and spoil the appearance of the plants, particularly by the sooty mould which grows on the excreta left by them on the fronds. The best time to deal with these is when the young scale-insects emerge from the parent scale case and search for a suitable feeding spot. Derris liquid can be used without harm, but a more beneficial preparation is diazinon, a member of the organophosphorus group of chemicals, which gives a much greater degree of success. During the winter months one or two applications of malathion mixed with diazinon in equal proportions will control scale insect.

Mealy bug Can be controlled by spraying with diazinon and malathion.

Aphids Mainly appear on *Adiantum*. Providing no young growth in the pink unfolding stage is present, nicotine shreds may be used as a fumigant, but care must be taken in its use, and rare specimens should not be exposed to the fumes, unless previously known to tolerate the treatment without damage. Diazinon and malathion must not be used on *Adiantum*.

Slugs and snails These can be very destructive. A liquid slug-killer applied to benches and staging will give some protection, and slug pellets can be broken and placed in each pot or container.

Cockroaches These are particularly fond of the fern-ally *Lycopodium*, and eat the centres of the growing spikes, causing them to become blind. Baits can be tried, but general cleanliness is very important.

Glasshouse red spider mite Although not a prevalent pest of ferns, this does occur and can be controlled with diazinon.

Botrytis This is the main fungal attacker. It causes a lot of harm, and again the *Adiantum* group suffers most from its ravages if conditions are overcrowded or the atmosphere stagnant. Good plant husbandry should keep the effects of this to a minimum, but if persistent a spray of karathane may be used.

The frond eelworm Turns the fronds black. *Adiantum* again susceptible. These should never be watered from overhead, as this will cause the eelworm to spread rapidly. Badly infected fronds should be cut off and burnt.

Chapter 30

Orchids

The first orchid plants to arrive in Europe came from the West Indies in the mid-eighteenth century. These were of the species *Bletia verecunda (purpurea), Epidendrum rigidum,* various *Vanilla* species and *Epidendrum fragrans.* Later in the century came the first Asiatic orchids *Cymbidium ensifolium* and *Phaius tancervilleae.* Not until the beginning of the nineteenth century did orchids arrive from South America. Few orchids survived the long journey to Europe, but this only made them the more desirable. At first the cultural systems adopted contributed to the casualties. Irrespective of source, all orchids were kept in excessively hot, damp, humid conditions and poor light. It was a long time before it was realised that few orchids came from steaming jungles and that fresh air and cooler temperatures might bring more success.

Nowadays orchids are still imported but on nothing like the scale of the last century. This is due in part to nature conservancy and the restriction of exports, but even more to the production of hybrids. The first orchid hybrid, × *Calanthe dominyi,* between *Calanthe masuca* and *Calanthe furcata,* was made in the mid-nineteenth century by John Dominy of the firm of Veitch, and in 1859 he exhibited at a meeting of the Royal Horticultural Society in London five seedlings which were hybrids of *Cattleya guttata* and *Cattleya loddigesii* (× *Cattleya hybrida*). Gradually further hybrids involving other genera were made, frequently in a haphazard manner. In 1904 a breakthrough occurred. This was × *Odontioda vuylstekeae,* the result of crossing *Cochlioda noetzliana* with *Odontoglossum pescatorei,* the first bigeneric hybrid.

The production of hybrid orchids in quantity was limited by the symbiotic method of seed germination, which was the sowing of the seed on the surface of the compost of a healthy adult plant. Losses were heavy under this system. In 1922 Dr Lewis Knudson of Cornell University introduced an artificial medium, providing nutrition for the orchid seed chemically in a base of agar jelly (asymbiotic process), the seed sowing being done under laboratory conditions. This process revolutionised the raising of hybrid orchids, not only by enabling them to be produced in quantity, but because planned breeding programmes could now be carried out. Knudson's formula has been superseded by many variations of the original, particularly in the USA, Hawaii, southern Asia and Australia, where due to kinder climates most of the world's orchid raising is now done.

Meristem propagation

When an orchid hybrid is registered, all the seedlings of the cross receive the same name, even though they may vary tremendously in many respects. Selected plants of the cross may then be given varietal names. Until the introduction of the meristem method of propagation, such plants could only be multiplied by division of the original plant, a slow business which kept prices high. Now, however, the meristem process enables practically any number of identical plants to be brought to the flowering stage in 3–5 years, the time taken to produce a flowering seedling. Briefly this technique is as follows: a microscopic section of the growth tip of a young orchid shoot can be raised as if it were an orchid seed. If, however, the seed-raising medium is a liquid, ie without agar, and the medium constantly disturbed—the flasks containing the medium are placed on a rotating wheel—the original

Vanda sanderiana, one of the more unusual orchids that can be grown in the greenhouse. A native of the Philippines, it needs high temperatures.

growth tip will proliferate. The proliferations are then sectioned and each section treated as the original growth tip. The process can be continued until the desired number of propagations is reached, the rotation is stopped and the sectioned proliferations will then develop into plantlets. These are then treated as orchid seedlings. This method of propagation brings young plants identical to the world's most illustrious orchids within the reach of everyone. Seed raising is of course still necessary, since only by this method can new and better orchids be raised. The meristem process has not as yet been applied to all genera. It has, however, enabled commercial *Cymbidium* growers to upgrade their stock and amateurs to possess orchids which a few years ago would have been quite beyond their means.

Meristem propagation for amateurs is probably too difficult to carry out due to the equipment required, but in fact kits are available in America for this purpose though the original propagation is supplied ready for use. Seed raising is by no means beyond the careful amateur, since all the requirements for seed sowing are available in kit form both in Britain and in America and the simple equipment needed can readily be obtained. Raising the seedlings is more difficult than producing them, but temperature and light-controlled Wardian-type cases can be made or purchased.

Starting a collection of orchids

Until fairly recently prospective orchid growers experienced some difficulty in obtaining information of any kind on this subject. Nowadays more orchid nurserymen are advertising in the general garden press, most public libraries contain at least one or two orchid books, and the recently formed British Orchid Council means that it is only necessary to write to the secretary of that body to receive a list of orchid nurserymen and of the orchid societies in Great Britain, with one of whom an early contact should be made for advice. A further and most useful source of advice is one's local botanical garden where at least some orchids will be grown.

Greenhouses for orchids

Specially designed orchid houses are obtainable, but orchids may be grown in any kind of greenhouse if certain points are borne in mind. Glazed to the ground structures, due to their high heat loss, are only really suitable for growing *Cymbidium* in beds of compost at ground level. Any greenhouse, however, may be double glazed to help with the control of heat and humidity. Preferably this should be done with one of the transparent semi-rigid plastics. Concrete is better avoided for the floor surface unless the house is naturally a very wet one. Ash floors will retain water and provide humidity.

Which orchids to grow?

This depends not only on personal preference, but on the average temperature of one's greenhouse, particularly the winter temperature. While an occasional drop in temperature during severe winter conditions will do no harm, particularly if the house is kept on the dry side, there is no point in attempting to grow orchids at temperatures consistently below the optimum. Of the commoner genera, *Cymbidium* will do well at winter temperatures of 50–55°F (10–12.8°C), *Odontoglossum* at similar temperatures, *Cattleya* and *Paphiopedilum* at 55–60°F (12.8–15.6°C) and *Phalaenopsis* and *Vanda* at 65–70°F (18.3–21.1°C). With one of these as the main crop there are innumerable species available for each temperature range to provide variety.

General cultivation

The conditions required for growing orchids may be summarised as follows: adequate heating; shading from April to September, the amount depending on which orchids are grown and preferably provided by blinds; adequate fresh air combined with air circulation such as may be provided by an electric fan; a relative humidity of from 65 to 85 per cent day and night, provided by watering the green-

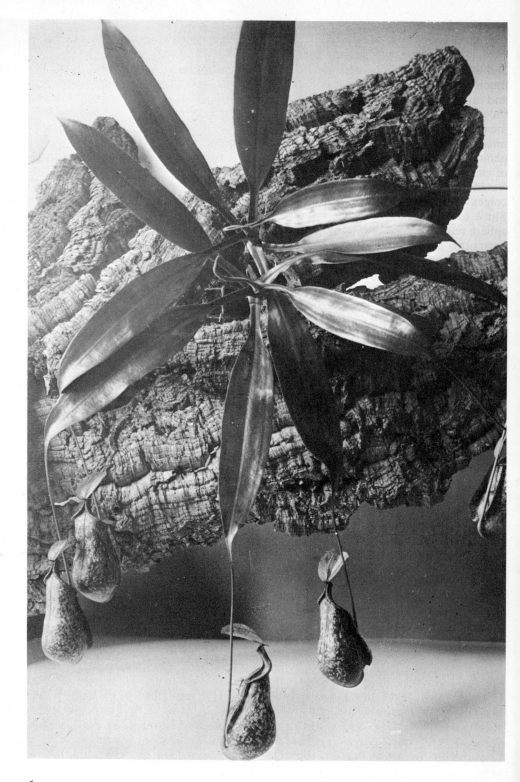

A nepenthes species
growing on cork bark in
an orchid house. Many
orchids can also be
grown on bark in this
way.

376

house by watering can, hose, or automatic mist spray system.

Watering is the key success factor in orchid growing. Many orchids require much water during the growing season and infrequent watering during the rest of the year. Much water with any orchid means pouring water through the compost until it is wet, then no more water until the plants require it—this is largely a matter of experience. It does *not* mean dribbling water every day until the compost becomes waterlogged and the orchid roots die. Since in fact orchids in a humid atmosphere require less frequent watering than most other plants, their culture lends itself particularly well to the automatic provision of heat, humidity and ventilation. Even automatic shading is available, although rather expensive.

Potting

Modern potting composts have done away with the principal chore of orchid cultivation. Economy composts were introduced to replace expensive osmunda fibre and

Orchids come in many weird and wonderful shapes, sizes and colours. The variations they produce on the simple theme of petals and reproductive organs are almost endless—and it is this that gives them their wide appeal.

have proved to be not only less expensive but easier and quicker to handle and frequently they produce better growth. Bark composts are often used for *Cattleya* and *Vanda*, particularly in the USA, and most genera will do well in equal parts by volume of fibrous, lumpy peat, Perlite or polystyrene granules and sphagnum moss, the aim being to provide a compost which will hold plenty of water but at the same time remain well drained. Where available locally, sphagnum moss alone is quite a useful compost, particularly for *Dendrobium* and newly imported orchids. As economy composts are generally lacking in nutrient, a slow-release fertiliser such as Magamp or Vitax Q4 is generally used. Due to the relatively poor light in Britain, few orchids will respond to as heavy a fertilising programme as they would in the tropics.

In botanic gardens many orchids are grown on pieces of bark or logs or in open teak or cedar baskets. Orchids may be divided into epiphytic and terrestial plants, the former normally growing on trees, not usually on the bare bark but in association with mosses and other epiphytic plants. Terrestial orchids normally grow on the ground. Most of the popular genera of orchids are epiphytic, but in the open composts mentioned will grow perfectly well in pots and these, if desired, may be hung from the roof of the greenhouse or on the walls. It may seem natural to grow epiphytic orchids without pots but such do require a great deal of attention to watering and spraying.

Chapter 31

The Alpine House

This romantic sounding name is given to the completely cold greenhouse (no artificial heat whatsoever) utilised for the culture of hardy low-growing rock plants including shrubs. It gives them protection to a certain degree from the extremes of weather and certainly from the ravaging effects of cold winds, enabling them to flower earlier and with more precision than if they were out of doors. It is a form of activity that can occupy an enthusiastic gardener over the winter and early spring months, and of course is a necessity for the rock-gardening enthusiast keen on exhibiting.

Many gardeners automatically think of all rock plants as being extremely hardy and able to withstand very low temperatures because they are indigenous to high alpine valleys on inaccessible rock shelves where, obviously, the average air temperatures are low. They forget, however, that for a major portion of their life many of these alpine plants are protected by a thick insulating blanket of snow which provides an even-temperatured congenial environment. Grown artificially below the snow-line in the variable autumn and winter conditions of a temperate climate, rock plants often quickly deteriorate.

Broadly speaking, any type of greenhouse will suffice, provided it is situated in a sunny position and—perhaps more important—provided it is well ventilated with both side and ridge vents to keep temperatures down.

Benches covered with inert gravel or pebbles are desirable and tiering is useful to give effect and better space utilisation. Plants are potted up in the summer, using clay pots for preference, and an appropriate compost—broadly speaking one of John Innes No 1 standard with either lime or no lime according to species. Good

Chamaecyparis obtusa
'Wissellii'

379

drainage is essential, using broken crocks or pebbles in the base of the pot. Pots are plunged to the rim in a shady sheltered position and kept moist, and the plants are lifted into the greenhouse early in October, where they must be kept cool and watered according to temperature, but generally sparingly. Small-flowered spring bulbs are potted in August or September and plunged in ashes in a cool shady frame for five or six weeks before being brought into the greenhouse.

It is essential to give continuous air day and night on the top ventilators at least, except during very cold frosty weather, and water very sparingly according to growth. It helps to keep plants moist and at the same time looking attractive if the

A selection of conifers suitable for growing in the alpine house.

Picea conica 'Albertiana'

Chamaecyparis obtusa gracilis

Juniperus squamata 'Mayerii'.

380

tops of the pots are dressed with a layer of inert chips of suitable colour, preferably grey, white or red.

Shrubs may be grown in much the same way, using larger pots, and there is obviously a vast range of species to choose from, size being the limiting factor. Full lists of species can be obtained from specialist nurserymen. The following are some of the more popular species grown:

Bulbs

Anemones   *A. apennina, blanda, fulgens* and *stellata*

Miniature daffodils *Narcissus bulbocodium* (hoop petticoat), *cyclamineus* (cyclamen-flowered), *minimus* (with tiny flowers) and *triandrus* (angel's tears)

Fritillarias

Winter-flowering crocuses

Plants

Alyssum	Mertensia
Androsace	Omphalodes
Draba	Primula
Eritrichium	Saxifrage
Gentiana verna	Sedum
Iberis	Sempervivum
Lewisia	Soldanella

Juniperus communis 'Compressa'

Dionaea museipula, the Venus fly-trap, an ideal plant for cultivation in a cool greenhouse, but needing rather special cultural conditions.

The alpine house is a
world of its own,
dominated by dwarf
conifers and high
mountain plants.

Chapter 32

Greenhouse cleansing

Whilst routine inspection of the growing plants is helpful in reducing the chances of disease and pest spread, the periodic cleansing of the glasshouse structure is also essential. To do this it is, of course, necessary to move out *all* plants to a suitable environment when a further examination of them can be made. The house should then be thoroughly washed down either with a proprietary cresylic acid solution or with dilute formalin (2 per cent) plus a wetting agent, making sure that cracks and crannies in the structure and on the bench are not neglected, and that old bits of string used for plant supports and remnants of plant material are removed and burnt.

Both formalin and cresylic acid can be applied by brush or by sprayer, but whatever method is used it is advisable to wear an eye-shield or goggles. When formaldehyde is used the structure should be completely closed for 24 hours after treatment,

and if possible the temperature should be raised to about 70°F (21°C) during this period. Following this treatment the house should be opened up and thoroughly ventilated until all traces of formaldehyde smell have gone.

In larger glasshouses it may be more convenient to wash down with a proprietary detergent solution and then to fumigate with formaldehyde or with sulphur (provided the main structure of the house is not made of metal). The formaldehyde can be vaporised either by placing the solution in a container over a heater, or by placing crystals of potassium permanganate in a twist of soft paper and dropping it into a *metal* bucket containing the formaldehyde solution. Approximately 1 pint of formalin and 4oz potassium permanganate are required for each 1,000cuft of house. Care should be taken to use a large enough *metal* container for the formalin since the addition of the potassium perman-

Tomato plants showing, on the right, a healthy, vigorous plant and, on the left, one affected by Verticillium wilt. Disease-resistant strains are now available.

ganate causes violent bubbling and evolution of heat during which the formalin is vaporised. Allowing a 1 gallon container for 1 pint of formalin should be satisfactory. When sulphur is used, it can be placed in small bags (approx 6½oz per 1,000cuft) with wood wool and ignited. Close tightly all the doors and vents in the house; these are subsequently opened after 24 hours (for formaldehyde) or 2–3 days (for sulphur) to allow the fumes to escape.

Safety

Many pesticides are relatively harmless, even when exposure to them is considerable, but some are quite toxic, and a few are *extremely dangerous* both in the concentrated and diluted state. It is, therefore, *essential to treat all pesticides with respect,* and to err on the side of extra care when storing and handling them.

The following points should be constantly borne in mind:

1 Store all pesticides (if possible under lock and key) out of reach of children, in clearly labelled containers. **DO NOT TRANSFER CHEMICALS TO SOFT DRINK OR OTHER TYPES OF BOTTLE.**

2 Amateur growers should obtain their fungicides and insecticides from the appropriate retail sources. Where possible, use chemicals that carry the seal of approval of the official Agricultural Chemicals Approval Scheme in preference to materials not carrying such approval. All officially approved chemicals have also been cleared for safety under the Pesticides

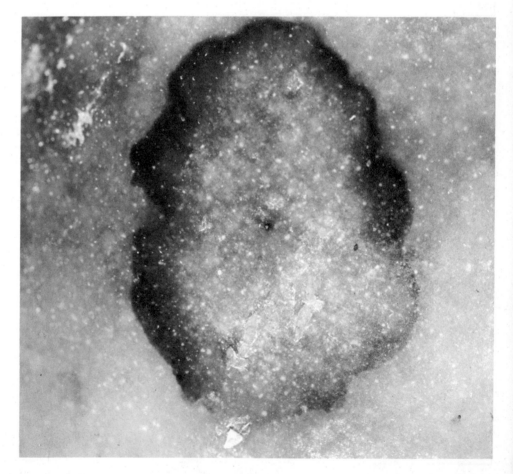

Buck eye rot of tomato (*Phytophthora parasitica*) greatly enlarged.

384

Tomato fruits affected by
blossom end rot. A
common disease,
usually easily avoided by
correct cultural
management.

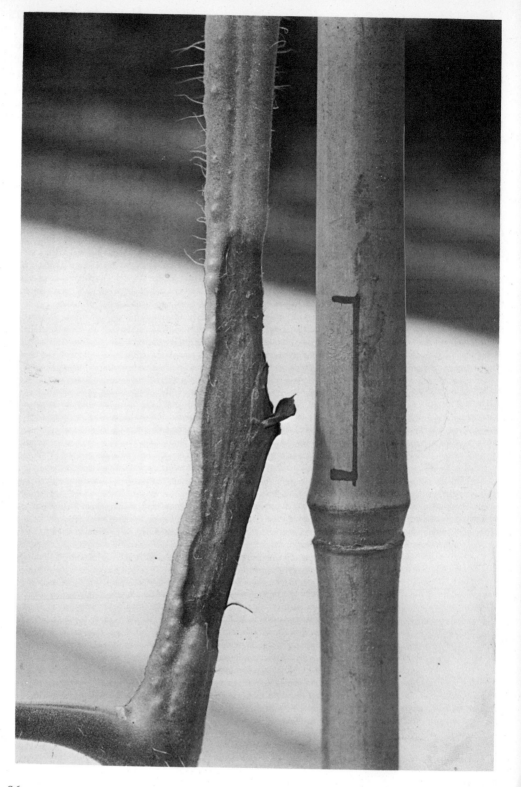

Didymella attack on the stem of a young tomato plant. The disease is less prevalent now than it used to be.

Safety Precautions Scheme (in the UK see MAFF booklets *Chemicals for the Gardener*, and *List of Approved Products and their Uses for Farmers and Growers*).

3 Carefully read the instructions on the pesticide container *and follow them*. Wear rubber gloves when handling pesticide concentrates and also when spraying. Also use a face mask and other protection if so instructed. A face mask should be worn when handling and applying certain dusts.

4 Thoroughly cleanse the spraying equipment after use.

5 Wash hands and face, and all protective clothing after spraying or dusting.

6 Do not eat, drink or smoke when spraying or dusting, nor until protective clothing has been removed and hands and face have been thoroughly washed.

Biological control

Just as the more stable environmental conditions of the greenhouse are favourable for pests they are also extremely suitable for some of the natural enemies of the pests (the parasites and predators). Concern over the hazards and expense of pesticides together with increasing problems of pest resistance to chemicals has recently re-focused attention on biological agents. The most notable of the techniques developed at the Glasshouse Crops Research Institute is the use of the predatory mite *Phytoseiulus persimilis* for the control of glasshouse red spider mite (*Tetranychus urticae*) on cucumbers and tomatoes. There are also techniques for the control of aphids and whiteflies on glasshouse crops.

Characteristics and treatment of some disorders and pests of greenhouse plants

In the following pages are described a number of disorders and pests which may affect some of the crops mentioned earlier in the book. It is obviously quite impossible to do more than cover the better-known disorders, and inclusion of particular diseases and pests in the section is based mainly on the likelihood of their occurrence in the greenhouse.

Where a disorder is caused by a pathogenic organism or is of physiological origin, the letters (F), (B), (V) or (Ph) are appended to indicate whether a fungus (F), bacterium (B), virus (V), or physiological feature (Ph) respectively is involved. Pest infestations are indicated by the letter (P). Features marked with an asterisk (*) are visible with a magnifying glass ($\times$ 10 magnification).

IMPORTANT NOTE Where a particular chemical is recommended for use against a pest or disease, it is essential (a) strictly to observe the maker's instructions regarding rates and methods of application, (b) to check that the chemical will not damage the variety being treated, and (c) that with an edible crop the stated minimum time should be allowed between the final fungicide or insecticide application before harvest and the picking and eating of the crop.

(a) **Tomato**

Disorder

Damping-off root and foot rots
Rhizoctonia solani, Pythium spp,
Phytophthora spp (all F)

Brown root rot and corky root
Pyrenochaeta terrestris (F)

Grey mould
Botrytis cinerea (F)

Stem rot
Didymella lycopersici (F)

Leaf mould
Cladosporium fulvum (F)

Blight
Phytophthora infestans (F)

Wilts
*Verticillium albo-atrum, V. dahliae,
Fusarium oxysporum* f. sp. *lycopersici* and
F. redolens (all F)

Buck-eye rot
Phytophthora sp (F)

Bacterial canker
Corynebacterium michiganense (B)

Tomato mosaic and Streak
Tobacco mosaic virus (V)

Symptoms	*Control*
Collapse of seedlings or young plants at soil level. Roots may be rotted.	Sterilise seed boxes, pots and compost. Ensure clean water supply. Drench soil surface with zineb, Cheshunt compound or proprietary copper compound; incorporate quintozene in compost if *Rhizoctonia* suspected. Sterilise border soil. Do not plant in cold soil (less than 57°F/13.9°C).
Plants unthrifty and wilt in bright weather. Soft brown rot, outer tissues of root lost. Later, brown uneven cork-like swelling of larger roots. Stem base rot and yellowing and withering of lower leaves.	Hygiene and soil sterilisation as for Stem rot. A stem base drench of nabam after planting helps to reduce infection.
Pale brown lesions on stem, with grey fur of fungus (under humid conditions). Fruit may show green rings with pinpoint brown mark at centre (Ghost spots) and grey soft rotting.	As for Stem rot. Also avoid checks to plant growth, and conditions of high humidity (ie ventilate and give a little heat if necessary to create buoyant atmosphere). Spray with benomyl after de-leafing. Tecnazene smokes can be used. Dichlofluanid sprays are recommended.
Brown, grey or blackish rot of base, or later the upper parts of stem. Dark pimples (fruiting bodies) on lesions may be present.* Roots rotted. Dark lesions at flower end of fruit.	Remove and destroy remains of previous tomato crop, including roots, strings and debris. Wash down house with detergent or disinfectant. Fumigate with formalin or sulphur (not in metal houses). Sterilise canes and boxes. Sterilise soil before planting. Inspect plants during cropping and remove primary infectors. Spray captan on stem bases and adjacent soil after planting, and repeat 3 weeks later. Maneb can be used similarly, but avoid applying to soil. A stem base drench (1 pint/plant) of benomyl after planting, with subsequent whole plant sprays have been found to be good.
Yellow patches on upper surface of leaves, with corresponding brown or purplish velvety fur of fungus on lower surface.	Avoid conditions of high humidity (ie ventilate and give a little heat to create buoyant atmosphere). Give reasonable space between plants. Crop hygiene important (see Stem rot). Grow resistant varieties. Spray regularly with benomyl or zineb.
Brown areas on leaves, with dark streaks on stem. Reddish-brown marbled patches on green fruit, which later shrivel and die.	Spray regularly with potato blight fungicides, such as zineb, maneb, or mancozeb, particularly if blight on neighbouring potatoes. Reduce humidity of atmosphere by ventilating and giving some heat.
Yellowing and/or wilting of leaves, progressively up the plant. Symptoms may be one-sided (especially with *Fusarium*). Wood often discoloured light-, dark-, or reddish-brown. Severely affected plants may die.	Hygiene and soil sterilisation as for Stem rot. A stem base drench (1 pint/plant) with benomyl after planting may reduce infection. Grow resistant varieties or use plants grafted onto resistant rootstocks.
Grey to reddish-brown zonate patches on fruit.	Support lower trusses up off ground to prevent fungus splashing from soil on to fruit. Spray soil surface and lower trusses with proprietary copper fungicide to prevent disease spread.
Small light brown areas on surface of leaves which coalesce and kill the leaf. Raised yellowish-white mealy areas on stem; skin separates easily from wood. 'Birds-eye' spotting (white spot with dark centre) on fruit.	Hygiene and soil sterilisation as for Stem rot. Reduce temperature by ventilation and cease overhead watering. Remove infected plants carefully and spray remaining plants with mild copper fungicide every 3 days until disease under control, then weekly.
Seedlings are checked and turn purple. On older plants, leaves are mottled light and dark green (Mosaic), with variable distortion. Leaf blades may not form, giving fern-leaf effect. Sometimes grey streaks form on stem and leaf stalks, and bronzing and sunken markings occur on fruit (Streak).	Use virus-treated and tested seed. Hygiene as for stem rot, except that washing down should be done with 3% tri-sodium phosphate. Fumigate with formalin or sulphur. Sterilisation with steam will reduce virus in soil; chemicals ineffective. During growth, handle obviously affected plants last when de-leafing, side shooting etc. Wash hands

389

Disorder

Aspermy
Tomato aspermy virus (V)

Other virus diseases
Spotted wilt virus, cucumber mosaic
virus etc

Blossom end rot (Ph)

Magnesium deficiency (Ph)

Iron deficiency (Ph)

Manganese toxicity (Ph)

Dry-set (Ph)

Flower abortion (Ph)

Flower drop (Ph)

'Missing' flowers (Ph)

Greenback (Ph)

Blotchy ripening (Ph)

Fruit splitting (Ph)

Symptoms

Control

before handling plants. Maintain well-balanced feeding of plants to minimise effect of virus. If fruit bronzing persistently bad, grow resistant varieties. Control of virulent disease by inoculation with attenuated strain of TMV currently under test.

Plant appears bushy, with distorted and mottled foliage. Fruits may be small and virtually without seeds.

Control aphids which can transmit the virus from neighbouring tomatoes or chrysanthemums which can also harbour the disease.

Mottling, bronzing, ringspots and distortion. Plants may be stunted or killed.

Control aphids and thrips which transmit some of the viruses.

Dark green circular patch at distal end of fruit, later becoming sunken and black.

Maintain uniform watering regime, since lack of water in soil can lead to blossom end rot. Do not over-feed as high salt concentration, especially if calcium is low, can also cause the disorder.

Interveinal yellowing and browning of the lower leaves, which later curl and die. Condition progresses up plant.

Spray with magnesium salts (Epsom salts). Reduce potash applications temporarily.

General yellowish-blanching of leaves with main veins standing out green. Younger growth affected first.

Most common under alkaline conditions, so adjust pH to less than 7 before growing tomatoes. To correct condition in growing crop, apply chelated iron to the soil around affected plants.

Brownish lesions on stems and petioles. Leaves may wither and droop. Condition generally transient.

Occurs most frequently in acid soils, particularly after steam sterilisation. Check pH of soil before growing the crop: if too low adjust to pH 6–6.5 by addition of suitable form of lime.

Fruit fails to set, or flowers drop off.

Since pollination fails if atmosphere too dry, damp down during morning on sunny days. Use proprietary hormone setting compounds, but avoid excessive application as distorted fruits may occur on lower trusses.

Although flowers fertilise, flower abortion later occurs and only 'chat' fruits develop. It is thought to be related to light input or day/night temperature relationship, producing flowers which are not fully viable.

Control propagation regime as much as possible. In poor light areas, use should be made of supplementary lighting or a growing room, ensuring standardisation of conditions under which early flower trusses are laid down, this occurring at an early stage and first and second trusses are initiated during the light treatment period.

Flowers drop off at 'knuckle' due to dry atmosphere, lack of moisture at the roots, or a high salt concentration in the soil.

Improve environmental control and carefully check the application of water and nutrients.

Flowers do not appear or only open partially although truss has formed. Due to excess of nitrogen and related to low salt content of the soil. Low night/high day temperatures can also contribute.

Adjust salt concentration and apply potash to harden growth. Day and night temperatures should be balanced.

The shoulder of the fruit stays green. Ailsa Craig and its offspring are susceptible. To avoid this trouble Moneymaker types were developed. Too hard defoliation, lack of potash, or excess sunlight can cause greenback.

Do not over-defoliate. Shade in extreme cases when very hot weather persists. Increase the application of potash.

Fruit has light patches which do not ripen. Caused by irregular feeding and watering which results in variable salt content of the soil. Those in the 'vigorous' categories tend to be most susceptible.

Ensure regular feeding, watering and even temperatures as far as possible.

The fruit cracks or splits due to irregular water uptake and sometimes to varying temperatures. More frequent in cold houses when fruit development has taken a long time and the skin has grown tough.

Keep temperatures as even as possible and shade if necessary to avoid excessive daytime temperatures. Ensure a regular watering pattern.

391

Disorder
Bronzing (Ph)

Oedema (Ph)

Leaf curling (Ph)

Silvering (Genetical)

Springtails
Collembola (P)

Thrips
Mainly *Thrips tabaci* (P)
Other species occasionally troublesome

Whitefly
Trialeurodes vaporariorum (P)

Aphids
Mostly the glasshouse-potato aphid
Aulacorthum solani or the peach-potato
aphid *Myzus persicae* (P)

Tomato moth
Laconobia oleracea (P)

Tomato leafminer
Liriomyza solani (P)

Red spider mite
Tetranychus urticae (P)

Symptoms

A dead layer of cells immediately below the skin due to excessively high daytime temperatures. Virus or boron deficiency can also be the cause.

Bumps or blotches on stems or leaves. Transpiration does not take place rapidly enough through the leaves. Due to excess humidity or the application of oil-containing sprays. More common on container-grown systems if excess water is allowed to lie about between troughs or containers.

Leaves curl upwards excessively, especially older leaves, due to a great variation in day/night temperatures, the plant being unable to cope with surplus carbohydrates.

Foliage turns light in colour on part of the plant and up to half the leaves may be affected. It is thought to be a genetical disorder associated with layers of tissue which may correct itself or persist.

Seedlings and young plants with pin holes or scraping of surface of foliage. Springtails (minute white or colourless, wingless insects) present in large numbers when soil floated in bucket of water.

Removal of sap causes wilting and scarring of foliage and fruit. Thrips are also important vectors of spotted wilt virus. Minute yellow-brown insect with strap-like wings.*

Small adults with white wings, larval stage scale-like. Adults fly away in clouds when foliage disturbed. Found in large numbers on young plants and growing point of old plants. Removal of sap causes chlorotic area and sugary waste product (honeydew) induces the growth of black moulds on foliage and fruit.

Removal of sap results in yellowing of foliage. *A. solani* is vector of tomato aspermy virus. Honeydew may spoil fruit. Small (1–1.5mm) dull green or yellowish green insects with or without wings.

Young skeletonise foliage and older larvae eat holes in fruit and stems and strip all leaves from May–July. Adults wing span dark purple-brown in colour. Caterpillars pale green head with yellow-brown body, dark stripes on back and yellow stripes on side. (Other species may also occur. Control as given.)

Adults feed on foliage causing pits; larvae tunnel into cotyledons of seedlings often killing them. Small pale orange larvae in tunnels mostly in S. England.

Foliage hard, parchment-like with yellow mottling on upper surface becoming completely yellow. Webs are produced on plants and all stages of pest are visible. Fruit and flowers spoiled by webbing. Mite has small (0.6mm) pear-shaped body with yellow/green or red coloration.

Control

Avoid high daytime temperatures and check for other troubles. The trouble does not usually persist for more than a few trusses.

Lower humidity by doing away with excess water. Ensure adequate ventilation, especially at night.

Adjust day/night temperature differential.

Apply gamma-BHC dust to soil, or drench soil with gamma-BHC or malathion.

Spray foliage with malathion. Two applications at 14 day intervals.

Spray with malathion or diazinon. Biological control possible.

Many alternative treatments include: on young plants, spray of demeton-S-methyl or dimethoate or malathion and repeat in 10 days; on mature plants gamma-BHC or nicotine smokes, or sprays of organophosphorus compounds which have systemic action. May develop resistance to certain organophosphorus compounds.

Spray with dichlorvos or trichlorphon at 1 week intervals. Do not spray young plants—try handpicking.

Spray soil and seedlings with diazinon.

Mites come out of hibernation in spring and breed rapidly. Resistance may occur as in aphids and treatment should be varied. Many acaracides are available including: on seedlings, sprays of dimethoate, demeton-S-methyl or tetradifon; on mature plants dicofol plus the above sprays, or smoke with azobenzene or tetradifon. Biological control very effective using predators. Remove old crop immediately after fruit finished to prevent hibernation of mites.

393

Disorder

Slaters or woodlice
Armadillidium spp (P)

Symphilids
Scutigerella immaculata (P)

Potato-cyst eelworm
Heterodera rostochiensis (P)

Root-knot eelworms
Meloidogyne spp (P)

(b) **Cucumber**

Disorder

Black root rot
Phomopsis sclerotioides (F)

Grey mould
Botrytis cinerea (F)

Stem and root rots
Rhizoctonia sp, *Pythium* sp,
Phytophthora sp (all F)

Black stem rot
Mycosphaerella melonis (F)

Gummosis
Cladosporium cucumerinum (F)

Powdery mildew
Erysiphe cichoracearum (F)

Mosaic
Cucumber mosaic virus (V)

Green mottle
Cucumber green mottle virus (V)

Symptoms

Stems of seedlings chewed through at or below soil level, roots stunted. Occasionally damage foliage by chewing holes. Grey/brown armour plated segmented body with numerous small legs on underside. Nocturnal feeders hiding under pots etc during day.

All stages feed on young roots causing wilting and blue discoloration, and encouraging infection by disease organisms. White body (about 6mm) with 12 pairs of legs. Fast moving and prefer moist soil.

Dwarf plants with slight purple discoloration and tendency to wilt. Large numbers of fibrous roots near surface of soil. From mid-summer white or golden pin-head cysts visible.*All other stages in life cycle microscopic.

Plants with pale lower foliage and severe wilting. Large irregular shaped galls on roots distinguish this pest from PCE above.

Control

Remove rubbish, boxes etc. Apply gamma-BHC spray or dust to soil.

Control when 10 or more are found at one root system. Drench soil with diazinon or gamma-BHC.

Plants may be helped by soiling up and extra water. Efficient soil sterilisation should be carried out next winter using steam or chemicals (metham-sodium). This pest is very easily spread by contamination from other *Solanaceae*, soil, boxes, tools etc.

Take care to purchase clean plants. If soil infested remove damaged plants and roots and steam sterilise or use D-D injection. If this is impossible use pot or peat culture methods (using sterilised materials). Grafts on KN or KNVF root-stocks are resistant to some species of the pest.

Symptoms

Plant wilts and dies. Rotting of stem base and roots. On smaller roots, black spots in outer tissues which slough off easily. Older rotted roots blackened.

Water-soaked lesions at nodes and at side shoots and leaf scars. Fruits rotted.

Light brown *(Rhizoctonia)* or dark brown *(Pythium/ Phytophthora)* lesions at stem bases of seedlings or young plants. Rotting of the roots.

Small pale green spots turning brown later on leaves. Edges of leaves water-soaked. Lesions on stems where leaf or side shoot removed. Soft greyish-green rot at distal end of fruit.

Grey sunken spots on young fruits exude a sticky liquid. Fruits split exposing inner tissues. Green fungal masses on diseased tissue.

White powdery growth on the leaves.

Yellow and light green mosaic, with star and ring symptoms and distortion of the leaves and fruits. Symptoms vary according to strain of virus occurring.

Inconspicuous light and dark green mottling on the young shoot leaves. No symptoms on older leaves or fruits. Marked loss of crop yield can occur.

Control

Sterilise border soil or re-soil, or grow plants on straw bales.

Remove infected tissue. Reduce humidity. Spray with benomyl.

Sterilise soil in seed boxes and bed. If *Rhizoctonia* occurs, apply quintozene dust to surface of bed and rake in. For *Pythium* and *Phytophthora* remove diseased plants and apply copper fungicide to bases of unaffected plants.

Thoroughly clean glasshouse and destroy debris. Reduce humidity. Cut out dead or diseased growth. Spray with thiram or zineb at first sign of disease and then at 14 day intervals, or dust with thiram.

Destroy affected fruit. Reduce humidity. Avoid low temperatures in house. Spray with zineb, thiram or captan at 10 day intervals. Grow resistant varieties.

Spray with dinocap, colloidal sulphur, quinomethionate or benomyl at 10–14 day intervals. Drench dimethirimol on the soil.

Destroy young infected plants. Do not handle uninfected plants after infected ones. Spray with insecticide to control aphid vectors.

Disease is seed-borne and easily transmitted by handling. Seed can be free of infection by heating it to 158°F (70°C) for 3 days. Destroy young infected plants by watering pots with disinfectant (eg formalin or cresylic acid at 2%) *before* removing. In border, carefully remove and destroy affected plants and adjacent plants to prevent spread. Wash hands and utensils with trisodium phosphate (5%).

Disorder
Seedling disorders (Ph)

General plant disorders
Causes not fully known (probably Ph)

Fruit disorders (Ph)

Springtails
Collembola (P)

Whitefly
Trialeurodes vaporariorum (P)

Aphids
Aphis gossypii (P)

Fungus gnats
Sciara spp (P)

Bees—domestic and wild (P)

Red spider mite
Tetranychus urticae (P)

French-fly
Tyrophagus dimidiatus (P)

Millepedes
Oxidus gracilis (P)

Root-knot eelworm
Meloidogyne hapla and
M. incognita acrita (P)

(c) **Lettuce**

Disorder

Damping-off
Pythium sp, *Rhizoctonia solani* (both F)

Collar rot
Rhizoctonia solani (F)

Grey mould
Botrytis cinerea (F)

396

Symptoms	Control
Uneven germination, collapse of seedlings and distortion of cotyledons.	Use reliable seed. Ensure that uniform watering and fertiliser incorporation are carried out and that temperature for germination is favourable ($80°F/27°C$). Avoid high salt concentrations (low pC) in seed boxes. Handle seedlings carefully to avoid damage.
Blindness or fusion (fasciation) of shoots. Marginal and interveinal leaf scorch associated with temporary wilting of plant.	Avoid damage to shoot tips which causes fasciation.
Distortion, or marked failure of fruit to develop. White or pale brown superficial corky scars. Fruit may split.	Avoid checks to plant growth. Ensure roots in good condition. Avoid draughts of cold air or sudden general drops in temperature when cucumbers forming.
See pest in (a). Leaves may be completely skeletonised. Young seedlings only.	Drench soil with gamma-BHC.
See pest in (a).	Spray with diazinon or malathion (older plants only). Biological control possible.
Yellow foliage and distorted fruitlets. Also a vector of cucumber mosaic. Small yellowish-green to black aphid with long feelers.*	Spray seedlings or young plants with demeton-S-methyl or dimethoate. Mature plants are also tolerant to sprays of malathion and smokes of nicotine or sulfotep.
Larvae feed on root hairs of seedlings slowing growth or causing collapse. May also feed on foliage causing holes. Larvae 6mm long translucent or white in colour with black heads.	Give extra water and drench beds with malathion. Treat soil with diazinon prior to sowing seed.
Swollen, bitter tasting fruit due to cross pollination.	Screen ventilators; or remove male flower/buds. Varieties without male flowers are now available.
See pest in (a). If not controlled, will kill all young growth.	As tomatoes, but do not use tetradifon on seedlings and use azobenzene smokes with caution.
In high temperatures become active and migrate to young plants causing minute holes which enlarge as foliage grows. Severe infestations cause blindness of shoot. NB. These are not flies—but mites visible as creamy-white globular organisms with many large bristles.*	Mites are brought in on straw and horse manure. Spray with diazinon or dicofol. Avoid using straw and manure which is infested.
Gnawing of stem above soil level destroys plant. Root damage may allow entry of disease. Flattened body 8mm long; brown in colour.	Drench soil with gamma-BHC and use sterilised compost for seedlings. Thorough cleaning of house essential after crop lifted.
See pest in (a).	As tomatoes, but no resistant root-stocks available. Culture on straw bales or in peat reduces incidence.

Symptoms	Control
Collapse of seedlings at soil level.	Sterilise seed boxes and soil for compost. Do not overwater. For *Pythium* remove affected seedlings and water with Cheshunt compound or with thiram. For *Rhizoctonia* incorporate quintozene into compost before sowing.
Brown lesions on stems of older plant at soil level. Extensive rotting results in collapse of plant.	Sterilise border soil. Incorporate quintozene into surface of soil.
Seedlings collapse with water-soaked lesions. On older plants, reddish-brown lesions develop on the stem at soil level. Leaves develop wet brown lesions.	Remove debris from glasshouse. Do not allow plants to wilt. Avoid humid atmosphere by ventilating and giving a little warmth. Rake dicloran dust into surface soil before sowing or planting. Spray or dust plants with thiram, or spray with benomyl. Use tecnazene smokes.

397

Disorder
Downy mildew
Bremia lactucae (F)

Mosaic
Lettuce mosaic virus (V)

Big vein
(believed to be V)

Tipburn (Ph)

Springtails
Collembola (P)

Aphids (P)
The lettuce aphid
Nasonovia ribisnigri
The glasshouse-potato aphid
Aulacorthum solani and several other species

Symphilids
Scutigerella immaculata (P)

Slugs and snails (P)
(several species)

(d) **Other vegetables**
In glasshouse borders such general soil pests as
leatherjackets, wireworms, millepedes and slugs
attack all vegetables, but are not generally as
widespread as they are out of doors.

Crop	*Disorder*
Brassicas (young cauli-flower and Brussels sprout plants raised for outdoor planting)	Clubroot *Plasmodiophora brassicae* (F)
French bean	Foot rot *Fusarium solani* f. sp *phaseoli* (F)
	Halo blight *Pseudomonas phaseolicola* (B)
	Aphids Various species (P)

Symptoms

Pale green or yellow angular leaf spots, with white fungal growth on underside of leaf.

Seedlings grown from infected seed are stunted, with mottling of the young leaves. Vein clearing, mottling, blistering and distortion occur on the leaves as the plant grows. Plants are dwarfed.

Yellow or white vein-banding makes veins appear prominent, especially at base of outer leaves. Distortion and puckering.

Marginal scorching of the leaves.

Leaves curled or blistered and plant stunted. Honeydew secretion forms sticky layer which holds dust and cast aphid skins on foliage. Some species penetrate to heart and spoil entire lettuce. Several species act as vectors of lettuce mosaic virus and cucumber mosaic virus. Pale or dull green colour, 2–2.5mm long.

Especially troublesome in frames. Foliage with ragged holes. Roots chewed. Slime trails visible, pests hide under cover during day.

Control

Pick off initially infected leaves. Avoid humid conditions by ventilating and giving a little warmth. Spray with thiram or zineb. Try resistant varieties.

Use mosaic-tested seed (containing less than 0.1% LMV). Spray with insecticide to control aphids which spread the disease.

Efficient sterilisation of the soil will kill the fungus (*Olpidium*) which carries the virus. Raising plants in pots of sterile soil before transplanting will delay infection.

Ensure adequate soil moisture during hot weather. Avoid applying excessive amounts of fertiliser.

See pest in (a).

Inspect regularly. Clear all aphid infested weeds and plant clean seedlings. Raise seedlings away from aphids and spray with demetion-S-methyl, dimethoate or malathion. Use above-sprays on growing crop giving thorough cover.

See pest in (a).

High organic matter and humidity encourage slugs. Remove weeds which give food and shelter. Use methiocarb or metaldehyde bait pellets, or spray soil with metaldehyde. May also be trapped under boxes, leaves, pots—then remove and destroy.

Symptoms

Elongated swellings on the roots and/or stem bases of seedlings and young plants.

Stem base shrivelled and brown. Leaves yellow progressively up plant.

Water-soaked spots with surrounding yellow halo on leaves, may coalesce to form brown necrotic areas. Pods similarly affected. Affected seeds may show blistering.

Foliage curled or distorted and flowers mis-shaped.

Control

Examine all plants carefully before transplanting and discard and burn any with unevenly thickened or swollen roots. Sterilise soil before using for seed sowing or potting. Ensure boxes and pots clean and free from contamination by the fungus.

Remove and destroy affected plants. Do not grow beans in soil for several years, or sterilise thoroughly before replanting in following year.

Do not sow blistered seed. Remove and destroy affected plants. Avoid overhead watering which spreads the bacteria. Spray with Bordeaux mixture. Resistant varieties are available.

Gamma-BHC smoke, gamma-BHC or malathion sprays.

Crop	Disorder
	Silver-Y-moth *Plusia gamma* (P)
	French-fly *Tyrophagus dimidiatus* (P)
	Symphilids *Scutigerella immaculata* (P)
Mint	Rust *Puccinia menthae* (F)
	Strawberry eelworm *Aphelenchoides fragariae* (P)
	Cuckoo spit *Cercopis sanguinea* (P)
Mustard and Cress	Damping-off *Rhizoctonia solani* *Pythium* spp (both F)
Rhubarb	Grey mould *Botrytis cinerea* (F)
	Rosy rustic moth *Hydraecia micacea* (P)
Vegetable marrow	Powdery mildew *Erysiphe cichoracearum* (F)
	Grey mould *Botrytis cinerea* (F)
	Mosaic Cucumber mosaic virus (V)
	Millepede *Oxidus gracillis* (P)
	Slugs and snails (P)

(e) **Fruits in pots and border**

Because of the protected cropping, at least for the period they are indoors, fruit trees in the greenhouse are probably less likely to contract the diseases which can seriously affect them out of doors. The most common disorder is probably powdery mildew, though grey mould can cause damage under humid stagnant conditions.

A wide range of outdoor pests may attack these crops but the ones most likely to be encountered are given in this table.

Crop	Disorder
Various fruit trees (and many herba- ceous and woody species)	Crown gall *Agrobacterium tumefaciens* (B)

Symptoms	*Control*
Holes chewed in foliage and frass granules on lower leaves. Caterpillars on plants in July about 15mm long; green body with dark brown head.	Spray with gamma-BHC.
	See pest in (b).
	See pest in (a).
Shoots and leaves thickened and distorted, on which yellow or brown, or, later in the season, black pustules are formed.	Plant runners from healthy bed only. Or spread straw on bed in autumn and burn. Lift runners and wash, then dip in water at 112°F (44.4°C) for 10 minutes. Wash in cold water and plant.
Black patches on foliage and distorted brittle shoots.	Try to obtain healthy plants. Runners for forcing can be treated by hot water method (10 minutes at 115°F (46.1°C) followed by rapid cooling).
Frothy masses on foliage and roots.	Drench soil with diazinon.
Dark, water-soaked lesions on stems at soil level. Plants collapse and die.	Sterilise seed boxes and propagating soil. Avoid over-watering, and check water supply for fungal contamination. For *Pythium*, water with Cheshunt compound. For *Rhizoctonia* mix quintozene with compost.
Soft brownish rotting of the leaves with grey fur of fungus growth.	Adequate ventilation will reduce the problem. Remove all mature sticks before they rot.
Tunnels in stems of mature plants. Foliage eaten.	Destroy plants and obtain new healthy stock.
	See disease in (b).
	See disease in (b).
Pale yellow wavy line or circle mottling on the leaves. Considerable puckering. Shortened internodes. Fruits mottled, with wart-like areas.	See disease in (b).
	See pest in (b).
	See pests in (c).

Symptoms	*Control*
More or less rounded growths with rough or smooth surface. Occur on both above- and below-ground parts of plant.	Destroy affected plants. Avoid damaging plants, as bacterium enters through wounds. Take care when grafting, particularly if crown gall present in nursery, by washing down benches with disinfectant and using clean knives etc. Cover graft unions with tape or wax.

Crop	Disorder
Apple	Powdery mildew *Podosphaera leucotricha* (F)
	Brown rot and blossom wilt *Sclerotinia fructigena* and *S. laxa* (both F)
	Scab *Venturia inaequalis* (F)
	Aphids Various spp (P)
	Common green capsid *Lygus pabulinus* (P)
	Fruit tree red spider mite *Panonychus ulmi* (P)
Apricot	Leaf curl *Taphrina deformans* (F)
	Brown rot and blossom wilt *Sclerotinia fructigena* and *S. laxa* (both F)
	Brown scale *Eulecanium corni* (P)
	Peach aphid *Appelia schwartzi* (P)
	Glasshouse red spider mite *Tetranychus urticae* (P)
	Walnut root-lesion nematode *Pratylenchus vulnus* (P)
Citrus fruits	Soft scale *Coccus hesperidium* (P)
	Palm thrips *Parthenothrips dracaenae* (P)
Fig	Canker *Phomopsis cinerescens* (F)

Symptoms	Control

Symptoms

Young shoots and leaves covered with white mealy mould. Infected leaves and blossoms wither and drop.

Cankers on branches. Withered flower trusses and spurs (blossom wilt). Fruits bearing greyish or buff-coloured sporing cushions, often in concentric circles. Fruits later mummified (brown rot).

Sooty blotches on leaves, and blistering of bark on twigs. Fruits bear dark scabs or spots and surface may be cracked. Sunken black saucer-shaped lesions on fruit in store.

Yellow or red discoloration, leaf curling or twig distortion and aphids visible.

Small holes in foliage which later turns brown. Misshaped fruit with scars.

Yellow specking of leaves later turning brown. Mites' eggs and cast skins visible on underside of leaves. Adult mites small 0.4mm long* red or yellow coloured.

Shoots stunted and covered in brown scales (3–6mm long). These scales do not move about on the shoot or twig but in a year or two completely cover the bark.

Severe leaf curl and leaf fall on young shoots. Globular brown aphids present.

See pest in (a).

Stunted plant with leaf chlorosis and poor root system.

Brown body 1.3mm long with yellow legs. Accumulate on foliage.

Canker lesion on branch, with bark roughened at site of infection. Branch may die if canker extensive.

Control

If feasible, pick off diseased young shoots in winter, and infected blossoms and buds in spring and summer. Spray with DNOC in petroleum oil in Dec–Jan, and with binapacryl, dinocap, lime sulphur, or benomyl from blossom time at weekly intervals until mid-July. Check that varieties are not susceptible before using copper or sulphur sprays.

Cut out cankers and infected spurs during spring or early summer when infection visible. Remove and destroy affected fruit and 'mummies', both on and off the tree. Pre-blossom spray with benomyl or lime sulphur (except on shy varieties) and tar oil winter washes will reduce blossom wilt. Control insects that can cause entry points for fungi.

Collect and burn fallen leaves. Prune and destroy diseased twigs before bud-burst. Spray with benomyl, lime sulphur, Bordeaux mixture, or other recommended fungicide at regular intervals from bud burst onwards. Check that varieties are not susceptible before using copper or sulphur sprays.

Use tar oil winter washes and spray prior to flowering with demeton-S-methyl, dimethoate or malathion.

Spray with gamma-BHC.

Use tar oil winter wash and summer sprays (just after petal fall) of demeton-S-methyl, dimethoate or malathion.

See disease on Peach in this section.

See disease on Apple in this section.

Treat when dormant with tar oil winter wash or try spray of diazinon in growing season.

After blossom apply spray of demeton-S-methyl, dimethoate or malathion. Repeat if further infestation occurs.

Apply spray of chlorbenside, chlorfenson, demeton-S-methyl or tetradifon in mid-May and 3 weeks later.

Remove plant and buy clean stock. Sterilise soil with D-D or use fresh soil.

See pest on Fig in this section.

Spray with diazinon, or nicotine.

Cut off and burn diseased branches, ensuring that no snags are left where infection can lodge. Paint wounds with suitable protectant paint (eg white lead).

Crop	Disorder
	Die-back and fruit rot *Botrytis cinerea* (F)
	Fig cyst nematode *Heterodera fici* (P)
	Soft scale *Coccus hesperidium* (P)
Grape vine	Powdery mildew *Uncinula necator* (F)
	Grey mould *Botrytis cinerea* (F)
	Shanking (Ph)
	Scald (Ph)
	Greenhouse mealy bug *Planococcus ciri* (P)
	Wingless weevils *Otiorrhynchus* spp (P)
Melon	Gummosis *Cladosporium cucumerinum* (F)
	Powdery mildew *Erysiphe cichoracearum* (F)
	Pests (P)
Nectarine	Leaf curl *Taphrina deformans* (F)
	Brown rot and blossom wilt *Sclerotinia fructigena* and *S. laxa* (both F)
	Pests (P)
Peach	Leaf curl *Taphrina deformans* (F)
	Powdery mildew *Sphaerotheca pannosa* f. *persicae* (F)
	Brown rot and blossom wilt *Sclerotinia fructigena* and *S. laxa* (both F)
	Pests (P)

Symptoms

Wilt and death of young shoots, and rotting of fruits which may remain mummified on the tree.

Lemon-shaped cysts* white to brown in colour protrude from roots.

Yellow/brown elongate—oval scales on midribs of leaves.

Grey or purplish areas on the leaves with powdery white patches of fungus both there and on the shoots. Flowers and young fruit may fall, and berries may be cracked.

Berries at tips of bunches develop spots and later wither. Berry stalks turn rusty colour. Fruits bitter.

Berries have scorched appearance.

Stunted growth foliage covered in stationary scales with mealy wax threads. Underneath many small yellow elliptical eggs.*

Wilting foliage and damaged roots together with U-shaped notches on foliage. White, crescent-shaped, legless grubs (5mm long) in soil. Adults nocturnal, climb foliage to feed.

Leaves distorted, thickened and yellowed. With tinges of red. Becoming darker red later, then wither and drop. Common outdoors but infrequent in the greenhouse.

Infected shoots stunted with narrow leaves. Powdery growth on leaves and shoots.

Control

See Grey mould in Table I (g).

Destroy plant and buy 'clean' replacements.

Spray with malathion.

Avoid overcrowding and checks to growth (eg too dry atmosphere or marked changes of temperature). Ensure adequate ventilation without draughts. Spray with dinocap or sulphur (i) when laterals are 12–15in long, (ii) just before flowers open, (iii) after berries have set. Spray when temperature not too high.

See Grey mould in Table I (g).

Remove affected trusses. Ensure adequate moisture and nutrient available to the roots. Do not allow too much fruit to develop, as shanking worst on overladen vines.

Avoid excessive sunlight and high temperature early in the day.

Spray with diazinon before berries swell, otherwise 'bloom' will be spoiled.

Drench soil and base of plant with gamma-BHC. Apply gamma-BHC dust to soil around plant.

See disease in (b).

See disease in (b).

See pests in (b).

See disease on Peach in this section.

See disease on Apple in this section.

See pests on Apricot in this section.

Pick off affected leaves and gather fallen leaves and burn. Spray before bud burst and after leaf fall with a proprietary copper spray or with lime sulphur.

Spray with proprietary sulphur fungicide, dinocap or quinomethionate at regular intervals.

See disease on Apple in this section.

See pests on Apricot in this section.

Crop	Disorder
Pear	Powdery mildew *Podosphaera leucotricha* (F)
	Scab *Venturia pirina* (F)
	Pests (P)
Plum	Rust *Puccinia pruni-spinosae* (F)
	Brown rot and blossom wilt *Sclerotinia fructigena* and *S. laxa* (both F)
	Pests (P)
Strawberry	Powdery mildew *Sphaerotheca macularis* (F)
	Grey mould *Botrytis cinerea* (F)
	Arabis mosaic Arabis mosaic virus (V)
	Other virus diseases, including yellow edge and crinkle viruses and green petal virus
	Strawberry aphid *Chaetosiphon fragaefolii*
	Shallot aphid *Myzus ascalonicus* (both P)
	Wingless weevils *Otiorrhynchus* spp (P)
	Glasshouse red spider mite *Tetranychus urticae* (P)
	Strawberry mite *Steneotarsonemus pallidus* (P)
	Stem eelworm *Ditylenchus dipsaci* (P)
	Leaf and bud eelworms *Aphelenchoides ritzemabosi*, *A. fragaeriae* (P)

Symptoms	*Control*
See disease on Apple in this section.	Spray from petal fall onwards as required with any of the fungicides used against apple mildew.
Dark brown velvety patches on leaves. Young shoots and flowers also affected. Similar scabs on fruits which may be misshapen and one-sided.	See Scab on Apple in this section.
	See pests on Apple in this section.
Yellowish spots on upper surface of leaves, and brown spots on lower surface.	Pick off initially affected leaves. Spray with Bordeaux mixture or a proprietary copper fungicide. Check infection on anemones.
	See disease on Apple in this section.
	See pests on Apple in this section.
	See pests on Apple in this section.
Dark areas on upper surface of leaves, with greyish powdery growth on underside. Leaf margins may curl upwards exposing undersides. Pedicils, flowers and fruits may be affected.	Spray with dinocap, lime sulphur, sulphur or benomyl at 10–14 day intervals from just before flowering onwards. Do not continue sulphur or lime sulphur when fruit commences ripening.
Soft rot of the flowers and fruits, with smoky grey fur of mould.	Avoid over-damp conditions around the plants. Spray with benomyl, captan or thiram at 10 day intervals from early flowering to harvest.
In late spring and autumn, yellow spots (bright red in some varieties) or blotches appear on the leaves. Distortion of the leaves, and dwarfing may occur.	Destroy affected plants. Kill eelworm vector *(Xiphenema diversicaudatum)* by DD injection in the autumn, or by incorporation of dazomet. Avoid replanting with infected runners.
Various symptoms, including chlorosis, distortion and stunting of the plants. Sepals enlarged, petals dwarfed and green with green petal virus.	Destroy affected plants. Control aphids since some of the viruses are aphid-transmitted.
Leaves curled and distorted and pale yellow or greenish brown aphids visible.	Spray with demeton-S-methyl, dimethoate or malathion prior to flowering and after picking is complete.
	See pest on Grape vine in this section.
	See pest in (a).
Very small* colourless mites feed on young folded leaflets causing them to remain small and wrinkled. Other leaves silvery brown.	Spray with dicofol 3 times at 28 day intervals from first signs of damage. Remove damaged leaves.
Leaflets crinkled, margins turned down, midribs underneath puffy and enlarged. Leaf and flower stalks short and swollen.	
Leaflets small and distorted with rough grey/brown areas. Leaves are almost hairless and stalks elongated. Main growth may be killed. Eelworms microscopic.	Always buy certified SS or A plants. Treat infested runners in hot water 46°C for 10 minutes (this will also control strawberry mite). Do not use eelworm infested soil for growing.

(f) Bedding plants

A wide variety of disorders affect plants used for bedding purposes, but most of them only occur after the plants have been set out. During the period prior to transplanting, the seedlings, cuttings and young plants are prone to the following diseases and pest infestations:

Disorder

Damping-off, stem and root rots
Pythium spp, *Rhizoctonia solani*, *Phyto-phthora* spp, *Thielaviopsis basicola* (all F)

Grey mould
Botrytis cinerea (F)

Slaters or woodlice, Symphilids
Various spp (P)

Millepedes, Slugs
Various spp (P)

(g) Herbaceous plants and shrubs in pots or border

Table I *Diseases which may occur on many crops*

Disorder

Damping-off and root rots
Pythium spp, *Rhizoctonia solani*, *Phyto-phthora* spp, *Thielaviopsis basicola* (all F)

Grey mould
Botrytis cinerea (F)

Powdery mildews
Various species of fungi including
Erysiphe, Sphaerotheca, etc (F)

Leaf spots
Various species of fungi including
Septoria, Cercospora, Phyllosticta etc (all F)

Springtails, Slaters (woodlice), Symphilids
Various spp (P)

Symptoms

Water-soaked lesions and shrivelling of tissue of stem at soil level. Plant unthrifty and may wilt, turn yellow and finally wither and die. Roots appear brown or blackened and rotted.

Control

Use sterilised soil in seed and potting compost, or use proprietary soilless mixes; ensure composts uniformly mixed. Sterilise seed boxes and pots. Check water supply from static tanks for fungal contamination; sterilise tank with potassium permanganate (1lb in 500 gal water). Sow seed thinly to avoid overcrowding. Do not over-water seedlings or allow them to dry out. Raise plants at recommended temperatures. If *Rhizoctonia* suspected, incorporate quintozene in compost before sowing. For other fungi, remove infected seedlings and water the remainder with Cheshunt compound or other proprietary copper fungicide. A drench with benomyl may be effective against *Rhizoctonia* and *Thielaviopsis*.

Soft wet rot of seedlings or rotting cuttings with development of smoky grey fur of fungal growth.

Avoid overcrowding and delay in pricking-out of seedlings. Remove diseased tissue carefully and destroy. Give adequate ventilation and warmth to create a buoyant atmosphere. Spray or dust with captan or thiram. Spray with benomyl, or use a tecnazene smoke. Dichlofluanid sprays may be useful.

See pests in (a).

See pests in (b).

Symptoms

Control

See Damping-off, stem and root rots in (f).

Soft rotting of the tissues, which later become covered with smoky grey fur of fungal growth. Spots may occur on leaves and flowers, which may later rot.

Remove diseased, moribund or dead tissue and destroy. Avoid overcrowding. Give adequate ventilation and warmth to create a buoyant atmosphere. Spray or dust with captan or thiram. Spray with benomyl or use tecnazene smoke. Dichlofluanid may also be used.

White powdery growth on shoots and surface of leaves. May cause some distortion and discoloration of the foliage.

Take care with watering to avoid drying out. Remove initially infected leaves. Spray regularly with sulphur, lime sulphur, dinocap, quinomethionate or benomyl. Check for toxicity of chemical to particular crop.

Localised separate spots of dead tissue, sometimes surrounded by a pale green or yellow halo. May coalesce to form larger areas of dead tissue.

Remove and burn affected leaves. Protectant sprays with copper or dithiocarbamate fungicides may be helpful. Check for any phytotoxicity before using extensively.

See pests in (a).

409

Disorder

Millepedes
Various spp (P)

Leatherjacket
Tipula spp (P)

Cutworms
Various spp (P)

Mice (P)

Table II *Diseases on specific crops*

Crop	Disorder
Abutilon	Variegation Abutilon mosaic virus (V)
	Mealy bug *Pseudococcus latipes* (P)
Achimenes	Chlorotic leaf spots (Ph)
Aloe	Mealy bug *Rhizoecus elongatus* (P)
Antirrhinum	Downy mildew *Peronospora antirrhini* (F)
	Rust *Puccinia antirrhini* (F)
	Peach-potato aphid *Myzus persicae* (P)
Asparagus plumosus nana and *A. sprengeri*	Basal rot *Pythium* sp (F)
	Root rot *Fusarium* sp (F)
	Yellowing (Ph)
Azalea	Gall *Exobasidium vaccinii* (F)
	Grey mould *Botrytis cinerea* (F)
	Chlorosis Iron deficiency (Ph)
	Bud drop (Ph)
	Glasshouse thrips *Heliothrips haemorrhoidalis* (P)
	Glasshouse whitefly *Trialeurodes vaporariorum* (P)

410

Symptoms	*Control*
	See pest in (b).
Plants wilting or chopped through stem near soil. Large dark grey 25–30mm wrinkled legless grubs present in soil.	Spray with gamma-BHC or fenitrothion. Use poison bran baits or pellets.
Stem cut through at, or just below, soil level. Large 25–30mm long green-brown caterpillars in soil.	Spray or dust with gamma-BHC.
Stems and foliage nibbled. Holes visible.	Use traps and/or poison baits.

Symptoms	*Control*
Variegation of the leaf coloration.	Since the virus causes the appearance of the desirable variegation feature, no control measures are required.
Twisted foliage and large colonies of pest.	Spray with demeton-S-methyl or malathion.
Pale ring-like spots may develop on the leaves.	See Saintpaulia chlorotic leaf spots in this section.
Small yellow structures on roots of plant covered in white wax. Plant showing poor growth.	'Quarantine' plant and treat soil with dilute wash of diazinon. Repeat at 14 days.
Plants stunted. Leaves curled with grey felty growth on underside.	Sterilise seed boxes. Destroy initially infected plants. Avoid cool humid atmosphere by ventilating and giving some warmth. Spray with zineb, thiram or copper fungicide.
Dark brown pustules on leaves.	Remove initially infected leaves. Spray with zineb or maneb.
Stunted plants with pink/yellow aphids (2mm) visible.	Spray with demeton-S-methyl, or malathion.
	See Damping-off, stem and root rots in (f).

Plant becomes yellow and dry. Basal shoots wither and die.	Sterilisation of border soil essential, by steaming if possible.
Tops become yellowed.	Often due to over-watering during winter or to an excessive amount of lime.
Small hard reddish swellings on leaves and flower buds, later become covered with white bloom of spores.	Remove and burn affected parts before the white bloom develops. Spray with Bordeaux mixture or other copper fungicide.
Flowers rot and are covered with grey fur of fungus.	See Grey mould in Table I in this section.
Yellowing between the veins, particularly on the younger leaves.	Water with chelated iron solution at recommended rate.
Flowers drop without opening.	Avoid draughts and marked changes of temperature. Ensure adequate but not over-watering.
Flowers and young leaves show patches or streaks of white. Small adults (1.5mm) brown in colour and yellow larvae found on plant.	Gamma-BHC or malathion smokes. Two applications at 14 day intervals.
	See pest in (a).

Crop	Disorder
Begonia	Grey mould *Botrytis cinerea* (F)
	Root and stem rots Various fungi
	Powdery mildew *Oidium begoniae* (F)
	Bacterial blight (on winter- flowering vars) *Xanthomonas begoniae* (B)
	Ringspot Tomato spotted wilt virus (V)
	Mosaic Cucumber mosaic virus (V)
	Glasshouse whitefly *Trialeurodes vaporariorum* (P)
	Broad mite *Hemitarsonemus latus* (P)
	Greedy scale *Hemiberlesia rapax* (P)
Cacti	Root and stem base rots *Pythium* sp (F) *Phytophthora* spp (F)
	Glassiness (Ph)
	Corky scab (Ph)
	False red spider mites *Brevipalpus* spp (P)
	Many pests including Scale insects, eg Greedy scale (P)
	Mealy bugs *Pseudococcus citri* and *P.* *longispimus* (P)
	Root mealy bugs *Rhizoecus* spp (P)
Calceolaria	Root rots *Phytophthora* sp, *Thiela-* *viopsis basicola* (both F)
	Spotted wilt Tomato spotted wilt virus (V)

Symptoms	*Control*
Leaves, stems and flowers may be infected.	See Grey mould in Table I in this section.
	See Damping-off, stem and root rots in (f).
See Powdery mildew in Table I in this section.	Care should be taken in the choice of fungicide as some varieties may be slightly damaged.
Brown spots with yellow translucent margins scattered on the leaves, which may fall prematurely. Stem may be attacked and plant die. Yellow bacterial slime may ooze from petiole when broken.	Destroy affected plants and thoroughly cleanse benches and pots. Avoid overhead watering if disease present. Keep pots well spaced. Select cuttings from healthy plants. Spray plants with Bordeaux mixture or other copper fungicide. Dip cuttings in fungicide.
Plants weak. Ring markings on leaf.	Destroy affected plants. Control thrips, which spread the virus, with insecticide. Cleanse and fumigate the greenhouse.
Yellow areas, with brown spotting, between the veins.	Destroy affected plants. Control aphids, which spread the virus, with insecticide. Cleanse and fumigate the greenhouse.
	See pest in (a).
Young leaves puckered and turned down. Sometimes brittle. Adults* visible in folds of leaves, light brown/grey.	Repeat sprays of dicofol, or use weekly light dustings of flowers of sulphur.
Small (2mm) scales with distinct cone on leaves and stem.	Spray with malathion.
	See Damping-off, stem and root rots in (f).
Dark green translucent spots, which later may become black. Decay may follow.	Decrease humidity and increase lighting. Note that some species are sensitive to excessive light.
Corky spots on stems of many species (especially *Opuntia*). Shoots may be so badly affected as to be killed. Surface tissues crack and curl back.	See Glassiness above.
Damage as red spider mite, but mites very small. Grey dry patches on skin.	Apply dicofol at 7 day intervals (not Epiphyllums).
See Begonia in this section.	Use demeton-S-methyl.
Soft oval scales with white wax and filaments.	Use several washes of nicotine or malathion (if tolerant).
See Aloe in this section.	Diazinon wash. (Care!)
	See Damping-off, stem and root rots in (f).
Plants stunted and distorted. Pale irregular blotches, or mottling and streaking on leaves. Flowers reduced and distorted.	See Begonia ringspot in this section.

Crop	Disorder
	Glasshouse whitefly *Trialeurodes vaporariorum* (P)
	Glasshouse-potato aphid *Aulacorthum solani* (P)
Callistephus (China Aster)	Damping-off, stem and root rots *Phytophthora* spp, *Rhizoctonia solani, Thiela- viopsis basicola* (all F)
	Wilt *Fusarium oxysporum* f. sp *callistephi, Verticillium albo-atrum* (both F)
	Peach-potato aphid *Myzus persicae* (P)
Camellia	Leaf blotch or spot *Pestalotia guepini* (F)
	Bud shedding (Ph)
	Scale insects, Mealy bugs Various spp (P)
Cineraria	Powdery mildew *Oidium* sp (F)
	Wilt *Phytophthora* spp (F)
	Grey mould *Botrytis cinerea* (F)
	Glasshouse red spider mite *Tetranychus urticae* (P)
	Aphids Various (P)
Cissus	Broad mite *Hemitarsonemus latus* (P)
Cyclamen	Grey mould *Botrytis cinerea* (F)
	Black root rot *Thielaviopsis basicola* (F)
	Mottled arum aphid *Aulacorthum circumflexum* (P)
	Vine weevil *Otiorrhynchus sulcatus* (P)
	Cyclamen mite *Steneotarsonemus pallidus* (P)
Daphne	Mosaic Cucumber mosaic virus (V)
Dracaena	Leaf spots *Macrophoma draconis* (F)

Symptoms	Control
	See pest in (a).
	See pest in (a) but care with malathion.
	See Damping-off, stem and root rots in (f).
Blackening at base of stem with *Fusarium,* but much less discoloration with *Verticillium.* Plant wilts from base upwards and leaves turn yellow.	Ensure adequate sterilisation of border soil if diseases suspected.
	See Antirrhimum in this section.
Roundish brown or grey spots or blotches on the leaves.	Remove and burn diseased leaves.
Buds drop off.	Avoid sudden changes of growing conditions, eg drought, over-watering, draughts, high or low temperature, or excess nitrogen, etc.
	See Cacti in this section.
See Powdery mildew in Table I of this section.	Formulations of dimethirimol are reported to be effective.
Root and stem base rot, resulting in wilting of the plant.	See Damping-off, stem and root rots in (f).
	See Grey mould in Table I in this section.
	See pest in (a).
Discoloration and honeydew spoilage.	Malathion spray.
	See Begonia in this section.
Spotting on the flowers.	See Grey mould in Table I in this section.
Plants become yellowed and unthrifty. Roots rotted and black.	Use sterilised soil for compost. Water with captan or benomyl at intervals.
Flowers and foliage infested with bright green aphid and much honeydew present.	Spray with demeton-S-methyl or malathion.
Marked stunted growth.	See pest on vines in (e).
Outer leaves curled upward. Flower buds rot or wither. Mites very difficult to see*.	See pest on strawberry in (e).
Pale yellow mottle of the foliage, with chlorotic spots, rings and flecks. Plants may be somewhat stunted.	Spray with insecticide to control aphid vectors.
	See Leaf spots in Table I in this section.

415

Crop	Disorder
	Palm thrips *Parthenotrips dracaene* (P)
	Oleander scale *Dynaspidiotus britannicus* (P)
	Mealy bugs Various spp
Euonymous	Powdery mildew *Oidium euonymi-japonici* (F)
	Bean aphid *Aphis fabae* (P)
Euphorbia (Poinsettia)	Damping-off Various fungi
	Black root rot *Thielaviopsis basicola* (F)
Fuchsia	Grey mould *Botrytis cinerea* (F)
Gardenia	Stem canker *Phomopsis gardeniae* (F)
	Grey mould *Botrytis cinerea* (F)
	Chlorosis (Ph)
	Mealy bugs Various spp (P)
	False red spider mites
Gloxinia	Foot rot and corm rot. *Phytophthora parasitica*, *P. cryptogea* (both F)
Hippeastrum (amaryllis)	Leaf scorch or tip burn *Stagonospora curtisii* (F)
	Mealybugs *Planococcus* spp (P)
Hydrangea	Damping-off *Rhizoctonia solani* (F)
	Grey mould *Botrytis cinerea* (F)
	Powdery mildew *Microsphaera polonica* (F)
	Chlorosis (Ph)

Symptoms	Control
Foliage discoloured with very small (1.3mm) yellow and brown adults visible.*	Gamma-BHC smokes or dusts, or malathion sprays.
Light brown convex scales 2mm diameter.	Spray with diazinon at 14 day intervals.
	See pest on Cacti in this section.
	See Powdery mildew in Table I in this section.
Black eggs and adults clustered on twigs and foliage.	Spray with malathion.
	See Damping-off, stem and root rots in (f).
See Damping-off, stem and root rots in (f).	A post-planting drench with benomyl in place of the first watering is recommended against this disease.
Flowers may be rotted under very damp conditions.	See Grey mould in Table I in this section.
Brown area on stem near soil level, at first sunken, but later swelling and having a rough cracked surface. Branches also affected. Plant may be stunted or even die.	Destroy infected plants. Take cuttings from healthy plants. Ensure that rooting medium is sterile. When cutting blooms, do not leave snags where the fungus can enter. A spray with a dithiocarbamate fungicide may help to prevent infection.
	See Grey mould in Table I in this section.
Leaves become yellow.	Keep soil on the acid side (less than pH 7) and temperature above 68°F (20°C). If chlorosis due to iron deficiency, apply chelated iron to the soil.
	See pest on Hippeastrum below.
	See pest on Cacti in this section.
Rotting at base of plant spreads into the corm, and up into the leaves and flower stalks.	Remove and destroy the affected plants.
Purplish to red spots, or streaks of varying size on the leaves. Spotting also on flower stems and petioles. Infected bulbs small.	Discard suspected bulbs, or dip in 0.8% formaldehyde for 1 hour. Destroy affected parts. Avoid over-watering. Spray at shoot emergence, and at first sign of disease with zineb, mancozeb or copper fungicide to prevent spread.
Poor growth pest found in scales of dormant bulb and in neck of foliage.	Drench with demeton-S-methyl or malathion.
Cuttings liable to collapse under damp conditions in infected soil.	See Damping-off, stem and root rots in (f).
Rotting of flower heads.	See Grey mould in Table I in this section.
	See Powdery mildew in Table I in this section.
Yellowing of the leaves and pale colouring of the flowers.	Avoid alkaline conditions. Water with chelated iron to correct induced deficiency.

Crop	Disorder
Kalanchoe	Stem rots *Pythium* sp and *Rhizoctonia* sp (F)
	Powdery mildew *Erysiphe polyphaga* (F)
Matthiola (Stock)	Clubroot *Plasmodiophora brassicae* (F)
	Downy mildew *Peronospora parasitica* (F)
	Mosaic diseases Stock mosaic virus, Turnip mosaic virus, Cauliflower mosaic virus (all V)
Pelargonium	Rust *Puccinia pelargonii-zonalis* (F)
	Grey mould *Botrytis cinerea* (F)
	Blackleg *Pythium* spp (F)
	Black root rot *Thielaviopsis basicola* (F)
	Bacterial leafspot and stem rot *Xanthomonas pelargonii* (B)
	Leaf curl Pelargonium leaf curl virus (V)
	Ringspot Pelargonium ringspot virus (V)
	Glasshouse potato aphid *Aulacorthum solani* (P)
	Cyclamen mite *Steneotarsonemus pallidus* (P)
Peperomia	Ringspot Possibly cucumber mosaic virus (V)
Primula	Root rots *Pythium* spp, *Rhizoctonia* spp, *Thielaviopsis basicola* (all F)

Symptoms	*Control*
Rotting of stems at soil level.	See Damping-off, stem and root rots in (f).

See Powdery mildew in Table I in this section.

See disease on Brassicas in (d).

Leaves may be distorted, with fungal growth on under surface.	Reduce humidity by ventilation and some warmth. Spray with zineb, maneb, mancozeb, thiram, or a copper fungicide. Dichlofluanid may also be effective.
Mottling of the leaves and 'breaking' of the flowers. Plants may be stunted and distorted.	Destroy affected plants. Spray with insecticide to control aphid vectors.
Brown erumpent spore masses in concentric rings mainly on lower surface of leaves. Yellowish areas on upper surfaces.	Pick off and burn affected leaves. Destroy severely affected plants. Spray at least fortnightly with zineb, maneb, mancozeb or thiram. Grow plants on the dry side. Cuttings can be freed from infection by allowing them to wilt and then putting in a polythene bag at 100°F (38°C) for 48 hours. Remove basal 1 in of cutting before striking the cutting.
See Table I in this section.	Spray with dichlofluanid or benomyl. Reduce humidity.
Soft black rot of stem. Roots also rotted.	Take cuttings from healthy stock plants. See Damping-off, stem and root rots in (f) for general hygiene.
Plants turn yellowish and wilt. Roots show black rotting.	See Damping-off, stem and root rots in (f). Watering soil with benomyl may control this disease.
Slightly sunken water-soaked, later brown, spots on leaves. Water-soaked lesions near stem apex, spread slowly up and **down** and darken. Finally stems dry and shrunken. Cuttings infected at base appear similar to those infected by blackleg.	Check that stock plants healthy before taking cuttings. Ivy-leaved pelargoniums can be symptomless carriers, so keep away from other varieties. See Damping-off, Stem and Root rots in (f) for general hygiene.
Small pale green or yellowish spots, sometimes becoming star-shaped, on leaves. Leaves more or less crinkled and distorted. Symptoms most pronounced in spring.	Rogue out symptom-bearing plants in spring. Select plants from symptomless stock plants. Give good growing conditions, as starvation and drought will accentuate symptom expression.
Light green spots and ringspots on the leaves. Plants may be stunted.	Same as for Pelargonium leaf curl above.

See pest in (a).

See pest on Cyclamen in this section.

| Plant stunted, with distorted leaves bearing chlorotic or necrotic rings. | Discard affected plants. Insecticidal sprays control aphids which may spread the disease. |

See Damping-off, stem and root rots in (f).

Crop	Disorder
	Grey mould *Botrytis cinerea*
	Glasshouse whitefly *Trialeurodes vaporariorum* (P)
	Bryobia mite *Bryobia* spp (P)
Saintpaulia	Grey mould *Botrytis cinerea* (F)
	Crown rot *Pythium ultimum* (F)
	Chlorotic leaf spots (Ph)
	Cyclamen mite *Steneotarsonemus pallidus* (P)
Salvia	Glasshouse leaf hopper *Zygina pallidifrons* (P)
	Glasshouse whitefly *Trialeurodes vaporariorum* (P)
Zantedeschia (Arum lily)	Leaf spots Various fungi (F)
	Corm rot *Bacterium aroideae* and *B. carotovorum* (both B)
	Spotted wilt Tomato spotted wilt virus (V)
Zinnia	Grey mould *Botrytis cinerea* (F)
	Seedling blight *Alternaria zinniae* (F)

(h) Roses

Disorder

Grey mould
Botrytis cinerea (F)

Powdery mildew
Sphaerotheca pannosa (F)

Black spot
Diplocarpon rosae (F)

Symptoms	*Control*
	See Grey mould in Table I in this section.
See pest in (a)	(Don't spray under direct sun or when pots are very dry.)
Large numbers of green globular mites with hairy bodies.	Spray with malathion, demeton-S-methyl or dicofol.
	See Grey mould in Table I in this section.
Leaves wilt and plant becomes soft.	Destroy badly affected plants. Take healthy leaf cuttings. Use sterilised soil for rooting. Do not overcrowd or over-water.
Irregular yellowish rings and lines on the leaves.	Water from below. Avoid overhead watering, particularly with cold water. Shade from bright sun.
	See Cyclamen this section, but avoid flowers and do not spray in sunshine.
White or yellow spots on foliage which may extend to form bleached area. Adults (3mm long) are slender and angular, pale yellow with dark V bands on back.	Gamma-BHC smokes at 14–28 day intervals.
	See pest in (a).
Necrotic spots of various types on leaves, petioles, flower stalks or white spathes.	See Leaf spots in Table I in this section.
Soft rot of corm. Plant wilts and dies.	Destroy infected plants. Thoroughly clean and disinfect benches on which plants will stand. Wash down or fumigate greenhouse.
Leaves may be distorted. Whitish, later brown, spots and streaks. Flowers mis-shapen. Spread by thrips.	Control thrips with insecticides.
Particularly damaging to the flower buds and open flowers, causing rotting. Stems and leaves also affected.	Remove diseased leaves and flowers regularly. Reduce humidity. Dust with tecnazene at regular intervals.
Dark brown cankers on the stems and somewhat angular reddish-brown spots on the leaves.	The fungus is seed-borne, and a seed-dressing with captan will reduce infection. Spray seedlings with zineb or proprietary copper fungicides.

Symptoms	*Control*
Brown spotting of the petals and rotting of the blooms under excessively humid conditions.	See Grey mould in Table I (g). Ensure adequate potash levels in the soil.
	See Powdery mildew in Table I in (g)
Purple or black blotches with ragged margins on upper surface of leaves. Leaves turn yellow and are shed prematurely. Occasional under glass.	Pick off and burn initially infected leaves. Spray at first sign of disease (or if disease present previously, after pruning) with captan, maneb, mancozeb/zineb or dichlofluanid. Repeat at fortnightly intervals if disease persists.

(i) **Carnations**

Methods are now available for detecting the presence of the various bacterial and fungal wilts in carnation cuttings so that only healthy ones are selected for propagation. Similarly, by heat treatment of cuttings and subsequent culture of excised meristem tips, virus-free carnation clones can be established. Since equipment and expertise are required for both these techniques, they should only be considered by the grower of commercial stocks (full details of the methods are given in the MAFF Bulletin No 151, *A Manual of Carnation Production*). The amateur gardener can protect his stocks by obtaining cuttings which have been indexed for the above disorders.

Symptoms	*Control*
Orange pustules on the leaves during the summer, with darker brown ones later in the year. Occurs infrequently under glass.	Remove and burn infected leaves. Spray regularly with maneb, mancozeb/zineb, or thiram if disease observed. Control rust on nearby outdoor roses, as above, also particularly destroy winter prunings.
Red-brown or purplish areas on young green wood of stem, later forming a canker with a rough irregular margin. Darker brown lesions and cankers can also affect the point of grafting.	Cut away and burn diseased tissues. Take care when grafting to avoid leaving unprotected wounds through which infection can take place. Use proprietary paint to protect wounds. Fungicide sprays of little use.
Irregular yellowish-grey or purple spots on upper surface of leaf, with grey fungus beneath. Flowers and flower stalks may be spotted.	Avoid high humidity and condensation at night by giving adequate ventilation and warmth. Collect and burn fallen leaves. Spray at regular intervals with copper/petroleum oil emulsion, or zineb.
General yellowing of the leaves.	May be a lime-induced iron deficiency. Soil pH can be lowered by incorporation of sulphur. Water chelated-iron solution onto soil.
Stems spotted with white circular and oblong scales (3mm diameter) with red-brown larveal skin in the centre.	Diazinon or malathion sprays repeated at 21 day intervals.
2mm long green/yellow clusters on foliage.	Spray with malathion or demeton-S-methyl or dimethoate.
3mm long pink/green on young buds.	Spray with malathion or demeton-S-methyl or dimethoate.
See pest in (a).	*Do not* smoke with azobenzene.
Stunting of growth and poor roots with small galls due to pest in soil.	Remove affected plants and sterilise or remove soil.

Symptoms	*Control*
Cuttings or newly-rooted plants may be attacked. Lesion at stem base may be pale or dark brown, depending on causal fungus. Stem breaks at a node at or just above soil level with *Rhizoctonia* infection. Orange or pink pustules may be present on cutting stems with *Fusarium* infection. Small purple leaf spots, which may enlarge to brown necrotic areas with purple margins, are caused by *Alternaria*.	Ensure thorough soil sterilisation. Avoid over-watering. Maintain buoyant atmosphere. Incorporation of quinto-zene into top 3–4in of border soil before planting will control *Rhizoctonia*. Spray stock plants with captan or maneb at 7–10 day intervals. Select cuttings from healthy plants and spray or drench with captan during rooting. Spray with zineb, maneb, mancozeb or thiram against *Alternaria*.

Disorder

Grey mould
Botrytis cinerea (F)

Powdery mildew
Oidium sp (F)

Wilts
1 *Phialophora cinerescens* (F)

2 *Fusarium oxysporum* f. sp *dianthi*
F. redolens (both F)

3 Slow wilt
Erwinia chrysanthemi (B)

Rust
Uromyces dianthi (F)

Greasy blotch
Zygophiala jamaicensis (F)

Anther smut
Ustilago violacea (F)

Fairy ring spot
Didymellina dianthi (F)

Virus diseases
Various viruses (V)

Split calyx (Ph)

Hollow flowers (Ph)

Onion thrips
Thrips tabaci (P)

Glasshouse-potato aphid
Anlacorthum solani (P)

Peach-potato aphid
Myzus persicae (P)

Carnation tortrix moth
Cacoecimorpha pronubana (P)

Red spider mite
Tetranychus cinnabarinus (P)

Symptoms	Control
Rotting of stems, with wilting of the shoots. Fluffy fungal growth may be visible. Petals rot and flowers may be destroyed.	See Grey mould in Table I (g).
Whitish powder on the leaves and occasionally on the calyces.	See Powdery mildew in Table I (g)
Rapid, and often initially one-sided wilting. Plants become greyish-green, with the affected leaves purplish-red. Gradually die and become straw-coloured. Vascular tissues brown. Plants do not pull up easily, as roots not rotted. Plants show slight chlorosis, with affected leaves purplish-red. Effect often one-sided. Vascular tissues brown. Plants pull up easily as roots rotted. Die fairly quickly. Infected plants grow very slowly compared with healthy plants. Wilting gradual and death may take 6–8 months.	Take cuttings from healthy plants or obtain indexed material. Use disinfected cutting boxes and sterilised soil for compost. Sterilise the border soil. Disinfect house if *Fusarium* present previously. If wilt appears in a small area, immediately remove affected plants and those for about 3ft around. Remove soil to 2ft depth and sterilise with formalin drench. Fill with clean soil. For more widespread infections, mark affected area and cultivate deeply after clearance of crop. Sterilise with metham-sodium or formalin, followed if possible by thorough steaming. Soil drenches with benomyl will contain *Fusarium* or *Phialophora* infection.
Brown pustules on stems, leaves and flower calyces. Cuttings may be infected.	Select cuttings from healthy plants. Destroy badly affected plants and leaves on less severely infected ones. Reduce humidity and overhead watering. Spray at 10–14 day intervals with mancozeb/zineb, thiram or zineb.
Web-like patches on the leaves, may extend to give the surface an oily appearance.	Reduce atmospheric humidity.
Plants stunted with many weak side shoots, giving a bushy habit. Flower buds short, and calyces tend to split. Flowers have black sooty appearance due to fungus spores replacing pollen.	Remove diseased plants before flowering. Take cuttings only from healthy plants, since fungus is systemic in infected plants.
Round or oval brown spots on the leaves and stems. Dark powdery spores produced in concentric rings on the lesions.	Reduce atmospheric humidity. Spray with zineb.
Symptoms range from slight or moderate mottling to more or less severe necrotic flecks and rings, or streaks of red or yellow on the leaves.	Most of the viruses are spread by handling and/or by aphids. Rogue diseased plants, and spray with insecticide to control aphids.
Calyx splits down side, petals spill outwards, so that flower loses its compact shape. Associated with the formation of additional whorls of petals which cannot be contained.	Select non-splitting varieties. Control of day and night temperatures, to avoid marked and rapid changes which stimulate production of secondary whorls of petals.
Number of petals reduced so that flower appears 'single'.	Maintain adequate watering and prevent excessively high temperature by ventilation.
	See pest in (a).
	See pest in (a).
	See pest in (a).
Young shoots and leaves spun together into tents by green caterpillars. Pupa, black, in foliage. Flower buds also attacked.	Difficult to control but use repeated sprays of gamma-BHC.
Small white spots and later leaves become pale. Red/brown mites just visible.	Spray with diazinon, dimethoate, or formothion.

425

(j) Chrysanthemums

Disorder

Root rots
Phytophthora spp, *Rhizoctonia solani*,
Fusarium spp, *Thielaviopsis basicola* (all F)

Root rot
Phoma sp (F)

Stem rot
Sclerotinia sclerotiorum (F)

Grey mould
Botrytis cinerea (F)

Petal blight
Itersonilia perplexans (F)

Powdery mildew
Oidium chrysanthemi (F)

Ray blight
Mycosphaerella ligulicola (F)

Rust
Puccinia chrysanthemi (F)

Wilt
Verticillium albo-atrum, V. dahliae (F)

Aspermy. Flower distortion
Tomato aspermy virus (V)

Stunt
Crysanthemum stunt virus (V)

Other virus diseases (V)

Mineral deficiencies (Ph)

Earwig
Forficula auricularia (P)

Glasshouse whitefly
Trialeurodes vaporariorium (P)

Peach-potato aphid
Myzus persicae (P)

Symptoms	*Control*
Rotting of roots on cuttings and older plants.	See Damping-off, stem and root rots in (f).
Plants stunted, with yellowing of lower leaves. Stem may crack at soil level. Pink flecks on roots which rot.	Sterilise border soil thoroughly, or drench with nabam before planting. An attack may be contained by drenching the soil with nabam at 7–10 day intervals in place of the normal watering. Captan or zineb similarly applied may also be useful in this respect.
Light brown lesion on stem becomes covered with whitish fungal growth in which hard black bodies (sclerotia) may be embedded. Sclerotia also present inside stem.	Ensure soil is properly sterilised before planting. Destroy affected plants. Incorporating quintozene into the surface soil may help to prevent spread of the disease.
Water-soaked spots on the petals and general rotting of the flowers. Stems and leaves may rot. Cuttings affected.	See Grey mould in Table I (g).
Pin-point reddish spots on the petals coalesce to form water-soaked lesions. Tips of outer florets affected first, later spreads to affect whole bloom.	Can be largely controlled by reducing humidity with ventilation and warmth. If necessary, spray with zineb (preferably freshly prepared from nabam plus zinc sulphate) at coloured bud stage and subsequently at weekly intervals.
Powdery white growth on surface of leaves.	See Powdery mildew in Table I (g).
Dark lesions on cuttings and on stem and leaves of older plants. Dark brown lesion starting at centre of flower head extends often to affect only one side of bloom.	Sterilise border soil to eliminate infected debris. If possible, use steam, as value of chemical sterilisation uncertain. Spray regularly with captan, maneb, or mancozeb.
Yellowish-green spots on upper surface of leaves, rusty brown pustules beneath.	Reduce humidity. Pick off infected leaves and burn. Destroy severely affected plants. Select cuttings from healthy stocks only. Hot water treatment of stools against eelworm may reduce rust infection there as well. Spray with zineb or thiram when the disease first appears, or as a routine if disease occurs commonly. Spray regularly.
Lower leaves turn yellow, then brown and wilt. Symptoms spread up the plant. Wood at base of plant may be brown. Bark separates easily from the wood.	Sterilise border soil thoroughly. Select cuttings from healthy stocks. If disease appears in isolated patches, remove affected plants, and apply benomyl drench to soil around neighbouring plants.
Flowers smaller than normally, and more or less severely distorted with 'breaking' of the flower colour.	Select cuttings from healthy stock plants. Control vector aphids with insecticidal sprays.
Whole plant miniaturised. In some varieties leaf spotting or flecking occurs, and flowers develop earlier and may be of poor colour and quality.	Select cuttings from healthy stock plants. Destroy affected plants.
Various symptoms of mottling or necrosis of the leaves, and discoloration and/or malformation of the flowers may be associated with virus infection.	Stocks should be examined regularly and plants bearing symptoms on leaves or flowers should be destroyed. Routine insecticidal spraying should be carried out to control possible aphid and thrip virus vectors.

Chrysanthemums are sensitive to mineral deficiencies, which are dealt with in general terms in Chapter 12.

Flowers and buds ragged and chewed.	Spray with gamma-BHC and use boards, tiles or sacks as traps.
	See pest in (a).
	See pest in (a).

427

Disorder

Mottled arum aphid
Aulacorthum circumflexum (P)

Bishop bug
Lygus rugulipennis (P)

Angleshades moth
Phlogophora meticulosa (P)

Chrysanthemum leafminer
Phytomyza syngensiae (P)

Chrysanthemum gall midge
Diarthronomyia chrysanthemi (P)

Glasshouse red spider mite
Tetranychus urticae (P)

Leaf and bud eelworm
Aphelenchoides ritzemabosi (P)

Sparrows (P)

(k) **Bulbs**

For hot water treatment of rots see MAFF Bulletin No 201 *Hot Water Treatment of Plant Material*. In addition to bulb disorders clearly associated with pathogen or pest attack, there are physiological disorders frequently associated with pre-treatment (or preparation) to induce flowering out of normal season. This may result from incorrect preparation or conditions prior to or after treatment (particularly over-heating in transit).

Crop	Disorder
Many bulb crops	Grey mould *Botrytis cinerea* (F)
	Aphids Various spp (P)
	Glasshouse whitefly *Trialeurodes vaporariorum* (P)
	Large narcissus fly *Merodon equestris* (P) Small narcissus fly *Eumerus tuberculatus* and *E. strigatus* (both P)
	Bulb mite *Rhizoglyphus echinopus* (P)

428

Symptoms	Control
	See pest on Cyclamen in (g).
Stem, leaves and flowers mis-shapen and distorted.	Gamma-BHC spray or smoke.
Holes in foliage and buds and flower petals trimmed at outside. Caterpillars dark green-brown with white dorsal stripe and V-shaped grey marks. Nocturnal feeders.	Spray with gamma-BHC.
Fine white spots on foliage (adult feeding marks) followed by the development of silvery white snake-like mines (due to larvae tunnelling).	Spray with gamma-BHC or diazinon.
Stems and leaves covered in cone-shaped galls 2mm long where larvae feed.	Spray with gamma-BHC or diazinon at 10 day intervals.
	See pest in (a).
Leaves with yellow-brown blotches which extend and blacken until leaf withers. Buds may turn black.	Remove all withered leaves and discard plant after flowering. Take new cuttings from healthy stock and use hot water treatment prior to taking cutting. Remove all infested soil.
Buds ragged. Petals also ragged and many lying on ground.	Net vents and doors and use black thread as extra deterrent.

Symptoms	Control
Leaves, stems and flowers may rot, with smoky grey fur of spores, under densely grown humid conditions.	See Grey mould in Table I (g).
Foliage and bulb with heavy infestations of greenfly. Distortion of foliage.	Spray or drench with malathion.
	See pest in (a).
Bulbs feel soft and basal plate may be rotted. A longitudinal cut shows a feeding cavity with either one single plump yellow maggot (15mm) or several small (8mm) white maggots. Result: failure to produce a shoot, or production of many adventitious grass-like shoots. Adults resemble blue bottles and house flies.	Nothing can be done after the attack and new infestatic.is on indoor bulbs are unlikely. Buy good quality produce which has been hot water treated.
Large (2mm) creamy white globular mites. Slow moving on lower foliage and bulb scales. Damage is secondary in nature following disease or eelworm activity.	Hot water dip for 4 hours at 110°F (43.3°C). *Not* suitable for tulips for forcing.

Crop	Disorder
	Bulb scale mite *Steneotarsonemus laticeps* (P)
	Stem eelworm *Ditylenchus dipsaci*
Freesia and Gladiolus	Fusarium yellows and corm rot *Fusarium oxysporum* (F)
	Core rot *Botrytis gladiolorum* (F)
	Dry rot *Sclerotinia gladioli* (F)
	Gladiolus thrips *Taeniothrips simplex*
Hyacinth and Muscari	Black slime *Sclerotinia bulborum* (F)
Hyacinth and Tulip	Grey bulb rot *Sclerotium tuliparum* (F)
Iris	Ink disease *Mystrosporium adjustum*
	Angle shades moth *Phlogophora meticulosa*
	Mites *Bryobia* spp (P)
Lily	Leaf blight *Botrytis elliptica*, *B. cinerea* (both F)
	Mosaics and mottles Various viruses (V)
	Tulip bulb aphid *Dysaphis tulipae* (P)

Symptoms	*Control*
Stored bulbs are very dry with scales sticking close to bulb. If bulb is cut through 6mm below neck small brown pieces of tissue will be seen at tips of scales. Mites microscopic (0.2mm). Ingrowing bulbs—foliage abnormally bright green, distorted and later flecked with yellow. Flower stem with 'saw edge' effect and flower killed or distorted.	Buy healthy bulbs. If infestations arise use hot water dip, 4 hours at 110°F (43.3°C) or use thionazin as a bulb dip.
Cross-section of bulb shows concentric rings of brown scale. May be white thread like mass of dead eelworms at base of bulb. Growing bulb will eventually die but initial symptoms include yellow swelling (spickels) on foliage, or foliage may be dwarfed and twisted.	Hot water treatment 3 hours at 112°F (44.4°C) or dip bulbs in a solution of thionazin (0.23%).
Brown zonate lesions on surface of gladiolus corms. Yellowing of the leaves with reddish-brown discoloration of vascular and surrounding tissue in the corms.	Discard diseased corms. Dipping the corms in benomyl suspension before storing in a dry well-ventilated store may be effective. Thoroughly sterilise border soil before planting. A soil drench with benomyl at 4–6 week intervals from the 4-leaf stage reduces disease in freesia crops grown from seed.
Centre of corm may rot, spreading out to destroy it completely.	Discard affected corms. Protect by dusting corms with quintozene. Sterilise border soil.
Small black lesions on flesh of the corm. May extend and destroy the corm. Leaves turn yellow and rot at soil level, leaving a stringy dry rot bearing minute black sclerotia. Sclerotia may also be present on the corms.	Discard diseased corms. Sterilise border soil. Primulinus varieties more susceptible than large-flowered varieties.
Small dark brown adults (1.5mm) and orange larvae may be visible. Foliage with silvering and stickiness due to leaking of sap.	Spray with malathion at 14 day intervals.
Leaves turn yellow and collapse. Bulbs decay, with black sclerotia between and within the scales.	Remove and destroy affected bulbs. Thoroughly sterilise border soil before replanting.
Shoots may fail to emerge, or may shrivel and die after emergence. Soil sticks to nose of bulb. Rotting, initially at nose portion, spreads and destroys the bulb which is covered with mycelium bearing brown or black sclerotia.	Discard diseased bulbs. Sterilise border soil or thoroughly incorporate quintozene dust in surface layers of soil.
Outer scales of bulb discoloured, as if stained with ink. Leaves may bear dark blotches, and turn yellow and die.	Discard severely affected bulbs. Less damaged bulbs may be soaked in 2% formalin for 1 hour before drying and storing in sand after lifting.
	See pest on Chrysanthemum in (j).
	See pest on Primula in (g).
Water-soaked or brownish spots develop on the leaves, flower stalks and buds under humid conditions. Seedlings may be infected and damp off.	Discard diseased bulbs. Sterilise soil for compost, or border soil before replanting. Spray affected plants with proprietary sulphur or copper fungicide; benomyl may be used. Destroy old stems and leaves at end of season.
Leaves distorted and mottled. Flower petals do not open, but remain together at the tips.	Destroy affected plants. Spray with insecticide to control insect vectors. Propagate from known healthy stock or from seed.
Grey coloured aphids below outer skin of bulb. Numbers increase rapidly after planting producing stunted growth. Vector of 'lily-symptomless' and 'tulip break' viruses.	15 minute dip in gamma-BHC solution (0.01%) or dust with gamma-BHC.

Crop	Disorder
Narcissus	Basal rot *Fusarium oxysporum* (F)
	Smoulder *Botrytis narcissicola* (F)
	Fire *Sclerotinia polyblastis* (F)
	Stripe Narcissus stripe virus (V)
	Blindness (Ph)
	Dry set (Ph)
Orchids	Virus diseases Various viruses (V)
	Springtails *Collembola* (P)
	Scale insects Various spp (P)
	Wingless weevils *Ottiorrhynchus* spp (P)
	Fungus gnats *Sciara* spp (P)
	Slaters or woodlice *Armadillidum* spp (P)
Tulip	Fire *Botrytis tulipae* (F)
	Shanking *Phytophthora* sp (F)
	Breaking One or more viruses (V)
	Streak Tobacco necrosis virus (V)
	Chalkiness (Ph)

432

Symptoms

Bulb initially soft, with rot at base. Chocolate brown rot spreads upwards with white or pinkish mycelium between scales. Infected bulbs either rot away or produce a few stunted chlorotic leaves.

Bulbs may show small flat black sclerotia under outer scales. Bulbs may rot. Shoots attacked after emergence decay, particularly under humid conditions. Infection less severe under warm dry conditions, but spotting of leaves and flowers may occur.

Small brownish spots on the flowers, and elongate lesions on the leaves, which may be killed under very damp conditions.

Longitudinal pale green to yellow stripes on the leaves. The surface of the leaves may feel rough to touch in some varieties when infected.

No flower emerges, or shoot may be stunted and poorly developed.

Flowers papery and shrivelled.

Symptoms of ringspots, mottling and chlorotic or necrotic streaking on the leaves. Colour breaking of the flowers occurs in some instances.

See pest in (g), several parts.

Sunken circular lesions with raised margins under outer scales on bulb. Black sclerotia present. Shoots may die. Spots on leaves and flowers.

Flower stalk may not emerge or may droop and die. Flower may fail to open. Growth generally poor. Brownish rot up centre of bulb.

Marked colour patterns on flowers. Little effect on leaves.

Leaves distorted with marked brown streaks, which may coalesce to give larger withered areas. Plants stunted or killed.

Inner tissues of bulbs become hard and chalky in appearance. Penicillium storage rot and mites are often associated.

Control

Handle bulbs carefully and store in a cool place. Discard any soft bulbs. Inclusion of formalin (0.5%) in the hot water treatment against eelworm, controls basal rot infection.

Discard diseased bulbs before planting, and severely affected plants after emergence. Sterilise border soil. Spray plants with zineb to prevent spread if disease is severe.

See Leaf blight of Lily in this table.

Roguing plants during the early growth stages should largely eliminate this problem.

May be caused by incorrect pre-treatment, or to forcing too soon by grower before bulb adequately developed.

May be caused by incorrect pre-treatment, or to forcing at too high a temperature.

Discard diseased stocks.

See pest in (a).

Use malathion only.

See pest on Vine in (f).

See pest in (b).

See pest in (a).

Discard obviously affected bulbs. A soak in benomyl after lifting may be effective, or dust the bulbs with quintozene and incorporate dust in the surface soil before planting. Sterilise border soil. Remove any primary infector plants. Spray the plants with captan, maneb, zineb, mancozeb/zineb or dichlofluanid to help prevent spread in cases of severe infections.

Ensure that compost and containers for growing are thoroughly sterilised with steam or formalin.

To prevent virus spread, keep unbroken stocks separate, and rogue out any infected plants as soon as possible. Spray with insecticide, to control vector aphids.

Rogue out diseased plants. Sterilise soil to kill the fungus which transmits the virus.

Avoid damage during handling. Store under best possible conditions, particularly avoiding exposure to hot sunshine after lifting.

Crop　　　　　*Disorder*
　　　　　　　Topple (Ph)

　　　　　　　Hard scale (Ph)

　　　　　　　Tulip aphid
　　　　　　　Dysaphis tulipae (P)

434

Symptoms

Flower stem kinks and flower falls over.

Outer skin of bulb very hard, so that roots fail to penetrate and hence grow upwards between outer skin and fleshy scales. Growth poor. Blindness.

Control

May be associated with conditions during raising and pre-treatment of bulbs. Bulb forcers should take care not to force too soon or at too high a temperature. A preventative spray with calcium nitrate may be applied to varieties known to suffer particularly from topple.

Cut outer skin before planting.

See Lily in this section.

Appendix

METRIC AND OTHER CONVERSION FACTORS

Definition	To convert	Into	Multiply by
Temperature rise	deg F	deg C	0.55
and fall	deg C .	deg F	1.8
Length	in	mm	25.4
	mm	in	0.0394
	ft	metres (m)	0.3048
	m	ft	3.2808
Area	ft²	m²	0.0929
	m²	ft²	10.7639
Volume	ft³	m³	0.0283
	m³	ft³	35.3148
Mass	lb	kg	0.4536
	kg	lb	2.2046

BUILDING HEAT LOSS DATA

Thermal transmittance:

U-value	Btu/ft² deg F	W/m² deg C	5.678
	W/m² deg C	Btu/ft² deg F	0.176

Useful data:

20 fluid ounces = 1 pint

1 gallon of water weighs 10lb

Cubic capacity is calculated by multiplying
length × breadth × average height

TEMPERATURE CONVERSION TABLE

°F	°C	°F	°C	°F	°C
86	30.0	60	15.6	34	1.1
85	29.4	59	15.0	33	0.6
84	28.9	58	14.4	32	0.0
83	28.3	57	13.9	31	—0.6
82	27.8	56	13.3	30	—1.1
81	27.2	55	12.8	29	—1.7
80	26.7	54	12.2	28	—2.2
79	26.1	53	11.7	27	—2.8
78	25.6	52	11.1	26	—3.3
77	25.0	51	10.6	25	—3.9
76	24.4	50	10.0	24	—4.4
75	23.9	49	9.4	23	—5.0
74	23.3	48	8.9	22	—5.6
73	22.8	47	8.3	21	—6.1
72	22.2	46	7.8	20	—6.7
71	21.7	45	7.2	19	—7.2
70	21.1	44	6.7	18	—7.8
69	20.6	43	6.1	17	—8.3
68	20.0	42	5.6	16	—8.9
67	19.4	41	5.0	15	—9.4
66	18.9	40	4.4	14	—10.0
65	18.3	39	3.9	13	—10.6
64	17.8	38	3.3	12	—11.1
63	17.2	37	2.8	11	—11.7
62	16.7	36	2.2	10	—12.2
61	16.1	35	1.7		

Formulae for conversion: Celsius to Fahrenheit $= (°C \times 1.8) + 32$
Fahrenheit to Celsius $= (°F - 32) \times .55$

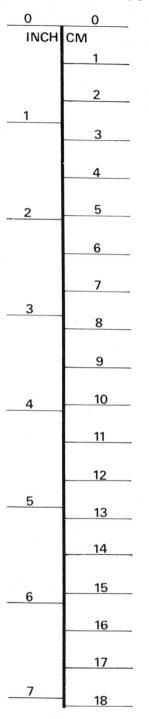

Index

Index

Index